# "LOOKING UP AT DOWN"

The Emergence of Blues Culture

# "LOOKING UP AT DOWN"

The Emergence of Blues Culture

## WILLIAM BARLOW

Temple University Press
Philadelphia

Temple University Press, Philadelphia 19122
Copyright © 1989 by Temple University. All rights reserved
Published 1989
Printed in the United States of America

**Library of Congress Cataloging-in-Publication Data**

Barlow, William.
    "Looking up at down" : The emergence of blues culture / William
Barlow.
      p.    cm.
    Bibliography: p.
    Includes index.
    ISBN 0-87722-583-4 (alk. paper)
    1. Blues (Music)—History and criticism.    I. Title.
ML3521.B36    1989
784.5'3'00973—dc19                            88-15921
                                                 CIP
                                                 MN

For poem and song lyric permissions, see page 403.

This book is dedicated to
Sunnyland Slim
and to the memory of
Sterling A. Brown (1902–1989).

# Acknowledgments

The final version of this manuscript was a long time coming. It has gone through a number of revisions, and along the way many people have made important contributions to its development. First and foremost were the blues musicians and scholars I interviewed. Their thoughtful and detailed recollections are the raw material of this book—it is their stories that make up the whole. They are Sterling A. Brown, Roy Byrd (Professor Longhair), Sam Charters, Peter Chatman (Memphis Slim), Sam Chatmon, Arnett Cobb, Willie Dixon, Honey Boy Edwards, John Lee Hooker, Sam "Lightnin' " Hopkins, Big Walter Horton, John Jackson, B. B. King, Milt Larkin, Robert Jr. Lockwood, Albert Luandrew (Sunnyland Slim), Brownie McGhee, Little Brother Montgomery, Hammie Nixon, Paul Oliver, William Perryman (Piano Red), Esther Mae Scott, Johnny Shines, Victoria Spivey, Houston Stackhouse, Hubert Sumlin, Roosevelt Sykes, Sonny Terry, Willa Mae "Big Mama" Thornton, Henry "Mule" Townsend, Ira Tucker, Big Joe Turner, Sippie Wallace, Junior Wells, Big Joe Williams.

I would also like to acknowledge and thank my professors, colleagues, and friends who contributed encouragement, criticism, and support for this project as it unfolded. They are, at the University of California at Santa Cruz and in the San Francisco Bay Area: Lucia Birnbaum, Herman Blake, Carl Boggs, Norman O. Brown, Julianne Burton, Larry Davis, Harry Duncan, Karlene Faith, Lorenzo Milam, Paul Niebanck, Nancy Shaw, Page Smith, Chris Strachwitz, Queenie Taylor, Howie Winnant; at Howard University and in the Washington, D.C./Baltimore area: Henri Bourgeois, Sterling A. Brown, Ben Caldwell, Grace Cavalieri, Larry Coleman, Jannette Dates, Daphne Duval Harrison, Abbas Malek, Paula Mantabane, Bishetta Merritt, Bernice Johnson Reagon, Natalie Reuss.

The major research facilities that assisted me while I conducted my blues research included the Library of Congress (especially the Folk Archives), Washington, D.C.; the DeSable Museum, Chicago, Illinois; the Rutgers University Institute for Jazz Studies, Newark, New Jersey; the Moorland–Springharm Collection, Howard University Library, Washington, D.C.; and the Blues Archives at the Center for the Study of Southern Culture, University of Mississippi, Oxford, Mississippi. I would also like to thank the staff at Temple University Press and my editor there, Janet Francendese, for their help in editing and proofreading the manuscript for publication. And finally, I owe special thanks to my long-time blues mentors, Sterling A. Brown and Sunnyland Slim, to whom this book is dedicated. Sterling A. Brown passed away in January 1989. He will be missed by many blues lovers throughout the country.

# Contents

# Before the Blues

When West Africans were first brought into the United States as slaves, their shared enslavement and their shared oral traditions and folkways gave them a common base for social intercourse. Eugene Genovese, in his landmark history of the African-American slave community, *Roll Jordan Roll: The World the Slaves Made,* argues that building a "separate black national culture" was essential to the survival of African-Americans during slavery.[1] This culture of resistance included traditional African cultural practices and those selectively appropriated from the dominant white culture. Although the slaves' native languages were suppressed and they were forced to adopt the English language of their captors, they spoke English with African nuances, molding it to their traditional cultural practices. Their religion came from their white captors too, but it focused on biblical images, themes, heroes, and proverbs that reinforced their opposition to slavery.

The slaves' culture of resistance was articulated in their secular and sacred songs—as well as family histories, verbal games, folktales, aphorisms, proverbs, sermons, riddles, toasts, hexes, and jokes. Like the other components of the oral tradition, the songs illuminated the slaves' growing consciousness of their collective struggle for freedom during the antebellum period. The widespread existence of slave songs and the "coded" messages they conveyed has been thoroughly documented in Dena Epstein's *Sinful Tunes and Spirituals: Black Folk Music to the Civil War* and John Lovell Jr.'s *Black Song: The Forge and the Flame.*[2] The evidence these books present demonstrates that spirituals and secular songs were an important part of the slave community's oral tradition and that that tradition was the engine driving their cultural resistance to slavery and white supremacy.

In *Black Culture and Black Consciousness: Afro-American Folk Thought from Slavery to Freedom,* Lawrence Levine surveys the recorded folk thought found in African-American humor, toasts, proverbs, aphorisms, legends, tall tales, spirituals, and secular folksongs during the nineteenth and twentieth centuries. He concludes that secular song played a pivotal role in the cultural life of the black populace:

> It gave a sense of power, of control. If it did not affect the material well being of its creators, it certainly did have an impact upon their psychic state and emotional health. It allowed them to assert themselves and their feelings and their values, to communicate continuously with themselves and their peers and their oppressors as well. . . . Black secular

song, along with other forms of the oral tradition, allowed them to express themselves communally and individually; to derive great aesthetic pleasure, to perpetuate traditions, to keep values from eroding, and to begin to create new expressive modes. Black secular song revealed a culture which kept large elements of its own autonomous standards alive, which continued a rich internal life, which interacted with a larger society that deeply affected it, but to which it did not completely succumb.[3]

Jesse Lemisch argues that historians should write history from the point of view of the masses at the bottom of the social order: "To study the conduct and the ideology of the people on the bottom—this is nothing less than an attempt to make the inarticulate speak."[4] Folk music scholar Charles Wolfe echoes this insight. He believes that the black populace speaks to the historian through secular song. Specifically, he regards the blues as an ideal vehicle for "getting at the thought, spirit and history of the very segment of the Negro community that historians have rendered inarticulate through their neglect."[5]

The blues have always been a collective expression of the ideology and character of black people situated at the bottom of the social order in America. The blues originated as a folk music on the cotton plantations in the South during the 1890s and came to fruition in the tenderloin ghettos of urban America over the next four decades. The blues tradition is therefore interwoven with the social conditions, concerns, conflicts, and shifts in consciousness among working-class African Americans over this period. For a folk art, the music has been relatively well preserved, in part because of the continuity of the black oral tradition, much of which has been captured in print, and in part because of the advent of the record industry in the twentieth century, which has preserved an abundance of audio documentation of the development of the blues tradition, especially since the 1920s. This reservoir of historical data, including recordings of the music itself and of oral histories and interviews, makes it possible to trace the evolution of the music within the context of the history it commented on. The following chapters attempt to do just that—to bring to life the emergence of a blues culture that documents from the bottom up the historical trajectory of African-American cultural resistance to white domination.

# Part I
## Rural Blues

# Introduction

Developed by a new generation of black agricultural workers in the South—the first to be raised free of the shackles of slavery—the blues represented a significant new voice in the black community, one that updated the social concerns and critical vernacular of African Americans. The simple blues song structures and the reservoir of floating verse that became associated with them were products of the African-American practice of returning to traditional folk sources for renewal and revitalization. As historian Lawrence Levine has noted, "Simply because it remained closer to its folk roots than other forms of American music in the twentieth century, Afro-American song retained a high degree of redundancy in both its musical structure and its stock of poetic forms."[1] Like the spirituals and slave seculars—forerunners of the blues in the oral tradition—the blues became an important component of the indigenous communication system used by the black population in the post-Reconstruction years. This was a reactionary period, a period when African Americans faced economic servitude, political disenfranchisement, social segregation, and a wave of brutal lynchings.

The earliest folk blues were sung by nameless African Americans living and working in the South's cotton belt in the 1880s and 1890s—in particular, the region from the Mississippi Delta to East Texas, which gave birth to several rural blues styles that were especially popular among the younger members of the local black population. If, as Sam "Lightnin' " Hopkins put it, the original folk blues "come out of the fields,"[2] they nevertheless captured the imagination of the entire African-American working class. Their popularity spread quickly among the army of laborers involved in lumbering, milling, and turpentine production in the South's "Piney Woods" forest belt, among the stevedores working the docks of southern seaports and riverports, among the workers building and repairing the levees along the Mississippi River and its tributaries and those building and maintaining the South's new railroad system, and among the growing legions of black domestics in the cities.[3] Even before the emergence of the "race" record industry in the 1920s, the blues were easily the southern black population's most popular form of secular music.

The simple musical form used to create the blues incorporated three practices that were fundamental to African-American folk music, all having their antecedents in West African musical traditions. Cross-rhythms, the centerpiece of African-American music, were used extensively in the blues. In essence, these were simple polyrhythms, which have always been the foundation of West African drumming. The most common means of creating them was to separate the melodic line from the groundbeat, thereby putting the two in rhythmic conflict. This could be easily accomplished by a solitary musician singing or playing in a manner that emphasized the off beat. The second major innovation with roots in African music was the melodic tendency to express rising emotions with falling pitch; it was accomplished by bending or flattening certain notes of the diatonic scale, using one's voice or a musical instrument. This technique, which was also practiced by the Akan people of Ghana, produced what are now known as "blue notes." Finally, blues musicians used a variety of vocal techniques, from coarse gutteral tones and slurs to falsetto and melisma, to color the melodic line and give it identity and expressiveness. All these techniques had counterparts in West African vocal styles.[4]

The rural blues were a vocal music used to articulate the personal and social concerns that arose in the daily lives of African Americans. As black music scholar John W. Work Jr. has put it, "The blues singer translated every happening into his own intimate inconvenience."[5] Blues lyrics were drawn from two major sources—the folk artists' individual observations of the world around them and the black oral tradition. Thus, there was both an immediate and a historical dimension to the content of the early folk blues. They were a mix of personal sentiments and collective memory. They were focused on the present, but they were framed in the folklore of the past. Many rural blues were "cautionary folktales" designed to uphold traditional values and foster group cohesion; they were commonsense lessons on how to survive in America as have-nots.[6]

The critical role the rural blues played in revitalizing the black oral tradition during the post-Reconstruction era has yet to receive proper recognition. The black population in the South was still overwhelmingly agrarian and non-literate. The oral tradition was still a primary communication channel between individuals and the community and between one generation and the next. As such, the black oral tradition shaped—and in turn was shaped by—both the social consciousness and the social intercourse of African Americans. From their inception, the rural blues made significant and far-reaching secular contributions to the oral tradition. Blues songs documented the temper of the times and thus preserved the historical legacy of a people still confined to the lowest echelon of the social order. In addition, they presaged the social upheaval implicit in the impending black migration out of the cotton belt and into the urban ghettos.

The conventions that grew up around the performance of the rural folk blues contributed directly to the power and magnetism of the music. Like the participants in traditional African musical performances, blues musicians and audiences collectively participated in a cultural ritual that was often cathartic. At the social gatherings where the blues were performed, the music making— singing, playing musical instruments, dancing, stomping, handclapping, shouting, and so on—involved all those present in spontaneous, expressive, and emotional communication. Voices, musical instruments, and body movements created an atmosphere that allowed the group to release pent-up emotions and act out their feelings. The early folk blues were extensions of the sounds and rhythms of common struggles and pleasures. They dramatized the cultural vitality and rebelliousness of the participants, evoking race and class solidarity.

The pioneering rural blues artists were, quite naturally, the key cultural workers in the dissemination of this new music to the various sectors of the black population. A high percentage of these first-generation blues musicians came from poor farming families, and their choice of vocation figured in a larger rebellion against the established white social order. Their role as innovators in the formative years of the blues tradition has been well documented by blues scholars and historians.[7] Their role as cultural rebels, however, needs to be given more attention. They were the makers and carriers of a music that resisted cultural domination in both form and content. They used traditional African musical practices to spread the rebellion and to reinforce the powerful hold that African traditions had on African Americans living in the South. By choosing a life of travel and recreation rather than unrelenting labor and unrewarded abstinence, they signaled their alienation from the established cultural norms in their communities. To older and more conservative religious members of the black population, their music was blasphemous and they were characterized as the Devil's disciples. And it is true that they acted as proselytizers of a gospel of secularization in which the belief in freedom became associated with personal mobility—freedom of movement in this world here and now, rather than salvation later on in the next.

Rural blues bards had certain similarities with black preachers. Both groups were active in shaping the oral tradition and both drew upon traditional African performing styles to impart their messages. However, they were also in competition for the loyalty and allegiance of their audiences. Moreover, the texts of their respective messages had little in common. Although they both recognized the perilous situation confronting African Americans in the South after the collapse of Reconstruction and the resurgence of white racism, they differed in their responses to the crisis. Black preachers had strong ties to the "old-time" religion of their slave forebears. Because they embraced the religious traditions and beliefs used as survival mechanisms during slavery, their cultural outlook had a conservative orientation. They looked to the past for their inspiration, urging self-reliance, social restraint, and religious resistance to prejudice and discrimination. In contrast, the rural blues artists identified with an emerging secular consciousness critical of the oppressive social order. They advocated personal rebellion and resistance as a means of combatting their oppressors.

The rural blues were not the result of a few isolated incidents of individual genius. Instead, they were a broadly based cultural movement occupying the time and energy of large numbers of black farm workers in the South's cotton belt. Nurtured and popularized by enclaves of black musicians and songsters, many of whom toiled as fieldhands and unskilled laborers to make a living, their appeal was initially strongest among the younger members of the workforce. The music and the cultural activities surrounding it generated race and class traditions, practices, and preferences that sharpened the contradictions between the black community and the reigning white social order, while reinforcing the black community's self-esteem and solidarity. The ideology of the early folk blues elucidated these two tendencies. Critical assessment of the working conditions, the living conditions, and the treatment of African Americans by the white-controlled criminal justice system in the South helped to sharpen the contradictions between the black and the white social orders, while the encouragement of rambling, hedonism, and rebelliousness among the lower-class black population born after the end of slavery helped to reinforce self-esteem and solidarity. These tendencies infused the rural blues with an ethos of revolt expressed in the tongue-in-cheek humor, the sexual double entendres and erotic fantasies, the magic charms and animal totems, the general rowdiness, and above all the self-parody typical of the blues tradition from its inception.

For at least three decades rural blues flourished as part of the recreational life of segregated black farming communities. During that period, local blues traditions matured at a leisurely pace, since outside influences were minimal until the 1920s. But even as they grew and prospered in close proximity to their folk roots, the rural blues articulated the call for urban migration. There is a clear historical connection between the rebellious and restless spirit of these folk blues musicians and the black exodus from the cotton belt in the first half of the twentieth century. Many rural blues artists were in the forefront of this exodus; they were the oracles of their generation, contrasting the promise of freedom with the reality of their harsh living conditions, using their imagination and insight to reformulate the common complaints and aspirations of African Americans. In particular, they represented the emerging consciousness of a younger generation of African Americans living in a new historical era—seeking personal freedom, social mobility, and better compensation for their labor.

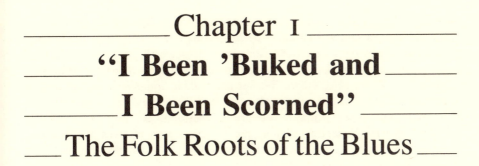

# Chapter 1
# "I Been 'Buked and I Been Scorned"
## The Folk Roots of the Blues

### Blues Origins and Influences

The popular African-American music commonly referred to as the blues has been a unique and compelling expression of black culture in the United States since the late 1800s, when it first emerged as a clearly indentifiable folksong genre.[1] The blues evolved from the secular and sacred folk music of African Americans living in the South during slavery and Reconstruction. They were an amalgam of African and European musical practices—a mix of African cross-rhythms, blue notes, and vocal techniques with European harmony and ballad forms. In particular, the blues were fashioned out of worksongs, field hollers, and ballads popular among rural African Americans in the last half of the nineteenth century. All the necessary elements for this new folksong family had coalesced by the 1890s. Then, over the next two decades, the blues grew to be the most popular folk music in America.

The sudden ascendency of the blues helped to strengthen the black oral traditions at a critical juncture in the history of African-American cultural resistance to white domination. It is no accident that the blues came to the forefront of black culture at a time when African Americans were confronting a serious decline in their collective economic and political status in the South. The blues were part of a widespread cultural response to renewed white oppression. They infused the black oral tradition with a new assessment of the urgency of the situation and a mandate to change it.

The legions of folk musicians and songsters who created and sustained the blues in their infancy were African-American variations on the famous West African "griot" tradition. The griots were talented musicians and folklorists designated to be the oral carriers of their people's culture; in some regions, such as the Western Sudan, they were a hereditary caste. Griots preserved the history, traditions, and mores of their respective tribes and kinship groups through songs and stories. They composed songs of praise for tribal chieftains

or powerful clans. But they were also known for their complaint songs, which
often got them branded as dissidents by their tribal leaders. Griots were both
admired and feared by their fellow tribe members since they were thought to
consort with trickster gods and even evil spirits. While many griots confined
themselves to one village, others roamed about their homelands entertaining
and educating people in one village after another. Since they lived in a culture
organized around an oral tradition, the griots functioned as "the libraries" of
West African tribal societies "by supporting among themselves successive
generations of living books." A well-known West African proverb states:
"When an old man dies, a library burns to the ground."[2]

The African-American songsters who synthesized the blues from earlier
genres of black folk music were descendents of the griots, carrying forward
the historical and cultural legacy of their people even while they were setting a
new agenda for social discourse and action. Their songs were the collective
expression of the experiences of a new generation of African Americans born
after slavery but still living with its legacy, still caught up in a life-or-death
struggle for survival and freedom. As one folk historian put it, "The blues
started when black people began to discover that being free as they
thought . . . well, being free wasn't as free as it was said to be."[3]

## Blues Basics

The blues in their standard form were songs of personal experience characterized by a twelve-bar, three-line (AAB) stanza structure and a basic topic
(I)-subdominant (IV)-dominant (V) chord sequence. Within the stanza pattern,
the first line was repeated with minor variation in the second line; the third
vocal line responded to the first two. The repetition of refrains strengthened
the song's sense of personalization. Enveloping the vocal patterns was the instrumental accompaniment, usually a guitar, which established the groundbeat
and chord progression and also responded to each vocal line. The stanza structure was simple and flexible enough to be open to innovative diversification,
including eight-bar (AB), twelve-bar (AAA), and sixteen-bar (AAAB) blues
patterns. In addition, the twelve-bar pattern was easily altered to eleven bars,
or thirteen bars, or fourteen bars. This suggests that the earliest folk blues
were irregular in structure and length, and that the twelve-bar pattern became
standardized later.

The first recorded use of the word "blue" to designate something other
than the color was in the English expression "to look blue," which dates to
the 1500s, when it was used to connote an anxious and troubled state of mind.

By the 1600s, the term "blue devils" was in common usage in England to refer to evil spirits that brought on depression and despair. The colloquial use of the term "blues" in the United States has been traced back to the early 1800s, at which time it seems to have been used interchangeably with the phrase "blue devils" to describe a mood of low spirits and emotional stress.[4]

At some point near the end of Reconstruction, African Americans in the rural South began to apply the expression "the blues" to a certain style of folksong evolving in their midst.[5] The earliest known rural blues were constructed out of black folk music and folklore. They were solo compositions that borrowed freely from traditional song formats and from the stock of folk sayings, proverbs, and poetic images in the African-American oral tradition. Black American musicians and songsters improvised their songs from these common folk resources, but they approached the music through their individual experiences of postbellum southern life. The rural blues thus represented both a break with and a return to the past. It was this tension between innovation and tradition that endowed the blues with a capacity to illuminate the emotional life and social consciousness of the African-American people.

## Spirituals

The influence of the antebellum spirituals on the blues stemmed from their central role in the black oral tradition. Collectively, they formed a mosiac of the African Americans' sacred cosmos, a mythical world of Old Testament heroes and fables selectively constructed with their own situation in mind. In the spirituals, the slaves again and again paid tribute to "Brudder David's" clever triumph over the mighty giant Goliath, "Brudder Joshua's" stunning victory at the Battle of Jericho, and "Brudder Samson's" final apocalyptic destruction of his tormentors. They identified with the plight of the Hebrew slaves in Egypt, and in particular with their spectacular escape from bondage while "Ole Pharaoh" and his army perished. They celebrated the redemption of Noah in the ark, Jonah in the belly of the whale, and Daniel in the lion's den. The religious symbols and parables chosen by the slaves were cultural paradigms of good and evil, justice and injustice, or sin and retribution, while the biblical heroes served as race prophets and redeemers. They demonstrated that faith, perseverance, and acceptance of a higher authority could lead to ultimate triumph over slavery.

African-American spirituals, like other slave folksongs, were communally composed to fit the current social context and tended to have both an underlying thematic unity and a regional individuality. In an essay, "Negro Spiritu-

als,'' written in 1865, Thomas Wentworth Higginson commented on this folk
dynamic:

> True, the individual songs rarely coincided; there was a line here, a cho-
> rus there—just enough to fix the class, but this was unmistakable. It was
> not strange that they differed, for the range seemed almost endless, and
> South Carolina, Georgia, and Florida seemed to have nothing but the
> generic character in common, until all were mingled in the united stock
> of camp melodies.[6]

James Miller McKim, a minister from Philadelphia, collected slave spirituals
during the Civil War and tried to find out how they were created. He recorded
an interview with a slave.

> I asked one of these blacks—one of the most intelligent I had met—
> where they got these songs. ''Dey make em, sah.'' ''How do they make
> them?'' After a pause, evidently casting about for an explanation, he
> said, ''I'll tell you; it's dis way. My master call me up and order me a
> short peck of corn and a hundred lash. My friends see it and is sorry for
> me. When dey come to de praise meeting dat night dey sing about it.
> Some's very good singers and know how; and dey work it in, work it in,
> you know; till dey get it right; and dat's dey way. . . .

> No more driver call me
> No more driver call
> No more driver call me
> Many thousand die!

> No more peck of corn for me
> No more peck of corn
> No more peck of corn for me
> Many thousand die!

> No more hundred lash for me
> No more hundred lash
> No more hundred lash for me
> Many thousand die![7]

It is interesting to note that this song's verse structure is closely related to the
blues AAB verse structure. This suggests that the two song genres may have
shared some common verse structures early on.

Those spirituals that most resemble the blues in tone and structure are sol-
emn and mournful songs based on long-phrased melodies. They include the
well-known spirituals ''I Been 'Buked,'' ''Deep River,'' and ''Motherless

Child." This style was drawn from both the more traditional hymnody of the Protestant church and an African taproot of lullabies and "sweet plaintive airs" sung by slaves, which W. E. B. Du Bois would later call "sorrow songs."[8] In general, the spirituals were a moving call for deliverance from oppression and exile as a race and for redemption from individual hardships and suffering. These concerns would remain ongoing ones for black people in the United States even after slavery was abolished. The spirituals would continue to express the moral and social conflicts inherent in the times and the communal hope for a brighter future:

> Oh brethren
> Oh sistern
> You got a right
> I got a right
> We all got a right
> To de tree of life.[9]

After the Civil War, African Americans would generate new song forms—like the blues—and extend their thematic reach; as long as the struggle for freedom persisted, the music would continue to support it.

## Seculars

Seculars were folksongs of satire, complaint, caution, derision, or praise that articulated some of the social tensions of plantation life. Known as "kaiso" in West African Bantu dialects,[10] these songs were transported to the southern United States, where they re-emerged as a common feature of the slaves' musical vocabulary. Some of these songs satirized the slaves' illegal exploits, often carried out in defiance of the local white authorities. For example, a northern traveler visiting Kentucky on Christmas Eve in 1858 wrote down this bit of verse sung by the song leader of a group of slaves:

> Oh lord have mercy on my soul,
> De hens and chickens I have stole.

The entire group responded to each line of the verse by shouting a "jubilant chorus."[11] A similar folksong was recalled by a former South Carolina slave who participated in an oral history project late in her life. It went in part:

> Sorry dat if I leave my home,
> I gwine to my shack
> Wid de chicken on my back,
> Nobody business but mine.[12]

A former slave, Solomon Northup, in his narrative account of slavery, recalled this escape scenario:

> Harper's creek and roarin' ribber,
> Thar my dear we'll live forever.
> Den we'll go to the Ingin Nation.
> All I want in dis creation
> Is pretty little wife and big plantation.
>
> Up dat oak and down dat ribber,
> Two overseers and one little nigger.[13]

In the context of master-slave relationships, the slave trickster was a prominent figure in the seculars. A good example is the following verse from the song "Away Down in Sanbury," first published in 1867:

> O massa take that bran' new coat
> And hang it on the wall.
> That darky take the same ole coat
> And wear it to the ball.[14]

Another slave bragged

> I fooled old master seven years,
> Fooled the overseer three.
> Hand me down my banjo
> And I'll tickle your bel-lee.[15]

Closely related to poking fun at plantation authority figures were the folk seculars that criticized white society and the institution of slavery. One of the most common and long lasting included the following verse, first published in 1853 by a fugitive slave:

> The big bee flies high,
> The little bee makes the honey.
> The black folks make the cotton
> And the white folk gets the money.[16]

The same theme is represented in a song Frederick Douglass recorded in his autobiography:

> We raise de wheat,
> Dey gib us de corn.
> We bake de bread,
> Dey gib us de crust.
> We sif' de meal,
> Dey gib us de huss.
> We peel de meat,
> Dey gib us de skin.
> And dat's de way
> Dey take us in.
> We skim de pot,
> Dey gib us de liquor
> And say dat's good enough for nigger.
> Walk over, walk over,
> Your butter and fat.
> Poor nigger, you can't git over dat,
> Walk over.[17]

In general, the musical satire of the enslaved African Americans was used to expose the most glaring social contradictions of slavery to recognition and ridicule. However, slaves also used these folk seculars to complain about each other publicly. One example recalled by a former slave spoke of the practice of "puttin' 'uh o duh banjo."[18] When a slave was guilty of misconduct in the eyes of his or her peers, a song was made up exposing the misconduct to the entire slave community. The practice of exposing misdeeds through song was often reported among the black slave population throughout the South during the antebellum period. Larry Levine traced the source of this practice back through the oral tradition to Africa: "The African tradition of being able to verbalize publicly in song what could not be said to a person's face not only lived on among Afro-Americans throughout slavery, but continued to be a central feature of black expressive culture in freedom."[19]

## Worksongs

Worksongs, like other forms of secular African-American folk music, retained their traditional African mold while adapting to the New World environment, and in so doing became an important component of early rural blues. Many West African tribes used songs to coordinate collective labor in the fields and domiciles. Weaving, boating, planting, and harvesting crops, preparing meals, doing household chores—all had their musical counterparts. Once in the United States, the enslaved Africans continued to sing close approximations of these songs where and when they were appropriate. They were widely reported not only among fieldhands but also among hemp spinners, stevedores, tobacco workers, and firemen on the early steamboats.[20] Worksongs were generally encouraged by the slaveowners, who saw them as means of increasing the slaves' work output and maintaining their morale. For the slaves, however, the nature of their work was punishment, not self-fulfillment. As Frederick Douglass explained, their use of worksongs was linked to their resignation or resistance to forced labor:

Slaves are generally expected to sing as well as to work. A silent slave is not liked by masters or overseers. . . . This may account for the almost constant singing heard in the southern states. . . . I have often been utterly astonished, since I came north, to find persons who could speak of the singing among slaves as evidence of their contentment and happiness. It is impossible to conceive of a greater mistake. Slaves sing most when they are most unhappy. The songs of the slaves represent the sorrows of his life; and he is relieved by them only as an aching heart is relieved by its tears. At least such is my experience.[21]

The composing of worksongs, like most African-American folk music, was done spontaneously and collectively; it usually expressed an immediate concern or referred to a recent event in the lives of the slaves. Thomas Wentworth Higginson recorded one such incident. While in South Carolina, he spoke with a black boatsman:

"Once we boys," he said, "went for tote some rice and de nigger-driver he keep a-callin' on us; and I say, "O de ole nigger-driver." Den anudder said, "Fust ting my mammy tole me was notin' so bad as nigger-driver." Den I made a sing, just puttin' a word, and den anudder word."

Then he began singing, and the men, after listening a moment, joined in the chorus, as if it were an old acquaintance, though they evidently had never heard it before. I saw how easily a new "sing" took root among them.

O de ole nigger-driver
O gwine away!

> First ting my mammy tell me
> O gwine away!
> Tell me 'bout de nigger-driver
> O gwine away!
> Nigger-driver second devil
> O gwine away!
> Best ting for do he driver
> O gwine away!
> Knock he down and spoil he labor
> O gwine away![22]

Another southern traveler, J. Kinnard Jr., commented on the communal and improvisational dimensions of antebellum African-American folksongs:

> The blacks themselves leave out old stanzas, and introduce new ones at pleasure. Traveling through the South, you may in passing from Virginia to Louisiana, hear the same tune a hundred times, but seldom the same words accompanying it. This necessarily results from the fact that the songs are unwritten, and also from the habit of extemporizing, in which performers indulge on festive occasions.[23]

The stress on musical inventions and process in the slaves' culture of resistance was based on long-standing African musical traditions. These traditions were of vital importance because they were antithetical to the European musical traditions prevalent in the dominant white culture—especially the emphasis on the ability to "read music" and on the "authority of the text." African-American musicians often "crossed over" to perform and compose European-style music, but they also built their own separate musical culture on an African foundation. It proved to be an integral part of the black oral tradition, and hence of the struggle for freedom.

After the Civil War, worksongs were maintained on southern prison farms, where black convicts were forced into gang labor, well into the twentieth century. The more popular of these songs were also well known among the general black populace and were often sung in the fields, on the levees, in the lumber camps, or wherever African Americans were involved in manual labor. The worksongs continued to stress oppressive work conditions, the hardships of the laborers, the injustice of their situation, and their yearnings for freedom and for loved ones far away. Some of them, like "Old Riley," "Another Man Done Gone," and "Lost John," were escape epics that helped to replenish the African-American oral tradition in the postbellum era. "Lost John" was the saga of a legendary black prisoner who escaped from a convict farm and eluded his trackers by putting additional heels on the front of his shoes. Lafcadio Hearn recorded in print one of the earliest accounts of this worksong:

> One day, one day,
> I were walkin' along
> And I heard a little voice,
> Didn't see no one.
> It was old Lost John,
> He said he was long gone,
> Like a turkey through the corn,
> With his long clothes on.
> He had a heel in front,
> Had a heel behind,
> Well you couldn't hardly tell,
> Well you couldn't hardly tell,
> Whichaway he was goin',
> Whichaway he was goin'.[24]

The Lost John legend followed in the mold of John de Conquerer, the trickster folk hero in the popular cycle of slave folktales involving "John and Old Marster" that had previously flourished in the antebellum South. Both figures demonstrated the will and the ingenuity needed to resist slavery or its prison-farm legacy.[25]

Through the worksongs, black laborers were able to carry forward their long-standing sense of being treated unjustly by their white overlords. There is a large reservoir of folk rhymes and sayings reflecting this resentment. A classic protest verse first noted by collectors of African-American folksongs around the turn of the century was the following:

> Nought's a nought, figger's a figger,
> Figger for the white man, nought for the nigger.
> Nigger and a white man playin' seven-up,
> Nigger won the money but was feared to pick it up.[26]

Many versions of this verse reappeared in the blues; its use was widespread among the rural black population during this period.

Some of the more common worksongs were very closely related to the rural blues in emotional tone and lyrical imagery. These included songs like "Diamond Joe," "Look Down That Long Lonesome Road," "Long Hot Summer Days," and "Go Down Old Hannah." Diamond Joe was another African-American redeemer figure:

> Ain't gonna work in the country
> And neither on Forest's farm.

>I'm gonna stay until Maybelle comes
>An' she gonna call me home.
>
>Diamond Joe, come a-gittin' me
>Diamond Joe, come a-gittin' me
>Diamond Joe, come a-gittin' me
>My black Joe.[27]

In the mournful "Go Down Old Hannah," the theme was again the grueling effects of manual labor:

>Go down old Hannah,
>Don't you rise no more,
>Don't you rise no more.
>Why don't you go down old Hannah,
>Don't you rise no more.
>Well I looked at old Hannah,
>She was turning red,
>She was turning red.
>Well I looked at old Hannah,
>She was turning red.
>
>Well I looked at my partner,
>He was almost dead,
>He was almost dead.
>Well I looked at my partner,
>He was almost dead.[28]

The tempo and tonality of these a cappella dirges were similar to those of the earliest rural blues. In addition, blue notes were used in both. The only major difference was that the rural blues featured some sort of guitar accompaniment, not just singing to the rhythms of work.

## Arhoolies

Another family of black folk music sung without instruments, yet still closely related to the blues, comprised the whoops, hollers, calls, cries, and arhoolies, as they were called, that had been commonplace among southern African Americans since the antebellum plantation days. Whooping, a form of yodeling, is a musical practice traditional among the tribes of Angola and the

Congo, especially the pygmies in the area, who use whoops as musical embellishments. Frances Ann Kemble, residing in 1839 on a Georgia plantation, left the first written account of a field holler. She described it as "an extremely pretty, plaintive air, there was but one line which was repeated with a wailing chorus."[29] The calls appear to have been most prevalent among the black vendors, peddlers, and craftsmen in southern seaport and riverport towns. They were usually linked to a product being sold or a service being offered. Cries and arhoolies, on the other hand, tended to be sung in the fields while farm work was in progress. Initially, they were short signature pieces—the vocalization of a fieldhand's identity and mood. Later they began to be turned into verbal phrases and then rudimentary impressions of life put to verse. All that these hollers needed to become blues songs was an instrumental accompaniment.

Son House, an early Mississippi Delta bluesman, credits the hollers with being the source of the rural blues: "All I can say is that when I was a boy we always was singing in the fields. Not real singing, you know, just hollering. But we made up our songs about things that was happening to us at the time, and I think that's where the blues started."[30] Echoing this notion of the blues' origins was Texas bluesman Sam "Lightnin' " Hopkins, who stated in a recorded interview: "Blues come out of the fields, baby. That's when you out there under the hot sun, bending down pickin' that cotton and singin' 'Oh God, have mercy on po' ole Lightnin'!' "[31] Sonny Terry, representing the Piedmont blues tradition, agreed. He told me:

I'll tell you where the blues began. Back there working on them cotton farms, working hard and the man won't pay 'em, so the people started singin', "Ohhh, I'm leavin' he one of these days and it won't be long." See, what's happenin' is givin' them the blues. "You gonna look for me one of these mornings and I'll be gone, ohhh yeah!"[32]

## African-American Ballads

African-American folk ballads were another major influence on the formation of a rural blues tradition. These narrative folksongs were loosely modeled after the traditional Anglo-American ballads sung all over the South, but particularly in the Appalachian region. The Anglo-American ballads were simple folksongs with a plaintive tone; they were characterized by a long series of stanzas that told a story, usually of epic proportions, about a momentous event, a tragic love relationship, or an ill-fated folk hero. When postbellum black songsters took over this ballad form, however, they reshaped it to meet the needs of their own people and culture—just as the slaves had reshaped Anglo-American hymnody into African-American spirituals. The black ballads are yet another historical manifestation of an oral tradition that resisted assimilation by a dominant cultural order. Thus, the form and the content of the traditional Anglo-American ballad underwent certain key transformations when it was adopted by African Americans. For example, the form was made less repetitive by the interjection of refrains between the stanzas. This variation on the West African call and response song pattern allowed for more breaks in the music, more rhythmic input, and more audience participation. Moreover, the narrative content was reconstructed to accommodate a pantheon of black folk heroes, tricksters, and outlaws who would be venerated and immortalized in the new folksongs.

The folk heroes in the black ballads were often modeled after actual historical figures, many of whom had died bravely and tragically. George Washington Cable translated this Creole ballad, recited to him by a former slave, about a rebellious slave's tragic ending:

> Aie! Young men, come to lament
> For poor St. Malo out there.
> They hunted him with dogs,
> They fired guns at him.
> They brought him from the cypress swamp,
> His arms they tied behind his back.
> They tied him to a horse's tail,
> They dragged him to the city.
> Before the men of the Cabildo,
> They accused him of a plot
> To cut the throat of all the whites.
> They asked him who his comrades were,
> But poor St. Malo was silent.
>
> The judge read out the sentence
> And they then prepared the gallows.
> They drove the horse—the cart moved off
> And left poor St. Malo hanging there.
> The day was an hour old
> When they hanged him.
> They left his body swinging
> For the carrion crows to eat.[33]

Folklorist B. A. Botkin collected a ballad named after Gabriel Prosser, the Virginia slave insurrectionist who was executed in 1800 after his plans to seize the city of Richmond were discovered. Entitled "The Escape of Gabriel Prosser," it suggests that Prosser escaped his captors with the aid of another slave and thus was elevated to the status of victorious black folk hero.

> Dere wuz two a-guardin' Gabr'l's cell
> An' ten mo' guards in the jail about;
> An' two a-standin' at the hangman's tree,
> An' Billy wuz dere to git Gabr'l out.
>
> Billy bus' chains an' Billy bus' bolts
> An' Billy bus' all dat's in his way;
> Ontwell he come to Gabr'l's do'
> An' he bus' dat too, right silently.
>
> Dere wuz musket shot an' musket balls
> Betwiz' his neckbone an' his knee;
> But Billy took Gabr'l up in his arms,
> An' he carried him away right manfully.
>
> Dey mounted a hoss an' away dey went,
> Ten miles off f'om dat hangin' tree
> Ontwell dey stop whar de river bent,
> An' dar dey rested happily.
>
> An' den dey called fo' a vic'try dance,
> An' de crowd dey all danced merrily;
> An' de bes' dancer 'mongst dem all
> Wuz Gabr'l Prosser who wuz jes' sot free![34]

## African-American Folk Heroes

John Henry, the archetypical postbellum black folk hero, was in real life an African American who died while driving steel for the railroad in West Virginia in the early 1870s. John Henry worksongs and ballads were first noticed by folklorists just after the turn of the century, when many versions were already being sung throughout the country. The enormous appeal of the John Henry legend among African Americans stemmed from their pride in his herculean exploits in the face of an untenable labor situation. The pressures from industrial mechanization and the rising influx of immigrant laborers were combining to trap black workers at the lowest level of the new industrial system. There they were forced to take on the dirtiest and most dangerous jobs. John Henry was a symbol of this economic plight as well as a symbol of resurgent racial dignity. He was not a slave but a "natural born" man who, although doomed, triumphed over the steam drill before dying, hammer in hand. As a tragic hero of African-American stock, John Henry had no equal in the last decades of the nineteenth century. He represents the conflicts between blacks and whites, labor and capital, men and machines. Understandably, his legend ignited the collective imagination of African Americans during this period, and his fame took on a national dimension.[35]

Ballads immortalizing famous black desperadoes were also widespread in the postbellum South. Like the folk hero legends, they were usually built upon real life characters who had died in some tragic and sensational manner. Unlike the folk heroes, however, these black renegades operated beyond the laws of society, preying on both their white antagonists and their own people. John Hardy, for example, was a notorious black steel driver (often confused with John Henry) who was hanged for murder in West Virginia in 1894. Railroad Bill (a pseudonym for Morris Slater) was a black turpentine worker from Alabama who became an infamous fugitive from justice after killing a white lawman in 1893; Slater eluded capture for over two years, during which time he robbed trains and killed another law officer before being gunned down by bounty hunters.[36]

Although much more self-aggrandizing than their revolutionary forebears, outlaws such as John Hardy, Railroad Bill, Stagolee, Roscoe Bill, Eddy Jones, Lazarus, and Aaron Harris symbolized resistance to harsh political repression and rigid segregation. Both John Hardy and Railroad Bill were characterized in the ballads that immortalized them as fearless "bad niggers" who belligerently transgressed white society's legal and moral order. In this respect, they were emblematic of a new generation of lower-class African-American insurgents who replaced slave insurrectionists like Nat Turner, Gabriel Prosser, Denmark Vesey, and St. Malo as the harbingers of race retribution. Their tactics of terror and intimidation were no less brutal than those used by the vigilantes of white supremacy; in fact, the wanton violence of the black badmen could be viewed as a spontaneous response to the official and unofficial violence the African American people were subjected to throughout the region. Even when humorous, the black badman ballads often revealed both a contempt for the laws and morals of the dominant white social order and a penchant for wrecking havoc on it:

> I's Wild Nigger Bill
> Frum Redpepper Hill,
> I never did work, an' I never will.

> I's done kill the boss,
> I's knocked down the hoss,
> I eats up raw goose without apple sauce.[37]

English historian Eric Hobsbawn, in his pioneering studies on social banditry, characterizes bandits as pre-political or "primitive rebels" in revolt against a newly established social order, "avengers" of those sectors of the lower-class population that were the most dislocated and oppressed by the changes in the political economy. Hobsbawn's observations, when applied to the American setting, are helpful in probing the cultural significance of the black outlaw ballads that originated in the last decades of the nineteenth century and were widely known among African Americans throughout the South in the early decades of the twentieth. Whether confronted with disenfranchisement and economic peonage in the rural South or with socio-economic inequality in the burgeoning urban centers of both the South and the North, American black people found their power and status during this period at their lowest ebb since slavery. The "bad nigger" ballads were folk antidotes calculated to negate the feelings of powerlessness and to avenge victimization by the dominant white social order. In this respect, they would share a kinship with the rural blues.[38]

## African-American Tricksters

A more indirect and certainly more strategic response to oppression was manifested in the emergence of trickster ballads that accented the continuing popularity of trickster folk heroes and folktales in the oral tradition. Animals with human personalities were usually central chracters of the trickster fables. Their stories invariably involved weak animals triumphing over stronger adversaries or a hostile environment through the use of their superior wits. Ananse, the clever spider in numerous West African folktales, Brer Rabbit, the trickster hero of the slaves' Uncle Remus fables, and the modern, urbanized Signifying Monkey—all habitually overcame their more formidable opponents with guile and a certain amount of bravado and by cunningly inverting the status quo of normal power relations. In so doing, they launched a sneak attack on the values of the dominant white culture.

A major characteristic of the commonplace animal trickster of the postbellum era was its indestructibility. The boll weevil was the most omnipotent folk symbol cast in this mold. The feisty weevil crossed into Texas from Mexico in the 1860s and began systematically to ravage the state's cotton crops. By the early 1900s, these tiny but seemingly invincible pests had pushed eastward, all the way to Georgia, leaving ruined cotton fields in their wake and hastening the collapse of the cotton economy in the South. Although black farm workers were themselves victimized by the boll weevil's insatiable appetite for cotton, they still felt a kinship with the weevils' dogged determination in "just looking" for a home. Furthermore, they viewed the misfortunes that the boll weevil brought the white plantation owners as retribution for the exploitation of black farm workers. The black folk ballads that sprang up to immortalize the boll weevil reflected these attitudes. One version has the weevil playfully nesting in "the capt'n's Sunday hat," while another version has him brashly confronting a merchant:

> Boll weevil said to the merchant, better drink you cold lemonade.
> When I get through with you, gwine drag you out of the shade.
> I have a home, I have a home.[39]

The boll weevil ballads eventually evolved into a popular folk blues, which was noticed in Mississippi by W. C. Handy as early as 1902.[40]

Another animal trickster ballad figure of the postbellum period, especially popular among African Americans in East Texas, was the Gray Goose, who was also prominent for her indestructibility. According to Leadbelly, who learned the ballad on a Texas prison farm, the Gray Goose was a metaphor for the prisoners' defiance of their captors.[41] As Alan Lomax stated in his introductory notes to a version of this folk ballad on a Library of Congress field recording:

> The folk have always loved humble heroes who were absolutely invincible, who could endure any hardship or torture without fear or harm. For the southern Negro, faced with the problem of sheer survival under slavery and later as a sub-standard economic group, this pattern has dominated his ballads and folk tales. The ballad of the heroic goose, who, after being shot, picked, cooked, carved and run through the sawmill, was last seen with a large, derisively honking flock of goslings, flying over the ocean, epitomized the Negro's belief in his own ability to endure any hardship.[42]

African-American ballads, arhoolies, and worksongs were the cultural products of an era that was rapidly disappearing. With the advent of the twentieth century, they became obsolete in the South at the same time that the rural blues were on the upswing, filling a musical vacuum for younger black people. Nonetheless, the ballads, arhoolies, and worksongs each made separate but critical contributions to the growth of the rural blues. Ballads supplied folks heroes, fables, metaphors, and melodies. Field hollers supplied vocal techniques and tonality. More than likely the "blue notes" had their origins in the arhoolies. Worksongs supplied antiphony, cross-rhythms, and important thematic material. Together, they provided the bedrock for the rural folk blues.

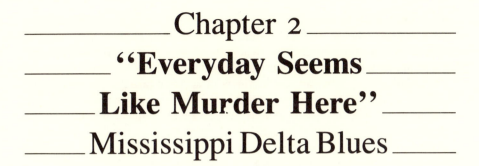

# Chapter 2
## "Everyday Seems Like Murder Here"
## Mississippi Delta Blues

### Rural Blues and the Plantation Economy

After the defeat of the Confederacy, the South was forced to free the slave population, but it did not abandon its plantation economy. Instead, the system was modified to take better advantage of the former slaves' vulnerable economic position. Knowing no vocation other than farming, the large majority of the black population had little choice but to remain in the rural South after the Civil War as tenant farmers or sharecroppers. Under these similar forms of agricultural peonage, the black farmers were forced to deduct a substantial share of their crops for the use of the land and tools, as well as for the credit extended them by the plantation owners for food, shelter, and clothing. After the harvest, they usually found themselves still in debt to their landlords. A major consequence of the postbellum plantation economy was that African Americans were confined to cotton farming and, for the most part, effectively blocked from owning their own land or from moving into more lucrative occupations. This situation existed from the end of the Civil War until World War II. In 1862, 92 percent of the black population lived in the rural South; by 1900, that figure had dropped only a few percentage points because of a slight migration into southern cities.[1]

The postbellum plantation economy proved to be a powerful bulwark against the political ascendency of black freedmen and their Republican allies during the Reconstruction era. In the aftermath of Reconstruction, with the upsurge in vigilantism and lynchings, the imposition of Jim Crow segregation laws, and the disenfranchisement of black male voters, African Americans in the South were relegated to a lower legal and political status and denied basic civil rights. The pre-industrial social order stubbornly reasserted its hegemony over southern race relations. However, the South's economy deteriorated steadily as a result; allegiance to the plantation system of tenant farming and sharecropping inhibited the quest for greater cotton productivity, newer methods of commercial farming, and agricultural diversity as well as industrialization. By 1900, the per capita income in the South was 51 percent of the national average, having declined steadily for four decades. As could be expected, the rural black population was the most impoverished social group.[2]

The blues sprang from this environment of agrarian poverty and racial segregation, a folk music indigenous to the cotton belt farming communities and seeming to flower in those regions most heavily populated by African-American farm workers. The Mississippi Delta, East Texas, and the Piedmont were the key regions where the blues emerged as a popular form of folksong before they rose to national prominence during the second and third decades of the twentieth century. Each of these early blues cultural formations contributed to a truly original folk music that matured in relative isolation from the dominant white culture.

## Delta Blues Origins

The home soil of the Delta blues was the flat fertile farmland on either side of the Mississippi River stretching from Memphis, Tennessee, some two hundred miles south to Vicksburg, Mississippi. The eastern border of the Delta was formed by the barren hills of central Mississippi; its western border was the Ozark plateau in Arkansas.

Beginning in the 1840s, the lower eastern segment of the Delta emerged as one of the richest cotton-producing areas in the South. It attracted white planters and their slaves, who first cleared the land and then toiled in the fields, planting, cultivating, and harvesting the cotton crops. There was a further influx of planters and farm workers after the Civil War into the upper, more remote Delta hinterlands, where the plantations were organized into many smaller sharecropping parcels farmed by individuals or families. By the 1890s, African Americans were more heavily concentrated in the Delta region than anywhere else in the South and outnumbered the white population by three to one. The influx continued until World War I, at which time the black population in the Delta outnumbered the white by four to one. During that thirty-year period, the entire region was transformed from a swampy frontier wilderness into a bustling labor-intensive agricultural assembly line. The Delta now had two cash crops; in addition to the resurrection of King Cotton, there was a booming lumber industry. Moreover, complementing the Mississippi waterway was a new network of railroads linking the area to the outside world from all directions.

Yet, as we have seen, for the black sharecroppers the plantations were feudal in character. This concentrated black population tied to the plantation economy and segregated from the average white citizenry, combined with the general backwardness of the region, provided the cultural mesh in which the Delta blues would take root, grow, and eventually flourish.[3]

The first Delta blues were made up by rural laborers at work, according to most of the primary sources on the music's origins. The earliest known blues in this region were closely akin to the worksongs and field hollers still prevalent at the time. Delta-born bluesman Albert Luandrew, also known as Sunnyland Slim, who grew up in Vance, Mississippi, in the early 1900s, recalled:

They were singing the blues in Mississippi and Louisiana ever since there were colored peoples living there to my way of knowing. They sang in cotton fields and in the prison camps and the levee camps. Peoples on the county farm cutting trees with an axe sang, "Oh Captain, believe it's quitting time." People picking cotton were crying out, "Oh, I'm a poor boy long way from home." They weren't doin' it for no money or nothin' like that. No, they was doin' it 'cause it just sound so good to them, you know, it allowed for 'em to express themselves. People standing out for miles along the railroads and highways singing, "Oh it ain't gonna rain no more," and "Sun gonna shine in my door someday, yeah." This was the oldest blues I ever knowed.[4]

Fellow Mississippian McKinley Morganfield, better known as Muddy Waters, also remarked on the influence of rural work habits on the music of the Delta, in this case, his own:

You just make things up when you're working out on the plantation. You get lonesome and tired and hot and you start to sing you something. And so all that stuff come to me real good. I can remember that a lot of the records I have made, I first made those songs up during my workdays out on the farm.[5]

The earliest written description of a Delta blues song text dates to 1901. In June of that year a Harvard archeologist named Charles Peabody, who was excavating an Indian burial site close to Stovall, Mississippi, hired a group of black workers in Clarksdale as diggers. Peabody kept detailed notes on the folk music he heard performed by the black workers he hired and later used them in an article, "Notes on Negro Music," published in 1903 in the *Journal of American Folklore*.[6] The songs he documented in the article included work-

songs, field hollers, ragtime songs, and a few blues verses that proved to be
very popular throughout the South. Some of the worksongs were improvised
on the spot by Ike Antoine, the workers' designated song leader. One pointed
example—

> I'm so tired I'm 'most dead,
> Sittin' up there playin' mumbley peg[7]—

was actually composed while Peabody and another white man were playing the
knife game in front of the black work crew. The article describes field hollers
as "strains of apparently genuine African music," and quotes a "ragtime"
folksong with a guitar accompaniment that poked fun at black preachers:

> Some folk say preachers won't steal,
> But I found two in my cornfield.
> One with a shovel and t' other with a hoe,
> A-diggin up my taters row by row.[8]

Another kind of folksong that Peabody heard his work crew sing in the evenings was the "hard luck tale." Among the lyrics he wrote down were:

> They arrested me for murder
> And I never harmed a man.[9]

> Well I thought I heard that KC whistle blow,
> Blow lak' she never blew befo'.[10]

> The reason I love my baby so
> 'Cause when she gets five dollars she give me fo'.[11]

Folklorist Howard Odum visited the Mississippi Delta as part of a fieldtrip
through the South's cotton belt between 1905 and 1908. Half the songs he
collected from the African-American "songsters" and "musicians" he encountered were blues or blues-related. In addition, many of the songs he heard
featured a guitarist using a slider—a technique common among Delta blues
musicians. Odum wrote down one line that enjoyed widespread use throughout
the cotton belt: "I got the blues and can't be satisfied."[12]

For the most part, overt protest was absent from the early Delta blues. The
social commentary was confined to descriptions of the hardships and injustices
experienced by African Americans in the region; there were no frontal assaults
on segregation or political disenfranchisement. Yet protest was implicit in

these new blues songs because they described events and expressed feelings from the perspective of a group relegated to the lowest levels of the Delta's rigid caste system. Such an outlook, based on the collective experience of rural black workers, was bound to come into conflict with the ideology of the dominant white culture.

Although the Delta blues initially came out of cotton farming and the work routines of black farm workers, they soon gravitated toward the recreational activities of the region's segregated black enclaves, especially social gatherings such as picnics, barbecues, fish fries, sporting events, holiday parties, and country dances. Music was an integral part of the entire spectrum of social activity—from the spirituals and gospel songs of the Sunday morning church meetings to the uptempo rags and party tunes played at the Saturday night dances—but, as could be expected, the infectious rhythms and candid lyrics of the blues found a more receptive audience at the Saturday night celebrations.

The Saturday night social gatherings were communal rituals of resistance that originated during slavery. Since the slaves worked six days a week from sunup to sundown, Saturday evening was the only time they had for recreational activities. Most plantation owners allowed their slaves to hold a dance or to attend one on a nearby plantation, and these get-togethers were the highlight of the week. One ex-slave recalled:

> Law me, us had a good time in demdays.
> Us danced most ebry Sattidy night
> And us made de rafters shake wid us foots.[13]

Besides shaking rafters, the Saturday night gatherings also facilitated communication and group solidarity. Sometimes the talk centered on Africa, where the slaves before losing their freedom had "done what they wanted."[14] Such gatherings were one of the ways that their desire for freedom was kept alive during captivity.

After the Civil War, the tradition of the Saturday night dance continued on many of the resurrected cotton plantations in the South. During this period, the dance evolved into a festive and at times rowdy gathering where African-American men and women came together to socialize and seek release from a long week of work. Dances were held either in local homes or outdoors if the weather permitted; much later, "juke joints" were opened to accommodate these parties on a regular basis. Coal lamps provided the lighting. Freshly cooked food, homebrew, and moonshine were sold cheaply. There was usually some gambling, talking, and flirting on the periphery of the gatherings, but the center of activity was the dancing.

Music for the Saturday night dances traditionally had been the purview of black fiddlers. The fiddle was the most widely used instrument among

African Americans until the Civil War, surpassing even the banjo. Most black fiddlers who grew up after emancipation learned their musical techniques and repertoire from former slaves. Delta bluesman Sam Chatmon recalled that his father, a former slave from Mississippi who died in 1934 at the age of 109, learned to play the fiddle from an older fellow slave. They often played to gether at white plantation dances, as well as at dances in the slave quarters. Their favorite tunes, played at both occasions, included "Little Lisa Jane," "Chicken in the Birdbath," and "Old Grey Mare"—all of Anglo-American origin. The elder Chatmon had a large extended family and taught many of them to play the fiddle or the four-string banjo, which was the instrument that Sam Chatmon first played as a youth. Butch Cage was another second-generation Mississippi fiddle player who learned his instrument from older black musicians. The first tunes he was taught to perform were also mid-nineteenth-century Anglo-American standards like "Dixie," "Arkansas Traveler," "Old Mule," and "Hell Broke Loose in Georgia." W. C. Handy's grandfather played the fiddle as a slave and told him about an early method of making rhythm for the dance music by having a second person drum on the fiddle strings with a set of knitting needles. Later, Handy's uncle, also a traditional fiddler, taught him how to master the knitting-needle percussive technique and allowed his nephew to accompany him occasionally at country dances. Each of these accounts of postbellum black male fiddlers suggests that they drew heavily on Anglo-American fiddle tunes but played them in their own style. The dance music they played syncretized the folk materials and instrumental techniques from both traditions and was played before both black and white audiences.[15]

The Delta blues represented a definitive break with the "old-time" country dance music. Although African Americans danced to the blues, the dances changed, since the music was primarily drawn from folk sources other than the Anglo-American fiddle tradition. Square dancing gave way to slow and intimate couple-dancing or upbeat "hip-shaking" routines. Moreover, the early Delta blues used different musical instruments—the guitar and the harmonica rather than the fiddle and the banjo. In particular, the adaptation of the guitar to the rural blues idiom proved to be a major innovation that would have far-reaching consequences.

In the Delta, black guitarists either began by learning to play instruments like the banjo or the mandolin and adapted those playing techniques to the guitar or began their musical training on a homemade guitar, often with just one string. Musicians who came to the guitar from other instruments were likely to have more formal training and to be able to play more styles of black folk music than just the blues. They often came from families like the Chatmons and the Handys that had well-established traditions as schooled musicians and grew up listening to and learning to play the music of their parents and grandparents on many different musical instruments. Thus, their approach to the guitar and the blues overall was both more sophisticated and more conventional than that of the self-taught Delta bluesmen.

The self-taught Delta guitar players were often, paradoxically, both the most traditional and the most original interpreters of the rural blues: original because they developed a sound that was unprecedented in both African-American and Anglo-American folk music; traditional because the one-string instruments they learned on were the progeny of the ancient musical bow, a common folk instrument for centuries in West Africa. The cultural practices associated with making and playing the musical bow were diffused throughout the African diaspora: in Brazil it was called the "berimbau"; in the southern United States it was known to the children who used it as a "didley bow" or a "jitterbug." One-string instruments in the Delta were usually made by attaching a taut wire to the side of a house or a barn. The aspiring musician plucked out repetitive, one-measure figures with one hand while using the other to slide some sort of hard, smooth device along the wire to get the desired tone. Mississippi bluesmen Big Joe Williams, Big Bill Broonzy, Muddy Waters, Elmore James, Fenton Robinson, and B. B. King all began their musical careers on homemade one-string instruments.[16]

A similar musical technique found throughout the Mississippi Delta was the practice of pressing an object like a rock, a knife, or a bottleneck against the resonating strings of various types of string instruments to produce extended musical phrases that sounded like the human voice. This practice of imitating vocal timbre and diction was adopted at an early stage in the development of Delta blues. W. C. Handy described his first encounter with the soon-to-be-famous Mississippi Delta "bottleneck" or "slide" guitar style while stranded at the Tutwiler, Mississippi, train station in 1903:

A lean, loose-jointed Negro had commenced plucking a guitar beside me while I slept. His clothes were rags; his feet peeped out of his shoes. His face had on it some of the sadness of the ages. As he played, he pressed a knife blade on the strings of the guitar in a manner popularized by Hawaiian guitarists who used steel bars. His song, too, struck me instantly:

Goin' where the Southern cross the Dog.

The singer repeated the line three times, accompanying himself on the guitar with the weirdest music I had ever heard.[17]

Handy erred in tracing the slide guitar style to Hawaii; from all indications, it was simultaneously developed in the Delta.

The appearance of black slide guitarists in the early 1900s has often been linked to the popularization of a similar technique by Hawaiian guitarists, but slide guitar wasn't native to Hawaii; it was introduced there between 1893 and 1895 reputedly by a school boy, Joseph Kekaka. It did not spread from Hawaii to the mainland until 1900, when it was popularized by Frank Ferera, and by that time black guitarists in Mississippi were already fretting their instruments with knives or the broken-off necks of bottles.[18]

The slide technique was especially appealing to the early blues musicians because it allowed them to approximate on their guitars the sounds and the phrasings of the arhoolies. The use of a slide was a key innovation, unique to folk music in the United States. In time, it would become inseparable from the Delta blues tradition.

## Delta Blues Pioneers

The earliest blues singers and musicians to become well known in the Delta were fieldhands whose musical activities were most often secondary to their cotton farming. They played on weekends and holidays for free drinks and tips at local parties and social events, perhaps with a few other musicians. By performing with others before their friends and neighbors, they gained valuable support that helped them to develop a repertoire and a performing style. Because the music was learned through repetition but played intuitively on each occasion, it continued to be a spontaneous expression of the African-American oral tradition in the Delta area. As long as there was a functional relationship between the rural blues and the black-belt farming communities in which they originated, the folk roots of the music remained intact and exhibited an ongoing vitality. By the turn of the century, some of the more talented and determined of the blues musicians in the Delta were gaining wider recognition. They began traveling to surrounding black enclaves to perform their music before larger audiences and attracting young apprentice musicians.

### Big Bill Broonzy: "Goin' Down the Road Feeling Bad"

William Lee Conley Broonzy, known affectionately as "Big Bill," was born on a tenant farm in the Mississippi Delta on June 26, 1893. His parents had grown up during slavery, and the family was poor, religious, and large. There were twenty-one children in all; most of them worked in the cotton fields with their parents, but a few were allowed to go to school. Because Broonzy grew tall and strong at an early age, he had to work in the fields. At the age of seven, he started working as a plowhand; it was to be his primary vocation until his flight to Chicago fifteen years later. Broonzy was ten years old when his uncle, Jerry Blecher, taught him the rudiments of playing a homemade fiddle fashioned out of a cigar box. Blecher played a five-string banjo; his repertoire and the repertoires of his fellow musicians included many of the region's earliest folk blues: "Goin' Down the Road Feeling Bad," "Mindin' My Own Business," "Crow Jane," "See See Rider," and "Joe Turner Blues." The first two are standard folk blues in the AAB stanza pattern:

> Goin' down this road feeling bad, baby,
> I'm goin' down this road feeling so miserable and sad.
> I ain't gonna be treated this way.

> Take six months to tend my business, six months to leave
>     other people's alone,
> Six months to tend my business, six months to leave other
>     people's alone,
> By the time I do that, I declare the whole twelve months
>     is gone.[19]

"Joe Turner Blues" is built around the more archaic AAA pattern:

> They tell me Joe Turner been here and gone,
> Lord, they tell me Joe Turner been here and gone,
> They tell me Joe Turner been here and gone.[20]

According to Broonzy, the song pays tribute to a good samaritan who helped out black families during a devastating Mississippi River flood in 1892. Another version of "Joe Turner" popular in the Memphis region is about a malevolent lawman named Joe Turney, who took black prisoners to the Tennessee State Penitentiary in Nashville between 1892 and 1896; W. C. Handy published his rendition of this folk blues in 1915. Broonzy also talked about an itinerant Delta bluesman called C. C. Rider, who played a one-string fiddle and claimed to have written the "See See Rider Blues," after himself. However, there are no other accounts of such a character in the early oral histories of the blues in the Mississippi Delta.[21]

### Charley Patton: "Moon Going Down"

Charley Patton was the heart and soul of the early Delta blues tradition. In his prime he was the most famous blues artist in the region. One of his protégés referred to him as "a great man," and his principal biographer calls him "the conscience of the Delta."[22] Patton was born on a farm near Bolton, and Edwards, Mississippi, two small towns located just west of Jackson, the state capital. His birth is listed in the 1900 census as having occurred in April 1891, which would make him one of the youngest of the first-generation Delta bluesmen. He was one of twelve children, seven of whom died before reaching their teens. This was an unusually high child mortality rate, even for a poor rural black family, and it no doubt had an impact on Patton. Death would be a prominent theme in his later blues and spiritual compositions. His mother, Annie Patton, was part African American and part Native American; his father, Bill Patton, had African-American, Native-American, and white ancestors. Bill Patton was a farmer, a lay preacher, and a stern disciplinarian who used his bullwhip on his son in a futile effort to prevent him from becoming a blues musician.

While still a child, Charley Patton learned to play a guitar in the company of the Chatmon clan, who lived close by. The Chatmons were a large family with a tradition of performing music together that was in its third generation. They played stringband music for white square dances and black social gatherings. Their repertoire did not include the blues until after the turn of the century, and it is unlikely that Charley Patton was introduced to this new folk music before moving with his family to Dockery's plantation farther north in the Delta near Drew, Mississippi, between 1901 and 1904.[23]

Drew was a new town built in the 1890s on land taken back from the Mississippi River. It had previously been swampland but was cleared and cultivated after the construction of a levee system to protect the land from the annual spring floods that plagued the entire Mississippi basin. Will Dockery founded his plantation, called Dockery Farms, near Drew in 1895 on forty square miles of wild, wooded, swampy bottomland. The son of a slaveowner who lost most of his wealth during the Civil War, Dockery worked tirelessly to establish his own cotton kingdom near Drew and across the river in Arkansas. His empire-building spirit ultimately inspired him to have his own railroad line constructed, linking Dockery Farms to the nearby town of Cleveland. Called the "Pea Vine" by the black fieldhands because of its circuitous route to and from Dockery's, it was eventually immortalized by Charley Patton in "Pea Vine Blues." In the heyday of the plantation, Dockery employed up to eight hundred black workers and issued paper money for use in the general store. Many of the workers lived in the residential camp, which they called "the Quarters,' a reference to the old slave living quarters on antebellum plantations and, by implication, to the lack of change in the postbellum era. The Quarters consisted of about a dozen boarding houses for single men and women and a smaller number of separate family dwellings. In most accounts, Will Dockery was a benevolent and paternalistic "bossman" by Delta standards. He employed African Americans as middle-level managers of his company town, sponsored "free" picnics for his workers, and encouraged music making on his plantation.[24]

At Dockery's, young Charley Patton came under the influence of a small group of older black musicians, who introduced him to the blues. The standout of this group was Henry Sloan, who was twenty years older than Patton. Sloan had lived for a time in the "hill country" west of Jackson and had moved to Dockery's around 1900. He is remembered as the leading musician on the plantation before Charley Patton's ascendancy and as the man most responsible for Patton's early blues style and repertoire. Sloan moved to Chicago during World War I and dropped out of sight. He was never recorded, but he was clearly one of the founding fathers of the Delta blues tradition.[25]

By the 1910s, Patton was emerging as the most influential blues musician in the Drew area, and Dockery's plantation became a focal point of local blues activity. In addition to Patton and Sloan, the Dockery group included Jack Hicks, Ben Maree, Dick Bankston, Jim Holloway, Mott Willis, and Jake Martin; they were all transitional folk musicians, spanning the gap between the established songster tradition and the newly emerging blues tradition. Equally important, Patton and the rest of the Dockery group were beginning to attract younger disciples like Willie Brown, Kid Bailey, and Tommy Johnson and, later, Son House, Robert Johnson, Bukka White, and Chester Burnett, also known as Howling Wolf. These men would be instrumental in establishing the Delta blues tradition as one of the most formidable in the entire South.

Those who knew Charley Patton remember him as a small, vigorous man with a coarse, rasping voice. A photograph taken of him while still a young man reveals the light complexion, large ears, curly, slicked-down hair, crooked bow tie, and Huck Finn facial features that led a fellow musician to say, "He looked like a Mexican."[26] A flashy dresser who always wore expensive suits, ties, and shoes and a Stetson hat, Patton went through eight marriages and once had his throat cut by a jealous husband. He was also a mercurial rambler and a rowdy, fun-loving prankster who loved to drink and socialize and cut up. In one of his songs he boasts:

> I love to fuss and fight,
> I love to fuss and fight,
> Lord, and get sloppy drunk off a bottle of bond
> And walk the streets all night.[27]

Ultimately, Charley Patton was remembered as a flamboyant and charismatic blues performer. Once in front of an audience, he not only sang but also danced, told tall tales, bantered with fellow musicians, and played his guitar behind his head, between his legs, or lying on his back. Patton's guitar playing emphasized rhythms over melodies. He played the guitar more like a drum than a string instrument, picking propulsive bass runs, hammering out percussive patterns on the treble strings, and hitting the "sound box" or hollow guitar body with the palm of his hand like a bass drum. According to Robert Palmer, "Most of the rhythmic devices that Patton uses have counterparts in West African drumming, and he uses them in an African manner, stacking rhythms on top of each other in order to build up a dense, layered rhythmic complexity."[28] Patton also made use of African-derived vocal technique. He habitually used his voice like a musical instrument. It is often hard to understand his lyrics because he alters his speech patterns to achieve certain rhythmic effects. He also uses a call and response framework for many of his songs. For example, in "Spoonful Blues" Patton creates four separate voice parts that engage each other in a call and response dialogue. There are his regular singing voice, his falsetto singing voice, his spoken word voice, and the voice of his guitar "singing" the phrase "spoonful" with the help of a slider.[29]

Charley Patton's repertoire was indicative of his rural upbringing and lifestyle, as well as his semi-professional status as a leading Delta bluesman. Several of the songs he performed were his own renditions of traditional spirituals such as "I'm Going Home," "I Shall Not Be Moved," "Nearer My God to Thee," and "Old Ship of Zion." He also composed his own sacred songs, which he often included in the sermons he preached from time to time in local churches. His favorite hymn, according to his niece, contains the verse:

> Jesus is my God, I know his name,
> His name is all my trust.
> He would not put my soul to shame
> Or let my hopes be lost.[30]

Patton's calling as a preacher was eclipsed by his attraction to secular song—ballads, ragtime, and especially the blues. He was well schooled in the entire spectrum of black folk music popular in his locale, but the blues he composed and sang were his most personal achievements. To create his melodies, he generally reworked three basic blues "tune families" over and over again; hence, many of his songs sound similar. As for his lyrics, he fused vignettes of Delta life and love with his favorite epigrams and folk sayings from the black oral tradition (for example, "I'm worried now, but I won't be worried long," "Handful of gimmie and a mouthful of much obliged," "Hard times at your front door, blues all around your bed," "Blues come down like showers of rain"). His better-known compositions contain numerous references to local people, in particular his women friends and fellow musicians, but also white lawmen and plantation owners, references to Delta towns like Belzoni, Clarksdale, Lula, Greenville, Joiner, and Vicksburg, and references to local events he was caught up in, such as an ordeal in jail ("High Sheriff Blues") or the flooding of the Mississippi basin in 1927 ("High Water Everywhere") or the 1929 Delta drought ("Dry Well Blues"). A niece of Patton's recalled that he would often "dream a song . . . , get up and write it down."[31] (Dreams were an important source of inspiration for many of the rural blues artists in the South.)

Charley Patton recorded a total of fifty titles at four different sessions between 1929 and 1934; thirty-five are blues, ten are sacred numbers, three are black folk ballads, and two are ragtime songs.[32] His blues songs are pregnant with rural metaphor and social commentary. His signature piece, "Pony Blues," for example, celebrates social mobility in a rural setting:

> Hey, hitch up my pony, saddle up my black mare,
> Hitch up my pony, saddle up my black mare,
> I'm gonna find a rider, baby, in the world somewhere.[33]

The underlying emphasis on freedom of movement is tied to the search for a "rider" or mate, which in turn is linked to the promise of personal satisfaction. It can only be found "somewhere" beyond the confines of the immediate social reality. This is a recurrent theme in rural folk blues, one that was often expressed in the songs of the early Delta blues artists.

Critical social commentary is more explicitly evident in songs like "High Sheriff Blues," which describes Patton's incarceration in the Belzoni jail. The lyrics give a fleeting glance at the sharp race and class divisions prevalent in the Delta during this period:

> I was in trouble ain't no use screamin' and . . .
> When I was in prison it ain't no use screamin' an' cryin',
> Mr. Purvis in his mansion he jes' pay no mind.[34]

Or consider these verses from "Down the Dirt Road Blues":

> I'm goin' away to a world unknown,
> I'm goin' away to a world unknown,
> I'm worried now, but I won't be worried long.

> Everyday seems like murder here (my God I'm gonna sing 'em),
> Everyday seems like murder here,
> I'm gonna leave tomorrow, I know you don't bit more care.[35]

In other songs, Patton extends his social concern to a wider milieu. In
"34 [1934] Blues," Patton sings bitterly about being ordered off Will Dockery's plantation and links his hardship to the suffering of others through the
depression:

He run me from Will Dockery's, Willie Brown, hunt you a job,
He run me from Will Dockery's, Willie Brown, hunt you a job
   (wonder what's the matter),
He went an' told Papa Charley, don't want you hangin' round on my
   job no more.

Further down the country it almost make you cry,
Further down the country it almost make you cry (my God, Children),
Women and children flaggin' freight trains for rides.

And it may bring sorrow, it may bring tears,
It may bring sorrow, Lord, it may bring tears,
Oh, Lord, oh Lord, spare me to see a brand new year.[36]

"Revenue Man Blues" conjures up the specter of white vigilantes on the
prowl—

Aw the revenue men is ridin', boy, you'd better look out—[37]

though this most likely refers to the local lawman assigned to uphold the Prohibition laws of the 1920s. "Tom Rushing" is about a deputy sheriff in Boli-
var County assigned to tracking down moonshiners and bootleggers who had
arrested a bootlegger named Holloway, a friend of Patton's:[38]

Once you get in trouble, there's no use screamin' an' cryin',
When you get in trouble, there's no use screamin' an' cryin',
Tom Rushing will take you back to Cleveland flyin'.[39]

"Mean Black Moan" is about a railroad strike in Chicago, which Patton
visited in the late 1920s and early 1930s. It is the only topical blues that he
recorded that takes place outside the Delta:

Ninety men were laid off at a railroad shop,
Ninety men were laid off, Lord, at a railroad shop,
And the strike in Chicago, Lordy Lord, it just won't stop.[40]

In the song Patton expresses concern for the plight of the workers, who are hungry and unable to pay their rent as the strike goes into its third month with no end in sight.

"High Water Everywhere" is a frantic portrait of the devastating 1927 Mississippi River flood. Spring rains and a swollen river caused the levees to break at several locations in the Mississippi basin, including one just north of Greenville, Mississippi. The flooding caused a three-hundred-mile-wide lake in the Delta. African Americans living in the area were forced to take refuge in a hastily constructed tent city on high ground near Greenville, where they were confined for two months while the waters receded. Many were also pressed into work gangs by the National Guard, which had been put in charge of cleaning up and keeping order. One black man was shot dead by the guardsmen for refusing to work. Overall, 125 people were killed in Mississippi as a result of the flood and thousands of homes were destroyed.[41] Patton recounts his own troubles when the rising flood waters "drove poor Charley down the line." He exclaims, "I would go to the hill country but they got me barred," a reference to the state of emergency being enforced by the white guardsmen that restricted African Americans to the tent cities. After assessing the situation at Greenville and Leland and even across the river in Blytheville and Joiner, all of which were under water, Patton ends his narrative by eulogizing "fifty men and children, come to sink and drown, . . . women and children sinking down, Lord have mercy."[42]

Throughout his career in the 1910s and 1920s, Charley Patton was constantly on the move in the Delta and the hill country to the south where he was born. He was prosperous enough to own a car, which gave him the freedom of movement so important to rural blues performers, as well as a certain amount of prestige and status. As a result, he was able to cultivate an extensive audience for his music not only among the black populace but also among white people, who often hired him to perform at their social affairs. On occasion, he traveled north to Memphis, St. Louis, and even Chicago to perform. By the onset of the depression, when he began his recording career, his fame as a blues artist was without an equal in the Mississippi Delta, and it was beginning to spread to other regions of the country. But Patton was unable to achieve national recognition before he died. In the early 1930s he began to experience heart problems, which caused fatigue and shortness of breath. In 1934, under the care of a doctor, he traveled to New York for his last recording session, in which he recorded his version of "I Know My Time Ain't Long"; he retitled it "Oh, Death." This song and his earlier sacred records, "The Prayer of Death" and "You're Gonna Need Someone When You Die," attest to his enduring fear of death. Soon after he returned to the Delta, he was bedridden with bronchitis. He lay in bed for a week preaching from the Book of Revelations and then died. He had just turned forty-three. The black newspapers that advertised his records failed to mention his passing, but his funeral was attended by hundreds of friends and fans.[43]

## Delta Blues Networks

Charley Patton's prominence in the formative years of Delta blues culture stems from his charisma as a folk artist and his life-long association with an informal network of fellow blues musicians and apprentices. Patton was at the center of a nexus of blues artists destined to become the region's most famous exponents of the music. While the evidence suggests that there were numerous informal networks, "extended families," or "schools" of blues musicians in and around the Delta region—especially after the turn of the century—it is also obvious that Patton and his associates gained the most popular acclaim. As a consequence, their lives and music have been more thoroughly documented than have most of their contemporaries'. Thus while they are certainly not the only Delta blues network or "tree" of relationships to take root and grow to maturity during this period, they are representative of those that did, and the abundance of information on them makes it much easier to discern how that came about.

The three most influential of the younger Delta bluesmen who played with Charley Patton during his heyday were Willie Brown, Tommy Johnson, and Son House. Willie Brown spent most of his life in the Delta, where he worked as a sharecropper and played music in his spare time. He joined Patton on Dockery's plantation around 1911, when he was still in his teens, and played regularly with him thereafter. Willie's trademark was his versatile guitar playing. He was admired for his masterful approach to the standard blues line and was always in demand as a second guitarist backing up other Delta bluesmen. Brown composed only a few of his own blues, and most of those relied heavily on material garnered from Patton. His best-known composition, "Future Blues," was an adaptation of Patton's "Moon Going Down"; however, its rhythmic guitar accompaniment was a classic piece of Delta blues much emulated by rural guitarists attracted to the idiom. Willie Brown appears to have been an unassuming blues musician who formed strong bonds of friendship with his fellow bluesmen. He is mentioned prominently in the blues lyrics of Charley Patton and, later, Robert Johnson. He was indispensable to Patton when he was performing in the Delta, and then he teamed up with Son House for a time before he died in the mid-1940s.[44]

Willie Brown was married to Josie Bush, an older blues singer and guitarist from nearby Florence, Mississippi. They met in the Drew area around 1911 and often played together in public. Bush was generally considered to be the best female blues musician in the region. Her much-copied signature piece, "Riverside Blues," is a song she had learned in her youth from a blues singer named Willie Love, who came from south of the Delta. The prevailing social conditions made it difficult for black women to join the growing ranks of the semi-professional blues performers; it was much more dangerous for them than for their male counterparts to live in the rough-and-tumble milieu of the itinerant blues musicians. If a young black woman was inclined toward music during this period, more than likely she sang in a church choir or joined a traveling minstrel troupe. Those few women in the Delta who proved to be the exceptions were Josie Bush, Louise Johnson, Lucille Davis, and Mattie Delaney. Davis and Delaney were also guitarists; Johnson played the piano. Johnson was a companion of Charley Patton and Willie Brown; she accompanied them on an excursion north in 1930 to a recording session where she recorded four piano blues, including her signature piece, "On the Wall." Delaney also was recorded during this period, but she and Johnson were the only two women participating in early Delta blues culture who were recording artists.[45]

### Tommy Johnson: "Canned Heat Killin' Me"

Tommy Johnson, another talented pupil of Charley Patton's, absorbed much of his mentor's performing style and repertoire before moving on to establish himself as a major Delta blues artist in his own right. Johnson was born sometime before the turn of the century in Crystal Springs, Mississippi, a small town south of Vicksburg; he grew up in a large family that seems to have been musical. He and one of his brothers spent time near Dockery's during World War I, and then again in 1921. During his visits to the Delta, Johnson developed a taste for alcohol, women, and the Devil. He told his brother how he sold his soul to the Devil in return for his talents as a blues musician. It happened—so the legend goes—at a deserted Delta crossroads at midnight during a full moon where Johnson was sitting, playing the blues on his guitar. A large black man appeared from nowhere, took his guitar, tuned it, played a blues number, and then gave it back. The crossroads is the traditional domain of Legba, a Yoruban trickster god who became identified with Satan, the Christian Devil, during slavery. The African Americans' version of the Christian Devil remained a trickster figure in their folklore, and it was this trickster persona that Tommy Johnson reveled in. He took to wearing a large rabbit's foot around his neck and was delighted to be known as someone in league with the Devil. It went with his act. He developed into a flamboyant showman, playing his guitar behind his back, over his head, and between his legs much like Charley Patton. As Delta bluesman Houston Stackhouse recalled:

He'd clown sometimes. He'd kick the guitar, flip it, turn it back of his head and be playin' it, then he'd get straddled over it like he was ridin' a mule; pick it that way. All that kind of rot. Oh, Tommy Johnson would tear it up, man. People loved to see that. People went for his jive, what he was putting down.[46]

In the mid-twenties, Tommy Johnson moved to Jackson, Mississippi, on the southeast periphery of the Delta farmlands, where he played regularly and built up a substantial reputation as the top blues performer in town. At the time, Jackson was fast becoming a hub of blues activity. It was the home base for the Chatmon brothers' popular blues-oriented string band, the Mississippi Sheiks, as well as for other regional blues musicians like the McCoy brothers, James Cole, Walter Vincent, Babe Stovall, Skip James, Tommy Bradley, "Memphis" Minnie Douglas, Eddie Dimmitt, and Ishman Bracey. In addition, Jackson was the home of the only record company talent scout in the Deep South, H. C. Spiers, who owned a furniture store there and was responsible for most of the authentic Delta blues recorded in the late 1920s and early 1930s. Charley Patton, Willie Brown, Son House, and Tommy Johnson all had their first recording sessions arranged by Spiers.[47]

Johnson was a consummate composer who carefully crafted set guitar accompaniments, personalized lyrics, and fragments of folk poetry into striking blues compositions. "Maggie Campbell," named after a former wife of Johnson's with whom he had a tempestuous relationship, uses the following standard folk verses:

> Now sun gon' shine in my back door someday, my back
>      door someday,
> Sun gon' shine in my back door someday,
> And the wind gon' change, gon' blow my blues away.
>
> Now see see rider, see what you done done, now see
>      what you done done,
> You done made me love you, now you trying to put
>      me down.[48]

"Big Road Blues," a refashioning of Patton's "Down the Dirt Road Blues," was one of Tommy Johnson's most popular songs. Once again, the theme is freedom of movement—the call of the "big road," which was destined to help launch the African-American exodus out of the Delta in the coming decades.

> I ain't goin' down that big road by myself
>      (hear me talkin' to you, pretty baby),

I ain't goin' down that big road by myself,
If I don't take you, I'll take someone else.[49]

Tommy Johnson spent his declining years drifting back and forth between Jackson and Crystal Springs, playing his blues at black social gatherings or in the street for tips. An alcoholic, he would drink Sterno or denatured alcohol in shoe polish when nothing else was available. In his most haunting, autobiographical blues composition, "Canned Heat Blues," he reveals the addiction that was destroying him:

Cryin' canned heat, canned heat, mama, cryin'
    Sterno's killin' me,
Cryin' canned heat, mama, Sterno's killin' me,
Takes alcorub to make these canned heat blues.

I woke up this morning with canned heat 'round
    my bed,
Run here somebody, take these canned heat blues,
Run here somebody and take these canned heat blues.[50]

### Son House: "Down on the Killing Floor"

While Son House was active on the Delta blues scene, he, like his close friend Willie Brown, was most admired for his guitar style. Where Brown had primarily expanded the rhythmic possibilities of the blues accompaniment in his playing, Son House perfected the sliding bottleneck guitar technique, making it the cornerstone of his sound.

Son House was born in 1902 on a farm close to Lyon, Mississippi, in the heartland of the Delta. He grew up singing church music and only began to play guitar in his late twenties, after hearing a local musician named James McCoy use a bottleneck on the strings of his guitar while playing a blues tune. At that time, the bottleneck was replacing the knifeblade as the device commonly used to produce the distinctive voicelike whining sound. House had spent most of his youth with family in Louisiana and had only recently returned to Lyon, which may explain why he was unfamiliar with this Delta guitar style, even though it was becoming a fixture in the region by the 1920s. In any event, House immediately went out and purchased a second-hand guitar, persuaded McCoy to teach him how to play the blues with a bottleneck, and ended up playing with him at dances and parties.

In 1928, House shot and killed another man at a house party near Lyon. He pleaded self-defense and served two years on Parchman Farm before being paroled in 1930. At that time he began his association with Charley Patton and Willie Brown. They played together regularly throughout the Delta, and it was Patton who arranged for Son House's first recording session for Paramount Records in Grafton, Wisconsin. House recorded only three of his standard blues numbers at the session—"My Black Mama," "Preachin' Blues," and "Dry Spell Blues"—but since all three were excellent vehicles for his virtuosity with a bottleneck, they helped further his reputation as the Delta's foremost slide guitarist. "My Black Mama" is a Delta standard that was later copied by Robert Johnson as "Walking Blues" and by Muddy Waters as "Country Blues." "Preachin' the Blues" juxtaposes the sacred and the profane. In the first verse, House lampoons the Baptist preacher:

> Oh I'm go' get me religion, I'm goin' to join the Baptist church,
> I'm goin' be a Baptist preacher and I sure won't have to work.

Then he focuses on his own dilemma:

> Oh I had religion, Lord, to this very day,
> But the women and whiskey, well they would not let me pray.

Finally, he resolves the conflict by exclaiming: "I swear to God I've got to preach these gospel blues."[51] "Dry Spell Blues," the most original of the three, is a powerful portrayal of the rural poverty in the region:

> The dry spell blues are falling, drove me from door to door,
> Dry spell blues are falling, drove me from door to door,
> The dry spell blues have put everybody on the killing floor.
>
> Now the people down South soon won't have no home,
> Lord, it's the people down South soon won't have no home,
> 'Cause this dry spell has parched all their cotton and corn.
>
> Pork chops forty-five cents a pound, cotton only ten,
> Pork chops forty-five cents a pound, cotton only ten,
> Can't keep no women, no, no, not one of them.
>
> So dry old boll weevil turn up his toes and die,
> So dry old boll weevil turn up his toes and die,
> Now ain't nothing to do but bootleg moonshine and rye.[52]

Son House remained an active Delta bluesman throughout the depression and into the war years. Then, after the death of his close friend Willie Brown, he moved to Rochester, New York, where he retired. The classic Delta bottleneck guitar style he was so instrumental in developing had by then become inseparable from the rural blues culture indigenous to the region and would prove to be the seminal influence on the music of younger Mississippi Delta blues giants like Robert Johnson, Bukka White, Muddy Waters, and Elmore James.[53]

### Robert Johnson: "Hellhound on My Trail"

Robert Johnson was the key transitional figure working within the Mississippi Delta's blues culture. He bridged the gap between the music's rural beginnings and its modern urban manifestations, but he died before receiving any national recognition. Over the years, both his stature as a Delta blues trailblazer and the legends surrounding his life have grown considerably.

Johnson was born south of the Delta in Hazelhurst, Mississippi, on May 8, 1911. He was raised by his mother, who lived with a series of men and moved around routinely from place to place in the mid-South. While Johnson had close family ties in the Delta, he was also one of its uprooted. He moved from Hazelhurst to the Delta, then to Memphis, and back to the Delta before he reached the age of eight. The rest of his youth was spent at a sharecroppers' settlement called Commerce on Richard Leatherman's plantation near Robinsonville, Mississippi. He was married when he was nineteen years old, and in less than a year he lost his sixteen-year-old wife in childbirth. He never remarried or settled down again.

Johnson's restless spirit was indicative of the changing social consciousness among the rural black population still living and working in the South. A recurring message at the heart of his blues was epitomized in the line "Travel on, poor Bob, just can't turn you 'round." Johnny Shines, a fellow bluesman and traveling companion of Johnson's, said of him: "People might consider him wild because he didn't think nothing of just taking off from wherever he was, just pack up and go. He had that about traveling."[54] Johnson spent time in Memphis, St. Louis, Chicago, Dallas, San Antonio, and Helena, Arkansas, but he was always drawn back to the region he was obsessed with leaving. He was murdered in the Delta town of Greenwood, Mississippi, in 1938. He was twenty-seven.[55]

Robert Johnson started out in the blues as a skinny teenager who "blew a pretty good harp" (short for harmonica) at the local Saturday night dances around Robinsonville. Here he met Charley Patton, Willie Brown, and Son House, who got him interested in the guitar. He was particularly keen on Son House's bottleneck slide technique, which he made the centerpiece of his own playing style, but his musical tastes ventured beyond the Delta tradition. His guitar work was also influenced by the recordings of Kokomo Arnold, Scrapper Blackwell, Willie Newbern, and Lonnie Johnson, who also influenced many of his vocal inflections, along with Leroy Carr, Peetie Wheatstraw, and Skip James. Johnny Shines recalled that Robert Johnson had a sensitive ear and that he listened to music from many different sources:

> Robert didn't just perform his own songs. He did anything that he heard over the radio. ANYTHING that he heard. When I say anything, I mean ANYTHING—popular songs, ballads, blues, anything. It didn't make him no difference what it was. If he liked it, he did it. He'd be sitting there listening to the radio—and you wouldn't even know he was paying any attention to it—and later that evening maybe, he'd walk out on the streets and play the same songs that were played over the radio. Four or five songs he'd liked out of the whole session over the radio and he'd play them all evening, and he'd continue to play them.[56]

In the mid-thirties, Johnson spent time with Esther Lockwood in Helena, Arkansas, and taught her son, Robert Jr. Lockwood, to play the guitar. Lockwood's impressions of Johnson echoed those of Johnny Shines and most of the other musicians who knew him:

> Robert was a strange dude, I guess you could say he was a loner and a drifter. . . . He could pick a song right out of the air. He'd hear it being played by someone or on the radio and play it right back note for note. He could do it with blues, spirituals, hillbilly music, popular stuff. You name it, he could play it. . . . Then I heard he was poisoned by some jealous woman in Greenwood. Sonny Boy was runnin' with him at the time. He said Robert drank some whiskey that had been poisoned and he fell out. Crawled on the floor and howled like a dog before he died. It was a sad day when we heard the news. Robert was a good guy and a hell of a blues musician. He sure could play.[57]

Don Law, the record producer for Johnson's recording session in San Antonio, was particularly impressed with Johnson's dexterity with a guitar—his touch and hands astounded him: "He had the most beautiful hands I've ever seen—long slender fingers."[58]

Robert Johnson's only recording sessions were held in San Antonio late in 1936 and then in Dallas early in 1937; he recorded a total of twenty-nine blues selections. In San Antonio he was arrested for vagrancy. While he was in jail he was beaten by the police and his guitar was broken. Don Law bailed him out of jail.

The impact of Johnson's guitar style would be far-reaching. As blues historian Samuel Charters puts it:

As a guitarist he almost completely turned the blues around. His tightening of the rhythmic line was the basis for the instrumental blues scene that followed him in Chicago—letting the upper strings play a free melodic part, but using the thumb for a hard rhythm in the lower strings that was almost like a drum part. When Muddy Waters started his first bands in Chicago six or seven years later all he had to do was have the bass player and the drummer pick up on the treble. Elmore James took less from Robert, but his various versions of ''Dust My Broom,'' and all the other versions he did of the same melody with different words, caught the rough excitement of one part of Robert's style.[59]

Blues scholar Robert Palmer comments:

He made the instrument [guitar] sound uncannily like a full band, furnishing a heavy beat with his feet, chording innovative shuffle rhythms and picking out high treble-string lead with his slider, all at the same time. Fellow guitarists would watch him with unabashed, open mouth wonder. They were watching the Delta's first modern bluesman at work.[60]

Robert Johnson's recordings are either blues borrowed from other sources or his own compositions, which tend to be the more poetic. In the former category are selections such as ''Walking Blues,'' a tune that borrows its melody and guitar accompaniment from Son House's ''My Black Mama.'' ''Sweet Home Chicago'' is copied from both ''My Black Mama'' and Kokomo Arnold's ''Old Original Kokomo Blues,'' while ''32-20 Blues'' is based on Skip James's ''20-20 Blues.'' ''If I Had Possession over Judgment Day'' and ''Traveling Riverside Blues'' both use the traditional ''rolling and tumbling'' tune family or blues core first recorded by Willie Newbern as ''Roll and Tumble Blues'' in 1929; it is directly related to ''Brownsville Blues,'' which was initially recorded by Sleepy John Estes, also in 1929. Basically, a blues core of this nature is a constellation of lyrics, melody, and guitar parts that can be used interchangeably. The ''rolling and tumbling'' blues core was a well-known favorite both in Memphis and in the Delta.[61]

Johnson also recorded a number of blues selections that are strikingly original, including ''Hellhound on My Trail'':

I got to keep moving, I got to keep moving,
Blues falling down like hail, blues falling down like hail,
Ummm blues falling down like hail, blues falling down like hail,
And the day keeps on reminding me there's a hellhound on my trail,
Hellhound on my trail, hellhound on my trail.[62]

Leaving and painful separation are the themes of his poignant "Love in Vain":

> I followed her to the station with her suitcase in my hand,
> And I followed her to the station with her suitcase in my hand,
> Well it's hard to tell, it's hard to tell when all your love's in vain,
> All my love's in vain.
>
> When the train rolled up to the station, I looked her in the eye,
> When the train rolled up to the station, I looked her in the eye,
> Well I was lonesome, felt so lonesome and I could not help but cry,
> All my love's in vain.
>
> When the train left the station with two lights on behind,
> When the train left the station with two lights on behind,
> Well the blue light was my blues and the red light was my mind,
> All my love's in vain.[63]

In songs like "Milkcow's Calf Blues" and "Traveling Riverside Blues," Johnson made erotic love the dialectical counterpoint to unrequited love and developed clever double entendres with obvious delight. In "Terraplane Blues," the sexual metaphor is extended to the mechanics of the automobile:

> I'm goin' to get deep down in this connection, keep on
>    tangling with your wire,
> I'm goin' get deep down in this connection, uum keep
>    tangling with your wires,
> And when I mash down on your starter,
> your spark plug will give me power.[64]

The social themes and images that dominate the landscape of Robert Johnson's songs are representative of those found in early rural blues in the Delta and throughout the cotton belt. Their mixture of personal observations and folklore proved to be instrumental in updating and invigorating the black oral tradition in the region. In blues like "Walking Blues," "Rambling on My Mind," "Dust My Broom," and "Sweet Home Chicago," he used mobility as a metaphor for personal freedom. Two verses from Johnson's "Preaching Blues" alludes to the bleak situation, that is "the blues," that made flight so urgent:

> And the blues fell mama child and they tore me all upside down,
> Blues fell mama child and they tore me upside down,
> Travel on, poor Bob, just can't turn you 'round.

Well the blues is a achin' old heart disease (Do it with you,
   gonna do it),
The blues is a low down achin' heart disease,
Like consumption, killin' me by degrees.[65]


In tandem with Robert Johnson's obsession with freedom of movement at
any cost is his fatalistic assessment of the forces arrayed against him—both
social and supernatural. He expresses that fatalism most eloquently in "Hellhound on My Trail" and in "Crossroad Blues," a song that simultaneously
evokes the terror of the Delta social order as experienced by African
Americans relegated to its lowest echelons and the spirit of Legba, the
Yoruban god associated with the crossroads. In Yoruban folklore, a crossroads
symbolizes the junction between the physical and the spiritual worlds, the human and the divine, where mortals sought out the god Legba in order to learn
their fate:


I went to the crossroad, fell down on my knee,
Went to the crossroad, fell down on my knee,
Asked the Lord above to have mercy, save poor Bob if you please.

Uumh, standing at the crossroad, I tried to flag a ride,
Standing at the crossroads, I tried to flag a ride,
Didn't nobody seem to know me, everybody passed me by.

Uumh, the sun going down, boy, dark gonna catch me here,
Uumh, dark gonna catch me here,
I haven't got no loving sweet woman that loves and feels my care.

You can run, you can run, tell my friend, poor Willie Brown,
You can run, tell my friend, poor Willie Brown,
Lord, that I'm standing at the crossroad, babe, I believe I'm
   sinking down.[66]


In many respects, Robert Johnson's flirtations with the Devil are an extension of the fatalism implicit in his philosophy. Like Tommy Johnson, he is
known to have encouraged the legend that he had made a pact with Satan:


Early this morning when you knocked on my door,
Early this morning, uumh, when you knocked on my door,
I said, "Hello Satan, I believe it's time to go."

Me and the Devil was walking side by side,
Me and the Devil was walking side by side,
I'm going to beat my women until I get satisfied
  (now baby, you know you ain't doing me right).

You may bury my body down by the highway side
  (baby, I don't care where you bury my body when I'm dead
  and gone),
You may bury my body, down by the highway side,
So my old evil spirit can get a Greyhound bus and ride.[67]

Johnson's fatalism implies a capitulation to overwhelming social constraints: he makes a deal with Satan because he has nothing to lose. But there is also an element of defiance in this pact with the forces of darkness, a defiance of the dominant white culture that enforces its social constraints with the help of its official religion, Christianity. It is also important to note that the Devil is the ultimate trickster figure in Johnson's blues, a reincarnation of Legba at a Delta crossroads. Once again, cultural resistance is made manifest in the use of an African icon, here disguised as Satan, to reaffirm African custom and tradition.


## Telling It Like It Was


The harsh and foreboding nature of Robert Johnson's blues compositions— their condensed rage mixed in with gloom and apocalyptic doom—stems from his experiences growing up in the Mississippi Delta, becoming a male adult in a social environment that denied him his manhood. When Johnson composed his songs, the region was still a backward, almost feudal, agricultural stronghold dominated by a small group of wealthy white plantation owners and merchants. The black population continued to outnumber the white population by nearly four to one, and African Americans remained confined to the Delta's lowest social stratum. Barred from voting and from holding public office, they were denied their basic civil rights and often were deprived of legal rights as well. Rigidly segregated from whites, they had limited access to public education and health care. Moreover, the living conditions for African Americans in the Delta were crude and often unsanitary. Their homes lacked plumbing and electricity; their diets lacked nourishing foods. As a result, the death and disease rates for African Americans residing in the region before World War II were much higher than those of the white population.[68]

White supremacy in the Delta was maintained by subjecting the black population to repressive social practices such as curfews and cross burnings and to the constant threat of violent acts such as beatings and lynchings. The level of violence in the region remained high in comparison to the national norm. After World War I, the violence escalated and frequently pitted black war veterans against white vigilantes. African Americans who had fought to "end war" were not inclined to endure unfair treatment at home. In the early 1920s, for example, near Drew, Mississippi, not far from Dockery's plantation, a black veteran killed a white plantation owner he worked for in a dispute over money. He was pursued by a white posse and killed four of them before being captured, paraded through the streets of Drew, and then lynched in public.[69] Robert Johnson, Son House, Tommy Johnson, Willie Brown, Charley Patton, and several other Delta blues pioneers were living and playing in the midst of continual violence and could not remain untouched by it. Johnson was poisoned to death, House killed a man in a gun fight, and Patton was cut badly on his neck in a knife fight.

Like the living conditions in the Delta, the working conditions were also fraught with peril and hardship. The cotton plantations were the major source of employment for black workers in the Delta, but the region was also notorious for its levee contract labor system. The levee construction along the Mississippi River and its tributaries was the only line of defense against the periodic floods that imperiled the entire river basin. After the Civil War, the task of maintaining, extending, and upgrading the levee system was taken over by the federal government, which hired contractors to do the job. These white contractors leased convicts, most of whom were African Americans, to do the grueling manual labor necessary to keep the levees intact. After the turn of the century, this convict lease system was gradually abandoned in favor of a new system that proved to be just as invidious. The local labor contractors hired a workforce, once again predominantly black, and set up levee camps near the worksites where the laborers were billeted. Discipline was enforced by armed guards called "strawbosses" on the job and "shack bullies" in the camps. In addition, the workers were charged exorbitant fees for their food, water, clothing, shelter, and recreation. As a result, they invariably owed the contractors more than they were getting paid. This system of peonage was remarkably similar to the system that already existed on the Delta's cotton plantations. Black workers performed back-breaking labor from sunup to sundown, lived in squalid and unsanitary facilities, and were perpetually in debt to the labor contractors or plantation owners.[70]

By the 1930s, there were sixty-five federally funded levee camps along the Mississippi River; most of these were in the Delta region. In an article titled "Mississippi Slavery in 1933," published in the NAACP journal, *Crisis,* Roy Wilkins described the plight of the black levee workers in detail after investi-

gating the situation first hand. He made note of the low wages ("$1.00 a day
for common laborers"), the long working hours (from twelve to eighteen
hours a day), the poor working conditions, and the built-in pay deductions.
Wilkins also indicated that many of the labor contractors apparently failed to
pay workers the agreed-upon wage: "The men grumble over small pay, the
long hours, the cursing, the beating, the food, the tents, the commissary
fleecing, but they reserve their greatest bitterness for the contractor who
'won't pay you even that little you got coming.' "[71]

Many Delta blues musicians worked on the levees and in the levee camps
entertaining the workers confined there on the weekends. Their musical repertoire usually included popular folk blues like "Levee Camp Moan" and
"Shack Bully Stomp," which registered the black workforce's collective protest against the levee contractors and their hired thugs. Big Bill Broonzy, Peter
Chatman (also known as Memphis Slim), and Big Joe Williams all worked for
the infamous Lowrence brothers, a large family of levee contractors reputed to
have operated the biggest and most brutal levee camps in the region. As Memphis Slim remembered them:

> They was seven or eight of them Lowrences and they was all mean, but
> that Charlie Lowrence was the worst one I ever knowed. Would work a
> man to death and pay it no mind. Work you from can see to can't see—
> you know from time the sun come up until it went down. You couldn't
> say you was tired and wanted a break 'cause they'd crack you upside
> your head with a club. Them straw bosses would beat you dead. Mister
> Charlie say, "Kill a nigger, hire another. But kill a mule you got to buy
> another." You see they treated a mule better than a Negro back then in
> those camps. They was bad mens those Lowrence and they all got rich.[72]

Big Joe Williams described life in a Greenville, Mississippi, levee camp run
by "Captain Charlie Lowrence" as follows:

> We worked until there wasn't no more light, and we would start at day-
> break—long hours and you only made a dollar a day, dollar fifty for
> mule skinners. The straw boss had a club and a gun. He'd beat you if
> you tried to rest a bit. We slept in old tents on filthy mattresses. The lice
> and mosquitos eat you up. Food was just as rotten and there wasn't
> much of it. It was a tough life on that levee, man.[73]

Williams later recorded "Levee Camp Blues," which he said was based on his
levee work experience. It goes, in part:

Yea, I been workin' on the levee, I been workin' night and day,
Yea, I been workin' on the levee, oh, I been workin' night and day,
That's somewhere around Greenville, Mississippi.

Yes every Saturday night I went to Clarksdale, Mississippi,
Charlie Lowrence tell me, Big Joe Williams, you ain't got no pay.

My lead mule crippled and my off mule blind,
My lead mule crippled and my off mule blind,
How can I drive here buddy, when I ain't got me a loaded nine?
Bring me a loaded nine.

I ain't gonna work both night and day,
I hate to tell you, Captain Charlie,
I ain't gonna work both night and day,
I can't help you build your levee, oh well,
And you won't give me no pay.[74]

Sunnyland Slim also worked as a muleskinner—a teamster who drove the mules used to haul the dirt and rocks to the levees for fill. Like Big Joe Williams, he used a "loaded nine" tail whip on the animals:

> Yea I worked as a muleskinner down on them levees around Memphis and Arkansas. Boss man had me out there all day in that hot sun drivin' that ole mule. Had me a team of old worn-out mules at first. But I drive 'em best I could. Use the whip on 'em and I'd sing too. "Well good morning captain, my mule is tired and slow, what time is it captain, quittin' time for sure." Sing those little ole things for the boss man 'cause he liked to hear that. Liked his boys to sing. Them were hard times, only rough mens could work on them levees. Had to be 'cause you could get yourself killed if you weren't.[75]

When there was periodic flooding in the Mississippi Delta basin, local black residents were often pressed into labor gangs. The gangs worked around the clock to shore up the levees in order to save the cotton crop. Work camps with armed guards, often called "relief camps," were set up to coordinate and control the efforts of the illegally conscripted black labor force. Those who refused to work without compensation were denied emergency relief supplies and shelter provided by the Red Cross; sometimes, they were also beaten or jailed. The worst incident of this kind occurred during the famous 1927 Mississippi River flood. Thousands of homeless black farm workers were lured into government-sponsored Red Cross camps near Greenville, Vicksburg, and

Yazoo City, held there against their will, charged for the relief services, and pressed into forced-labor gangs to clean up after the flood.

Constant exploitation and humiliation eventually helped to provoke a full-scale black exodus from the Delta's fertile farmlands. The African-American population in the region began to decline slowly for the first time ever in the 1920s and would continue to do so at an accelerated pace for the next three decades.[76]

It was the economic dynamics of the plantation system in the Delta, however, that necessitated black migration. Sharecropping and its variations—share-renting and land-renting—all led to debt and dependency on the plantation owners. Very few African-American tenant farmers were able to get far enough ahead to buy their own land. Sociologist Hortense Powderhouse's study of the Delta region around Indianola, Mississippi, completed in 1932, estimated that at least 70 percent of the black tenant families living there were cheated by their landlords. Only 17 to 18 percent made even a slender profit from their labors. On the average, the African-American families she surveyed moved every other year. It was common knowledge that the only way to get out of debt to the plantation owner was "to walk out."[77]

In the forefront of this migration were many of Mississippi's finest blues musicians, whose music often encouraged the exodus. Henry Sloan, Joe Hicks, Frank Stokes, Furry Lewis, Gus Cannon, Jim Jackson, J. D. Short, Big Joe Williams, and Big Bill Broonzy all had abandoned the state for points north by the 1920s. During the depression and the war years, they were followed by Robert Johnson, Howling Wolf, Sonny Boy Williamson II, Tommy McClennan, Bukka White, Big Boy Crudup, Sunnyland Slim, John Lee Hooker, Muddy Waters, and many others who were not as well known. These migratory Mississippi bluesmen were eventually responsible for focusing national attention on their music and fusing it with the emerging urban blues cultures in the midwestern industrial centers.

Many other Mississippi Delta blues musicians who were standouts and acknowledged as critical to the Delta blues culture in its formative years stayed in the Delta and were never recorded. Only their names and reputations survive: Josie Bush; Charley Patton's mentor, Henry Sloan; Son House's bottleneck slide guitar instructor, Willie Wilson; and Gus Cannon's slide guitar teacher, Alex Lee, belong to that community of musicians who are remembered but whose contributions are now difficult to assess. We know more about others who remained in the general region and managed to make a few commercial recordings in the late twenties and early thirties—Skip James, Mississippi John Hurt, William Harris, Sam Collins, Rubin Lacey, King Solomon Hill, Kid Bailey, Joe Reynolds, Garfield Akers, and Roosevelt Graves. For these men and women, who had little formal education and who made their livings as farm workers, music was a leisure-time activity, but they were also creative musicians who developed individual blues styles and repertoires with minimal outside help. Inspired by the indigenous Delta blues culture, they drew upon various elements of the Delta style—the bottleneck slide technique, percussive instrumental techniques, a heavy emphasis on drawing out individual notes, intensely passionate vocals, and the use of falsetto, moaning, and ostinato. With their help, the Delta blues matured, but the migrants were ultimately responsible for carrying the music to areas where it would be transformed and would itself transform popular American music in the postwar decades.

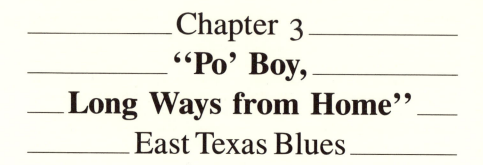

# Chapter 3
# "Po' Boy,
# Long Ways from Home"
## East Texas Blues

### The Lone Star State: Slavery's Last Refuge

The Gulf of Mexico's coastal plain covers most of eastern Texas. The rural landscape is flat, monotonous, and barren, except for a scattering of yellow pine-tree clusters and ramshackle farming structures. The center of the area is known as the Texas cotton belt, a three-hundred-square-mile stretch of country rimmed by Houston to the southeast, Austin to the southwest, and Dallas to the north. Two key rivers run through this section of the coastal plain, the Trinity to the north and the Brazos to the south; they are both bordered by grassy swamplands, well suited for sugarcane cultivation.

Southern planters, using the labor of slaves, built the first large plantations in this region just before the Civil War. Most Southerners who moved to Texas in the 1850s were fleeing from areas like the Tennessee River basin in northern Alabama or farther east in Georgia and South Carolina, where the soil had been severely depleted by an overemphasis on cotton production. During the Civil War, the migration to Texas became more pronounced; over 150,000 slaves were moved into the state in an effort to avoid the Yankee armies and the enforcement of the Emancipation Proclamation. Those who were brought to Texas in this turbulent era initially traveled the last leg of the journey by boat from the ports of Natchez, Mobile, or New Orleans southwest to the port of Galveston, or northwest and then due west on the Red River. After the Union captured the South's seaports, the journey was made overland.[1]

Two well-known folk blues associated with Texas, "Po' Boy, Long Ways from Home," or simply "Poor Boy Blues," and "Red River Blues" commemorate this historic voyage. The first line of "Red River Blues"—"Which way do that blood red river run?"—has been traced to an antebellum spiritual based on a biblical passage. The line took on a new dimension in Texas, however, because the Red River, which is part of the Texas-Oklahoma border and runs north before bending west, captured the imagination of the transient slave population. They supplied the answer: "It runs north and south." To the slaves, traveling north meant escaping from bondage, and so, just as many other spirituals evoked the desire for freedom, this one undoubtedly also helped to keep that goal in mind. Sometime after the Civil War, the call and response format of this spiritual was recycled into an early rural folk blues song popular not only in East Texas but throughout the South. It is interesting to note that in the Piedmont region, where it was also an early standard, the common answer to the question was that the Red River "runs from my window to the rising sun," which would be east, toward the Atlantic Ocean.[2]

The East Texas version of "Poor Boy Blues" recounts a boat journey from Louisiana to Texas. The experience of being afloat was a major preoccupation in the version recorded by Texas bluesman Willard "Rambling" Thomas in the 1920s:

> Po' boy, po' boy, long ways from home,
> If your home's in Louisiana what you doin' here,
> Said my home ain't in Texas and I sure don't care,
> Po' boy, po' boy, po' boy, long ways from home.
>
> I don't care if the boat don't never land,
> I can stay on the water as long as any man,
> Po' boy, po' boy, po' boy, long ways from home.
>
> Hey my boat come a rockin' just like a drunken man,
> And my home's on the water and I sure don't like land,
> Po' boy, po' boy, po' boy, long ways from home.[3]

Like "Which way do that blood red river run?" the line "Po' boy, long ways from home" turned up in the early blues of regions other than East Texas. Its earliest documented appearance seems to have been in the Mississippi Delta, where Gus Cannon remembered learning it from a slide guitar player named Alex Lee around 1900.[4] Other bluesmen who recorded renditions of "Poor Boy Blues" in the 1920s include Robert Hicks from Atlanta and Sam Butler from Mississippi. All these early folk blues and their regional distinctions demonstrate the continuity and adaptability of the black oral tradition.

## "Ain't No More Cane on the Brazos": The Texas Prison Farms

In the aftermath of the Civil War, East Texas, like other cotton belt enclaves, continued to maintain much of the antebellum plantation economy through sharecropping and tenant farming arrangements imposed on the vulnerable population of former slaves. Most of the earliest postbellum prison farms were located along the Brazos River; later, farms were also set up along the Trinity River. The state of Texas owned up to one hundred thousand acres of land adjàcent to these rivers and operated a number of sugarcane plantations. It used convict labor for public construction and farm work in the area. Soon after the war, the fledgling Texas prison system was leased to private operators, who in turn began to lease convict labor gangs to white landowners living close to the prison farms. In 1883, the Texas prison system was repossessed by the state because of high escape rates, excessive physical abuse of the convicts by their captors, and the deplorable health standards that existed on the farms. Conditions improved very little, however, even with the state of Texas back in command. The squalid living conditions, harsh corporal punishment, and convict leasing business all persisted well into the twentieth century. Furthermore, Texas lawmen and judges made certain that African Americans made up the bulk of the prison population on these farms, even though they constituted only 25 percent of the state's total population after the 1880s. Large numbers of black men in Texas were given prison sentences for vagrancy, debt, or even trumped-up criminal charges.

Once on the prison farms, it was not unusual for prisoners to be worked and driven until their health failed. African American convicts resisted this victimization as they had resisted slavery before. They regularly attempted to escape, malingered when the opportunity arose, and even resorted to self-mutilation, severing an Achilles tendon rather than do the grueling manual labor demanded of them day after day from sunup to sundown. As a result, the Texas prison system soon gained a reputation as the most brutal, strife-ridden, and oppressive in the entire South.[5]

The infamous Texas prison farms were indirectly responsible for the survival of a powerful worksong tradition among the black inmates. The continued use of gang labor in the cane and cotton fields, in the pine forests, or in construction work allowed the worksong to remain functional in prison work and life. The call and response patterns in the music supplied the appropriate rhythms to accompany the backbreaking labor of the chain gangs. The folk verses documented the convicts' feelings and registered their defiance, most often covert, of the individuals and institutions that controlled their lives. Although worksongs were sung on prison farms throughout the South, in Texas the worksong tradition seemed to be particularly resilient, and it significantly influenced the formation of a regional blues style in the East Texas cotton belt.

Some of the more famous Texas prison worksongs identify historical figures who were part of the penal system. Perhaps the most notorious was Bud Russel, the state's assistant prison transfer agent from 1908 to 1912 and then the chief transfer agent until the early 1940s. Russel traveled around the state collecting prisoners for the camps; he reportedly handled 115,000 convicts during his time on the job.[6] A former Texas prison inmate remembered seeing Bud Russel come to Fort Worth in his early years as a transfer agent:

> He would have the guards lined up with machine guns. The convicts would come out chained by the ankles and by the necks and by the hands. Come out in what we call the "Chinese Shuffle." . . . Everybody would be there to watch Bud Russel take the men to prison. And it used to be like that for years.[7]

Russel's menacing figure appears in the lyrics of many traditional worksongs sung on the Texas prison farms. He came to symbolize the enemy to African Americans living in his territory. As recently as the 1960s, Bruce Jackson collected a version of "Go Down Old Hannah" in a Texas prison that includes this verse:

> Well I see Bud Russel, little boys,
> With his ball and chain, little boys,
> He gonna take you back to Sugarland.[8]

A similar verse appears in the popular resistance song "Midnight Special":

> Here come Bud Russel, how in the world do you know?
> Well we know him by his wagon, and the chains he wo',
> Big pistol on his shoulder, big knife in his hand,
> He's comin' to carry you back to Sugarland.
>
> Let the Midnight Special shine her light on me,
> Let the Midnight Special shine her ever lovin'
>    light on me.[9]

The "Midnight Special" was a train that regularly left Houston at midnight heading for the West Coast. Some thirty miles outside the city it passed by Sugarland, one of the prison farms on the Brazos River. The train and its headlight, which passed over some of the prison buildings that housed the convicts, became a metaphor for their long-enduring hope for freedom.[10]

Another group of Texas worksongs focused on white landowners who had convicts leased out to them. Among the more notorious were Tom Moore and his three sons, who owned a large plantation near the Brazos River. They are the subject of many tall tales and worksongs:

> Well who is that I see ridin', boy,
> Down on the low turn row?
> Nobody but Tom Devil,
> That's the man they call Tom Moore.[11]

Another name that appears with some regularity in the Texas worksongs is that of Mister Cunningham. There were actually two men with that name who played a role in the history of the Texas penal system: A. J. Cunningham, one of the first landowners to lease convicts after the Civil War, and J. B. Cunningham, chief transfer agent for the prisons and predecessor of the infamous Bud Russel.[12] The name turns up in the blues standard "Don't Ease Me In," first recorded in the 1920s by Texas bluesman Henry Thomas:

> Don't ease, don't you ease, ah don't you ease
>     me in,
> It's all night long, Cunningham, don't ease me
>     in.[13]

## Early East Texas Blues Sources

Many other folksongs seem to have originated as prison worksongs and then passed into the early rural blues tradition centered in East Texas. Some of the more common were "Ain't No More Cane on the Brazos," "Roberta," "Long Hot Summer Days," "Shorty George," "Alberta," "Make a Long-time Man Feel Bad," and "Two White Horses Standing in a Line." These prison worksongs were a principal influence on the formation of an indigenous blues repertoire and vocal style. All the major rural blues standouts from Texas were influenced by them; the blues of "Ragtime Texas" Henry Thomas, Blind Lemon Jefferson, Huddie Ledbetter, Willard Thomas, and Texas Alexander are preoccupied with prison life. By focusing on prison conditions and the experiences of those imprisoned, the worksongs and the rural blues continually reminded African Americans of their still vulnerable and precarious position in relation to the dominant white social order and of the struggle against institutionalized racism and oppression. The songs helped to galvanize resistance to the regressive white power structure in the South.

Another cultural theme that was common in the early rural blues of East Texas, but certainly not unique to the Texas coastal plain, was travel. The metaphor has a recognizable historical dimension among African Americans, much in evidence in the slave spirituals, where traveling on to heaven is synonymous with being finally released from bondage. Within the pervasive system of southern tenant farming and sharecropping, moving was one of the few defiant options open to African-American farm workers in the cotton belt; frequent moves from plantation to plantation in search of a more equitable labor arrangement and a better livelihood were fairly common. This independence of movement for black farm workers and their families offered only a limited means of rebelling against their economic servitude, given that work conditions and opportunities for landownership did not vary much throughout the South. Moreover, traveling could be dangerous because of an upsurge of white vigilantism and lynchings after the 1870s. Nonetheless, a general pattern of restlessness and movement was discernible among the black masses concentrated in the cotton belt until significantly worsened economic conditions provided the impetus for the mass movement north.

### "Ragtime Texas" Henry Thomas: "Don't Ease Me In"

As in the Delta, the early Texas bluesmen came to represent an important aspect of the African Americans' revolt against post-Reconstruction white cultural hegemony. They traveled around a lot, worked in the fields as little as possible, and sang about their exploits and hardships in the black community. Through their music and their lifestyles, they kept the spirit of resistance alive. Representative of this rebellious cultural profile was "Ragtime Texas" Henry Thomas, father figure of the East Texas blues tradition.

Thomas was born in Upshaw County, Texas, in 1874. He was the son of former slaves who worked as sharecroppers, one of nine children who grew up in a shanty on a bleak northeastern Texas cotton plantation. Henry Thomas quickly grew to hate cotton farming, and especially the inequities built into the sharecropping system. (Later in his life he would sing sarcastic songs about the sharecroppers' chances of profiting from their labors.) As a youth, he apparently taught himself how to play the quills and then the guitar. He left home as soon as he was able to pursue a career as a wandering singer, riding the rails for transportation. The introduction of railroads to rural regions like East Texas during this period inspired many African Americans to explore new horizons. For Thomas, the quest became a way of life. He was soon a legendary musician and vagabond along the Texas and Pacific Railroad line between Dallas and Shreveport. He seems to have centered his musical activities on the trains or in the depots and parks of the small East Texas towns along this route. As was true with many of the early Delta blues musicians, his movements were somewhat circular, and he remained tied to the East Texas terrain of his youth. Although he hoboed as far north as St. Louis in 1893 and later to Chicago during the 1920s, Thomas invariably returned to his homeland and his favorite railroad strip, where he was best known.[14]

Henry Thomas fashioned his music from the rural folk traditions indigenous to the black farming communities he played in. His guitar style varied according to the kind of folk music he happened to be making. His dance tunes featured hard-strumming guitar work, accented by foot stomping. This style is found in his recording of "Old Country Stomp," which also features verses that resemble traditional square dance calls. On popular folksongs like "Alabama Bound," he limited himself to playing, in standard beats, conventional chord progressions. On one of the blues numbers he recorded, "Shanty Blues," he used a knifeblade in a manner reminiscent of the early Mississippi Delta blues guitarists. This technique was widespread by the 1920s, when Henry Thomas made his recordings for Paramount Records, but no doubt there was some interaction between Delta and Texas blues musicians before that decade. Thomas's guitar style on some original blues numbers, in particular, "Texas Worried Blues," "Cottonfield Blues," and "Texas Easy Street Blues," suggests that here was the beginning of a distinctive regional blues style. His thumb provides the repetitive groundbeat, while he picks the melody line higher up the guitar neck. He also has a tendency to brush backward on the upper strings of the guitar with his fingers in these blues recordings.

Henry Thomas also played the quills, a traditional African-American folk instrument made from cane reeds. Several of these reeds cut to specified lengths were tied together in a row. By blowing across the openings on the tops of the reeds, a musician could produce a simple folk scale and fashion folk melodies. The quills sounded like high-pitched whistles and were a likely precursor to the use of harmonicas in blues instrumentation. In the recordings that Thomas made with his quills, he alternates vocal lines with responses from the quills; the effect is to create a haunting musical dialogue. Thomas's voice is high and plaintive; there is little slurring of notes or word syllables, and even less embellishment of the melody. The sound of his voice is clear, intense, and challenging, its slow, rocking cadences constantly evoking the rhythms of an agrarian culture.

Henry Thomas's recorded repertoire of twenty-three songs, although probably only a fraction of the songs he actually played, demonstrates his indebtedness to the African-American oral tradition. Most of the recordings are blues; the next largest group is the country dance tunes; then come a few gospel numbers; and finally two well-known black ballads. He recorded "John Henry," a rarity among Texas musicians. He also did a version of "Bob McKinney," the ballad of a notorious St. Louis badman. He sang about ordinary life in the folksy and fun-loving "Fishing Blues," and he portrayed cotton farming as a woeful and dreary way of life in "Cottonfield Blues." His travel songs include "When the Train Comes Along," "Alabama Bound," "Texas Easy Street Blues," and his classic tribute to riding the rails, "Railroadin' Some":

I leave Fort Worth, Texas, and go to Texarkana,
And double back to Fort Worth,
Come on down to Dallas,
Change cars on the Katy,
Coming through the Territory to Kansas City,
And Kansas City to Saint Louis,
And Saint Louis to Chicago,
I'm on my way but I don't know where,
Change cars on the T.P.,
Leaving Fort Worth, Texas,
Going through Dallas,
Hello, Terrell,
Grand Saline,
Silver Lake,
Mineola,
Tyler,
Longview,
Jefferson,
Marshall,
Little Sandy,
Big Sandy,
Texarama,
And double back to Fort Worth,
Change cars on the Katy,
Leaving Dallas, Texas,
Coming through Rockwell,
Hello, Greenville,
Celeste,
Denison,
South McAlester,
Territory,
Muskogee,
Hello, Wagner,
Parsons, Kansas,
Kansas City,
Sedalia,
And I change cars and jump in Saint Louis,
Hello, Springfield,
I'm on my way to Chicago,
Bloomington,
Joliet.
Can the Highball pass on through?

Highball on through, Sir.
Grand Crossing,
Thirty-first Street Depot,
Polk Street Depot,
Chicago.[15]

Nowhere in the early rural blues recorded in the 1920s is there a more vivid and intense recollection of railroading. The cadences of the song depict the restless lifestyle of the vagabonds who rode the rails and their boundless enthusiasm for the mobility it gave them.

Prison farms and resistance to incarceration are recurring themes in many of Thomas's recordings, including "Don't Ease Me In" and "Run Molly Run." In "Shanty Blues," the refrain goes:

I'll make it to my shanty if I can, if I can, if I can,
I'll make it to my shanty if I can,
Dogs on my track, man's on his horse,
Make it to my shanty if I can.[16]

"Bull Doze Blues" refers to the unsavory practice of flogging (bulldozing) African Americans in the South before and after slavery. The song is a hodge-podge of floating blues lyrics centered on the refrain, "I'm goin' where I'll never be bulldozed."[17]

Thomas's themes—farming, travel, prisons, and relationships between the sexes, which included celebrating sexual pleasure and promiscuity—combine to evoke a sense of the content and quality of life for the black inhabitants of the East Texas farming communities during his four-decade career as a wandering bluesman, from the 1890s to the 1930s. Much of what he recorded was well within authentic folk traditions and represented black people's efforts to shape and reshape their own culture in the face of continuing oppression and adversity.

Henry Thomas was sixteen years old and still living in Upshaw County when the first written record of a blues song in Texas was made in 1890. That was the year folklorist Gates Thomas noted a song called "Nobody There," which is structured much like the traditional AAB blues stanza:

That you nigger man, knockin' at my door?
Hear me tell you nigger man,
Nobody there no more.[18]

Immediately after the turn of the century, Gates Thomas wrote out lyrics to some traditional folk blues classics, including "C. C. Rider," "Alabama

Bound," and "Baby, Take a Look at Me"; archaeologist Charles Peabody noticed the last song during the same period in the Mississippi Delta. Will H. Thomas wrote down the lyrics to a song called "Railroad Blues" that he collected in Texas in 1912. It contains the well-known line, "I got the blues, but I'm too damn mean to cry." Three years earlier in Mississippi, E. C. Perrow had noted a similar line: "Got the blues, I'm too damn mean to talk." Perhaps the most unusual early Texas folk blues were collected by Prescott Webb in 1915. In a Beeville, Texas, poolhall he came across a blues bard named Floyd Canada who played guitar, banjo, and harmonica. Canada sang for him a folk blues epic he called "Dallas Blues." It is an autobiographical stream of consciousness that rambles on for eighty stanzas about home and family, women troubles, hoboing around the state, and trouble with Texas lawmen. The piece may be several blues run together; but because it is the only historical reference to Canada recorded for posterity, the origins and the composing method remain a mystery.[19]

### Blind Lemon Jefferson: "See That My Grave Is Kept Clean"

Dallas was an important center of blues activity for itinerant black musicians after the turn of the century, and it was a favorite stopping-off place for the most renowned country blues oracle in Texas, Blind Lemon Jefferson. He was one of seven children born into a poor sharecropping family on a farm outside of Couchman, Texas, in 1880. Because Jefferson was born blind, he turned to music at an early age; it was one of the very few means of self-support for blind African Americans. The struggle for independence and self-sufficiency against overwhelming odds was central to both his life and his music. Classic blues singer Victoria Spivey, who knew him in Texas, remembered that Jefferson always used the expression "Don't play me cheap" in his conversations with others. Okeh talent scout Polk Brockman recalled that when Jefferson was in Atlanta for a recording session, he asked the record producer, Tom Rockwell, for a five-dollar advance. As a joke, Rockwell gave him a dollar bill, but Jefferson immediately recognized it as such and protested angrily. Blindness compelled him to constantly remind people that he was their equal. In his songs, Jefferson invariably took the side of the underdog, giving voice to the desires and concerns of the downtrodden.[20]

Jefferson began his career as a bluesman at local community picnics and Saturday night dances. His cousin Alec Jefferson described the "country suppers" where Blind Lemon performed: "Of course, my mother don't let me go to them country suppers often. They were rough. Men was hustling women and selling bootleg and Lemon was singing for them all night. They didn't even do proper kind of dancing, just stomping."[21] The rural blues of Jefferson and the other pioneering bluesmen from the East Texas cotton belt were particularly popular among black farm workers, whose dancing to the blues at these weekend socials sharply contrasted with formal social dance genres and intentionally defied the established legal and moral institutions of respectable, middle-class Americans—black and white—in the postbellum South. As we have already seen, the uninhibited dancing involved the audiences in a cathartic ritual of collective release and regeneration. In this respect, the Saturday night country suppers recalled the secret prayer meetings among slaves.

Blind Lemon Jefferson's music was grounded in the folk culture prevalent in the East Texas farming communities. He was remembered as being diversified enough to perform at country suppers, picnics, and dances, on the street corners of the towns in the region, and on at least one occasion at a Baptist social in Buffalo, Texas. Like Henry Thomas and Charley Patton, he recorded a few traditional religious songs, which were released under the pseudonym Deacon L. J. Bates. First-generation rural bluesmen had repertoires of folk music appropriate for a variety of social functions. Probably Jefferson came to local get-togethers prepared to provide the music, whether the occasion demanded sacred hymns, secular ballads, country dance tunes, or the blues.[22]

Details about Blind Lemon Jefferson's adult life are sketchy. After he established his reputation in the farming communities around his birthplace, he ventured into the red-light districts of Dallas and Galveston, where he could earn a better living as a blues performer. In the early 1920s, he married a young woman from his home region named Roberta, who gave birth to a child soon after. However, Jefferson continued to travel much of the time; throughout the twenties, he made many trips outside of Texas to Oklahoma, the Mississippi Delta, Atlanta, Virginia, and eventually Chicago, where he did most of his recording for Paramount Records. Bluesman Arron "T-Bone" Walker, who grew up in Dallas, recalled traveling with Jefferson to Oklahoma City, and Tulsa, Oklahoma, while still in his teens. He first worked with Jefferson on the Dallas streets: "He had a cup on his guitar and everybody knew him, you know, and so he used to come through on Central Avenue singing and playing his guitar. And I'd lead him and they'd put money in his cup."[23] Mississippi Delta bluesman Houston Stackhouse remembered seeing Jefferson perform for an overflow crowd in his hometown:

I saw Blind Lemon in 1928. I believe it was when I saw him. He came to Crystal Springs and was playin' in some little show for a doctor. . . . They had it in Freetown there at the colored school. There was plenty of people there. It was a big school and crowded all indoors, people couldn't get to see him. They had to bring him out to the front, on the porch. They come to see him, he was a big name then. Said he was comin' in town, why everybody was right there. . . . He played many a song that night. Yeah he played great. He played that "Wonder Will His Matchbox Hold His Clothes" and all that.[24]

Stackhouse was at the time a young protégé of Tommy Johnson's; he recalled that Johnson knew much of Jefferson's recorded repertoire and spoke of regularly playing with him in Jackson, Mississippi. Charley Patton's sister recalled that her brother had played with Blind Lemon Jefferson in the Delta region and that they had both worked on the same traveling medicine show for a while. Jefferson recorded a couple of Patton's blues standards, including his signature piece, "Pony Blues," which Jefferson renamed, "Black Horse Blues." Jefferson roamed as far east as southwestern Virginia; there he is remembered drawing overflow crowds on three straight nights playing in a schoolhouse for the local black community. In the mid-1920s, he was "discovered" in the streets of Dallas by a Paramount Records executive named A. C. Laibley, who invited him to Chicago to make some records. Jefferson was successful in his first recording venture, and he returned to Chicago to record regularly. Between 1926 and 1929, he proved to be the most commercially successful of the rural bluesmen who were recorded; his high-pitched voice and eclectic guitar style were especially popular in the South among his own people. Blind Lemon Jefferson was in Chicago for a recording session during the early winter months of 1929 when he died of an apparent heart attack. His body was taken back to Texas for burial by a woman who claimed to be his widow.[25]

Jefferson's highly irregular guitar style was unique among the early East Texas bluesmen; he used it in juxtaposition with his equally unusual voice, the two carrying on an intense and competitive dialogue. While strumming a repetitive bass figure low on his guitar strings, he would construct playful single-string arpeggios high up the neck of the guitar, which moved the melody of his songs forward in tandem with his voice. Another characteristic of his guitar playing was his habit of taking periodic breaks in the rhythm to highlight his short solo runs; he seems to have been one of the earliest rural blues guitarists to have regularly used improvisation in his playing. Jefferson's tenor voice ranged over two octaves. His diction was relatively clean and even, his ever-present humming or moaning pliant and tinged with melancholy. There was an ordinary quality to his singing that was comforting and easy to identify with, which may in part account for his widespread popularity in the rural South once his records were made available.

The blues repertoire that Blind Lemon Jefferson developed in his youth and later recorded in Chicago reflects the range of familiar themes prevalent in the black oral tradition in the South at the turn of the century. Among the recordings he made in the late 1920s were his renditions of some traditional folk blues from his East Texas homeland; these included the gambling classic "Jack

o' Diamonds,'' a version of "Two White Horses Standing in a Line" renamed
"See That My Grave Is Kept Clean,'' the ubiquitous "See See Rider,'' which
he refashioned into "Corina Blues,'' and the legendary "Boll Weevil Blues,''
a folksong thought to have originated in the Texas cotton belt since Texas was
the first southern state afflicted by the boll weevil.

The mosquito rivaled the boll weevil as a public nuisance, especially in the
more humid regions of the South. In "Mosquito Moan,'' the insect's perseverance is thwarted by Jefferson's deadpan humor and clever resistance:

> Now I'm sittin' in my kitchen, mosquitos all around my
>     screen,
> Now I'm sittin' in my kitchen, mosquito all around my
>     screen,
> If I don't arrange to get a mosquito bomb, I'll be
>     seldom seen.
>
> I believe I'll sleep under a tin tub just to let them
>     bust their bad old bills,
> I believe I'll sleep under a tin tub just to let them
>     bust their bad old bills,
> Well, mosquitos so bad in this man's town keep me away
>     from my whiskey still.[26]

Travel as a response to the vicissitudes of work and personal relationships in
the cotton belt is also a theme in Jefferson's blues compositions. In "Bad Luck
Blues,'' he advises:

> Sister, you catch the Katy, I'll catch the Santa Fe,
> Doggone my bad luck soul,
> Sister, you catch that Katy and I'll catch that
>     Santa Fe,
> I mean Santa, speakin' about Fe,
> When you get to Denver, pretty mama, look around
>     for me.[27]

In one of his best-known songs, "Matchbox Blues,'' he laments:

> Sitting here wondering will a matchbox hold my
>     clothes,
> I'm sitting here wondering will a matchbox hold my
>     clothes,

I ain't got so many matches, but I gots so far to
  go.

I wouldn't mind marrying, but I can't stand settling
  down,
I wouldn't mind marrying, but, lord, settling down,
I'm gonna act like a preacher so I can ride from town
  to town.[28]

Here again, physical mobility is equated with individual freedom. To the extent that moving elsewhere continued to evoke expectations of better working and living conditions, it remained a powerful metaphor in the early blues lyrics. In these songs mobility appears to be a mordant and individualistic response to the social malaise, but its widespread use as a theme signals its importance as an expression of feelings shared by much of the population of the black belt.

Blind Lemon Jefferson's recordings also emphasize the sexual themes associated with the blues from their inception; perhaps his best-known recordings were the three records in the lascivious ''That Black Snake Moan'' series. The following lyric combines a rather menacing sexuality with slapstick comedy:

Ummm better find my mama soon, better find my mama
  soon,
I woke up this morning, black snake was making such
  a ruckus in my room.

Black snake is evil, black snake is all I see,
Black snake is evil, black snake is all I see,
I woke up this morning, he was moved in on me.

Ummm black snake was hanging around,
Ummm black snake was hanging around,
He got inside my living room and broke my only bed
  down.[29]

His views of women were largely conventional; he regarded them as desirable and virtuous (''good gal,'' ''sugar,'' ''baby,'' ''honey'') or misanthropic and untrustworthy: (''wild,'' ''dirty mistreaters,'' ''deceitful brownskins,'' ''cunning as a squirrel''). A verse from ''That Crawling Baby Blues'' warns:

The woman rock the cradle and I declare she
  rules the home,

> Woman rocks the cradle and I declare she rules
>     the home,
> Many a man rocks some other man's baby and the
>     fool thinks he's rocking his own.[30]

This verse is drawn from an African-American proverb that dates to the days of slavery.[31] In other songs Jefferson holds his female companion responsible for his pneumonia ("Pneumonia Blues"), a prison sentence ("Prison Cell Blues"), robbing him ("Deceitful Brownskin Blues"), and cheating on him ("Peach Orchard Mama"). In all these blues scenarios, the women break male hearts and egos with abandon and apparent delight.

Blind Lemon Jefferson sang to and for his people, especially those who suffered from chronic poverty and oppression. In "Tin Cup Blues," he speaks for the poor and destitute:

> I stood on the corner and almost bust my head,
> I stood on the corner and almost bust my head,
> I couldn't earn enough money to buy me a loaf
>     of bread.
>
> My gal's a housemaid and she earns a dollar a week,
> I said my gal's a housemaid and she earns a dollar
>     a week,
> I'm so hungry on payday, I can't hardly speak.
>
> Now gather around me people, let me tell you a true
>     fact,
> I said gather around me people, let me tell you a
>     true fact,
> That tough luck has struck me and the rats is
>     sleeping in my hat.[32]

"Rising High Water Blues," which refers to the devastating Mississippi River flood in 1927, is about the flood's victims, among whom Jefferson included himself:

> People, cinch it's raining, it has been for nights
>     and days,
> People, cinch it's raining, has been for nights and
>     days,
> Thousands of people stands on the hill looking down
>     where they used to stay.

Children standing screaming, "Mama, we ain't got no
    home";
Ohh, mama, we ain't got no home,
Papa says to the children, "Backwater left us all alone."

Backwater is rising, coming in my windows and doors,
The backwater is rising, coming in my windows and
    doors,
I leave with a prayer in my heart, backwater won't
    rise no more.[33]

As St. Louis bluesman Henry Townsend recalled, Blind Lemon Jefferson's blues compositions express "sympathy for the fellow." This was particularly true of his songs dealing with prison life, even though he is not known to have spent time in jail. Jefferson recorded five prison-related blues numbers, and in them he always empathizes with the convicts. Moreover, his vision of imprisonment was harsh and desolate; at its most powerful, it conjures up a nightmarish existence. In "Prison Cell Blues" there is the verse:

Got a red eyed captain and a squabblin' boss,
Got a mad dog sergeant, honey, and he won't
    knock off.[34]

Dropped into the middle of "'Lectric Chair Blues," there is a striking proverb, adopted from the folklore of prison life in the South:

I wonder why they electrocute a man after the one
    o'clock hour of the night?
I wonder why they electrocute a man after the one
    o'clock hour of the night?
Because the current is much stronger when the folks
    turn out all the lights.[35]

There is also mention of a regional town close to Jefferson's birthplace, where justice for black people was known to be one-sided and oppressive:

Take Fort Worth for your dressing and Dallas,
    Texas, for your style,
Take Fort Worth for your dressing and Dallas,
    Texas, for your style,
But if you want to go to the state penitentiary,
    go to Groesbeck for your trial.

> I hung around Groesbeck, I worked in hard showers
>     of rain,
> I hung around Groesbeck, worked in hard showers
>     of rain,
> I never felt the least bit uneasy 'til I caught that
>     penitentiary train.[36]

A final theme of these prison blues is the familiar longing for freedom, for a full and unshackled life beyond the prison walls:

> So nice to be where it's sunshine, I mean snow
>     or rain,
> It's so nice to be where it's sunshine, I mean
>     snow or rain,
> Because I can't go acuttin' and carrying a ball
>     and chain.[37]

## Leadbelly: "Midnight Special"

An early associate of Blind Lemon Jefferson's was Huddie Ledbetter, better known as Leadbelly. He was a rough-and-tumble itinerant bluesman who did time on two different Texas prison farms, where he was renowned for his herculean feats of labor. Jefferson and Leadbelly were apparently a popular duo in Dallas and the surrounding Texas countryside between 1905 and 1917, the year Leadbelly was first imprisoned at Huntsville, Texas.

Huddie Ledbetter was born in 1885 and grew up on a farm in the Lake Cado district of Louisiana, close to the Texas border. His father, Wes Ledbetter, was a stern, hardworking sharecropper who was eventually successful, against great odds, in his quest to buy his own land in the backwoods region of the district. His mother, Sally, was half black and half Cherokee; she worked alongside her husband, clearing and cultivating the new land. Their relationship was remembered as a stormy one that sometimes led to physical violence. The farm they owned was isolated, even for a rural location, and the work growing cotton was strenuous and never ending.

Although Leadbelly, by his own account, was a top-notch farmhand who could pick more cotton than any man in Lake Cado country except his father, he was also attracted to a life of music and good times, and while still in his teens, he began to attend—and then perform at—the weekly country dances, called "sooky jumps," in his region. Leadbelly was a natural and gifted musician who quickly developed a reputation as a flamboyant performer at the

Saturday night sooky jumps. His first instrument was a small accordion his uncle taught him to play, but he later graduated to guitar, mandolin, harmonica, and piano. He also became well known as a ladies' man and a dangerous man in a fight because of his size, strength, and quick temper. Leadbelly's rebellious behavior eventually enraged both his father and the local community; when he fathered his second child out of wedlock, public pressure led to his abrupt departure from the area.[38]

Leadbelly headed for the disreputable Fanin Street red-light district in Shreveport, where he encountered a new blues piano style known as barrelhouse. He would later cite the bass figures of barrelhouse blues piano as the inspiration for the rhythmic strumming prominent in his guitar style. Next he journeyed to "Deep Ellum" and the "Central Track" (Elm Street and Central Avenue) in Dallas's black tenderloin district. It was during this Texas sojourn that he teamed up with Blind Lemon Jefferson, adopting renditions of Jefferson's "Matchbox Blues" and "See See Rider" as his own and learning to use a knifeblade as a slide. Sometime during this period, Leadbelly also began to play the twelve-string guitar, an instrument common among Mexican folk musicians but used by very few East Texas bluesmen. Immersed in the lusty night life of the black lower classes—gambling, drinking, whoring, dancing, fighting—he eventually killed a man in a fight over a woman late in 1917 and was sentenced to thirty years in Huntsville, plus five more for an unsuccessful escape attempt.[39]

In prison Leadbelly continued to play his music. His skill at improvising new songs won his release in 1925. Texas Governor Pat Neff issued an official pardon after Leadbelly composed an impromptu song for him while Neff was conducting an inspection tour of the prison.

> Nineteen hundred and twenty-three,
> The judge took my liberty away from me,
> Left my wife wringin' her hands and cryin',
> "Lawd have mercy on de man of mine."
>
> I am your servant compose this song,
> Please Governor Neff, lemme go back home,
> I know my wife will jump and shout,
> Train rolls up, I come stepping out.
>
> Please, Honorable Governor, be good an' kind,
> If I don't get a pardon will you cut my time?
>
> Had you, Governor Neff, like you got me,
> Wake up in the morning and I'd set you free.[40]

After his release, Leadbelly returned to the Lake Cado district, where he resumed his life as the areas's best-known blues performer and hellion. Blues-woman Esther Mae Scott lived in Louisiana during this period; she was a friend of Leadbelly's and played with him on several occasions. In 1979 she recalled:

> He was like a chunky, big black bull! The thing about Leadbelly . . . he wanted women and he loved women. He'd love to have them around and play around—a playboy. But his girlfriend—don't fool around with her! He was a jealous man and that's the part I didn't like him for. I just couldn't understand that. He wasn't my cup of tea, but he was a very dear friend of mine. Leadbelly was just so much greater than I was. He could make anything rhyme. He's just smart, let's put it like that. I wasn't quick like that. Leadbelly was just a performer, a real performer from the heart.[41]

Leadbelly's rowdy behavior eventually caught up with him again. In 1930, he was convicted of an assault charge and sentenced to ten years in the state prison at Angola, Louisiana. By chance, folklorist John A. Lomax met and recorded him while doing fieldwork at the Angola prison farm in 1934. Among the songs recorded was another plea for a pardon, this one addressed to the governor of Louisiana, O. K. Allen. Lomax delivered the recording to Governor Allen, who set Leadbelly free that same year.

Leadbelly rejoined John Lomax in Texas, recorded another series of folk-songs and blues for him, and soon thereafter embarked on an extensive tour of white colleges and concert halls in the Northeast, with Lomax as his manager. While performing in the North, Leadbelly was married to Martha Promise, and they settled in New York City. With the exception of a brief return to Shreveport, he remained in New York the rest of his life. He continued to record his broadly based repertoire for John Lomax and his son, Alan, at the Library of Congress. The cumulative selection of blues, ballads, spirituals, prison worksongs, country dance tunes, and even cowboy songs constituted the most extensive collection of black folk music recorded at that time.

In addition to his recording efforts under the direction of the Lomaxes, Leadbelly also became associated with the "proletarian folk revival" spon-sored by white leftists in the late 1930s and early 1940s. This cultural move-ment, which was centered in New York City, relied heavily on sacred and secular African-American music; hence, Leadbelly and other black performers such as Paul Robeson, Josh White, Sonny Terry, and Brownie McGhee were much in vogue among the white radicals attracted to it. Leadbelly appeared regularly at the gatherings of the folk revival movement and readily shared his unique folk repertoire with white singers like Woodie Guthrie, Burl Ives, and the Almanac Singers. By exposing many of the era's white radicals, intellectuals, and folksingers to a large body of African-American folksongs, he helped to bring the music more into the mainstream of American culture. Moreover, he directly contributed to the politics of the leftist folk-revival movement by composing topical protest songs, including a spirited defense of the "Scottsboro Boys" and his exposé of segregation in the nation's capital, "Bourgeois Blues." Yet Leadbelly's involvement in white leftist cultural politics in New York City removed him permanently from his rural southern homeland and the daily struggles of his own people there. Hence, he became something of an anomaly. Separated from the blues culture that spawned his rebellious lifestyle and music, he was often viewed as a novelty in the North, even by those who courted him. Although still a legendary figure among African Americans in Louisiana and East Texas, Leadbelly soon lost his appeal in New York City. After the novelty wore off, he slowly faded into obscurity and then poverty. He eventually died in New York's Bellevue Hospital.[42]

### Texas Alexander: "Mama's Bad Luck Child"

In contrast to Leadbelly, whose odyssey took him beyond regional and racial boundaries, most of the other first-generation East Texas bluesmen may have left the state periodically, but they always returned. Alger Alexander, better known as Texas Alexander, was one of them.

Alexander was born in 1900 near Jewett, Texas, a small town located in Leon County, midway between Houston and Dallas. As a youth, he labored in the cotton fields and developed an unusual blues vocal style modeled after the mournful sounds of the field holler and the chants of prison work gangs. Alexander never learned to play the guitar, but he carried one with him in his travels and often found someone who could accompany his singing. He sang original blues compositions that drew readily on folksy witticisms, proverbs, floating verse, and rhymes from the black oral tradition. The focus of the songs was invariably the day-to-day concerns and experiences of African Americans living in the Texas cotton belt. There were ongoing references to the drudgery of farm work and gang labor; Alexander often worked as a laborer on railroad section gangs in his home county of Leon.[43] In "Section Gang Blues," he recreated the black workers' impressions of gang labor as first person narratives:

> I been working on the section, section thirty-two,
> I'll get a dollar and a quarter, won't have to work
>     hard as you,
> Lord, I'll get a dollar and a quarter and I won't
>     have to work hard as you.

Oh captain, captain, what's the matter with you?
If you got any battle axe, please sir, give me a chew,
Oh captain, captain, what's the matter with you?

Water boy, water boy, bring your water 'round,
'Til you ain't got no water, fetch your bucket down,
Water boy, water boy, bring your water 'round.

Oh captain, captain, what time of day?
Oh, he looked at me and he walk away,
Umm, oh captain, what's the matter with you?[44]

Alexander also spent time incarcerated in a Brazos River camp, perhaps on more than one occasion. Many of his blues numbers allude to these events; one of the most forceful is "Levee Camp Moan," which includes the widely used floating verse:

Lord, they accused me of murder, murder, murder,
I haven't harmed a man,
Ohh, they accused me of murder,
And I haven't harmed a man.
Oh, they accused me of forgery,
And I—I can't even write my name,
Lord, they accused me of forgery
I can't even write my name.[45]

It is interesting to note that these two social protest blues numbers were the first that Alexander recorded when the opportunity arose; they were done for Okeh Records in New York City in 1927. This was one of the few times he ventured out of the state for a recording session. Most of the other forty titles he recorded before 1930 were done at sessions in San Antonio, Texas.[46]

The revolving themes prevalent in Alexander's recorded blues include travel ("Frisco Train Blues," "Saint Louis Fair Blues"), death ("Death Bed Blues"), farming ("Farmhand Blues," "Bell Cow Blues," "Boe Hog Blues"), superstitions ("Blue Devil Blues," "Mama's Bad Luck Child"), skin color ("Yellow Gal Blues"), and the ubiquitous battle of the sexes ("98 Degree Blues," "No More Women Blues," "Mama, I Heard You Brought It Right Back Home"). Like the songs of his fellow first-generation East Texas bluesmen, Alexander's songs deal with the daily concerns and routines of rural black people living in the post-Reconstruction South. They are composed of a mixture of material drawn from his personal experiences and the black oral tradition; hence, they provide further testimony on life as the African Americans perceived it, just before mass migration to the industrial centers of the North and the West Coast.

Since Texas Alexander did not play the guitar himself, he recorded and worked with an impressive string of Texas-based or -bred guitarists, many of whom went on to become established blues performers in their own right. A youthful Lonnie Johnson was the first guitarist he recorded with in the late 1920s. Johnson was the first blues guitarist to fuse jazz into his playing technique and perhaps one of the top two or three blues innovators of the 1920s. He would play an important role in the development of a distinctive urban blues guitar style. Blind Lemon Jefferson played with Alexander in and around Dallas from time to time. Lowell Fulson was Alexander's guitarist before migrating to the West Coast, where he was to be a key figure in the urban blues resurgency after World War II. Two lesser-known accompanists were Little Hat Jones, who played with him on a few of the recordings made before 1930, and Funny Paper Smith, who worked the country fairs, picnics, and ballgames with Alexander during the depression. Sam "Lightnin' " Hopkins, a cousin of Texas Alexander's, recalled encountering him at a ballgame in Leon County between Leona and Normangee, the small town where Alexander's family lived. The spectators were also having a picnic and, as Hopkins put it, "a little old hoe down":

> So I got down there and I seen a man standing up on a truck with his hand up to his mouth and, man, that man was singing. That was Texas, my cousin, I didn't know. Alright, I goes on there and that man was singing so and he like to broke up the ballgame. People was paying so much attention to him instead of the ballgame.[47]

Texas Alexander's performances were festive events that galvanized the African-American audiences around him. His blues were honest and earthy; they spoke directly to the desires and the needs of the rural black masses. Not only did they register covert protests against white society's arbitrary and unjust domination of the land, the economy, the politics, and the social institutions of the postbellum South, but they also were representative of the subsequent cultural resistance in the agrarian black communities through affirming their commitment to a music and a culture of their own choosing and their own making.

Like the Mississippi Delta, East Texas was relatively isolated from the tentacles of the American entertainment industry. The black vaudeville shows and the race record enterprises penetrated the region only belatedly. This allowed the rural East Texas blues culture to mature free from commercial influences and imperatives. The styles and the repertoires developed by these first-generation folk blues musicians became the foundation of a music that was soon exported to the Southwest and the West Coast along with the large-scale black migration of the 1930s and the war years. It would prove to be the catalyst for the postwar rhythm and blues upsurge in those areas.

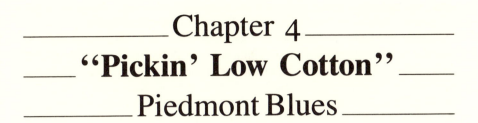

# Chapter 4
# "Pickin' Low Cotton"
# Piedmont Blues

## The Political Economy of the Piedmont

As a geographic region, the Piedmont extends from Richmond, Virginia, south to Atlanta, Georgia. Bordered by the Appalachian Mountains on the west and the Atlantic coastal lowlands on the east, it is a land of rolling foothills and placid, muddy brown rivers that undulate down the alluvial valleys like earthworms. The soil is colored with red clay. Clusters of oak and long-needle pines are commonplace where the land has not been cleared for farming. The Piedmont has traditionally been an agricultural region, with cotton and tobacco the dominant crops. In the pre-industrial South, tobacco predominated, for the most part, in the northern section of the Piedmont, from the agricultural lands around Richmond, Virginia, down to the Winston-Salem–Durham–Raleigh area of North Carolina. The cotton kingdom prevailed on the farmlands south of the tobacco fields, from Charlotte, North Carolina, down to Columbia, and Augusta, South Carolina, and from there westward to Macon, and Atlanta, Georgia. This region comprised the eastern end of the South's famed cotton belt.

Black slaves were essential to the production of both cotton and tobacco; hence, they constituted the bulk of the agricultural labor force at the onset of the Civil War. Emancipation, the Reconstruction era, and its bleak aftermath were not much different for black people living in this region than they were for those in the Mississippi Delta or East Texas. If anything set the Piedmont apart from other southern regions in the post–Civil War period, it was the fact that, because the area had been settled relatively early in the history of the South, its agricultural lands had been in use the longest; thus, they were not as rich and productive as more recently settled farmlands. The soil depletion in the region was hurried along by the omnipresence of the one-crop economy, which tended to disrupt the soil's ecological balance. This left the Piedmont particularly vulnerable. When the pre-eminence of American agriculture began to decline in the late decades of the nineteenth century, both black farm laborers and white farmers were left without suitable land, work, and a regular income.

The white leaders of the South's agrarian revolt and subsequent Populist movement recognized these basic similarities and attempted to form an alliance between the impoverished farmers of both races based on their common economic self-interests. Georgia Populist Tom Watson even went so far as to proclaim that racial antagonism in the South perpetuated the rule of the rich at the expense of the poor. Unfortunately, racism was still deeply embedded in the dominant southern culture, and racist demagogues ultimately won the allegiance of the lower-class white southern farmers, usually by blaming the African American for all their misfortunes. Moreover, the Southeast's ruling economic and political elites sought to resurrect the region's faltering economy through a program of industrialization. Critical to this strategy to build a "New South" was the initiation of a "Cotton Mill Campaign" in the Piedmont cotton belt. The South would now both grow the cotton and transform it into exportable textiles, thereby eliminating the Yankee middlemen. The new industry would provide its owners with a lucrative source of profits while also opening up exclusive job opportunities for the region's poor whites. Thus, the economy could be revived and workplace segregation among the lower classes in the Piedmont could be reinforced simultaneously. Coupled with the political strategy of disenfranchising the black male, the Cotton Mill Campaign succeeded in reconstructing southern hegemony along racial, as well as class, lines. While the displaced poor white farmers went to work in the textile factories for the South's new captains of industry and commerce, the black population was kept subordinate, segregated, and relegated to the lowest levels of the occupational pyramid.[1]

## Piedmont Blues Roots

The Piedmont's early folk blues, like those in East Texas and the Mississippi Delta, were a collective response to new regional manifestations of racism and oppression. However, the blues seem to have emerged as a distinct folksong genre in the Piedmont region later than they did in the Delta or East Texas. There are two arguments that attempt to explain this lag. One attributes it to the long-standing presence of an Anglo-American folk music tradition, especially among the poor whites living in the Piedmont and the Appalachian Mountains to the west. The traditional Anglo-American music in this regional center may have exerted a strong influence on the African-American music and playing styles in the same area, thereby partially dominating its makeup and development. On the other hand, as Samuel Charters has suggested, because the African-American musical traditions were older and more established in the Piedmont, they may have also been more fixed in their ways and less open to innovation and change than was newly transplanted black folk music. Given the social conditions prevalent in the Southeast during the postbellum decades, Charters' explanation of the blues lag in the area is the more plausible. Factors such as rigid segregation and heightened racial antagonism, as well as the absence of radios and phonograph records, probably kept the two folk traditions in the region relatively separate until at least after the turn of the century. At most, they influenced each other indirectly and peripherally.[2]

The black Piedmont folk tradition—instrumentally—can be traced to African slaves from the Wolof and Mandingo tribes, who brought the banjo and the kora playing style with them to America. The banjo became the favorite instrument of slaves in the antebellum South. The kora playing technique of using an alternating thumb to strum the strings down low in order to establish the groundbeat while also finger picking the melody line higher up the neck of the instrument became the major playing style. This style was later adapted to the guitar when it arrived on the scene in the late 1800s, and it eventually showed up in the playing of many of the region's earliest blues musicians.

Whatever the reasons for the lag, the blues were not noticed among rural African Americans in the Piedmont until after the turn of the century, more than a decade after their appearance in the Mississippi Delta and East Texas. Folklorist Howard Odum, an early collector of African-American folksongs and rhymes, recorded hearing at least three songs that could be considered folk blues in Newton County, Georgia, between 1906 and 1908; they were called "Baby, What Have I Done?" "No More Good Times," and "Look'd Down the Road" with the lines:

> I got the blues, but too damn mean to cry,
> I got the blues, but too damn mean to cry.[3]

He may well have heard more. Since Odum, a white southern academic, was unfamiliar with the term "blues" and unaware that a new folksong style and genre was in the making, he may have inadequately transcribed any number of the early folk blues because he did not describe the music, and he often neglected to indicate the repetition of a line or a phrase in the texts he wrote down and later published. This would have especially affected his transcriptions of the more primitive AAA folk stanzas, from which the three-line AAB standard blues stanza seems to have emerged.

The Piedmont's proximity to the urban centers of the Northeast and the early efforts to industrialize its agrarian economy resulted in the area's being less isolated from mainstream American culture than were the Mississippi Delta and East Texas. As a result, the folk blues from the region were more likely to be mixed in or fused with other popular styles of music, such as minstrel songs and ragtime. Ragtime had emerged in the Mississippi Valley out of the African-American practice of "ragging" popular European melodies. "Ragging" was in essence the age-old West African practice of separating the melody from the basic time scheme by positioning notes slightly ahead of or behind the groundbeat. The effect produced a pattern of simple cross-rhythms. Piano players accomplished this by establishing the groundbeat with left-handed bass figures while "ragging" the melody with the right hand. Although ragtime music was primarily identified with piano and marching band compositions, it was also influenced by the popular dance music of country stringbands, and the technique of ragging dance tunes was being used among black musicians even before the Civil War. Coinciding with the national ragtime craze in popular American music, which began in the 1890s and extended into the second decade of the twentieth century, was a regional penchant for playing instrumental rags on the tenor banjo and, later, the guitar. Many of these tunes became part of the repertoire of early Piedmont rural bluesmen.[4]

A second major factor in the makeup of a regional rural blues tradition in the Piedmont was the legacy of minstrels. Minstrel and medicine shows featuring black performers and musicians had been in existence since the Reconstruction era and had a well-established following among the black belt population in the Southeast. Before the emergence of the blues, the musicians played marches and dance tunes in ragtime, while the singers relied on a big repertoire of ballads and minstrel songs geared toward the preferences of their rural black audiences. African-American ballads like "John Henry," "The Titanic," "Gray Goose," and "Boll Weevil" were commonplace in the repertoires of these songsters, as were some ballads more identified with the Anglo-American tradition, like "Old Blue" and the "Wreck of Old 97."

It was the minstrel songs, however, that were the mainstays of the road shows. One of the best-known black minstrel songs was "Travelin' Man," a popular standard identified with Jim Jackson, the venerable medicine show performer from Hernado, Mississippi, who first recorded it in Memphis in the 1920s. His version tells the story of a foot-loose "travelin' man" who made his living stealing white folks' chickens, while traveling around from place to place. His speed afoot was as legendary as his ability to outwit his white adversaries:

> Well, they sent the old travelin' man one day,
> I asked for one pail of water,
> And where he had to go was two miles and a quarter.

He went and got the water alright, but he stumbled
   and fell down,
He run three miles and a half and got another pitcher,
Caught the water 'fore it hit the ground.

Another verse has him on the Titanic:

He ran and jumped on this Titanic ship,
And started up that ocean blue,
He looked out and spied that big iceberg,
And right overboard he flew.
All the white ladies on the deck of the ship,
Said that man certainly was a fool,
But when the Titanic ship went down,
He's shootin' craps in Liverpool.

But eventually the "travelin' man" is gunned down by the authorities:

And he wouldn't give up and he wouldn't give up,
'Til the police shot him down,
And he wouldn't give up and he wouldn't give up,
'Til the police shot him down.[5]

"Travelin' Man" was a favorite among early Piedmont bluesmen. Two of them, Luke Jordon and Virgil Childers, made separate commercial recordings of it in the late 1920s. In addition, it was a long-time favorite of Pink Anderson, who worked the medicine show circuit in the Southeast from 1914 into the 1950s.[6]

The first generation of Piedmont musicians and songsters who incorporated the blues into their repertoire were, for the most part, born in the 1890s and later, about a decade after their earliest counterparts in the Mississippi Delta and East Texas. Two pioneering Piedmont guitarists born before 1900 and attracted to the blues in the early stages of their development were Gary Davis and Willie Walker, both associated with the early blues scene in Greenville, South Carolina, where they were playing in a stringband together before World War I. Pink Anderson, whose home was in nearby Spartanburg, South Carolina, was born in 1900. Julius Daniels, a rural bluesman who lived near Charlotte, North Carolina, was born in 1902. Blind Willie McTell was born in McDuffie County, Georgia, in 1898. Other prominent Piedmont blues musicians, such as Blind Boy Fuller (1908), Sonny Terry (1911), Buddy Moss (1914), and Josh White (1914), came even later. Only Blind Simmie Dooley, born in Hart County, Georgia, in 1881, and Joshua Barnes "Pegleg" Howell, born in Eastonton, Georgia, on March 5, 1888, came close to rivaling Charley Patton or Henry Thomas as father figures of the rural blues in the South's cotton belt, and that claim would be a regional one at best.


## Rural Blues in Georgia


The cotton farming region southeast of Atlanta where Pegleg Howell grew up was an influential hotbed of local blues culture. Research by folklorist Bruce Bastin has uncovered an extensive network of black musicians in Newton, Morgan, and Walton counties who had incorporated the blues in their repertoires by the 1920s. The earliest record of this indigenous folk tradition goes back to sociologist Howard Odum's research in Newton County between 1906 and 1908. During his stay, Odum collected folksong texts from sixty-five residents of the region, forty-three of whom were born in the county. As previously mentioned, a handful of these song texts have been identified as early folk blues. In the late 1960s and early 1970s, Bastin interviewed a number of older black musicians who had been involved in the blues activity in the region beginning in the 1920s. They included two musicians from the small town of Porterdale in Newton County, "Sun" Foster and George White. Born in nearby Henry County in 1893, Foster learned to play the banjo at the age of nine, and by the time he was twenty he was also playing guitar. In 1915, he moved to Covington in Morgan County, and then on to Porterdale, where he first met George White. White was born in Jackson, Georgia, in 1901, then moved to Newton County with his family in 1905. He learned to play the banjo and then the guitar from older members of his extended family. Both Foster and White used the slide technique in their guitar playing and both were playing the blues by 1920.

Throughout the 1920s, Foster and White were an integral part of an ensemble of black musicians who were in great demand at local parties—black and white. The white parties were mostly square dances at which Foster and White took turns as the callers. At the black dances, songs such as "Candy Man," "Don't Let the Deal Go Down," and "Atlanta Favorite Rag" were popular. While the music was different at the black and white dances, the method of paying the musicians was the same. At some point, a hat was passed around and a collection was taken up, but the musicians also got all the free food and drink they wanted. Other black musicians associated with the Porterdale group include guitarists Nehemiah Smith, Judd Smith, Maylon Parker, and John Hardeman; harmonica players Robert Smith and Pete Coleman; fiddler Vince Hardeman; and banjo player Jesse English. In addition, a cadre of younger

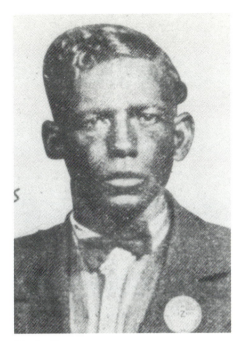

Charley Patton

Tommy Johnson

Son House

Clarksdale, Mississippi, 1939

Juke joint, Memphis, Tennessee

"Blind Lemon" Jefferson, c. 1927

Huddie Ledbetter ("Leadbelly")

Sam "Lightin'" Hopkins

Joshua Barnes "Pegleg" Howell

"Blind" (Arthur) Blake

Joshua Barnes "Pegleg" Howell and gang

"Blind Boy" Fuller

"Blind" Willie McTell

musicians like the Hicks brothers, Curley Weaver, and Eddie Mapp were involved and influenced by the group before moving to Atlanta, where they became important blues figures in the late 1920s.[7]

### Blind Blake: "Mr. Diddie Wa Diddie"

The best-known and most successful blues recording artist of the 1920s from the Southeast was Blind Blake, born Arthur Blake in Jacksonville, Florida, in the early 1890s. Very little is known about Blake. He apparently spent some of his youth in Georgia and was familiar with Geechie dialect and music, since on one of his instrumental recordings, "Southern Rag," he suddenly breaks into a Geechie monologue:

> Hey Mamma, I wanna match an' you cin light my pipe, yeah!
> Go on ole geechie, I ain't talkin about you.
> I know this sweet mess begin to roll.
> I could help you pick this cotton.
> You cain't dig potatoes—either one!
> I can stock more sugar cane than you cin stock in ten years!
> Now we gonna do that dance now.
> We call it the Geechie Dance.
> I'm gonna give you some music we call the Geechie music now.
> That's my gal!
> Get away from here!
> Play 'em![8]

Blake had an established recording career in Chicago, where he made seventy-nine commercial recordings with Paramount between 1926 and 1932. After his 1932 recording session, he left Chicago to tour with a traveling minstrel show and then dropped out of sight. He was never heard from again.[9]

Blind Blake is most remembered for his innovative blues and ragtime guitar techniques. He had a flair for improvisation. His style was to use an alternating thumb stroke to establish a groundbeat, which he often varied to embellish the rhythmic complexity of his playing. On the upper strings he sometimes made use of arpeggio, and sometimes finger-picked clusters of notes while deftly alternating the chordal harmonies on the song. The overall effect was a fluid and upbeat sound well suited for dancing.

Blake continued to return to his homeland in the Southeast, where he was widely known as an itinerant bluesman. Bill Williams recalled first meeting Blind Blake in Bristol, Tennessee, in 1922. Baby Tate heard him play in Elberton, Georgia, in 1926. Josh White ran across him in Charleston, West Virginia, in 1929. Blake also played at the Pekin Theatre in Savannah in 1929–30,

sometimes with a local jazz band led by Herman Quillion. There also are reports of him playing in Ohio, Virginia, North Carolina, and South Carolina.

When in Chicago, Blind Blake recorded with some of that city's most talented musicians, including New Orleans jazzmen Johnny Dodds and Jimmy
Bertrand, as well as banjo players such as Gus Cannon and Charlie Jackson.
In an interview much later in his life, Cannon remembered him vividly as a
heavy drinker with an uncanny sense of direction.

> We drank so much whiskey! I'm telling you we drank more whiskey
> than a shop. And that boy would take me out with him at night and get
> me so turned around I'd be lost if I left his side. He could see more with
> his blind eyes than I with my two good ones.[10]

While living in Chicago in the late 1920s, Blind Blake rented an apartment
at the corner of 31st Street and Cottage Grove Avenue. There was a piano in
the main room and consequently the apartment became a hangout for a group
of piano players who performed with Blake at the Southside house parties held
on the weekends. Among these blues pianists were Charlie Spand, Little
Brother Montgomery, and Roosevelt Sykes. Montgomery fondly remembered
the gatherings in Blake's apartment.

> We called them rehearsals. Usually we had them on Mondays when ev-
> eryone was free. We'd all get together over at Blake's place. Be a few
> piano players there—me, Spand, sometimes Roosevelt Sykes. Guitar
> players like Blake and maybe Tampa Red or Big Bill Broonzy. We'd
> drink moonshine and trade songs. Everyone was just like family and
> these were our little get-togethers.

As for the host of these gatherings, Blind Blake, Little Brother Montgomery
recalled:

> He [Blake] could play that guitar of his. He kept good time and he knew
> the changes in all the popular songs back then. He would play it all and
> he was good in a band, too, but he mostly played blues and ragtime
> tunes. Blake loved the blues most. He always wanted us to play blues.
> Funny thing, he drank a lot of moonshine, especially when he played his
> blues. But he never lost his senses and he always knew where he was.
> That boy could hear himself all around the Southside. He didn't need a
> guide. He could hear everything on the street. Hear the cars, the curb,
> the buildings, the people. So he knew where they were. That's why he
> was such a great musician, because he could hear things so well.[11]

Blind Blake's songs reflect many influences and experiences. There are the customary blues about being mistreated and having a broken heart, and there also are sexually suggestive nonsense songs. In "Diddie Wa Diddie" Blake sings:

> The little girl 'bout four feet four,
> Told papa hey give me some mo',
> Your diddie, your diddie wa diddie,
> I wish somebody would tell me what diddie wa diddie means.
>
> I went out and walked around,
> Somebody yelled hey look who's in town,
> Mister diddie wa diddie, Mister diddie wa diddie,
> I wish somebody would tell me what diddie wa diddie means.
>
> I said, sister, I soon be gone,
> Just give me that thing you sittin' on,
> My diddie wa diddie, my diddie wa diddie,
> I wish somebody would tell me what diddie wa diddie means.[12]

In contrast, there are traditional "cautionary folktales" warning African Americans against getting caught up in the criminal justice system. They include "Rope Stretching Blues," "Doin' a Stretch," "Police Dog Blues," "Search Warrant Blues," "What a Low Down Place the Jailhouse Is," "He's in the Jailhouse Now," and "Third Degree Blues." In addition, there are warnings of the ravages of alcoholism, perhaps based on personal experience. "Fightin' the Jug" concludes:

> When I die folks, without a doubt,
> When I die folks, without a doubt,
> You won't have to do nothin' but pour me out.
>
> I'm deep down in a hole somebody else has dug,
> I'm deep down in a hole somebody else has dug,
> Gettin' sick an' tired of fightin' that jug.[13]

In contrast to the rural imagery of "Southern Rag," a small but significant number of Blind Blake's blues are stories about the new urban experience that African Americans were confronting in increasing numbers. "Steel Mill Blues" records how black men felt about working in the mills.

Workin' in the steel mill, makin' pig iron all day,
Workin' in the steel mill, makin' pig iron all day,
When I come home, mama, have somewhere for me to lay.

Have dinner ready, don't let my coffee be cold,
Have dinner ready, don't let my coffee be cold,

Don't forget, mama, please save my sweet jellyroll.
When I look into that blast furnace it's already hot with ore,
When I look into that blast furnace it's already hot with ore,
If I catch you cheatin' ain't comin' back no mo'.

Every payday when I get my check,
Every payday when I get my check,
After I pay our bills I'm a nervous wreck.

Pig iron and bills eatin' out all my shoes,
Pig iron and bills eatin' out all my shoes,
That's the reason I got these lowdown steel mill blues.[14]

Songs like this reflect the fact that he lived in Chicago, where there were many steel mills that employed black immigrants.

### Pegleg Howell: "Georgia Skin"

Joshua Barnes "Pegleg" Howell was raised on a small farm in Eastonton, Georgia, run by his father, where he went to work full time as a plowhand in his early teens. The first music he encountered was the rural folk music popular among his family and neighbors, much of which was sung without accompaniment in the cotton fields and churches. His musical interests were strong enough to impel him to take up the guitar in about 1909, at the age of twenty-one. According to his own account of his life, he was a self-taught musician. The name "Pegleg" became his trademark in 1916, when a brother-in-law shot him in the leg during an altercation and he lost the leg as a result. Because of the amputation, he could no longer rely on farmwork for a livelihood. He recalled working in a fertilizer plant in Madison, Georgia, for a year, but other than that, he just "messed around" until the early 1920s, when he drifted into Atlanta. Before he reached Atlanta, he was undoubtedly playing music and singing for whatever he could get at the country dances, picnics, barbecues, and Saturday night parties, as well as on the streets and around the depots of the small rural towns. Pegleg may have also been engaged in moonshining enterprises while still living in the Georgia cotton belt. Certainly he was selling bootleg whiskey to customers in Atlanta soon after his arrival there because he acknowledged being arrested for it and spending a year at the River Camp prison farm.[15]

After completing his prison sentence, Pegleg Howell returned to playing for tips along Atlanta's Decatur Street, where in 1926 he was "discovered" by a Columbia Records talent scout. Soon after that he recorded four blues numbers under the auspices of Columbia: "New Prison Blues," "Fo' Day blues," "Tishamingo Blues," and "Coal Man Blues." "New Prison Blues," the first to be recorded, is a song he had learned on the prison farm. "Fo' Day Blues" is typical of the early rural blues in that it contains several traditional floating verses that are varied in length and are impressionistically arranged in a random order. It goes in part:

> I woke up this mornin', 'tween midnight and day,
> I woke up this mornin', 'tween midnight and day,
> I woke up this mornin', 'tween midnight and day,
> I felt for my rider, she done eased away.
>
> My rider got something they call it the stingaree,
> My rider got something they calls it the stingaree,
> I woke up this morning, it was worryin', worryin' poor me.
>
> Say the Mississippi River, man, it's long and deep and wide,
> The Mississippi River, long and deep and wide.
> Mississippi River, long and deep and wide,
> I got a lovin' rider, she's on the other side.
>
> I'm goin' up the country, mama, honey, and I would carry you,
> I'm goin' up the country, mama, I would carry you,
> Ain't nothin' up the country, sweet mama, you can do.
>
> I'd rather drink muddy water, sleep in a hollow log,
> I'd rather drink muddy water, sleep in a hollow log,
> Than to be in Atlanta treated like a dog.[16]

It seems likely that the initial rural blues compositions in the Piedmont drew heavily on folk material from the black oral tradition and that only later were the first-generation country bluesmen in the Southeast comfortable enough with the new medium to craft the lyrics to express their personal concerns more directly and individually. "Coal Man Blues" contains a similar hodgepodge of folk verse drawn from ballads, street vendor cries, and standard blues lyrics. It tells a story about an accident involving a coal man:

> Let me tell you something I seen,
> Coal man got run over by the five fifteen,
> Cut off his arms and crushed his ribs,
> Did the poor man die? No, the poor man lives.

Then followed the street vendor calls:

> Hard coal, stove wood man,
> Hard coal and the stove wood man,
> I ain't got but a little bit left,
> If you don't come get it, gonna burn it myself.

Eventually there is a fusion of the street calls with the blues lyrics:

> Sell it to the rich and sell it to the poor,
> Sell it to the rich and sell it to the poor,
> Sell it to the rich and sell it to the poor,
> Sell it to the nice brown that's standin' at the door.

> Furnish your wood, furnish your coal,
> Furnish your wood and I furnish your coal,
> Furnish your wood and I furnish your coal,
> Make you love me doggone your soul.

The final verse is pure blues:

> Let me tell you, mama, what's the matter now,
> Let me tell you, mama, what's the matter now,
> Let me tell you, mama, what's the matter now,
> You don't want me, take me anyhow.[17]

After his initial recording session, Howell remained based in Atlanta, where he frequently played in the streets with a small string band that featured Howell on guitar, his close friend Eddie Anthony on fiddle, another guitarist named Henry Williams, and sometimes a second fiddler named Ollie Griffin. This was the group that recorded as Pegleg Howell and His Gang at a second session for Columbia Records in 1927. The session produced "Jelly Roll Blues" and "Beaver Slide Rag," Howell's most successful commercial recording. "Jelly Roll Blues" is a folksy and titillating number that Howell had learned from an older country musician named Elijah Lawrence before moving to Atlanta. "Beaver Slide Rag" is a raucous country dance tune featuring Eddie Anthony's raw and unrestrained fiddle playing backed up by the rhythmic strumming of the guitarists; throughout the number, Pegleg hollers encouragingly, "Do the papa stomp!" "Do the deadeye!" "Do the Mister Eddie!"[18]

In stark contrast to the lively country dance music of Pegleg and His Gang are the solo blues that Howell continued to record; these tended to remain similar in style and content to his initial blues recordings. Subdued, mournful, and understated, these songs drew heavily on the folk lyrics and folklore current in the black oral tradition. Two prime examples of this tendency, and perhaps Howell's most important recorded legacies, are "Ball and Chain Blues" and "Skin Game Blues." "Ball and Chain Blues" is a dreary song about prison life modeled after the widely known Piedmont folk blues "Crow Jane." "Skin Game Blues" is his version of a song commemorating the legendary card game called Georgia Skin popular among African Americans in the Southeast. Its lyrics evoke an image of yet another outlaw figure from the reservoir of black folklore—the gambler:

> When I came to Georgie, money and clothes I had,
> Babe, all the money I had done gone,
> My Sunday clothes in pawn, Sunday clothes in pawn,
> Sunday clothes in pawn, lovin' babe, my Sunday
>     clothes in pawn.
>
> Dollar more, the deuce beats a nine,
> Dollar more, the deuce beats a nine, lovin' babe,
> Dollar more, the deuce beats a nine.
>
> When I did the skin game last night, thought I'd have
>     some fun,
> Lost all the money that I had, babe,
> Had to pawn my special gun, lovin' babe, had to pawn my
>     special gun,
> Had to pawn my special gun, lovin' babe, had to pawn my
>     special gun.
>
> Say you better let a deal go down, skin game comin' to a
>     close,
> And you better let the deal do down.
>
> Well, gambled all over Missouri, gambled all through
>     Spain, babe,
> Police come to arrest me, babe, and they didn't know
>     my name,

And they did not know my name,
And they did not know my name, lovin' babe,
And they did not know my name.

Better let the deal go down, skin game comin' to a
    close,
And you better let the deal go down.

Gambled all over Missouri, gambled through Tennessee,
    babe,
Soon as I reached ol' Georgie, the niggers carried a
    handcuff to me,
The niggers carried a handcuff to me, babe,
The niggers carried a handcuff to me, lovin' babe,
And the niggers carried a handcuff to me.

Better let a deal go down, skin game comin' to a close,
And you better let the deal go down.[19]

Joshua "Pegleg" Howell's brief recording career ended in 1929. However, he continued to play locally in Atlanta up until 1934, the year his friend and fellow band member, Eddie Anthony, died. A second band member, Henry Williams, had died in jail a few years earlier. These deaths had a traumatic effect on Howell. Apparently losing interest in music, he dropped out of the Atlanta blues scene altogether and went back to being a bootlegger for a while. He eventually lost his other leg because of diabetes and ended up an invalid. In 1963, at age seventy-five, he was rediscovered in Atlanta by country blues enthusiast George Mitchell, who interviewed Howell and recorded him for the last time.

### Blind Willie McTell: "Big Star Fallin' "

By far the most extraordinary blues artist to emerge from the Georgia cotton belt was Blind Willie McTell. He was born in McDuffie County in 1898 but spent most of his youth in the small town of Statesboro, where he moved with his mother in 1907. McTell was not born blind but apparently lost his sight slowly while in his teens. He took up music as a child. He was touring with a minstrel show in 1916, but he remained based in Statesboro until the death of his mother in 1920. He then seems to have suspended his musical activities to attend a series of schools for the blind in Macon, Georgia, as well as in the states of Michigan and New York, before launching his recording career back in Atlanta in the late 1920s. Presumably, he was totally blind when he started his studies at the school in Macon in the early 1920s. Once he started recording in Atlanta, McTell and his blues became a fixture along Decatur Street, the major African-American corridor. Over the years he recorded for half a dozen different labels, using a new pseudonym with each company with which he negotiated a contract, but varying his material and his style very little.[20]

Blind Willie McTell's initial recording sessions for the Victor and Columbia record companies included the earliest versions of his greatest blues compositions, "Mama, 'Tain't Long 'fo' Day," "Statesboro Blues," and "Broke Down Engine Blues." "Mama, 'Tain't Long 'fo' Day" was cut at McTell's first session for Victor in 1927; for this blues, he used a six-string guitar with a slide accompaniment. His guitar style was already very intricate and polished. He alternated between using the slide to answer the vocal line, and finger picking a response; in both instances, his deft touch produced a fluid and delicate sound. His high, poignantly adolescent voice blended smoothly with the guitar. He pronounced the words to the song clearly and distinctly, yet there was a fragile and helpless quality of his vocal delivery. The lyrics were pure poetry:

> Wake up, mama, don't you sleep so hard,
> Wake up, mama, don't you sleep so hard,
> For it's these old blues walkin' all on your yard.
>
> I've got these blues, reason I'm not satisfied,
> I've got these blues, I'm not satisfied,
> That's the reason why I stole away and cried.
>
> Blues grabbed me at midnight and didn't turn me loose
>     'til day,
> Blues grabbed me at midnight, didn't turn me loose 'til
>     day,
> I didn't have no mama to drive these blues away.
>
> The big star fallin', mama, 'tain't long 'for' day,
> The big star fallin', mama, 'tain't long 'for' day,
> Need a little sunshine to drive the blues away.[21]

In 1928, McTell was again recorded by Victor. It was at this session that he first used the twelve-string Stella guitar that would become his trademark. Atlanta was a hotbed of twelve-string guitar playing; the Hicks brothers, Charlie and "Barbecue Bob," were well known as virtuosos on the instrument. McTell seems to have adopted it after relocating in the city the year before.

The second Victor session produced his undisputed masterpiece, the haunting and wistfully restless "Statesboro Blues," named after his hometown:

> Wake up, mama, turn your lamp down low,
> Wake up, mama, turn your lamp down low,
> Have you got the nerve to drive Papa McTell from
>     your door?
>
> My mother died and left me reckless, my daddy died
>     and left me wild, wild, wild,
> My mother died and left me reckless, daddy died and
>     left me wild, wild, wild,
> Lord, I'm not good looking, but I'm some sweet
>     woman's angel child.
>
> She's a mighty mean woman to do me this a way,
> She's a mighty mean woman to do me this a way,
> When I leave this time, pretty mama, I'm going away
>     to stay.
>
> I once loved a woman better than I'd ever seen,
> I once loved a woman better than I'd ever seen,
> Treated me like I was a king and she was a doggone
>     queen.
>
> Sister tell your brother,
> Brother tell your aunt,
> Now auntie tell your uncle,
> Uncle tell my cousin,
> Now cousin tell your friend,
> Goin' up the country, mama, don't you want to go?
> May take me a fair brown, may take one or two more.
>
> Big Eighty left Savannah, lord, it did not stop,
> You oughta saw that colored fireman when he got that
>     boiler hot,
> Reach over in the corner, mama, and hand me my
>     traveling shoes,
> You know by that I've got them Statesboro blues.
>
> Papa got 'em,
> Sister got 'em,

Auntie got 'em,
Brother got 'em,
Friend got 'em,
I got 'em,
I woke up this morning, I had them Statesboro blues,
I looked over in the corner, grandma and grandpa had
    'em too.[22]

Love, travel, trains, their black firemen, home, and family are common themes in the rural blues, but no one combined them more lyrically than Blind Willie McTell, especially in these early recordings.

McTell remained based in Atlanta for the rest of his life. He married a woman named Kate in 1934 and continued to make commercial recordings periodically under various aliases. In 1940, he was both recorded and interviewed by John Lomax for the Library of Congress. Listening to the interview, one is struck by the precision of McTell's diction and his memory of places, dates, and names. McTell dates the origins of the blues from 1908 to 1914, adding that these "original blues" (i.e., rural blues) were augmented in 1920 by the "jazz blues" (i.e., vaudeville blues).

McTell was a multi-instrumentalist; besides the six- and twelve-string guitars, he played banjo, fiddle, harmonica, and accordion. As was true of Blind Blake, his loss of sight did not hinder his mobility; instead, it caused him to develop sonar. One of his cousins called it being "ear-sighted." As he aged, however, it became harder for him to survive as a street musician; he became increasingly dependent on alcohol, relied more and more on charity, and spent his final days as a ward of the Lighthouse for the Blind, a mission for the elderly blind in Atlanta.[23]

## The Greenville-Spartanburg Blues Network

Besides the Georgia cotton belt another important area of blues activity in the Piedmont was in and around the Greenville-Spartanburg region of South Carolina, where the blind guitarists Willie Walker and Gary Davis spent their youth and early manhood. Walker was born in South Carolina in 1896. He was born blind, most likely because of congenital syphilis. His family moved to Greenville around 1912 while he was still in his teens, and there he joined a local string band. The band developed a loyal following in the area even before World War I, and Walker quickly became the group's most prominent musician. He usually traveled with other musicians when on the move from place to place and from performance to performance. A youthful Josh White, also raised in Greenville, accompanied Walker on many such ventures. Walker often played with a second guitar player, Sam Brooks, a Greenville carpenter who was with him at his only commercial recording session in Atlanta in 1930.

Walker played the six-string guitar in a ragtime style and was considered by many to have the best playing technique in the region. Josh White rated him as the best blues guitarist in the entire Piedmont region—even better than Blind Blake. Others remember his guitar wizardry with equal admiration. Bluesman John Jackson recalled a visit by Willie Walker to his father's farmhouse in Culpepper, Virginia, in the early 1930s:

> My father knew Blind Willie Walker. Played with him some before he died. I reckon it musta been back in the depression years he come by the house once. I was just a youngster. Couldn't play any but I sure did like to listen to my daddy and his friends . . . and that Walker fella played his "South Carolina Rag." Boy that just about bowled me over even way back then. Never heard such playing. He was real fast and right on the number. Made you wanna jump up and dance.[24]

The two titles released by Columbia, "South Columbia Rag" and "Dupree Blues," give some indication of Walker's musical talent, if only briefly. "South Carolina Rag" clearly demonstrates his mastery over the ragtime idiom; his finger-picked runs at the bridges of the piece, between the standard verses, are especially bold and imaginative and are accomplished with amazing dexterity. "Dupree Blues" is a reworking of the black ballad immortalizing the convicted outlaw Frank Dupree, who was hanged in Georgia in 1922. On this song, Walker's clear and expressive voice is more prominently featured than his guitar playing. Unfortunately, these are the only recordings that Willie Walker released. He died in 1933 at the age of thirty-seven from the effects of the congenital syphilis.[25]

Walker's chief competitor on the guitar in Greenville was Gary Davis, born blind because of glaucoma in Laurens County, South Carolina, in 1896. In his childhood, Davis initially learned to play the harmonica, then he played the banjo, and by the age of seven, he had graduated to the guitar. In an interview much later in his life, Gary Davis recalled first hearing the blues at a carnival in 1911, about the same time his family moved to Greenville: "The first song that was a blues I heard was a man in a carnival singing, 'I'm on the road to somewhere, if the train don't break down, I'm on the road to somewhere.' "[26]

While living in Greenville, Davis became associated with the local string band that featured Willie Walker and sometimes included as many as eight musicians; the band was very popular and seems to have been active from about 1914 to the beginning of the depression. During these years, Gary Davis developed into an accomplished six- and twelve-string country guitar picker. His style and sound owed as much to the blues idiom as did Walker's playing.

Davis left Greenville in the late 1920s, not long after his wife left him for another blind guitarist named Joe Walker, who was also a member of the famous local string band and the brother of Willie Walker. He moved on to North Carolina, where he continued to work as a street musician.[27]

It is interesting to note that the Greenville-Spartanburg region was something of a haven for blind African-American blues musicians. Besides Gary Davis and Willie and Joe Walker, there were at least four other popular blind blues bards active in the area: John Henry "Big Boy" Arnold, Columbus Williams, Archie Jackson, and Simmie Dooley. These men usually traveled about with the help of young apprentice musicians who, in exchange for music lessons and a cut of the take, would act as guides. It was in this manner that many of the area's most talented second-generation rural bluesmen—Baby Tate, Roosevelt "Baby" Brooks, Josh White—got their start as guitarists and street singers.


### Blind Simmie Dooley

Only Blind Simmie Dooley had the opportunity to record, and from all accounts, he was the oldest and the most highly regarded of the four local musicians. More important, he is often mentioned as the earliest blues pioneer in the region. He was born in Hartwell, Georgia, in 1881, but nothing else is known of his life until he began singing and playing his guitar for tips in the streets of nearby Spartanburg, South Carolina, shortly after the turn of the century.

One of Dooley's early protégés was Pink Anderson, who grew up in Spartanburg during the time Dooley was becoming something of a musical institution there and who as a youngster sang and danced in the same streets for pennies. The two teamed up as a duo to play at the country picnics and Saturday night parties in the Greenville-Spartanburg area, and by 1916 they were the entertainers with "Doctor" W. R. Kerr's Indian Remedy Company Medicine Show. The show toured the small towns in the rural Piedmont during the summer and fall of the year. Anderson and Dooley would perform a mixture of popular minstrel songs, ballads, and blues to attract a crowd for the "Doctor" to hawk his wares and remedies to. In 1928, the duo recorded four songs for Columbia Records in Atlanta. Although their singing style—alternating verses and harmonizing on the choruses—owed much to the minstrel tradition, all the recordings were blues, and the guitar playing was reminiscent of other Piedmont bluesmen, particularly Pegleg Howell.

For reasons unknown, Simmie Dooley became inactive as a bluesman and medicine show performer at some point in the 1930s. Pink Anderson continued to work for traveling road shows, teaming up with a harmonica player from Rocky Mount, North Carolina, named Arthur Jackson. Both men later maintained that Dooley was the best blues stylist in their region, and an important influence on their music.[28]

### Josh White: "Blood Red River"

The most widely acclaimed and recorded member of the Greenville-Spartanburg blues network was Josh White. He was born in Greenville on February 11, 1914. His father was a fiery preacher whose outspoken opposition to racial discrimination and injustice was abruptly silenced by the local authorities during a period of heightened racial conflict after World War I. The elder White was beaten by the police and then incarcerated in a local insane asylum, where he eventually died. His seven-year-old son witnessed the beating, and it left an impression on him for life.

After the father's death, the boy's mother began to hire him out as a guide for the area's blind street singers. His first client was John Henry "Big Boy" Arnold, a giant-sized man over six feet tall and weighing between 260 and 270 pounds. One of their early outings took them to Waycross, Georgia, where they witnessed a black man being lynched by a white mob. In Jacksonville, Florida, during the same trip, White was roughed up by the police and then jailed for vagrancy. There is a direct link between these harrowing childhood experiences and Josh White's well-known disdain for the South, as well as his outspoken criticism of racial discrimination and injustice.[29]

In 1928, at the age of fifteen, White journeyed to Chicago with Blind Joe Taggart. He was Taggart's guide and also his backup guitar player on a series of recordings they made there for Paramount Records. The records indicate that White had already mastered the Greenville-Spartanburg playing style, especially the distinctive and sophisticated finger-picking techniques. Josh White next recorded as a solo artist in New York in 1932. Out of this session came five blues that were released under the sobriquet "Pinewood Tom" to prevent his mother from knowing that he was performing blues instead of sacred music.

Included in his earliest recorded blues is his rendition of the Piedmont version of "Red River Blues," which White called "Blood Red River":

> Which a way do that blood red river run?
> From my back window to the rising sun.[30]

This session also produced the blues song he is most associated with in the Greenville-Spartanburg region—and elsewhere in the Piedmont—"Pickin' Low Cotton":

> I been pickin' low cotton, no high cotton can I see,
> I been pickin' low cotton, Lord, no high cotton can I see,
> I be glad when this cotton picked, be happy as I can be.
>
> When you pick low cotton you get down on your bended knees,
> When you pick low cotton—get down on your bended knee,
> Wasn't fer this low cotton that gave me a dirty deal.
>
> If I was the President, I'd destroy this cotton that's worryin' us,
> I was the President, ohhhh,
> Penny an' a nickel make you darkies want to fight and cuss.
>
> I'm not the President, so there's nothin' I can do,
> I'm not the President, nothin' I can do,
> Cotton worryin' me just as it's worryin' you.[31]

During this period in the Piedmont, "low cotton" referred to the size of the plant in the region, which was shrinking because of the long-term soil depletion, and the price of cotton, which declined steadily from after World War I until late in the 1930s. That the hardships and frustrations associated with cotton farming were subjects most rural African Americans could still identify with in their own lives helps account for the popularity of "Pickin' Low Cotton."

Josh White left the Greenville-Spartanburg area permanently in 1934 and moved to New York. There he got married, established his home, and launched a new career, not as a bluesman, but as a folksinger. Like Leadbelly, White became associated with the leftist folk revival centered in New York City in the 1930s. The folk revival movement offered him opportunities to perform and a platform from which to denounce racial inequality and injustice. His performances were a mixture of traditional African-American folksongs—including the blues—and the topical protest songs then in fashion. These included songs he composed with other African Americans linked to the movement, including Langston Hughes and Richard Wright. White put music to "Red Sun," a blues poem by Langston Hughes, and to "Southern Exposure," a protest blues:

> Work all week in the blazing sun, [3]
> Can't buy my shoes, lord, when my payday come.

I ain't treated no better than a mountain goat, [3]
The boss takes my crop and the poll tax takes my vote.

I'm leavin' here 'cause I just can't stay [3]
I'm goin' where I'll get some decent pay.[32]

Both Hughes and Wright are credited with writing these lyrics. Since they are known to have worked together on some blues poems, this may have been a joint venture. In any event, Josh White provided the music and recorded it in the late 1930s. After World War II, he toured Europe with much fanfare and continued to make New York his home. He never returned to South Carolina.

# Bull City Blues

### Tobacco Strikes It Rich in Bull City

While the cotton farmers in the Piedmont suffered further setbacks in crop yield and pricing during the depression, the tobacco growers to the north prospered. With the help of mass advertising, especially by commercial radio, the tobacco industry had expanded its target audience to include women and college students. Cigarette sales climbed dramatically in the 1920s and continued to rise in the next decade. By World War II, smoking was a national pastime, along with listening to network radio and following professional baseball, and the tobacco industry did its bit for the war effort by donating huge quantities of cigarettes to American servicemen and servicewomen. The net result was that more Americans became habitual smokers. This translated into prosperous times for the tobacco centers in Winston-Salem, Greensboro, and Durham, North Carolina, even during the depression.[33]

Durham exemplified the prosperity and progress that resulted from the growth of the tobacco industry in the first half of the twentieth century. It is the hometown of the Duke family, the tobacco titans who founded the American Tobacco Company there in 1890. The company initially produced Bull Durham Tobacco, hence the nickname "Bull City." Durham grew up alongside the local tobacco industry. The Duke family invested in a variety of civic projects to forestall threatened antitrust litigation. Civic and economic growth fed into each other. By the 1930s, Durham was a thriving regional business and cultural center with prosperous white and black populations. The three giant tobacco factories located in the city, following the policy the Duke family established, employed black workers and paid them better wages than any of the other southern industries employing black labor. In addition, the local white business elite encouraged and financially supported the development of black businesses to service their own people in areas such as banking and insurance. North Carolina Mutual, a black insurance company set up in 1897 with white aid, went on to become the largest black-owned insurance corporation in the world. After the turn of the century, a black college—North Carolina College for Negroes (now North Carolina Central College)—was founded in Durham. By the 1920s, the black community in Durham had a growing middle class to augment its working-class population, which still constituted the vast majority of Durham's black community. During the depression years, the city continued to attract black workers hoping to find jobs in the tobacco industry. Mostly, they were fleeing the stagnant cotton farms farther south and were therefore still partial to the Piedmont blues.[34]

Thus it is not surprising that, in the 1930s, there was an influx of Piedmont blues musicians into Durham. They played on the street corners adjacent to the tobacco factories and warehouses during the week and at informal house parties or jook joints on the weekends. Author Glen Hinson, a native of Durham, wrote about these "sellins," as they were called locally:

> The party might be at a friend's place down in Bugs Button, or over at Peachtree Alley, or maybe out at Camel Grove. Or perhaps at one of the "houses" run by Minnie the Moocher, Big Mattie, or any of the other local bootleggers who worked in and out of Durham. The room you're in is large, with a few chairs off against the walls and a battered upright piano in the corner. A jar of moonshine for the musicians lays on the piano top. In a small room off to one side there's a table laden with barbeque, fried chicken and fish, chitlins, cakes and maybe some ice cream, all for sale. Behind that, a woman pours bootleg from a jar into small glasses. There's a one-eyed man tinkling the keys on the piano— that would be Murphy Evans—a guitarist picking a rag lead, a second guitarist playing the blues lines, and a washboard player rubbing his board with thimbles on his fingers. As the night wears on the musicians take breaks to dance or eat, and they are replaced by others with banjos or harmonicas. The room is crammed with people dancing the "Charleston Strut" or the "Hollywood Skip."[35]

A similar picture is painted by Zora Neale Hurston, who visited jook joints frequented by black migrant farm workers in Polk County, Florida, in the late 1920s:

> The jook was in full play when we walked in. The piano was throbbing like a stringed drum and the couples slow-dragging about the floor were

urging the player on to new lows. . . . "Jook Johnnie . . . jook it Johnnie! Throw it in the alley!" . . . Somebody had squeezed the alcohol out of several cans of sterno and added sugar, water and boiled-off spirits of nitre and called it wine. . . . The pay night rocks on with music and gambling and laughing and dancing and fights.[36]

Blind Gary Davis arrived in Durham in the early 1930s. He lived in Hayti, the city's black working-class district, and played for tips along Pettigrew Street, which was lined with cafes, pool halls, barbershops, a movie theater, and a dance hall. It was a rough neighborhood, but the years of travel and performing on his own—fending off con men and thieves, persevering through constant police harassment—had hardened Davis to the realities of southern life. To protect himself, he carried a large pocket knife, which he was known to use on people who attempted to cheat him or to steal from him.

Blind Gary Davis's guitar style had fully matured at this point in his career, and he quickly became the most admired blues guitarist in Durham. He was in great demand at the weekend house parties and he influenced other local blues musicians like Willie Price, Floyd Council, and Blind Boy Fuller. Fuller called him the "Daddy" of the local guitar pickers and credited him with showing him how to negotiate his famous bass runs on the guitar.

In 1937, Davis was ordained as a Baptist minister at Mount Vernon Baptist Church in Washington, North Carolina. He gave up drinking and playing blues at the weekend parties, and about a year later he stopped playing on the Durham streets altogether. He continued to play his guitar, however, performing "gospel blues" at revival meetings. In the early 1940s, Davis remarried and moved on to New York City, where he settled permanently.[37]

### Blind Boy Fuller: "I'm a Rattlesnakin' Daddy"

Blind Boy Fuller was born Fulton Allen in Wadesboro, North Carolina, around 1908, one of ten children of a poor sharecropper. Soon after his birth, the family moved on to Rockingham, North Carolina, where he grew up and learned to play the guitar. Ulcers behind the eyes slowly denied Fuller his sight, and by 1928 he was totally blind. He became an itinerant blues musician, working the streets and tobacco warehouses in Winston-Salem and then in Danville, Virginia. In 1929, he and his wife, Cora Mae, moved to Durham. Fuller soon became a familiar figure, playing along Pettigrew Street and around the nearby tobacco warehouses. His infectious singing and guitar style soon won him a local following in the area, and a cadre of aspiring young street musicians accompanied him from place to place. One of the cadre was George Washington, better known as Bull City Red. Red played blues guitar in the Piedmont style and was a strong singer, but he became best known as

Fuller's washboard player. Other younger bluesmen from the Durham area who played with Fuller include the Trice brothers, Richard and Willie, and Floyd Council and Sonny Jones, who may have first known him in Rockingham. Fuller was at the hub of a lively blues scene in Durham during this period.[38]

By 1935, both the Reverend Gary Davis and Sonny Terry had joined Fuller's blues entourage. One of eight children, Sonny Terry was born Sanders Terrell in 1911 on a Georgia farm near Greensboro, where he grew up. His father played the harmonica and started his son on the instrument at an early age, teaching him folksongs like "Lost John" and "Fox Chase." His mother sang in a local Baptist church, and Sonny Terry recalled singing with her at revival meetings. He improved his technique by listening to trains passing through the countryside and imitating their sounds on his harmonica. In addition, he was influenced by Deford Bailey, the famous black harmonica player featured on the "Grand Ole Opry" radio program, which was broadcast out of Nashville every week beginning in the late twenties.

After Sonny Terry lost his sight while in his teens because of two separate accidents, he became a full-time itinerant bluesman. He initially teamed up with another street musician, Bill Leach; they traveled around the North Carolina tobacco-warehouse circuit, playing for tips. At some point during this period, he met Blind Boy Fuller, who invited him to Durham. Sonny Terry arrived there late in 1935. He lived in Fuller's house and played with him, Bull City Red, and Gary Davis along Pettigrew Street and around the tobacco warehouses.[39]

That same year, Fuller was offered a recording contract by a local record agent, J. B. Long. Between 1935 and 1940, he was involved in many recording sessions in New York City and Memphis, Tennessee. For each of these sessions, Fuller brought along different members of his musical entourage, who would back him and also record some numbers on their own. At the first sessions for the American Record Company in New York, Fuller was with Bull City Red and Gary Davis. Davis and Red each recorded some separate songs, as did Fuller, but they also backed up Fuller on about half the material he recorded. (This proved to be Davis's last session for Long, who, he felt, underpaid him and cheated him out of his royalties.) Later sessions involved the Trice brothers, Floyd Council, and Sonny Terry.

Blind Boy Fuller, as he was called on these commercial recordings, made a total of 135 titles for three different labels. The most impressive blues were those done with either Gary Davis or Sonny Terry. The guitar duets with Davis on such numbers as "Rag Mama Rag" and "Baby, You Gotta Change Your Mind" are exuberant and free-wheeling ragtime pieces, perhaps the best to emerge from the entire Piedmont tradition. The numbers that Fuller recorded with Sonny Terry in the late 1930s are almost exclusively blues. They feature his light and polished guitar work in contrast to Terry's famous "whopping" harmonica-playing style. These duets are also original classics, rare recorded examples of the guitar and harmonica combination in the Piedmont's rural blues tradition.

Blind Boy Fuller was a diminutive man with an attractive face and a pleasing smile, but he also possessed a fiery temper. He was a smart dresser, and he usually carried a thirty-eight pistol, which on one occasion he threatened to use on his agent, J. B. Long. On another he did use it to shoot his wife, wounding her in the leg. He stayed out of jail with the assistance of his agent, J. B. Long, and because his wife refused to testify against him. A nephew of Sonny Terry's recalled yet another gun episode, this one involving his uncle and Fuller:

> Him and Unc' Son got into it. Once they both shot at each other. Unc' Son, he'll tell you about it. Unc' Son used to carry a knife and he went and got him a pistol, too. Blind Boy Fuller told him, "I ain't gonna get up on you. I know you got that big knife, but if you move I'll know where you at." Unc' Son, he said he heard where the shots was firing from and he shot back over there. Then Blind Boy Fuller says, "Oh, you got a gun too, ain't ya?" Unc' Son said, "Yeah, and it's mine." They was arguin' over a song.[40]

These gun incidents give us a glimpse of the rough and dangerous milieu of rural bluesmen. Like the lives of countless other bluesmen, Fuller's life was fast and often violent. Constant travel, playing in the streets, and heavy drinking eventually led to a kidney ailment, and in 1940 he was hospitalized for an operation. He failed to recover from surgery and died in his prime, at the age of thirty-three.

Blind Boy Fuller played a six-string National guitar. His style was representative of the rural Piedmont tradition, strongly influenced by Gary Davis and Blind Blake. J. B. Long recalled that Fuller learned much of his material by listening to recordings of Blake and other country bluesmen prominent in the late twenties and early thirties. Fuller's voice was medium range; on up-tempo numbers it was exuberant, while on the slow blues it was tinged with melancholy. One of his unique vocal characteristics was the optimistic way he shouted "Yeah!" to punctuate his guitar runs, or sometimes the groundbeat on the faster songs.

Fuller's repertoire of rural blues, ragtime, and even some gospel was an extensive one and a fine reflection of a fully matured regional tradition. He recorded such old standards as "Careless Love" and "Cat Man Blues," a song based on the Anglo-American ballad "Our Gudesman." He appropriated the regionally popular "Red River Blues" melody for several of his own blues pieces, including "Bye Bye Baby Blues" and "Pistol Slapper Blues"; the same technique was used to change Memphis Minnie's "Me and My Chauffeur Blues" into "Bus Rider Blues." He also recorded a number of uptempo ragged dance tunes, such as "Step It Up and Go," "Piccolo Rag," and his best-selling commercial release, "Rag Mama Rag," along with the whimsical "I'm a Rattlesnakin' Daddy."

The blues numbers that he recorded are a mixture of folk lyrics and melodies from the oral tradition, verses and tunes he learned from commercial recordings, and those that he composed himself to express his feelings and experiences. One of the best examples of Fuller's own compositions was about shooting his wife, called "Big House Bound":

> I never will forget the day they transferred me
>    to the county jail
> I never will forget the day they transferred me
>    to the county jail,
> I had shot the woman I love, ain't got no one to
>    come go my bail.
>
> Then I sent for my friends, please spare the rod,
> And I sent for my friends, Lord, please spare the
>    rod,
> Then my friends sent me word, Lord, this town is
>    too doggone hard.
>
> I got friends that got money, please tell them to
>    come and go my bail,
> I got friends that got money, please tell them to
>    come and go my bail,
> And my friends sent me word, had no business in
>    the county jail.
>
> Then I felt alright, till the judge turned around
>    and frowned,
> Then I felt alright, Lord, the judge turned around
>    and frowned,
> Say, I'm sorry for you buddy, but you're on your last
>    go 'round.
>
> I said hummm, ain't got nobody now,
> I said hummmm, ain't got nobody now,
> Well I got nobody, Lord, come and go my bail.[41]

After Blind Boy Fuller's death, the Piedmont's rural blues culture went into a decline. Many of the most important regional centers of blues activity had been diffused, and many of the area's most creative blues musicians joined the migration to the urban centers of the Northeast. Gary Davis and then Sonny Terry moved to New York City, where they continued to play in the traditional Piedmont styles. Unfortunately, their folksy blues material was out of place in Harlem, then the jazz capital of the world, and they would remain marginal to the black music scene there.

By this time, Sonny Terry had teamed up with guitarist Brownie McGhee, who had joined Fuller's Durham clan in the late 1930s. McGhee had been raised in Knoxville, Tennessee, where he learned to play the blues from his father. His proximity to the Piedmont blues style of Blind Boy Fuller, Gary Davis, and Blind Blake came from listening to their recordings and imitating them. He may have also been influenced by Carl Martin, who had moved to Knoxville from Greenville, South Carolina, where his father had played with musicians such as Gary Davis and Willie Walker. McGhee had a great admiration for Fuller's music; he wrote and recorded a famous tribute to him, "The Death of Blind Boy Fuller," soon after Fuller died. The musical partnership between Sonny Terry and Brownie McGhee was solidified in the early 1940s and remained viable up into the 1970s. For close to forty years they continued to play concert and club dates throughout the United States and Canada. They also made some commercial recordings in their original Piedmont styles, which changed very little over the years. As such, they were representative of the last vestiges of a rural blues culture that stubbornly maintained its folk roots in the face of a rapidly changing social environment.[42]

## The Piedmont Blues in Virginia

A final pocket of traditional rural blues activity in the Piedmont was located in southwestern Virginia, a region where the production of tobacco had long been the major industry. The process of handling and caring for the tobacco at each stage of its production was time-consuming work that required a great deal of manual labor. There was a constant need for workers in the fields where the crop was grown, in the warehouses where it was cured, and in the small local factories that processed it into the finished product, which was most often chewing tobacco. The industry had relied on slaves before the Civil War. After the war, it began to hire black laborers, and although the pay was at first minimal, the employment was fairly steady. By the turn of the century, there were numerous small black communities in the region, settled by African Americans who worked in some phase of tobacco production.

The black communities in Virginia's tobacco country, like most of the others located in the rural South, were close-knit cultural entities that sustained traditional African-American folk practices. Within these communities were well-developed networks of home-trained musicians, many of whom belonged to families in which making music together was the primary cultural activity. The musical instruments and playing styles indigenous to these black kinship groups had been passed down from one generation to the next since slavery. Kip Lornell, a leading blues historian of the region, documented this characteristic among a number of local blues musicians he interviewed:

> Virginia blues singers may have learned much from contact with local musicians, but for many of them, music education began at home. Turner and Marvin Foddrell, Richard Wright and Rabbit Muse all learned to sing from their fathers. William Richardson learned guitar from his father, Herbert, who learned it from his father, Tom. Blues is often associated with the stereotyped wandering performer, but music in the Piedmont was frequently a family affair. Posey Foddrell, whose wife was also a musician, taught all his children to play. Rabbit Muse was a member of a family band that included his parents and a cousin.[43]

Although these rural bluesmen were second- and even third-generation participants in the Piedmont blues tradition, they still maintained a folk ethos in relation to the music. Like their forebears, they continued to perform at weekend house parties and picnics, playing for free food, drinks, whatever came their way in tips, but most of all for the fun of it. More than likely, they had regular employment in the tobacco industry and did not see their musical talents as something that could earn them their livelihoods. Hence the orientation of this group of indigenous bluesmen was decidedly nonprofessional; they were the secular bards of the oral tradition and remained well within the folk continuum of the rural black culture.

In a second category were the more widely known itinerant blues singers who periodically visited Virginia's tobacco country, especially during the late summer, at the height of the tobacco auction festivities. Blind Lemon Jefferson was the most famous. Others more identified with the Piedmont in general included Blind Blake and Blind Boy Fuller, who lived in Roanoke for a few months early in his musical career. Several of the numbers each of them recorded found their way into the repertoires of southwestern Virginia's local blues musicians.[44]

Falling into neither of these two categories of rural blues performers were a handful of full-time street musicians who made the locale their home base of activity and who attempted to live on the income they made playing in public. Some of these musicians worked seasonally as crowd pleasers for traveling medicine shows, which crisscrossed the region in the late summer and early fall before moving farther south. Rabbit Muse is an outstanding example of a local street musician who regularly worked on the medicine show circuit. When not on the road, Muse played in the streets of his hometown, Rocky Mount, Virginia, where he was born in 1908. He sang both blues and minstrel songs, while accompanying himself on a ukelele, which he learned to play after seeing one used in a traveling minstrel show in the 1920s.[45]

Another avenue open to the region's semi-professional street musicians was to migrate to the larger towns such as Danville, Roanoke, or Lynchburg, where they performed whenever and wherever they could draw a crowd. The main streets and the parks were the best places to attract a following, as were the tobacco warehouses, especially on paydays. Foremost among the street singers of this stature was Luke Jordon, one of the few Virginia bluesmen to be recorded in the 1920s. Jordon was born on January 28, 1892, most likely in Campbell or Appomattox County. He grew up in a rural environment and apparently learned to play the guitar and to sing the blues before moving to Lynchburg around 1910. Once he relocated in Lynchburg, Jordon became a familiar figure in the town, playing and singing for tips at parties or in the streets. Black residents of Lynchburg who knew Luke Jordon remembered him as a fun-loving performer with a strong aversion to the standard employment available to African Americans in the town. He was also remembered for being fond of good liquor and fishing. His reputation as a country bluesman attracted the attention of Victor Records, which invited him to Charlotte, North Carolina, for a recording session in 1927. He followed this up with a second recording session for Victor, this time in New York City during November 1929. But this proved to be his final recording. He returned to Lynchburg and remained there, still performing regularly in the streets, until he died in the early 1950s.[46]

Jordon recorded only four titles at his initial session; among them were two blues numbers identified as his signature pieces by some of his Lynchburg acquaintances, the infamous "Cocaine Blues" and "Church Bell Blues." Another number he recorded was "Traveling Coon," the widely known black minstrel song. On these initial recordings, Jordon demonstrated a strong affinity for the traditional Piedmont blues style. His guitar playing was polished and precise; his touch was characteristically light and optimistic. He used the ragtime-influenced finger-picking technique preferred among the region's guitar and banjo players, but he was also capable of creating innovative solo runs—on occasion tinged with Latin rhythms—as bridges between the verses he sang. His voice was high pitched, yet quite expressive; he pronounced the words with clarity and exactness. The blues lyrics he fashioned into his best-known songs were a combination of the floating verse found in the black oral tradition and lines he himself created.

During World War II, the Piedmont blues culture was cresting as a movement involving hundreds of musicians and the many thousands more who sang along, danced, clapped their hands together, and shouted their approval. The Piedmont blues would not die out, but they would become a music of the past—preserved mostly by an older generation of African Americans. In their heyday in the 1920s and 1930s, they were on the cutting edge of the black oral tradition—recycling and updating from it the appropriate toasts, sayings, folktales, and testimonials. By the end of World War II, however, the Piedmont blues reflected a rural way of life pushed to the margins of the culture by urban migrations and industrialization.

As if to commemorate this passing of a tradition from the center stage of black culture, the first black folk music festival was sponsored by and held at Fort Valley State College, south of Macon in central Georgia. The festival was started in 1940 as part of an annual agricultural show. Its first director, Edgar Clark, put out a call for local folk musicians to come and participate in the festival; he was especially interested in musicians who performed African-American "ballads, worksongs, and folk blues":

> Some people look down on some of the folk music. This type of music may be what polite society calls gutter songs. Often these gutter songs or blues, as they are rightly called, are the very essence of Negro life; songs that men and women sang in their America. There is a human stir in them all. . . . Some made new songs, some changed old songs, and they are carried from place to place today. We at Fort Valley wish to keep these dying and forgotten songs of the Negro by presenting them as art—Negro art songs.[47]

The festival attracted many older black folk musicians from the Fort Valley–Macon region who played within the Piedmont blues tradition; the most popular were guitarists Gus Gibson, Bus Ezell, and Sam Jackson. In addition, luminaries such as W. C. Handy were honorary judges at the early festivals, and folk music scholar John Work from Fisk University was also on hand to record the participants. The Fort Valley Festival continued into the mid-1950s, at which time it was discontinued, but not before documenting one more active network of black musicians working within the Piedmont blues tradition, and not before setting the stage for the folk blues revival in the 1960s.[48]

Of the three major rural blues cultures, the Piedmont's proved to be the least adaptable to the emerging urban blues formats. The intricate and delicate ragtime-influenced guitar style was not enhanced by amplification any more than was the music of the small string-band groups that were also a trademark of the Piedmont tradition. In addition, the despairing and forlorn quality of the standard Piedmont blues material was the response of a rural black population to life in the post-Reconstruction era; it was not appropriate for the sounds and the texture of urban life. At its best, the Piedmont blues culture poignantly depicted the personal conflicts of rural African Americans and provided them with a carthartic release from social tensions. Although new blues forms would capture the imagination of urban America, the Piedmont blues remained an important aspect of the culture and the consciousness of the black farming communities in that region, especially those that sought to maintain their oral traditions and rural ways of life.

# Part II
# Urban Blues

# Introduction

As early as the turn of the century, with the vanguard of the black migration, the blues were trickling into the cities of the South and the Midwest. Once transplanted to an urban setting, they were significantly influenced by two disparate cultural forces—the music industry and the red-light districts. These forces transformed blues culture by reorganizing its sphere of production to make it into a profitable commercial enterprise, which in turn tended to separate it from its folk roots. And, in the process, the music became more susceptible to white economic control.

When first initiated during slavery, the expropriation of African-American song, dance, and humor by white entertainers for commercial gain resulted in the formation of the country's first native entertainment industry—blackface minstrelsy. As early as the 1790s, white actors began doing imitations of black song and dance in urban theaters catering to working-class males. Blackening their faces with burnt cork, they portrayed the slaves, as comic buffoons. By the 1840s, blackface minstrelsy had evolved into a distinct entertainment format requiring an entire troupe of actors for the show. Its standard portrayal of slaves as childlike, comical, and contented fueled the racist sentiments of the white male audiences in the South and the North. As historian Robert Toll has pointed out:

> Blackface performers were like puppets operated by a white puppet master. Their physical appearance proclaimed their non-humanity; yet they could be manipulated not only to mock themselves but also to act like human beings. They expressed human emotions such as joy and grief, love, fear, longing. The white audience then identified with the emotions, admired the skills of the puppeteer, even sympathized laughingly with the hopeless aspirations of the puppets to become human, and at the same time feasted on the assurance that they could not do so. Blackface minstrelsy's dominance of popular entertainment amounted to a half century of inurement to the uses of white supremacy.[1]

During Reconstruction, numerous black performers entered into blackface minstrelsy, and eventually succeeded in purging the minstrel format of its more blatant racial slurs and stereotypes. Black minstrelsy then emerged as a separate popular entertainment form for African Americans, though still controlled by white entrepreneurs. One custom that black minstrel performers continued was that of presenting African-American folk music in their stage acts. As a result, not long after the rural blues had been fashioned into a popular song genre in the South, they became an important component of black minstrel shows, moving from being a southern phenomenon to being popular with large black audiences throughout much of the United States.

The popularization of the blues by African-American minstrelsy had various consequences. On the one hand, the music was now being disseminated to, and adopted by, all sectors of the black working class; it had moved beyond its agrarian origins into the forefront of the great urban migration. On the other hand, the inclusion of the blues in black minstrel shows brought them to the attention of the commercial entertainment industry. The music's strong appeal among the black population meant that it could be packaged as a commodity and then sold back to African Americans at a considerable profit. The vaudeville theater circuit and the music publishing business were the first segments of the white-controlled entertainment industry to exploit this possibility. Theaters catering to black audiences began to include blues acts in their shows. Simultaneously, professional songwriters began to turn out blues compositions that they copyrighted and then sold as sheet music. For the most part, the music publishing business was centered in New York City along Tin Pan Alley. Songwriting there was organized on an assembly-line basis; popular songs were cranked out according to the prevailing song formulas. Tin Pan Alley was quick to expropriate well-known African-American folksongs—both ragtime and blues compositions—and transform them into commercial products to be sold in music stores. In the process, the music was standardized, its more complex rhythms diluted, and its lyrical content trivialized.

The rise of a nationwide recording industry in the initial decades of the twentieth century accelerated the incorporation of black folk music into the commercial marketplace. By the 1920s, the widespread popularity of the blues among African Americans attracted the attention of record company entrepreneurs, who saw them as a new musical fad they could exploit. In effect, the record industry began to absorb black folk music into its sphere of capitalist production. The blues performance was transformed into a mass-produced commodity. Capital now mediated the relationship between artist and audience, that is, between the producers and the consumers of blues disks. An expression of cultural resistance had been converted into a new form of capital capable of generating large profits for the record companies.

Once it was in place, the race record business had a two-sided effect on the further development of the blues. The mechanical reproduction of the music on phonograph disks made it available to far greater numbers of people. If the immediate authenticity of the blues performance suffered in the process, its potential to reach a mass audience on a regular basis was enhanced considerably. Localized rural and then urban blues cultures were infused with new songs and styles to an extent that was never before possible, giving way to a broader definition of the music. There can be little doubt that commercial blues disks were the last major catalyst in the expansion of the music from a regional to a national craze by the 1920s. And from all indications, aspiring blues musicians growing up during this era fully utilized the phonograph record in their learning process. In these respects, the recording industry played a progressive role in the support of an African-American art form in spite of its intentions. This transformation of a folk music into a commercial product had negative consequences. The record industry milked a lot of money from the black population by selling them their own music. In addition, the larger, more established record companies tended to replicate past successes with redundant song formulas, conventional arrangements, and cannibalized lyrics. If concerns about the music's authenticity could be put aside, quick profits could be made. These recordings diluted the content and the character of the blues, substituting a predictable imitation for the real thing, but they did not completely dominate the blues record market during this period (probably because the audiences were more demanding than cynical businessmen gave them credit for).

Record industry sales peaked in 1926 at $128 million. There are no solid figures for race record sales; estimates run from 5 percent to 15 percent of the industry's total volume during the same year. Competition from radio broadcasting and motion pictures, coupled with the depression brought the record business to a standstill. By 1933, the industry generated only $6 million in sales. The smaller record companies folded, while three major labels (Columbia, RCA, and Paramount) acquired a virtual monopoly on the marketplace.[2] The sharp decline closed down most of the race record labels for a while. This allowed the urban blues musicians time to develop their music free from restrictive commercial pressures.

When the record industry rebounded in the late 1930s, the blues again came to the forefront of the segregated race record market. The introduction of the jukebox, black-oriented radio shows, and a second wave of small independent record companies meant popular black music could now be heard and recorded all over the country. In the postwar decades, these smaller labels, with the help of black radio programming, were able to record and market a more authentic blues sound.

While the high road for blues migration passed through the world of show business, the low road led to the urban red-light districts of the South and North. Regardless of their location, these tenderloin or sporting districts were the hub of a local underworld economy, the site of a night-life subculture, and a haven for America's have-nots. The proliferation of red-light districts in the later 1800s and early 1900s—during an era of unprecedented industrial expansion, labor strife, and urban growth—was indicative of a troublesome fissure in the cultural hegemony of corporate America. They were pockets of resistance to the new urban social order that fostered the formation of an alternative culture. As such, they were bound to attract African-American migrants in general and blues musicians in particular.

The underworld economies based in the red-light zones organized vice along traditional business lines. In many ways they were throwbacks to the old days of laissez-faire capitalism and rugged individualism. The three principal vice operations were gambling, prostitution, and the sale of drugs, including alcohol. These activities were usually illegal. They also invariably generated huge profits, and they created a hierarchy of job opportunities—and hence social mobility—outside the dominant social order.

Within the red-light districts, the vice operations became an integral part of the formation of night-life subcultures. They blended well with certain legitimate forms of entertainment like popular music, dance, and vaudeville. The upsurge in red-light districts, especially after the turn of the century, was linked to the commercialization of night-life leisure in the cities. Theaters, dance halls, and cabarets sprang up alongside the saloons, gambling dens, and bordellos. The clients were no longer exclusively men. Women customers were also welcome to participate in urban night life.[3]

In the 1800s, the Irish, Germans, and Poles dominated the ethnic ghettos that overlapped the red-light districts. By the turn of the century, however, they were being replaced by a flood of Jewish and Italian immigrants. Most of the Italians came from southern Italy, especially from Sicily. New arrivals vied with earlier immigrants for local jobs and control of vice operations.[4]

African Americans migrating out of the rural South were the next major ethnic group drawn into the red-light districts. As early as the 1860s, waves of black farm workers began to relocate in cities like New Orleans, Atlanta, and Memphis. By 1900, 23 percent of the black population in the United States lived in metropolitan areas, mostly in the South. A second wave of one million African Americans settled in industrial centers like Detroit, Chicago, Cleveland, Pittsburgh, Baltimore, Philadelphia, and New York during World War I. Both "push" and "pull" factors influenced this mass migration. The upsurge of white supremacy in the wake of Reconstruction, the decline of biracial Populism, Jim Crow laws, the disenfranchisement of the black voter, and the economic plight of the black sharecropper and tenant farmer tended to push African Americans out of the South, while the outbreak of World War I and the curtailment of foreign immigration, both of which created an urgent demand for unskilled workers, pulled them toward industrial cities.[5]

The Irish who originally dominated the political economy of the red-light districts were inclined to organize gambling and prostitution along class lines.

The most expensive and lavish vice operations catered to a wealthy clientele that was usually white, while the more plebeian enterprises settled for any cash-carrying customer, regardless of race. The Irish restricted their neighborhood saloons to Irish men and used them exclusively for drinking, boisterous talking, and general rowdiness. Furthermore, Irish saloons and vice palaces rarely featured the popular music of the day or the music of their homeland, much less that of other nationalities. When Jewish and Sicilian gangsters began investing in their own saloons and nightclubs, they helped to usher in a series of cultural changes in the tenderloin night life. They presented live music in their establishments to facilitate both dancing and socializing. Black musicians were happy to be employed, even at rock-bottom prices, in the house bands or as solo performers. Wherever these two key groups—black musicians and immigrant underworld entrepreneurs—forged a business relationship, the music flourished, the night life was enlivened, and the red-light operations prospered.[6]

Blues musicians, like other black musicians, were drawn to these employment opportunities. Unable to make a living playing music in the black farming communities of the cotton belt, even the most talented blues artists were forced to augment what they made in tips or handouts with some other form of labor, usually working in the fields. In the urban tenderloins, however, they could supplement their incomes with tips from their audiences, and their employers often provided them with food, drink, and even lodging. More important, they were now moving toward becoming full-time professional musicians and could devote more time to their art. This change enhanced both their personal development as blues artists and their musical contribution to the new urban blues tradition.

The red-light districts' outlaw subcultures had other effects on the music and the lives of blues musicians. The blues discourse, now nurtured by an underworld ethos, remained in opposition to the prevailing white culture, but it now illuminated the day-to-day realities of African-American life in the tenderloin enclaves, not the cotton belt. And the blues artists did not escape the hazards of life in the tenderloin enclaves. Many talented blues musicians died violently before they were able to fulfill their artistic potential. Many others were incapacitated by drug and alcohol abuse, or contagious diseases. As a result, the ranks of the first-generation urban blues performers were depleted.

Yet despite these liabilities and hardships, the urban blues pioneers succeeded in establishing a radical new art form in the black ghettos of America's great industrial centers. The blues continued to be the oral literature of the black masses. As a message music dedicated to candid realism, it brought unpleasantness and controversy into the open. The release of frustration and torment, as well as humor and sexuality, gave the blues the paradoxical quality present in all great art. Richard Wright described them as "sad-happy" songs, while Ortiz Walton commented on their "melancholy" and "rapture."[7] This combination of opposites gave the music a healing power that helped African Americans in their ongoing struggles against urban poverty and racial oppression.

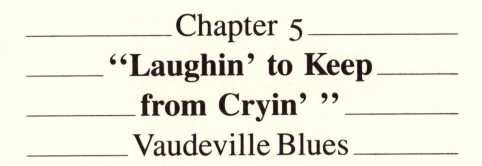

# Chapter 5
# "Laughin' to Keep from Cryin' "
## Vaudeville Blues

### Blues and the Music Industry

The expropriation of the blues by the American music industry had dramatic and far-reaching consequences for the music and its central role in the black oral tradition. A major reason for these changes was that the industry was owned and operated by white entrepreneurs, who became the middlemen between the blues artists and their audience. These men not only profited from the sale of the blues but also shaped the scope and the direction of blues culture. Once the blues' primary sphere of production shifted from a folk to a commercial setting, both artist and audience were confronted with a whole new set of constraints—economic, technical, legal, and organizational. Some of these constraints were the legacy of black minstrelsy.

Black minstrelsy, in its heyday in the late nineteenth and early twentieth centuries, was the most popular form of commercial entertainment in the black community. Among these southern-based African-American performing troupes, the best known were Silas Green's show out of New Orleans and the Rabbit Foot Minstrels out of Port Gibson, Mississippi; both organizations built up a following and longevity that was rare for black minstrel aggregations. They, and countless other lesser-known troupes with shorter life spans, made seasonal tours of the rural South, visiting tobacco regions in the spring and the cotton belt in the fall, as well as lumber, levee, and coal camps. The more successful black troupes traveled in special railroad cars and performed under large canvas tents. In their numbers were musicians, singers, dancers, comics, various novelty acts, and a work crew to set up and break down the tents, stage, and seating.

From its inception, black minstrelsy was dependent on white men who controlled the business end of the enterprise. From that vantage point, these white entrepreneurs also exerted considerable influence over the content of the shows, even though they were staged primarily for black audiences. While the black minstrel performers were able eventually to eliminate the more offensive racial stereotypes from their shows, they also had to accommodate the wishes of their white employers. As a result, fragments of the antebellum blackface minstrel tradition survived in black minstrelsy. For example, the practice of blacking up with burnt cork persisted even among African-American minstrel entertainers well into the 1920s. Because black minstrelsy was the first African-American beachhead in commercial entertainment, it established procedures and practices that carried over to later enterprises in the music industry involving black entertainers and audiences. The three major enterprises caught up in the commercial production of the blues were the Theatre Owners Booking Association (TOBA), the music publishing firms located along New York's Tin Pan Alley, and the phonograph record companies based in New York and Chicago.

In the early 1900s, the touring tent shows also began appearing before African-American audiences in urban theaters. The theaters were usually owned and managed by white businessmen who were notorious for the scanty wages they paid black entertainers and for their unwillingness to provide clean and adequate facilities for the performers. Nevertheless, these theaters became the metropolitan palaces for a black vaudeville circuit that flourished over the next two decades. As early as 1907, a white Memphis theater owner, F. A. Barrasso, attempted to organize a chain of theaters in the South featuring black entertainment into a vaudeville network. By formalizing the procedures for booking black performers at these theaters, he hoped to make them more efficient and thus more profitable for the owners, if not the entertainers. In 1909, his brother Anselmo took over the venture and founded the Theatre Owners Booking Association. He slowly built up a string of member theaters in the South and the Midwest, and along the eastern seaboard. By 1921, when the TOBA was taken over by a Nashville theater owner named Milton Starr and Charles Turpin, his TOBA counterpart in St. Louis, it was a prosperous enterprise with some forty theaters listed as members.[1]

To its credit, the TOBA provided valuable experience and exposure for innumerable black entertainers and musicians who might not have had an opportunity to break into show business otherwise. Some of the more established black performers like Bert Williams, Ben Harney, Bill "Bojangles" Robinson, Noble Sissle, and Eubie Blake also appeared in white vaudeville houses, where the salaries were more substantial. Harney was light enough to pass for white and sometimes did. Almost all the black entertainers, however, remained with the TOBA even though the facilities, wages, and working conditions inspired the well-circulated employee definition of TOBA: "Tough on Black Asses!" Yet the TOBA also offered entertainers the chance to perform before discerning African-American audiences throughout much of the country. And there was the allure of fame and fortune. Like the black minstrel shows it superseded, black vaudeville was one of the few means by which African Americans could acquire status and wealth. Overflow crowds flocked to the black vaudeville shows and lavished applause on the featured entertainers. The shows became a major cultural activity in the urban black communities, and their headline acts became cultural heroes and heroines. Hence, it is understandable that aspiring black performers took to vaudeville with such a passion and in such large numbers.[2]

The TOBA entertainment staged by black stock companies usually was organized around a major attraction. The shows all had their own band, and often a female chorus line. The acts that received top billing were a diverse lot: comedy teams, song-and-dance artists, instrumental virtuosos, theatrical troupes, novelty acts. A good number of husband-and-wife teams were active on the black vaudeville circuit. Jody and Susie Edwards, better known as Butterbeans and Susie, got married in a TOBA theater in 1917 and perfected a successful comedy routine satirizing their marriage squabbles; they also sang popular songs as a duet, occasionally including a blues number. Leola B. and Wesley Wilson—Coot Grant and Kid Sock Wilson—were seasoned vaudeville performers and songwriters with more than four hundred compositions to their credit, including one of Bessie Smith's trademarks, "Gimme a Pigfoot." A third well-known couple, George Williams and Bessie Smith—no relation to the "Empress of the Blues"—were vaudeville singers who performed both together and as soloists; George Williams played the piano and later recorded some material for Columbia Records that featured him both alone and with his wife.[3]

Women as well as men achieved star status on the TOBA, a notable change from the days of male-dominated minstrelsy. The leading male entertainers on the circuit, including Hamtree Harrington, Tom Fletcher, Sammy Lewis, Billy King, Ernest Hogan, and Dusty Fletcher, were complemented by a growing contingent of female stars, the most famous of whom were Fannie Wise, the Whiteman sisters, Sweet Mama Stringbean (Ethel Waters), Ada Myers, Ella Moore, Dianah Scott, and those women such as Ma Rainey, Ida Cox, and Bessie Smith who have more recently been labeled "classic blues singers." These were the women working on the TOBA or in the cabarets of New York and Chicago who first recorded the blues in the early 1920s. The TOBA peaked as an entertainment enterprise in the mid-twenties, when it had over fifty theaters employing hundreds of black performers who played to forty-five hundred paying customers a day. At the time, small communities of African-American performers were also flourishing in many of the larger cities. In Atlanta, the veteran black entertainer S. H. Dudley had established a local African-American repertory company, using Charles Bailey's 81 Theatre as a base of operation. A similar organization existed in Chicago, using the Grand Theatre as its base, under the direction of Billy King. Chicago and New York had the largest contingents of black entertainers and musicians, drawn there by the burgeoning entertainment and recording industries, which were slowly opening their doors to African-American talent.

The TOBA circuit began to falter by 1927, well before the stock market crash in October 1929. The advent of the radio and talking motion pictures played a large role in its demise. With the onset of the depression, the organization went out of business, leaving legions of black performers and the individual theater owners to struggle on as best they could.[4]

The growth of the theater circuit was complemented by the rise of "Tin Pan Alley" and the race record industry. In the late 1800s, the sale of sheet music for home entertainment was the major source of income for composers and their publishing firms. Many of the larger firms were located in New York City on 28th Street, between Broadway and Fifth Avenue. By the turn of the century, this corridor was commonly referred to as Tin Pan Alley. The music publishing business received a big boost in 1909, when the first copyright law was passed by Congress. The law stipulated that copyright owners had the exclusive rights to perform and to reproduce their works for profit and that record companies must pay royalty fees to the composers of the music they used or to the publishing firm that owned the composition's copyright. Five years after the new copyright law went into effect, the American Society of Composers, Authors, and Publishers (ASCAP) was founded in New York to monitor the commercial performances of its client members, collect royalty fees from the music users, and distribute that income to the appropriate composers, lyricists, and publishers. By the twenties, ASCAP had evolved into the most powerful trade organization in the music industry. As could be expected, very few "outsiders" were permitted to join, especially African Americans.[5]

By the 1920s, and with the help of ASCAP, Tin Pan Alley had consolidated its hold on the music industry centered in New York. The fifteen largest ASCAP publishing firms produced up to 90 percent of the commercial music of the era.[6]

African-American songwriters who worked for Tin Pan Alley during this period tended to be more respectful of their musical heritage, to value its authenticity and genius. Many of the specific themes and, to a certain extent, the stanza structures used in the songs they popularized were related to early folk blues. This was especially true when the composer was from the South and familiar with African-American folklore. The black oral tradition provided a large number of African-American commercial songwriters with a reservoir of material to draw on, just as it did for the rural blues musicians. Ben Harney's "Mr. Johnson, Turn Me Loose" (1896), for example, was based on a fourteen-bar AAB stanza; the repetitive statements were four bars long, while the response was six measures long. This was only a slight variation from the twelve-bar blues standard, and one that was also used by rural folk musicians.

Since Harney grew up in Kentucky and spent time in Louisville, an early hotbed of African-American musical activity, it is possible that he was introduced to the folk blues there.

The blues took a circuitous route to reach the American public. They were discovered by Tin Pan Alley songwriters soon after W. C. Handy moved to New York from Memphis in 1915. African Americans played a key role in popularizing the blues. Once this new song family was discovered by professional black entertainers like Handy and Ben Harney, the folk blues were incorporated into their compositions and their stage acts. The first written account of this transition was in 1898, the year folklorist John Jacob Niles observed a "shouter and moaner" named Ophelia Simpson who sang a number entitled "Black Alfalfa's Jailhouse Shouting Blues" in a medicine show headed up by "Doctor" Parker.[7] As the blues became more popular among the African-American population, they became the centerpiece of the remaining southern tent shows and those acts most in demand on the TOBA circuit.

Many of the more successful black composers who migrated to New York during this period, like many white composers, established their own music publishing firms. Handy and his partner, Harry Pace, went into business there in 1915. Other African Americans who formed their own companies include Sheldon Brooks from Mobile, Clarence Williams from New Orleans, Perry Bradford from Atlanta, and even Bert Williams. By having their own companies to copyright their songs, these songwriters could collect all the royalty fees, instead of splitting them with a middle party.[8]

W. C. Handy published his most renowned blues compositions in the 1910s: "Memphis Blues" (1912), "St. Louis Blues" (1914), "Yellow Dog Blues" (1914), "Jogo Blues" (1915), "Joe Turner Blues" (1916), "Beale Street Blues" (1917). All of them were based almost exclusively on folk blues that Handy had heard in his early travels in the South. Their subsequent popularity soon put the blues in a new cultural context. Handy's success demonstrated the blues' commercial potential, which in turn made the genre grist for the mills of the Tin Pan Alley song hacks. By the end of the decade, a blues craze was in full swing throughout the entertainment industry. They were the hottest items coming off the Tin Pan Alley assembly lines, being in great demand in vaudeville theaters, dance halls, and cabarets across the country. In short, they had entered into the mainstream of American popular music. As a 1917 Tin Pan Alley title proclaimed, "Everybody's Crazy About the Doggone Blues."[9]

The blues also caught on in the recording industry, which both encouraged and impeded their maturation. On the positive side of the ledger, the mechanical reproduction of millions of blues disks made the music far more accessible to the public in general, and black people in particular. Blues entered an era of unprecedented growth and vitality, surfacing as a national phenomenon by the

1920s. As a result, a new generation of African-American musicians were able to learn from the commercial recordings, to expand their mastery over the various idioms and enhance their instrumental and vocal techniques. The local and regional African-American folk traditions that spawned blues were, in turn, infused with new songs, rhythms, and styles. Thus, the record business was an important catalyst in the development of blues that also facilitated their entrance into the mainstream of popular American music.

On the other hand, the transformation of living musical traditions into commodities to be sold in a capitalist marketplace was bound to have its drawbacks. For one thing, the profits garnered from the sale of blues records invariably went into the coffers of the white businessmen who owned or managed the record companies. The black musicians and vocalists who created the music in the recording studios received a pittance. Furthermore, the major record companies went to great lengths to get the blues to conform to their Tin Pan Alley standards, and they often expected black recording artists to conform to racist stereotypes inherited from blackface minstrelsy. The industry also liked to record white performers' "cover" versions of popular blues to entice the white public to buy the records and to "upgrade" the music. Upgrading was synonymous with commercializing; it attempted to bring African-American music more into line with European musical conventions, while superimposing on it a veneer of middle-class Anglo-American respectability. These various practices deprived a significant percentage of recorded blues numbers of their African characteristics and more radical content.

The first black recording artist, and the only black entertainer to record on cylinder, was George W. Johnson, who recorded his "Whistling Coon" minstrel number for Thomas Edison's phonograph company. During the initial upsurge in the recording and marketing of disks, the leading record companies continued to virtually ignore African-American talent. The Columbia Record Company, founded in 1899, excluded black performers from their stable of exclusive recording artists until the 1920s. The Victor Talking Machine Company, founded in 1901, adopted a more liberal racial policy. Having been previously turned down by Columbia, Bert Williams recorded a total of fifteen titles for Victor, most of them show tunes or comedy routines from his stage repertoire. Victor also recorded the first authentic African-American folk music in 1902, when it released six sides of spirituals sung in the traditional African-American slow-meter style, without instrumental accompaniment, by a group called the Dinwiddie Colored Quartet. The next breakthrough for black musicians did not occur until 1914, when James Reese Europe's Society Orchestra recorded some dance music for the Victor Company as part of a series endorsed by the popular white dance team Vernon and Irene Castle.[10]

The major record companies released many recordings of African-American-inspired music interpreted by white performers during this period and throughout the next decade. Columbia Record's catalogue listed a "Negro novelty" section, while Victor boasted of "up-to-date comic songs in Negro dialect." The Russian-born vaudeville star Sophie Tucker, for example, had to wear blackface and perform "coon songs," in imitation of the antebellum "Mammy" stereotype, until she was able to prove to theater managers that she could be successful on the stage without them. Although she did away with the blackface and the coon songs, she continued to be a popularizer of African-American music and scored her greatest triumphs with ragtime and blues compositions written by black composers. These included her version of W. C. Handy's "St. Louis Blues," which became the first million seller in the blues category in 1917.[11]

## Vaudeville Blues

The leap from a handful of folk blues interpreters with direct links to the African-American oral tradition to a host of imitators with little feeling for or understanding of their subject matter led to a reformulation of the style and the themes of the music. This commercially motivated revisionism gave birth to a new popular song hybrid, "vaudeville blues."[12] The vaudeville blues were based on long-standing black musical traditions, but they were reproduced in a commercial setting as opposed to a folk community; hence, the intentions of the songwriters and the makeup of their audience changed dramatically. At their worst, the vaudeville blues were degrading burlesques of the music they attempted to duplicate. Their style was diffused and their content trivialized. Legions of Tin Pan Alley song manufacturers simply applied their clichéd song formulas to a standardized twelve-bar AAB stanza format. The result was a flood of third-rate imitations.

At their best, however, the vaudeville blues were the updated versions of real folk blues translated into popular standards by a relatively small group of African-American performers and composers. The best-known performers were female vocalists Ma Rainey, Ida Cox, Sara Martin, Alberta Hunter, Sippie Wallace, and Bessie Smith. These women also wrote some of their own lyrics. The most prominant black male composers of vaudeville blues were W. C. Handy, Perry "Mule" Bradford, James and Rosmond Johnson, Spencer Williams, Porter Grainger, Clarence Williams, and Thomas Dorsey. These men were also usually their own music publishers, and like their female counterparts, they were well acquainted with the South, where they were schooled in the performance and the application of black folk music. In an interview with E. Simm Campbell, a blues scholar, Clarence Williams stated:

Why, I'd never have written blues if I had been white. You don't study
to write blues, you feel them. It's the mood you're in—sometimes it's a
rainy day—cloud mist—just like the time I lay for hours in the swamp
in Louisiana. Spanish moss dripping everywhere. . . . White men were
looking for me with guns. I wasn't scared, just sorry I didn't have a
gun. I began to hum a tune, a little sighing kinda tune.[13]

Williams had a reputation as an opportunist in the race record business, and
he may well have been telling a tall tale to a white interrogator; nevertheless,
the final product was a blues grounded in experience, most likely taken from a
folk source, and difficult to duplicate on Tin Pan Alley.

W. C. Handy's approach to blues composition relied heavily on his first-
hand exposure to African-American folksongs. In his autobiography, he describes how he went about writing his earliest blues effort, "Mr. Crump,"
which he later retitled, "Memphis Blues":

The melody of "Mr. Crump" was mine throughout. On the other hand,
the twelve bar, three line form of the first and third strains, with its three
chord basic harmonic structure (tonic, subdominant, dominant seventh)
was already used by Negro roustabouts, honky tonk piano players, wan-
derers, and others of their underprivileged but undaunted class from
Missouri to the Gulf, and had become a common medium through which
any such individual might express his personal feelings in a sort of musical soliloquy. My part in their history was to introduce this, the
"blues" form, to the general public, as the medium for my own feelings
and my own musical ideas. And the transitional flat thirds and sevenths
in my melody, by which I was attempting to suggest the typical slurs of
the Negro voice, were what have since become known as "blue
notes."[14]

With other numbers, like "Yellow Dog Blues" and "Joe Turner Blues,"
Handy reconstructed the melodies and the lyrics of commonly known folk
blues from memory and published them under his own name; this was not an
uncommon practice in the record industry during the blues bonanza.

Perry "Mule" Bradford, along with Handy, played a crucial role in helping
to stimulate the commercial boom in vaudeville blues. Bradford was a seasoned vaudeville entertainer with an entrepreneurial flair. He was born in
Montgomery, Alabama, in 1895, but spent much of his youth in Atlanta,
where his family moved in 1902. The Bradfords initially lived in a house next
to the Fulton Street Jail. In the evenings, the jail's black inmates would pass
the time singing blues and other folksongs; this was where young Bradford
first heard the music that would become his livelihood and his claim to fame.

Like Handy, Bradford became an interpreter and a popularizer of the blues. In his autobiography, he cites two different blues numbers that he used in his repertoire by writing down their lyrical cores. Both of them were well-known folk blues that he had reconstructed:

> Baby, you don't know my mind. No—no—no.
> My gal's quit me—and treated me so unkind,
> So when you see me laughing—now
> I'm only laughing just to keep from cryin'.
>
> My gal walked the streets 'til she got soaked and wet,
> And this is what she said to every man she met,
> Don't want your dollars, just give me a lousy dime,
> So I can feed that hungry man of mine.[15]

The second verse was a variation of a blues that Ferdinand "Jelly Roll" Morton used in his repertoire; he credited it to Mamie Desdoumes, the first New Orleans singer to be identified with the blues.[16] The folk nature of the traditional blues popular before the emergence of the record industry allowed many singers to have their own versions of a song prominent in the black oral tradition. This became more difficult when copyrighting and then recording came along.

Perry Bradford broke into vaudeville in his hometown, Atlanta, as a singer, dancer, and piano player. In 1907, he went on the road with Allen's New Orleans Minstrels. He traveled to New Orleans and then on to New York, where he was involved in staging a musical revue, "Made in Harlem," which starred black singer Mamie Smith and showcased his "Harlem Blues." The song was a revision of a number he had learned in 1912 called "Nervous Blues." One of Bradford's pet schemes was to convince a major record company that there was a profit to be made by issuing blues records made by black artists. He argued that "fourteen million Negroes . . . will buy records if recorded by one of their own."[17] The two dominant record labels in the business, Victor and Columbia, turned Bradford down. A smaller label called Okeh, managed by a white businessman named Fred Hager for the General Phonograph Company, agreed to record a few of Perry Bradford's songs, but only if they were sung by Sophie Tucker. When contract commitments made it impossible for Tucker to do the session, Mamie Smith got the nod, and the title was changed to "Crazy Blues" to avoid a possible copyright suit by the backers of the musical revue. The backup group was five local black musicians called the Jazz Hounds; for this session, they included Johnny Dunn on cornet, Dope Andrews on trombone, Ernest Elliott on clarinet, Leroy Parker on fiddle, and Willie "The Lion" Smith on piano. The phenomenal success of

"Crazy Blues," issued in August 1920, proved that Bradford's prediction had been correct and opened the floodgates for the rush to record vaudeville blues sung by black women.

Okeh Records sold seventy-five thousand copies of "Crazy Blues" in the first month and surpassed the one million mark during its first year in the stores. Perry Bradford received close to twenty thousand dollars in royalty fees, according to his own records; this was less than half of what he was legally entitled to, given the sales figures and the fact that his copyrighted songs were on both sides of the record. Pressured by Okeh Records to waive his royalty rights to "Crazy Blues" when the record became a commercial success, he responded: "Please be advised that the only thing Bradford waives is the American Flag."[18]

## Blues Recordings in the Roaring Twenties

Several small, newly formed record companies were in the forefront of the upsurge in blues recordings following in the wake of Okeh's success with "Crazy Blues." The Arto label released Lucille Hegamin's "The Jazz Me Blues" and "Everybody's Blues" in February 1921. Later that year Emerson issued blues titles sung by Lillian Brown, and Gennett issued some by Daisy Martin. Other independent labels that attempted to capitalize on the blues boom in the early twenties included Perfect, Pathé, Ajax, Vocalion, and Paramount. Only a few of these smaller companies managed to survive the decade, however; promotion and distribution problems usually caused their early demise. When it became apparent that a new black record market did, indeed, exist, the two dominant companies in the recording industry, Victor and Columbia, also joined the blues bandwagon. Both were suffering from serious losses in revenues because of the popularity of commercial radio.[19]

The decade also witnessed the rise and fall of a few record companies owned by African Americans. W. C. Handy and his partner, Harry Pace, founded the Black Swan record label in January 1921 and immediately recorded Ethel Waters and Alberta Hunter. The company reported over $100,000 in sales during 1921, but three years later, it was deeply in debt and was forced to sell its remaining assets to Paramount. Two black record-store owners based in Los Angeles launched the Sunshine label in 1922 by issuing separate blues titles by Roberta Dudley and Ruth Lee, as well as a jazz instrumental by Kid Ory's jazz band. But after these three releases, the label never was heard from again. Winston Holmes's Meritt Records was formed in Kansas City in 1925. It lasted three years, but issued only seven disks. Female blues vocalist Lottie Kimbrough was Holmes's major recording artist; she was a native of Kansas City and well known in the town's red-light district. J. Mayo ''Ink'' Williams, Chicago's premier black talent scout in the 1920s, started his own label, called Black Patti, in 1927, but it folded in less than a year. Although Williams had access to the best African-American singers and musicians in the business, he was unable to distribute his product effectively, especially outside Chicago.

Overall, the smaller record companies were at a disadvantage in comparison to the major labels; they could not afford to advertise their product extensively on a national level, and they had no viable means of distributing their product beyond their home bases. As a result, they were invariably forced out of the industry, while the larger companies were able to take over the new markets they entered only belatedly. This was particularly true for the black-owned record labels, which never gained a foothold in the blues record business, even though it was aimed at a black consumer market. The economic structure of the industry, coupled with its biased cultural standards, ultimately proved to be an insurmountable obstacle.[20]

The three white-owned record companies that emerged as the leaders in the blues record market during the early twenties were Okeh, Columbia, and Paramount. Okeh, which initiated the trend in 1920, continued to set the pace for the next few years. Much of the credit for its success is given to Ralph Peer, who was primarily responsible for putting together the Okeh label's special 8000 series. By the end of 1922, forty selections had been released in the series—six jazz instrumentals, eleven gospel numbers, and twenty-three vaudeville blues. Okeh initially advertised this material in a ''Colored Catalogue.'' In 1922, however, it placed ads in the *Chicago Defender* for ''race phonograph stars'' and ''Okeh race records,'' and within a year, it had dropped the word ''colored'' from its advertising copy. Peer later claimed to have coined the term ''race records.'' In fact, he probably adopted it from the *Chicago Defender*, which used ''race'' as a progressive and positive adjective symbolic of black pride, militancy, and solidarity in the 1920s.

Louisville guitarist Sylvester Weaver was a typical Okeh race artist in the 1920s. He backed up the label's most consistent vaudeville blues vocalist, Sara Martin, on many of her records and also recorded several of his own compositions. Nine of those titles were copyrighted for him by the Clarence Williams Music Publishing Company. Williams had initially tried to buy Weaver's royalty shares from him but was turned down. Over a four-year period, Williams paid Weaver a meager $137.84 in royalty fees for the nine compositions. If Williams's figures were correct, and he was giving Weaver the same deal that Okeh offered its race artists, then the nine titles written by Weaver sold about twenty thousand copies on the commercial market. His most popular record was ''Guitar Rag'' and ''Guitar Blues''; he received under a hundred dollars for this guitar instrumental milestone—fifty dollars in recording fees and less than fifty in royalties. "Guitar Rag" was later recorded by Bob Wills and his Texas Playboys as "Steel Guitar Rag" and became one of the biggest country music hits of the 1930s. Weaver was not listed as the songwriter on the Wills recording and received no royalty money from it.[21]

Much of Columbia Records' success in the race market was due to its exclusive recording contract with Bessie Smith, the highly acclaimed "Empress of the Blues" during the culturally turbulent twenties. Smith was brought to the attention of Frank Walker of Columbia Records in 1923. Her go-between with Columbia was Clarence Williams, a well-traveled piano player and entrepreneur, who had befriended Smith when the two worked together with a touring minstrel troupe in the South. Williams negotiated her first contract with the label. Besides running his own music publishing firm, Williams worked as a talent scout for Walker, who supervised Columbia's race record series. Williams got Smith $125 a title, plus the royalties for her own material; however, the royalty checks went to his company, and he pocketed half her recording fees. When Smith discovered what kind of deal she was getting, she fired Williams and renegotiated her contract directly with Walker. This time, she got all of the $125 fee for each title, as well as a $1,500 guarantee for the year; however, Walker dropped her royalty clause, which allowed him to copyright her songs for Columbia Records. His own music publishing firms, Frank Music Company and later Empress Music, Inc., filed for the copyrights, which allowed him to collect a percentage of the royalties, while the balance went to Columbia. This was a common business practice among race record executives: Fred Hager of Okeh helped to found Helf and Hager's Music Firm; Ralph Peer started the Southern Music Publishing Company and the Peer International Corporation.[22]

Bessie Smith recorded 160 titles for Columbia from 1923 to 1933, 38 of them copyrighted in her name. She was paid a total of $28,575 by the company over the same period. One source estimated that her record sales averaged about 20,000 copies per release, but some of the biggest hits sold up to 780,000 in the first six months. Another estimate was that she sold between 6 and 10 million records.[23] Yet she never got a penny in royalties and, in all probability, knew nothing about the copyright law, which was true of most of the race record artists.[24]

The record business reached a highwater mark in sales in 1926—$128 million. The industry would not surpass that mark again until after World War II. The sales of race records were also on the rise during the twenties. On the basis of data from only three of the top race record labels, Howard Odum and Guy Johnson estimated that in 1925 African Americans were buying 5 or 6 million blues disks a year.[25] Blues scholar Jeff Titon has estimated that 10 million race records were purchased by African Americans in 1927, one for every black person living in the United States at that time. The number of race record releases peaked in 1928, when the yearly total of individual titles reached five hundred. Even latecomers like the front-running Victor label were now devoting a hefty portion of their catalogue, 21.7 percent in 1928, to race records.[26]

While the leading record companies were recording the vaudeville blues musicians in New York, they also started recording some of the African-American blues musicians living in the South and still grounded in their native folk traditions. Paramount Records was the first label to take full advantage of the wealth of talented black performers popular in the South. Started by the Wisconsin Chair Company in 1917 as an outgrowth of its phonograph manufacturing business, Paramount launched a race record series in New York in 1922 by issuing a handful of vaudeville blues titles sung by Harlem native Lucille Hegamin and Alberta Hunter. A key to the company's early success was a large mail-order operation. In 1924, Paramount established a second recording base in Chicago and hired J. Mayo "Ink" Williams to spearhead the race record operations there. Chicago already had a burgeoning black ghetto in its rundown Southside neighborhoods and a wide-open red-light district controlled by a constellation of underworld vice lords. This translated into jobs for black musicians, who came to Chicago from all over the country, but especially up the Mississippi River from the Mississippi Delta, a birthplace of the blues.[27]

Ink Williams's nickname stemmed from his ability to get the signatures of talented African-American entertainers on record contracts. After joining Paramount, he quickly signed up two of the most popular female blues singers on the black vaudeville circuit, Gertrude "Ma" Rainey and Ida Cox. Ma Rainey, the much-loved "Mother of the Blues," was at the height of her career as a performer. She recorded ninety-three selections for Paramount between 1923 and 1928; one-third of them were listed as her own compositions, while another nineteen listed no composer at all. The publisher for all the titles she recorded was the Chicago Music Publishing Company (CMPC). This firm was set up by Williams, and it filed for the copyrights to all the race recordings he supervised.[28] A gifted young Georgia musician, Thomas A. Dorsey, who worked as a studio pianist, arranger, and composer for Ink Williams in the 1920s, recalled: "A guy'd come in with a song, and he'd sing it. He had nobody to arrange it or put it down on paper. So I put it down on paper and then the company could copyright it."[29] The CMPC collected any and all royalty payments generated by the material it held the copyrights on; it was then responsible for passing some of that money on to the composer or performer.

Williams was also responsible for recording two of the race record industry's most popular rural folk blues performers, Blind Blake and Blind Lemon Jefferson. It is unlikely that Blink Blake got any royalties for his unique repertoire, even though his records were a commercial success. He was usually given a bottle for a recording session and was paid a flat fee for his guitar playing and singing.[30] The same is probably true for Blind Lemon Jefferson, the legendary Texas blues oracle who recorded seventy-five songs for Paramount between 1926 and 1930. Jefferson got composer credits on thirty-one of his recordings, while another twenty-four listed no composers. Most likely he also received a flat fee for his studio sessions and waived his royalties. The unfamiliarity of these rural blues musicians with copyright laws, coupled with the custom of providing free liquor at the recording sessions, made them especially vulnerable to the chicanery of race record entrepreneurs. In his autobiography, Big Bill Broonzy recalled how "Ink" Williams was able to trick him out of the copyrights to the songs he recorded at a 1927 session for Paramount:

> They had my head in a horn of some kind and I had to pull my head out of the horn to read the words and back in it to sing it. And they had Thomas put on a pillar about two feet high and they kept on telling us to play like we would if we was at home or at a party, and they kept telling us to relax and giving us moonshine whiskey to drink, and I got drunk. I went to sleep after the recording and when I woke up, on my way home, John Thomas told me that I had signed some paper, signed in ink. "You've let them make you drunk" Thomas said, "and you've signed our rights away."[31]

The successful marketing of the disks recorded by traditional African-American blues artists encouraged a number of field recording expeditions to southern cities by the record companies. The trend had been initiated in the early twenties by Ralph Peer, who took a unit to Atlanta, where he recorded blues singer Lucille Bogan. Peer focused on recording original songs and folksongs that he could copyright and assign to his publishing firms.[32] When he moved over to the Victor label in the middle of the decade to supervise their race catalogues, Peer continued to organize field recording ventures into the South. By this time, the development of portable electric recording equipment made it more feasible and profitable to do on-site recording sessions. Peer was the first to record a host of southern blues musicians, including Tommy Johnson, Blind Willie McTell, Furry Lewis, Gus Cannon and His Jug Stompers, and the Memphis Jug Band. Victor, Columbia, Okeh, Vocalion, and Gennett all recorded in the field. In addition, there was a network of white talent scouts in the South. These men usually ran furniture stores that sold phonograph machines and records. In conjunction with their business operations, they sought out talent for the race labels. The most successful were

Polk Brockman from Atlanta, Sam Price from Dallas, and H. C. Spiers from Jackson, Mississippi.

Generally, the rural African-American blues musicians who made commercial recordings in the twenties were paid much less than even the vaudeville blues performers. Georgia blues pioneer Pegleg Howell's record contract with Columbia in 1926 netted him fifteen dollars a side at a time when Bessie Smith was getting two hundred dollars a title from the same label. Mississippi John Hurt received twenty dollars a side from Okeh in 1928. Son House was promised fifteen by Paramount in 1930. Royalty fees for these rural bluesmen were habitually excluded from their contracts. Yet while the profits from better-selling race recordings went to the record companies, at least they documented a crucial period in the development of blues culture in the South and made that material available to black and white record buyers throughout the country.[33]

## Blues Recordings in the Depression Era

The onset of the depression quickly reversed the fortunes of the entire record industry; sales fell from over $100 million in 1927 to $6 million in 1933. Consequently, race record releases were drastically cut back, field recording ventures into the South were discontinued, the labels manufactured fewer and fewer copies of each title, and record prices fell from seventy-five to thirty-five cents a disk. Whereas the average race record on the market sold approximately ten thousand copies in the mid-twenties, it plummeted to two thousand in 1930, and bottomed out at a dismal four hundred in 1932. The smaller labels were gradually forced out of business, while the major record companies with large catalogues that went into debt were purchased by more prosperous media corporations based in radio and film. The record companies with race catalogues that totally succumbed to the economic downturn were Paramount, Okeh, and Gennett. By 1933, the race record industry appeared to be a fatality of the depression.[34]

The New Deal brought a new lease on life to the record business. The repeal of Prohibition revitalized the nightclubs and saloons of urban America. Simultaneously, the demand for popular records was stimulated by a new technical innovation, the jukebox, which began to supplant live music in bars and clubs. Although the curtailment of live performances tended to hurt professional blues musicians, it proved to be good news for the record manufacturers. By 1939, there were 255,000 jukeboxes in operation using 13 million disks. Record sales rebounded to $9 million in 1935, and the few surviving race record labels began to replenish the marketplace with new blues products. At this juncture, the major emphasis was on recording traditional rural blues performers and the newly coalescing urban blues bands. The vaudeville blues were a relic of the past. However, the industry's policy of segregated labels and markets remained intact, and the *Chicago Defender* and a few other black urban newspapers continued to be the major conduit of advertising for race records.[35]

Lester Melrose was a white native of Illinois who, along with his brother, ran a music store and publishing company in Chicago during the twenties. In 1934, he was hired as the local manager for RCA Victor's new race label, Bluebird. Melrose had published compositions by Jelly Roll Morton and Joseph King Oliver; he was familiar with African-American musicians in Chicago and had a good ear for their music. For almost two decades, he dominated the race recording operations there through his exclusive agent contracts with RCA Victor and also Columbia Records. By his own estimate, he was responsible for 90 percent of the blues recorded on these labels from 1934 to 1950.

Melrose's method of operation was similar to that of Ink Williams. Like Williams, he selected a close-knit group of local black musicians and songwriters to back up any outside talent he brought into the studio and also to make recordings on their own. This group was a who's who of Chicago blues during the depression and the war years. It included guitarists Lonnie Johnson, Big Bill Broonzy, Tampa Red, Amos Easton, Johnny Temple, and Memphis Minnie; pianists Blind John Davis, Black Bob, Little Brother Montgomery, Roosevelt Sykes, Walter Davis, Josh Altheimer, Memphis Slim, and Major "Big Maceo" Merriweather; female blues singers Victoria Spivey and Lil Green; harmonica players Jazz Gillum and Sonny Boy Williamson; bass players Ransome Knowling, Alfred Elkins, Bill Settles, and a youthful Willie Dixon. The studio drummer was usually Fred Williams. The major songwriters in the group were Broonzy, his half-brother Robert Brown, better known as "Washboard Sam," Amos Easton, who recorded as "Bumble Bee Slim," Tampa Red, Memphis Minnie, John Lee "Sonny Boy" Williamson, and Memphis Slim. Another similarity between Williams and Melrose was that both had an ear for folk blues talent, even if it was of an unpolished, downhome southern variety. Where Williams had found success recording rural bluesmen like Blind Lemon Jefferson and Blind Blake in the 1920s, Melrose sought to duplicate it in the following decade by recording country blues singers Bukka White, Big Joe Williams, Tommy McClennan, and Arthur "Big Boy" Crudup.[36]

RCA Victor's Bluebird label was quickly challenged in the race record market by Decca, which was launched in Chicago and New York late in 1935, under the direction of Jack Kapp, a crafty veteran of the recording business. Kapp had previously been Columbia's representative in Chicago, and then the head of the Brunswick/Vocalion race catalogue. The Decca label was financed by E. R. Lewis, the owner of the London-based Decca Record Company, but from the onset, Kapp called the shots in the United States. He hired Ink Williams as his chief black talent scout, and together they mapped out their recording strategy for Chicago. It had much in common with the operation of Lester Melrose and the one that Williams himself developed while working for Paramount in the 1920s. They hired a studio band to back up the local blues artists they contracted, including Johnny Temple, Rosetta Howard, and Frankie "Half Pint" Jackson. In addition, the studio musicians made their own recordings as the Harlem Hamfats. Over the next seven years, Decca released material in both blues categories: country blues by Kokomo Arnold, Blind Boy Fuller, and Sleepy John Estes; city blues by Peetie Wheatstraw, Louis Jordan, and the Harlem Hamfats.[37]

In 1938 the Columbia Broadcasting System bought the ailing Columbia label and launched a talent raid on RCA Victor and Decca recording artists that was reminiscent of the CBS raid on NBC radio talent earlier in the decade. Under John Hammond, a free-lance record producer for the Columbia label based in New York, Columbia signed up the Benny Goodman and Count Basie bands. Hammond had supervised Bessie Smith's last session for the label in 1933 and, during his early career with Columbia, was able to record an impressive list of the most important jazz and blues musicians of the era: Fletcher Henderson, Duke Ellington, Coleman Hawkins, Albert Ammons, Meade Lux Lewis, Teddy Wilson, Charlie Christian, Ida Cox, and Billie Holiday, to name just a few.[38] More important, he was honest in his business arrangements with black musicians, which separated him from most of his predecessors in the record industry.

## The Classic Blues Women

African-American women have always played a crucial role in maintaining and revitalizing the black oral tradition. During slavery they were an important creative source of spirituals, family histories, and cautionary folktales—the storytellers who taught their young about the grim realities of bondage and the constant dream of freedom. Sojourner Truth, for example, was as famous for her vocal renditions of spirituals like "There Is a Holy City" as she was for her fiery abolitionist oratory, and Harriet Tubman used spirituals to convey hidden messages about her underground railroad operation.[39]

Another important network of African-American women who combined an extensive knowledge of their oral tradition with a spiritual cause and calling were the "underground" priestesses who organized the surviving African "fetish" religions like vodun. These outlaw religious cults tended to be most prominent in the Caribbean, but they also persisted in the southern United States well into the 1900s, especially in the New Orleans area, the home of the legendary Marie Laveau, the most powerful and wealthy of the fabled "voodoo queens" of the pre–Civil War period. The "voodoo" songs these women sang as part of their sacred rituals evoked the magical omnipotence of African priestesses:

> They think they frighten me,
> Those people must be crazy,
> They don't see their misfortune,
> Or else they must be drunk.
>
> I—the Voodoo Queen,
> With my lovely handkerchief,
> Am not afraid of tomcat shrieks,
> I drink serpent venom!
> I walk on pins,
> I walk on needles,
> I walk on gilded splinters!
>
> I'm going to put gris-gris
> All over their front steps,
> And make them shake
> Until they stutter.[40]

There are strong thematic links between the prideful songs of the nineteenth-century voodoo queens and the "classic blues" sung by African-American women in the 1920s.[41] Both genres responded to adversity with self-confidence and determination; they symbolically encouraged and empowered black women to take control of their own lives. In the process, they fashioned a distinctly feminist outlook—one grounded in their unique social reality and primarily concerned with how black women were treated by the rest of society. This healthy preoccupation with black women's experiences and destinies tended to reinforce the broader racial struggles for political freedom and cultural self-determination because African-American women were burdened with the most social constraints in American society, given that they were its least privileged adult members. Viewed in this context, the classic blues women, like the voodoo priestesses and the abolitionist heroines before them, were another link in a long chain of black women who, from one generation to the next, worked to preserve and extend their culture through their use of the verbal arts.

The blues recorded by African-American women for commercial distribution in the 1920s were named "classic blues" by jazz historians writing in the 1940s and 1950s. The parallel notions of a classic genre and a classic period in the evolution of a black musical style was first used by these historians to characterize an early jazz era and style. The term was then applied to the black female vocalists who happened to have been involved in blues recordings during the same period. Rudi Blesh appears to have been the first to do so when he said, "With Gertrude 'Ma' Rainey, greatest of all blues singers, come the classic blues."[42]

The most insightful definition of the classic blues genre comes from LeRoi Jones's *Blues People*:

What has been called "classic blues" was the result of more diverse sociological and musical influences than any other kind of American Negro music called blues. Musically, classic blues showed the Negro singers' appropriation of a great many elements of popular American music, notably the music associated with popular theatre or vaudeville. The instrumental music that accompanied classic blues also reflected this development, as it did the Negro musicians' maturing awareness of a more instrumental style, possibly as a foil to be used with his natural vocal style. . . . Socially, classic blues and the instrumental styles that went with it represented the Negro's entrance into the world of professional entertainment and the assumption of the psychological imperatives that must accompany such a phenomenon. Blues was a music that arose from the needs of a group, although it was assumed that each person had their own blues and could sing them. As such, the music was private and personal, although the wandering country blues singers of earlier times had from time-to-time casual audiences who would sometimes respond with gifts of food, clothes, or even money. But again, it was assumed that anybody could sing the blues. If someone had lived in this world into manhood, it was taken for granted that they had been given the content of their verses, and as I pointed out earlier, musical training was not a part of African traditions—music, like any art, was the result of natural inclination. Given the deeply personal quality of blues singing, there could be no particular method for learning blues. As a verse form, it was the lyrics which were most important, and they issued from life. But classic blues took on a certain degree of professionalism. It was no longer strictly the group singing to ease their labors or the casual expression of personal deliberations on the world. It became a music that would be used to entertain others formally. The artisan, the professional blues singer, appeared; blues singing no longer had to be merely a passionately felt avocation, it could now become a way of making a living. An external and sophistocated idea of performance had come to the blues, moving it past the casualness of the ''folk'' to the conditioned emotional gesture of the public.[43]

Jones has described the crucial transition of the blues from a folk music to a commercially profitable popular music, and the entrance of the blues singer into American show business. These changes had revolutionary implications for black music in particular and American popular music in general. New infusions of African-American styles, rhythms, and consciousness were flowing into the mainstream of the dominant American culture. They made their initial appearance in the music and in the performance of the first wave of successful blues recording stars, most of whom were black women. There were social as well as economic reasons for this development. Black women tended to be more socially acceptable than black men to the white men running the music industry. They were less threatening physically, usually less experienced in business matters, and presumably easier to control. There may have also been some white male sexual fantasies at work in the equation. Moreover, black women were customarily paid less for their labor than were black men.

As a group, the classic blues women were an interesting cross-section of the African-American population. Like their black male counterparts in show business, they came primarily from the South. A few came from middle-class families, including Trixie Smith, who grew up in Atlanta and attended Selma University before embarking on a career in vaudeville and Edith Wilson, a native of Louisville, whose father was a college-educated school teacher. But the vast majority of the classic blues singers came from the bottom of the social order, where they experienced first hand the poverty and oppression confronting most African Americans. Maggie Jones was the daughter of a sharecropper from Hillsboro, Texas. Bertha ''Chippie'' Hill was one of nineteen children from a poverty-striken family in Charleston, South Carolina; she grew up in a hurry, leaving home to perform with a traveling minstrel troupe at age fourteen. Ethel Waters grew up in the streets of Chester, Pennsylvania, before taking to the road with a carnival; an illegitimate child, she had been cared for haphazardly by a series of relatives. Generally speaking, unlike most of the black population during this period, the classic blues women grew up in cities, and most had relocated to the larger centers of show business by the onset of the 1920s. Hence, they were in the forefront of the massive African-American migration into the cities that began in earnest during World War I.

The avenues the classic blues women used to enter the music business were an important aspect of their careers. To be sure, most of these women began singing in their local church choirs, but they soon moved on into various black entertainment enterprises. Ma Rainey, Clara Smith, Sippie Wallace, Ida Cox, and Lucille Hegamin all got their start in traveling tent shows. Those who began their singing careers on the more prestigious TOBA tour include Mamie Smith, who made the first recording breakthrough for black artists; Irene Gibson, a native of St. Louis who married Clarence Williams; her cousin, Katherine Henderson; Trixie Smith, from Atlanta; Lena Williams, from Charlotte, North Carolina; and Ada Brown, from Kansas City. A third group began their careers singing in the dance halls and cabarets of the nation's larger cities. Alberta Hunter and Edith Wilson started out in Chicago in the early 1920s, as did Georgia White and Lil Johnson in the late 1920s. Mary Johnson, Louise Johnson, and Alice Moore were the premier female blues singers in the St. Louis red-light district during the same era. Harlem's nightclubs, like Dash's Inn and the Capital Club, and dance halls, like the Roseland Ballroom, were the proving grounds for large numbers of women aspiring to follow in the footsteps of stars like Mamie Smith. Esther Bigeou and Lizzie Miles started singing professionally in New Orleans and Lottie Kimbrough started in Kansas City's wide open red-light district. Most of the women who were more successful with their original apprenticeships went on to work in all of the show business outlets accessible to them and were eventually featured on the classic blues recordings of the 1920s. The diversity of their backgrounds and the formative influences in their careers were especially reflected in the spectrum of blues styles they engendered.[44]

## Classic Blues Styles

In many respects, the style of blues recorded by the classic blues women was determined by the location of the recording session and, subsequently, the musicians chosen to back up the vocalists. In New York City, the hub of the recording industry, the session musicians were usually black jazzmen. These musicians had been playing instrumental blues for some time; they were responsible for adapting them to such European musical instruments as the tuba, trumpet, trombone, clarinet, and saxophone, in addition to the all-important piano and cornet, which were the dominant instruments in the studio bands. James Lincoln Collins, in his definitive jazz history, *The Making of Jazz*, pinpoints the three major changes that jazz musicians introduced to the blues when they began to build them into their repertoires. First of all, they standardized the blues time scheme, relegating it to a fixed twelve-bar pattern of three four-measure segments. This was in contrast to the more casual time schemes practiced by the early rural bluesmen, which were anywhere from eight bars to fifteen bars long. Next, the jazz musicians transformed the African-derived blue-note mode into a variation that could be played on the European diatonic scale. This necessitated substituting a minor third for the blue third, replacing the blue seventh with the so-called sixth note, and allowing the blue fifth note to simply atrophy. Finally, a standard tonic-subdominant-dominant harmonic system was adopted in lieu of the minimal concern for European harmony exhibited by the more traditional rural blues practitioners. Taken together, these transitions culminated in the birth of an urban blues genre.[45]

In contrast to the jazz-infused blues produced by New York City's African-American musicians are some of the field recordings made of black female vocalists in southern cities such as Atlanta, Memphis, St. Louis, and even New Orleans. In these sessions, string instruments such as the guitar and the banjo were more pervasive; guitar and piano duos were popular, as were jug bands with harmonicas, kazoos, and washboards. The session musicians were semi-professionals who were still more oriented toward the traditional rural playing styles.

Chicago was the one recording center in the country where both stylistic tendencies existed side by side, and in apparent harmony with one another. Black jazzmen from the South, especially New Orleans, had flooded Chicago even before the 1920s. Southern bluesmen, many of them from the Mississippi Delta, began their migration to the Southside Chicago ghetto soon after. Both groups were active backing up the classic blues women who recorded in Chicago during the next two decades.

In many respects, the classic blues women mediated the crucial transition from a rural folk blues to an urban popular blues. The best of them were neither modernists nor traditionalists in any strict sense; instead, they drew on both schools with equal facility. As vocalists, they were not as anxious to minimize the blue notes as were the jazz musicians. In fact, they often used blue notes to build their melodies around, and they also took advantage of the descending melodic line common in the earliest folk blues. Although they uniformly adopted a standardized twelve-bar time scheme and a standardized harmonic sequence, they likewise held tenaciously to the traditional African musical practice of separating their vocal lines from the accompanying ground-beat of the song. The greatest talents among this group of women proved to be important popular music innovators. Not only did they transform the lyrical content of the blues to coincide with their experiences and perceptions as black women, but they also created specific innovations in blue note patterns.

The best known of these was the practice of moving from a blue third note up to a major third note, an innovation that was used by Ma Rainey and became a trademark in many of Bessie Smith's recorded blues. Overall, the classic blues singers bridged the gap between the competing black musical traditions while developing their own personal genre of blues. They were in the forefront of the African Americans' entrance into the commercial music industry. They introduced the blues into the mainstream of American popular music, and thus to a new white audience. But most important, their record output represented the first significant plateau of achievement for an emerging urban blues tradition. The transplantation of the music and the transformation of its performers occurred simultaneously.[46]

## Classic Blues Recordings

The classic blues recordings of the 1920s included a wide range of material in their lyrics, some of it controversial and some of it banal. Here again, the commercial forces at work in the music business converged to impose Tin Pan Alley formulas and clichés on some of the recordings. On the other hand, many of the classic blues women also used material from the still resilient rural blues culture without diluting the message, or they fashioned their own lyrics out of their personal experience of urban life. This resulted in an uneven mix of material. The race record industry picked up sentimental Tin Pan Alley numbers about romantic love initially written for the vaudeville stage. Songs like Ethel Waters' "Oh Daddy" and "That Thing Called Love" are typical of this tendency:

> That thing called love, money cannot buy,
> That thing called love, will make you weep and cry,
> Sometimes you're sad, romantic and glad,
> The most wonderful thrill you ever had.[47]

The classic blues also retained Tin Pan Alley's "coon song" mentality, which resulted in the continuation of stereotypical images of African Americans. An example of this legacy was the Perry Bradford composition "Rules and Regulations (Signed Razor Jim)," recorded by Edith Wilson, which told the story of a black hustler in the big city who used a razor blade to enforce the rules at the dances he promoted. This image of the razor-toting, lawless, urban African-American male had antecedents all the way back in pre–Civil War blackface minstrelsy.

Another category of classic blues that reflects the influence of commercialism comprised the vaudeville-based novelty songs featuring graphic metaphors for sexual activity, which were often linked to culinary delights. Examples of these songs include "Whip It to a Jelly" by Clara Smith, "When the Wind Makes Connection with Your Dry Goods" by Martha Copeland, "I've Got Ford Movement in My Hips" by Cleo Gibson, and Lil Johnson's "Hottest Gal in Town":

> He's the kind of man that I want around,
> Handsome and tall and a teasing brown,
> He's got to wake me every morning 'bout half
>     past three,
> Kick up my furnace and turn on my heat,
> Churn up my milk, cream my wheat,
> Brown my biscuits, and chop my meat,
> He's long and tall, and that ain't all,
> He's got to be just like a cannonball,
> That's why I want him around,
> 'Cause I'm the hottest gal in town.[48]

One of the most popular songs of this type, and far removed from the realism of the blues, was the ditty composed by Thomas Dorsey and Tampa Red, "It's Tight Like That," first recorded by Clara Smith. Savory sexual metaphors were not uncommon in the black oral tradition, but once the race recording industry got involved, the material was often used to titillate prospective record buyers, as the advertisements for race recordings during this period demonstrate. The end result was that the classic blues sometimes became a burlesque of African-American sexuality.

When the classic blues women managed to use the more authentic floating folk lyrics from the black oral tradition, the lyrics of their blues numbers tended to resemble those of the rural precursors of the blues. This use of traditional lyrics was to be expected with the more common blues standards recorded by the female vocalists, examples of which were abundant. Songs like "See See Rider" and "Alabama Bound" were recorded again and again by the classic blues women. Bertha "Chippie" Hill was the first person to record Richard Jones's renowned blues composition "Trouble in Mind." Jones based his piece on the well-known spiritual of the same name from the days of slavery; he also made liberal use of a few other common expressions from African-American folklore.[49] The mixture gave birth to what must be considered the anthem of the classic blues genre:

Trouble in mind, I'm blue,
But I won't be blue always,
For the sun will shine in my back door someday.

Trouble in mind, that's true,
I have almost lost my mind,
Life ain't worth livin', feel like I could die.

I'm gonna lay my head on some lonesome railroad
    line,
Let the two nineteen train ease my troubled mind.

Well trouble, oh trouble,
Trouble on my worried mind,
When you see me laughin',
I'm laughin' to keep from cryin'.[50]

Similarly, three of Sippie Wallace's recordings, "Go Down Sunshine," "Shorty George," and "Section Hand Blues," are built around traditional worksongs common to her native state of Texas. In "Section Hand Blues," the folk lyrics were standard throughout most of the South.

If my captain ask for me,
Tell him Abe Lincoln set us free,
Ain't no hammer on this road,
Gonna kill poor me.

This ole hammer killed John Henry,
But this hammer ain't gonna kill me.

I'm headin' for my shack,
With my shovel on my back,
Although money's what I lack,
I'm goin home.[51]

Lyrics like this were far removed from the nonsense and "jive" rhymes that characterize the more commercialized classic blues recordings released in the 1920s.

Social themes reminiscent of those found in the early folk blues were more prevalent among the classic blues recordings than has been assumed by most blues historians. Female blues singers may have been more sensitive to the hardships of life than the men, since they were often discriminated against because of both their race and their sex. Their songs of city life frequently alluded to prostitution, gambling, excessive use of alcohol and drugs, crime, unemployment, poverty, and disease. Some of the best examples of these are Bertha "Chippie" Hill's release "Black Market Blues," about that illegal World War I enterprise, Mary Johnson's song "Barrelhouse Flat Blues," about bootlegging in St. Louis, Maggie Jones's recording "Goodtime Flat Blues," about a police raid on an illegal black after-hours club, and Victoria Spivey's own composition "Dirty T. B. Blues," a numbing tale of disease and desolation:

> Yes, he railroaded me to the sanatorium,
> It's too late, too late, but I've finished my run,
> This is the way all women are done,
> When they get dirty T.B.
>
> Yes, I've run around for months and months,
> From gin mill to gin mill to honky-tonk,
> Now it's too late, just look what I done done,
> Now I got the dirty T.B.[52]

In most of the southern states, black women convicted of crimes did time on prison farms, where they were also forced to work on labor gangs, just like black men. The classic blues women recorded many blues pieces with prison themes. Alice Moore's "Prison Blues" combines the experience of being incarcerated with that of being abandoned by a lover:

> The judge he sentenced me and the clerk he
>     wrote it down,
> Oh, the judge he sentenced me and the clerk
>     he wrote it down,
> My man said, I'm sorry for you babe, but you're
>     county farm bound.
>
> Six months in jail, seven months on the county
>     farm,
> Six months in jail, seven months on the county
>     farm,
> If my man had been good, he would have went my
>     bond.[53]

Sara Martin's first-person account, "The Prisoner's Blues," explains how she "went down for stealin' 'cause I didn't have a dime."[54] Victoria Spivey's "Bloodhound Blues" is a vivid re-creation of a black woman's escape attempt:

Well I poisoned my man, I put it in his drinking,
Now I'm in jail and I can't keep from thinking,
I poisoned my man, I put it in his drinking cup,
Well it's easy to go to jail, but lord, they set
  me up.

Well I broke out of my cell when the jailer turned
  his back,
I broke out of my cell when the jailer turned
  his back,
But now I'm so sorry, bloodhounds are on my track.

Bloodhounds, bloodhounds, bloodhounds on my trail,
Bloodhounds, bloodhounds, bloodhounds on my trail,
They want to take me back to that cold cold lonesome
  jail.

Well I know I done wrong, but he kicked me and blacked
  my —
I done it in a passion, I thought it was a fashion.
I know I done wrong, but he kicked me an' blacked my
  eye,
If the bloodhounds ever catch me, in the electric chair
  I'll die.[55]

Troubles and travels are major themes in the classic blues, building on similar material in the rural blues cultures. Alberta Hunter recorded her own composition ''I've Got a Mind to Ramble'' for Paramount Records. Edmonia Henderson cut a number called ''Traveling Blues.'' Ida Cox did her version of ''Rambling Blues.'' In ''Rolling Log Blues,'' Lottie Kimbrough captured the mood of the migrant's more somber moments:

I been drifting and rolling along the road,
Looking for my room and board,
Like a log I been jammed on the bank,
So hungry I grew lean and lank,
Get me a pick and shovel, dig down in the ground,
Gonna keep on diggin' till the blues come down.

I got the blues for my sweet man in jail,
Now, and the judge won't let me go his bail,
I been rolling and drifting from shore to shore,
Gonna fix it so I won't have to drift no more.[56]

Maggie Jones's "Northbound Blues" depicts the North as a haven:

> Goin' North, chile, where I can be free,
> Goin' North, chile, where I can be free,
> Where there is no hardship like in Tennessee.
>
> Goin' where they don't have no Jim Crow laws,
> Goin' where they don't have no Jim Crow laws,
> Don't have to work here like in Arkansas.[57]

So does Alberta Hunter's recording of Tony Jackson's "Michigan Water Blues":

> Michigan water tastes like cherry wine,
> Michigan water tastes like cherry wine,
> Louisiana water tastes like turpentine.[58]

Once settled in the North, however, African Americans were not free from hardships and discrimination. It is therefore understandable that the classic blues women also expressed some nostalgia for their southern homeland. In "Down South Blues," Ida Cox laments:

> When I was down South, I wouldn't take no
>     one's advice,
> When I was down South, I wouldn't take no
>     one's advice,
> Well I'm goin' home, let the same bee sting
>     me twice.
>
> I'm goin' where the weather suit my clothes,
> I'm goin' where the weather suits my clothes,
> Down where there ain't no snow,
> And the chilly wind don't blow.
>
> I don't want no Northern yellow, no Northern
>     black or brown,
> I don't want no Northern yellow, no Northern
>     black or brown,
> Southern men will stick with you when the
>     Northern men can't be found.[59]

Other recordings, such as Bertha "Chippie" Hill's tribute to her hometown, "Charlestown Blues"; Lillian Green's "Atlanta Blues"; "Shreveport Blues" and "Birmingham Blues," both recorded by Edith Wilson; and the many versions of "Vicksburg Blues" and "Gulf Coast Blues," all celebrate southern black communities. Typical of this attitude is Iva Smith's "Third Alley Blues":

> I just want to get back to Birmingham,
> I just want to get back to Birmingham,
> I got a gang in the Third Alley don't know
>     where I am.
>
> I'd rather be in Third Alley without a dime,
> I'd rather be in Third Alley without a dime,
> Than to be in Chicago wasting my time.[60]

Life at the bottom of the American social order is another major theme in the classic blues. Since being in this position was a long-standing grievance of African Americans in the United States, there was a wealth of proverbs, folk sayings, and floating verse already existing in the black oral tradition that could be drawn upon. Sippie Wallace's "Trouble Everywhere I Roam" expresses the pessimism associated with viewing society from the bottom up:

> There is trouble here, trouble everywhere,
> There is trouble here and trouble everywhere,
> Lord, I would go home, but there's trouble
>     over there.
>
> Ever since my dear old mother have been dead,
> Ever since my dear old mother have been dead,
> The rocks have been my pillow and the streets
>     have been my bed.[61]

This despairing view is echoed in Trixie Smith's "Mining Camp Blues," Ma Rainey's "Misery Blues," and Lucille Bogan's "Payroll Blues." Lucille Bogan's version of the standard "Tricks Ain't Walkin' No More" dramatizes both the plight of the female prostitute and her grim resolve to overcome all adversities:

> Times done got hard, money's done got scarce,
> Stealing and robbing is gonna take place,

Cause tricks ain't walking, tricks ain't walking
   no more,
And I've got to make my living, don't care where
   I go.

I'm gonna do just like a blindman, stand and beg
   for change,
And tell these 'rresting officers, change my
   tricking name,
'Cause tricks ain't walking, tricks ain't walking
   no more
And I can't make no money, don't care where I go.

          . . .

I got up this morning with the rising sun,
Been walking all day and I ain't caught one,
'Cause tricks ain't walking, tricks ain't walking
   no more,
'Cause tricks ain't walking, tricks ain't walking
   no more,
And I can't make a dime, don't care where I go.[62]

In a similar vein are Lottie Kimbrough's ''Wayward Girl Blues,'' which tells
the story of a prostitute's grief after learning that her mother had died, and Lil
Johnson's ''Scuffling Woman Blues,'' with the refrain:

Scuffling done got so hard until I can't hardly
   eat,
Scuffling done got so hard until I can't hardly
   eat,
Everywhere I turn, baby, the police is on my
   beat.[63]

A forlornness and a spirit of rebelliousness co-exist in Merline Johnson's
''Reckless Life Blues'':

I'm wild and reckless, can't even trust myself,
I'm wild and reckless, can't even trust myself,
'Cause my baby has quit me and I don't want
   nobody else.

I'm gonna buy myself a pistol and hang it on my
   side,
I'm gonna buy myself a pistol and hang it on my side,
I'm gonna join the gangsters and live myself a
   reckless life.

I'm gonna lock my cabin and turn my lights down
   low,
I'm gonna lock my cabin and turn my lights down
   low,
I've got these reckless life blues and I really
   got to go.[64]

In a similar mood of grim rage, Lillian Green exclaims:

A bucket of blood, a butcher's knife is all I crave,
A bucket of blood and a butcher's knife is all I crave,
Let me work in your packing house, daddy,
While I am your slave.[65]

Perhaps the angriest message issued on a classic blues recording was Julia
Moody's "Mad Mama's Blues":

Want to set this world on fire,
That's my mad desire,
I'm the devil in disguise,
Got murder in my eyes.

Now if I could see blood running through
   the streets,
Now if I could see blood running through
   the streets,
Could see everybody lying dead right at
   my feet.

Give me gun powder, give me dynamite,
Give me gun powder, give me dynamite,
Yes, I'm gonna wreck this city,
Gonna blow it up tonight.[66]

As a vivid expression of antisocial aggression—the total negation of the existing social order—these lyrics offered listeners a startling unleashing of pent-
up rage, a prophecy of an urban Armageddon.

The classic blues women also turned a critical eye on male-female relationships. In "Trixie's Blues," Trixie Smith admonishes her male friend:

> Now if you don't want me, baby, you have no right
>     to lie,
> Now if you don't want me, baby, that's no right
>     to lie,
> 'Cause the day you quit me, daddy, that's the day
>     you die.[67]

Most often, bad treatment elicits an angry response from the women. Viola McCoy recorded a number entitled "If Your Good Man Quit You, Don't Wear No Black." In "Bloodhound Blues," Victoria Spivey poisons her male companion after he beats her up. More typical is Jenny Pope's reaction to mistreatment in the concluding verse from "Doggin' Me Around Blues":

> I've been your dog, been your dog all of my
>     days,
> I've been your dog, been your dog all of my
>     days,
> The reason I'm leaving you, I don't like your
>     doggin' ways.[68]

In a lighter vein, Lil Johnson's recording "Press My Button" ridicules her male partner for his sexual ineptitude:

> Now tell me daddy what it's all about,
> Tryin' to fix your spark plug and it's all wore out,
> I can't see that thing—that ting-a-ling,
> I've been pressing your button and your bell won't ring.
>
> Here's my baby all out of breath,
> Been workin' all night and ain't done nothing yet,
> What's wrong with that thing—that ting-a-ling,
> I've been pressing your button and your bell won't ring.[69]

And in "Whip It to a Jelly," Clara Smith proclaims her sexual independence:

> I wear my skirt up to my knees,
> And whip that jelly with who I please.[70]

Clearly, these lyrics by the classic blues women present an explicit feminine view of male-female relationships, one diametrically opposed to the view expressed by the rural bluesmen on the same subject. In effect, they answer the bluesmen's sexual aggressiveness and braggadocio with an assertiveness and self-confidence of their own.

Self-reliance, self-worth, and self-assertion were interconnected themes in the classic blues that were at the heart of their feminist outlook. Sara Martin's "Mean Tight Mama" ties all three together with a savvy folk wit:

> Now my hair is nappy, and I don't wear no
>     clothes of silk,
> Now my hair is nappy, and I don't wear no
>     clothes of silk,
> But the cow that's black and ugly, has often
>     got the sweetest milk.
>
> Now when a man starts jivin', I'm tighter
>     than a pair of shoes,
> When a man starts jivin', I'm tighter than
>     a pair of shoes,
> I'm a mean tight mama, with my mean tight
>     mama blues.[71]

Other examples stressing women-identified solutions to their common problems include Lucille Bogan's "Women Don't Need No Men," Viola McCoy's "I Ain't Gonna Marry, Ain't Gonna Settle Down," and Ida Cox's signature piece, "Wild Women Don't Get the Blues":

> I've got a different system and a way of
>     my own,
> When my man starts kicking, I let him find
>     another home,
> I get full of good liquor and walk the
>     streets all night,
> Go home and put my man out if he don't treat
>     me right,
> Wild women don't worry, wild women don't have
>     the blues.
>
> You never get nothing by being an angel child,
> You better change your ways and get real wild,
> I want to tell you something and I wouldn't tell
>     you no lie,

> Wild women are the only kind that really get by,
> 'Cause wild women don't worry, wild women don't
>     have the blues.[72]

Taken as a whole, the lyrical content of the classic blues recordings created a fairly accurate mosaic of black urban culture in the 1920s from the perspective of African-American women. The classic blues singers mapped out new strategies for survival through their lively criticism of male supremacy and the dominant social order. They brought their common messages home to the black masses with humor, candor, and compassion. By relying on the oral tradition to enrich and embellish the lyrical content of their material, they helped to forge a vital link between their peoples' rural and urban cultural resistance. Moreover, they introduced the sensibilities of African-American women into the cultural dialogue, responding to the vicissitudes confronting them in the black community by creating new role models for feminine autonomy and solidarity. Nor did their sudden transformation into celebrated professional entertainers remove them from the struggles of their people, much less their traditional cultural roots. To be sure, there was some trade-off for commercial success in an entertainment industry controlled by white businessmen, and in certain instances it led to co-optation, as well as dilution of the blues. But an impressive number of the classic blues women remained true to an authentic rendering of the blues. As Alberta Hunter said:

> The blues? Why the blues are a part of me. To me the blues are—well, almost religious. They're like a chant. The blues are like spirituals, almost sacred. When we sing the blues, we're singing out our hearts, we're singing out our feelings. Maybe we're hurt and just can't answer back, then we sing or maybe even hum the blues. Yes, to us the blues are sacred. When I sing:
>
>> I walk the floor, wring my hands and cry
>> Yes, I walk the floor, wring my hands and
>>     cry
>
> What I'm doing is letting my soul out.[73]

## Classic Blues Women Profiles

Although the classic blues women were at the height of their popularity and influence in the 1920s, many of them had careers that spanned several decades. Ida Cox was active as a performer for over forty years. She was born

Ida Prather in Cedartown, Georgia, in 1889 and joined her first tent show as a dancer in 1903. By 1920, she was headlining at the 81 Theatre in Atlanta along with New Orleans jazz pioneer Jelly Roll Morton. Her repertoire at the time included novelty songs such as "Put Your Arms Around Me, Honey," traditional spirituals such as "Hard, Oh Lord," and the blues, especially "Jelly Roll Blues." During the 1920s, Cox recorded a total of eighty-eight titles; most were blues and many were her own compositions. She also managed her own vaudeville troupe, Ida Cox and Her Raisin' Cain Company. Their staging was from all reports quite elaborate, and she was the queen of the show. As one admirer put it: "Ida Cox was the best dresser of them all. For a headpiece she wore crown, jewels and feathers. Those jewels were not fake, they were real. . . . Her show had sixteen chorus girls doing dance routines—a jazz band, comedians, the works—it was a great show. People loved it."[74] Ida Cox's career concluded with a memorable appearance in the famous "Spirituals to Swing" concert at Carnegie Hall in New York City in 1939. Afterward she retired from show business but came back from time to time to make special appearances at recording sessions or concerts.[75]

Victoria Spivey was another classic blues woman who enjoyed a long and illustrious career in show business. She was born in Houston, Texas, in 1906 and grew up under the influence of a local pianist named Robert Calvin, who taught her to play and sing the blues. In 1926, at the age of twenty, Spivey wrote and recorded her biggest commercial hit of the decade, "Black Snake Blues." Like Ida Cox, Victoria Spivey was also a businesswoman and owned her own record company later in her career. But her real genius resided in her songwriting ability. She was a prolific composer of blues; they were her personal poetry about life and she learned to express herself elegantly through them. She was active as a blues songwriter until her death in 1976 and is credited with as many as fifteen hundred compositions. In an interview late in her life, Victoria Spivey, then known affectionately as "Queen Vee," summed up her approach to writing and singing the blues:

> To write the blues you got to experience life to the fullest. And by that I mean the good and the bad. The ups and the downs. Like my blues called "T.B. Blues." I did that way back in the 1920s. . . . There was a lot of T.B. goin' around then—especially among poor black folks. We had it down in Houston and that's where I got the idea for the song. Seein' those poor folks with T.B. in the streets, coughin' and sufferin' so . . . that's what I put in my blues, true things nobody wanna talk about.[76]

Alberta Hunter also excelled as a songwriter. She was born on April 1, 1895, in Memphis, Tennessee. Her father was a railroad porter who left home for good while she was still an infant. Hunter was then raised by her mother, who worked as a domestic in order to make ends meet. They lived in a poor black neighborhood near Beale Street, and for a while her mother worked as a maid in a local bordello. When they were finally able to move to a better neighborhood, the move proved to be traumatic for Hunter. She was molested by the white boyfriend of their landlady, then molested again by the black principal of her grade school.[77] No doubt these frightening experiences had an influence on her later decision to be involved exclusively in lesbian relationships.

Hunter moved to Chicago in 1911 at the age of sixteen to pursue a career as a singer. Her first job was at Dago Frank's Café for ten dollars a week. She worked her way up to the Elite #1 cabaret, owned by Teenan Jones, one of Chicago's most successful black underworld entrepreneurs. There she teamed up with the gifted New Orleans pianist Tony Jackson, learning to sing two of his most popular songs, "Some Sweet Day" and "Pretty Baby." By 1915 she had moved on to the Panama Café on the Southside; it was a showcase for black performers but catered to a white clientele from the Hyde Park area. At the Panama Café, Hunter was able to add new songs to her growing repertoire—in particular, Maceo Pickard's "Sweet Georgia Brown," Porter Grainger's "Michigan Water Blues," and W. C. Handy's "St. Louis Blues." In 1917, she began a five-year association with the fabled Dreamland ballroom, Chicago's most prestigious venue for black entertainers, and her salary rose to thirty-five dollars a week. In less than a decade, Alberta Hunter had become Chicago's most promising young black blues vocalist.

When the recording industry began to record the classic blues women in the 1920s, Alberta Hunter was one of the first to sign a contract. Initially, she recorded for W. C. Handy's Black Swan label in New York but quickly came to the conclusion that the company was more interested in showcasing Ethel Waters than her. Next, she recorded for Ink Williams at Paramount Records in Chicago. At Paramount, she worked with the talented pianist and arranger Lovie Austin, and wrote her first big blues number, "Down Hearted Blues." Austin helped with the arrangement and showed Alberta how to go about copyrighting it. However, she collected only $368 in royalties on the song after recording it for Paramount. Ink Williams surreptitiously sold the recording rights to Columbia Records, who had a big hit with it using Bessie Smith as the vocalist. Part of the deal gave the royalties to Williams. When Hunter learned what Williams had done, she stopped recording for him: "He was swiping my money," she later explained.[78]

In 1917, Alberta Hunter embarked on her first trip to Europe. She performed in Paris before enthusiastic audiences, then moved on to London, where she appeared in the English production of "Showboat" along with Paul Robeson. The trip was successful on all fronts. The Europeans treated her as an artist; their respect and even reverence made a lasting impression on her. Throughout the 1930s, Hunter divided her time between Europe and the United States. In Europe, she performed not only in France and England but also in Ireland, Denmark, Sweden, Greece, Turkey, and Egypt. She introduced more European and then Mediteranean audiences to African-American blues than did any other black performer of her generation.

Back in the United States, Alberta Hunter continued to travel and perform. With a depression in progress, bookings were slow, and recording sessions almost nonexistent. Still, Hunter prospered in comparison to most other African Americans in the music business. Having grown up poor, she knew how to stretch her resources, especially while living on the road. A companion of hers commented:

> She kept her money to herself, often up to eight hundred dollars in a money belt she wore all the time, and managed to save almost all her weekly pay. She lived off a loaf of bread and a pound of bologna, stored on the ledge of the window in their room.[79]

Yet if Hunter was tightfisted with her money, she gave freely of her time and energy to causes she considered worthy. She performed several benefit concerts for the NAACP and the children of Harlem. When World War II broke out, Hunter was one of the first black performers to tour with a USO show, playing for American troops at home and abroad. After the war, she retired from the music business and took up nursing, but she reappeared in New York in the 1970s for one final fling as a classic blues singer. It proved to be her last and greatest triumph.

### Ma Rainey: "Prove It on Me"

The most renowned of the classic blues women who emerged from the southern-based traveling minstrel shows was the legendary Ma Rainey, heralded as the "mother" of the blues. Born Gertrude Pridgett in Columbus, Georgia, in 1886, she was raised by her parents, who had moved there from Alabama. Her father died in 1896, at which time her mother got a job with the Central Railroad of Georgia to support the family.

Rainey was attracted to minstrelsy at an early age, appearing in a local minstrel show called "A Bunch of Blackberries" by the time she was fourteen.[80] In 1904, at the age of eighteen, she married William "Pa" Rainey, an older entertainer on tour with the Rabbit Foot Minstrels. From all indications, the marriage took place in Columbus, and soon after the two embarked on a career as a minstrel song-and-dance team that lasted for twelve years. During her early days with Pa Rainey, she acquired the nickname "Ma," even though she was still a young woman. The team became well known through-out the South, performing with many of the top black minstrel shows of the period. They followed the harvests in the summer and fall, spending the winter months in New Orleans. There, Ma Rainey sang with many of the city's top African-American musicians—Kid Ory, King Oliver, Sidney Bechet, Pops Foster, and a youthful Louis Armstrong. Ma and Pa Rainey's last job together as a duo was with Tolliver's Circus and Minstrel Extravaganza from 1914 to 1916, where they were billed as "Rainey and Rainey, Assassinators of the Blues." After two years with Tolliver's entourage, the team of Rainey and Rainey went their separate ways. Ma Rainey was already a well-established blues vocalist when she became a solo headliner; she, therefore, had little trouble making the transition. By 1917, she had formed her own troupe, which was billed as Madam Gertrude Rainey and Her Georgia Smart Sets. The show had a chorus line of female dancers and a five-piece band—violin, piano, guitar, bass, and drums.

There is some disagreement about when Ma Rainey first heard the blues and began to include them in her stage act. In an interview that took place late in her life, she told music scholar John Work Jr. that she first heard them in 1902 in a small Missouri town, where the minstrel show she was traveling with had stopped to give a performance. Work wrote down the following account:

> She tells of a girl from the town who came to the tent one morning and began to sing about the "man" who had left her. The song was so strange and poignant that it attracted much attention. Ma Rainey became so interested that she learned the song from the visitor and used it soon afterwards in her "act" as an encore. The song elicited such a response from the audience that it found a special place in her act. Many times she was asked what kind of song it was, and one day she replied in a moment of inspiration, "It's the blues."[81]

Since there is no mention of Gertrude Pridgett's touring that far from her hometown before her marriage to Pa Rainey on February 4, 1904, it seems more likely that she first heard the blues when she went on the road with her husband as a newlywed. It is also unlikely that she named the blues, since by 1904 the blues were an established folksong genre in the Deep South's cotton belt. Ma Rainey also told Work that she saved some newspaper clippings from 1905, which mentioned the new blues numbers in her stage act, but that the clippings were later destroyed in a fire. So it is fairly safe to assume that, by 1905, she had incorporated some of the rural folk blues she heard in her early travels with Pa Rainey into her repertoire. It is noteworthy that Gertrude Pridgett did not hear these "strange and poignant songs" while growing up in

Columbus, Georgia, between 1886 and 1904. This indicates that the folk blues had not penetrated the city, and perhaps the region, during that period, which lends credence to the assertion that the blues initially became popular as a song genre in the Mississippi Delta and East Texas, and only later spread to the Southeast.[82]

Ma Rainey's stage appearance was legendary. She was a flamboyant dresser who usually wore expensive floor-length gowns laden with glitter and frills and carried a huge, frosty ostrich fan. She also wore a tiara set with diamonds and a fine array of diamond rings, earrings, and necklaces. Jazz pianist Mary Lou Williams remembered that Ma was "loaded with diamonds" when she saw the blues mother on stage for the first time. Her most precious piece of jewelry, however, was a necklace made of gold eagles, twenty-dollar pieces with eagles stamped on them. She was so fond of the necklace that she had a huge eagle painted on the backdrop she used for her shows. The eagle was also the emblem of Paramount Records. The eagles were her trademark until the gold necklace was stolen. Ma then resorted to wearing imitation pearls, bangles, and beads around her neck.

Thomas Dorsey, who played the piano in Ma Rainey's band for a while, recalled her stage presence as follows:

> Then she would open the door and step out into the spotlight with her glittering gown that weighed twenty pounds and wearing a necklace of five, ten and twenty dollar gold pieces. The house went wild. It was as if the show had started all over again. Ma had the audience in the palm of her hand. Her diamonds flashed like sparks of fire falling from her fingers. The gold piece necklace lay like a golden armor covering her chest. They called her the lady with the golden throat. . . . When Ma had sung her last number and the grand finale, we took seven [curtain] calls.[83]

As Dorsey indicates, Ma Rainey's performances were no less mesmerizing than her stage appearance. She was blessed with a rich contralto voice that had both great depth and poignancy. It allowed her to belt out a raucous up-tempo dance tune or drag out a slow melancholy blues with equal effectiveness. Ma liked to moan along with a song during the breaks in the lyrics. She also used slurs and glissandos to emphasize her blue notes, much like the early rural blues singers. The songs she chose to perform were standard blues like "See See Rider" and "Boll Weevil Blues," material that was close to the common concerns and aspirations of African Americans. Many who worked with her or saw her sing in person have commented on her ability to strike a responsive chord in her audiences. The poet and newspaper columnist Langston Hughes maintained that black audiences' involvement in, and enthusiasm

for, a Ma Rainey concert was rivaled only by the spirited congregational ceremonies of the Holiness churches. African-American scholar and poet Sterling
A. Brown recalled: "She wouldn't have to sing any words; she would moan
and the audience would moan with her. . . . Ma really knew these people; she
was a person of the folk; she was very simple and direct. Her music went
straight to the heart."[84] Brown also captured a moving account of a Ma Rainey
concert in the poem he wrote in tribute to her, first published in *Southern
Roads*. It goes, in part:

> Oh Ma Rainey, sing your song
> Now you'se back where you belong
> Get way inside of us, make us strong
>
> Oh Ma Rainey, little and low
> Sing about the hard luck round our door
> Sing to us about the lonesome road we must go
>
> I talked to a fellow, an' the fellow say,
> "She jes' catch hold of us, somekindaway.
> She sang Backwater Blues one day:
>
> 'It rained fo' days an' the skies was dark as night
> Trouble taken place in de lowlands at night
>
> 'Thundered an' lightened an' the storm begin to roll
> Thousan's of people ain't got no place to go.
>
> 'Den I went an' stood upon some high ol' lonesome hill,
> An' looked down on the place where I used to live.
>
> An' den de folks, dey natchally bowed dey heads an' cried,
> Bowed dey heavy heads, shet de moufs up tight an' cried,
> An Ma lef' de stage, an' followed some de folks outside.
>
> Dere wasn't much more de fellow say:
> She jes' gits hold of us dataway.[85]

Ma Rainey's recording career came later in her life, when she had fully
matured as a blues vocalist. She made her first recordings in Chicago for Paramount Records in 1923, and her last sessions, for the same company, came in
1928. She recorded a total of ninety-two titles, a majority of them the standard
twelve-bar blues with AAB stanzas. There was not much variation in her ap-

proach to blues structure and the cadences of her songs. Like the rural blues-
men of her generation, she used a mere handful of blues melodies again and
again, fitting them with different lyrics so that they each told a different story.
In addition, her blues were full of folksy verse drawn from the African-
American oral tradition and common property among all blues musicians.
Fourteen of her recorded selections were traditional folk blues from the public
domain. As Ma Rainey expressed it in one of her numbers, entitled ''Last
Minute Blues'':

> If anybody ask you who wrote this song,
> Tell 'em you don't know but Ma Rainey put it on.[86]

Although Ma Rainey's blues were from a similar musical mold, her instrumental accompaniments were quite diverse. She recorded with a banjo, a banjo
and a guitar, a piano, a piano and a guitar, a hokem jug band, and a number of
jazz ensembles of various sizes. The jazz backup groups came early in her
recording career, and the jug bands toward the end. Ma was the first person to
record versions of some of the most popular rural folk blues. They included
her own version of ''Boll Weevil Blues,'' which she recorded on two separate
occasions, and the classic ''See See Rider.'' She also did her own version of
''Careless Love,'' which she retitled ''Blues, Oh Blues.'' Her recording ''Lost
Wandering Blues'' was the first to use the traditional floating verse ''I'm
standing here wondering will a matchbox hold my clothes?''[87] usually associated with Blind Lemon Jefferson's later title ''Matchbox Blues.''

Another point of common ground between Ma Rainey and the early rural
bluesmen was the choice of subject matter for their songs. The topics were
diverse, yet deeply rooted in the day-to-day experiences of black people from
the South. Ma Rainey's blues were simple, straightforward stories about heartbreak, promiscuity, drinking binges, the odyssey of travel, the workplace and
the prison road gang, magic and superstition—in short, the southern landscape of African Americans in the post-Reconstruction era. Foremost on her
list of lyrical preoccupations was the battle between the sexes. Blues scholar
Sandra Lieb has estimated that 75 percent of her songs touched on the theme
of love. She brought the feminist perspective of the classic blues women to
bear upon male-female relationships in the black community. Women were not
only pictured as being mistreated by men but were also represented as responding to the situation with a range of emotions—anger, gloom, humor,
hostility, passivity, rage. In her ''Hear Me Talkin' to Ya,'' she warns:

> Ya hear me talkin' to ya, I don't bite my tongue.
> Ya want to be my man, ya got to fetch it with ya
>     when ya come.[88]

A similar message is evident in the chorus of "Black Eye Blues":

> You low down alligator, just watch me soon
> or later,
> Gonna catch you with your britches down.[89]

In "Leavin' This Morning," a woman even threatens her man with bodily harm:

> When I get through drinking, gonna buy a
> Gatling gun,
> Find my man, he better hitch up and run.[90]

Many of Ma Rainey's blues demanded equal treatment and status with men. In "Barrelhouse Blues," she states:

> Papa likes his bourbon, Mama likes her gin,
> Papa likes his bourbon, Mama likes her gin,
> Papa likes his outside women, Mama likes her
> outside men.[91]

Her blues numbers that focus on love relationships always tell the story from the woman's point of view. Empathy for a woman's feelings of jealousy is the topic of "Jealous Hearted Blues," while criticism of male behavior is the theme of "Trust No Man." The most defiant feminist statement on sexual relationships and conventions comes in a composition of Ma Rainey's that may be partially autobiographical, entitled "Prove It on Me":

> They say I do it, ain't nobody caught me,
> Sure got to prove it on me.
> I went out last night with a crowd of my friends,
> It must a been womens 'cause I don't like no mens.
>
> Wear my clothes just like a fan,
> Talk to the gals just like any ole man.
> 'Cause they say I do it, ain't nobody caught me,
> Sure got to prove it on me.[92]

Ma Rainey's attraction to young women was no secret. Bessie Smith's cousin recalled an incident in Chicago when Smith had to go down to the local jail and bail out Ma Rainey and a coterie of females who had been arrested in the midst of an intimate party for women only.[93]

Ma Rainey was also fond of young men. Sterling Brown recalled that she looked him and John W. Work Jr. over closely when, as youthful scholars, they sought her out for an interview.[94] Jazz trombonist Clyde Bernhardt also commented on her fondness for young men, and how she built this affectation into her stage act:

> Oh yeah, she would tell jokes to the audience. . . . You know, "pig meat." . . . So she used to come out there and crack, "Yeah, I like my pig meat men. I like 'em young and tender. . . . If they be nice, I take care of 'em." . . . And she'd get up there and say, "I gonna tell you about my man." And then probably she'd start to singin' "A Good Man Is Hard to Find."[95]

Another one of her songs that developed a similar line of humor was "Lawd Send Me a Man Blues":

> Send me a zulu, a voodoo, any old man,
> I'm not particular, boys, I'll take what I can.
> I've been worried, almost insane,
> Oh lordy, send me a man,
> Oh lordy, send me a man.[96]

The other side of Ma Rainey's assertions of power are addressed in her blues dealing with loneliness, poverty, drinking problems, and jail experiences. Her descriptions of loneliness are always in the first-person singular, giving them a poignant authenticity. In "Blame It on the Blues," one line conveys the message with powerful simplicity: "This house is like a graveyard when I'm left here by myself."[97] She concluded her trademark version of "Boll Weevil Blues" with this verse:

> Lord, I went downtown and bought me a hat,
> I brought it back and put it on the shelf,
> Looked at my bed, I'm tired of sleeping by myself.[98]

Ma Rainey's blues put her in the place of problem drinkers, prostitutes, and people who had spent time in jail. "Dead Drunk Blues" assumes the persona of an alcoholic:

> Have you ever been drunk, slept in all your clothes,
> Have you ever been drunk, slept in all your clothes,
> And when you wake up, feel like you gotta go.

> I'm gonna get drunk just one more time,
> Honey, I'm gonna get drunk, Papa, just one more time,
> 'Cause when I get drunk, nothing don't worry my
>     mind.[99]

In "Hustlin' Blues," a prostitute gains her independence from a pimp by turning him in to the police. The plight of the black female offender caught up in the South's criminal justice system is the story line in "Chain Gang Blues." "Countin' the Blues" also focuses on the prison experiences of African Americans in the South; it contains the following verse:

> Lord, arrested at midnight, jailhouse made me lose
>     my mind,
> Lord, arrested at midnight, jailhouse made me lose
>     my mind,
> Bad luck and bo' weevil made me think of ole
>     moonshine.[100]

There is also a lighter aspect of the blues recorded by Ma Rainey in the 1920s. References to exotic superstitions and black magic appear in her lyrics: gypsies, black cats, charms and hexes, dreams and nightmares, bad and good luck are the subject matter of numbers like "Louisiana Hoo Doo Blues," "Black Cat and Hoot Owl Blues," and "Tough Luck Blues." In the last number she used a line similar to one used by Bert Williams's "Jonah Man": "If they was throwin' away money, I'd have on boxing gloves."[101] The ragtime dance song "Ma Rainey's Black Bottom" made use of the title's suggestive double entendre. The most humorous song she recorded was a piece that again projected Ma into the center of an experience known to all; it is entitled "Those Dogs of Mine (Famous Cornfield Blues)":

> Looka here people, listen to me, please be atellin'
>     the truth,
> If your corns hurt you just like mine you better see
>     what to do.
> Out for a walk, I stopped for a talk, oh how my
>     corns did burn,
> I had the people located over my feet to keep out
>     the light of the sun.
> Those dogs of mine, oh lordy those dogs of mine,
> They sure do worry me all of the time,
> The reason why for I do not know,
> Sometimes I soak them in the oleo,

> Lord I beg to be excused, Lord have mercy,
> I can't wear me no sharp soled shoes,
> Oh Lordy how the sun do shine,
> Down on these dogs of mine.[102]

The number was sung at a slow and mournful pace with mock deference to the topic. Ma Rainey must have elicited howls of delight and empathy from her audiences when she performed it in person. Another verse in her collection heaped good-natured abuse on the "highbrow stuff" associated with bourgeois culture, that is, European classical music:

> Grand Opera and parlor junk,
> I'll tell the world it's all bunk.
> That's the kind of stuff I shun,
> Let's get dirty and have some fun.[103]

The humorous blues were a significant part of Ma Rainey's repertoire and stage act but not as dominant as the more realistic stories, sketches, and images communicated in the majority of the blues numbers she sang. The candid, vivid, and simply constructed lyrics contained lodes of folk poetry that reflected the essence of the blues—that indomitable spirit of an uprooted race of people struggling to survive in an alien and hostile environment. "Lost Wandering Blues" contains the verse:

> I went up on the mountain, turned my face to the sky,
> I went up on the mountain, turned my face to the sky,
> I heard a whisper, said, Mama, please don't die.[104]

The final verse from one of Ma Rainey's own creations, "Southern Blues," briefly captures a philosophy of life at the heart of the early folk blues tradition:

> House catch on fire and ain't no water around,
> Yes your house catch on fire, ain't no water around,
> So you jump out the window, let it burn on down.[105]

The home is lost, but the person survives to build another one.

Ma Rainey recorded with the best black jazz and blues musicians in her day. For the first recording session in 1923, she used Lovie Austin and Her Blue Serenaders; the group consisted of Austin on piano, Tommy Ladnier on cornet, and Jimmy O'Bryant on clarinet. Lovie Austin could read music, and she worked both as the house pianist at Chicago's Monogram Theatre and as a studio musician for Paramount Records. She also wrote blues compositions for

Ma Rainey and several other female blues vocalists. Rainey recorded with Lovie Austin's group on several occasions, and she often worked with another female musician, pianist Lil Henderson. One gathering of musicians she recorded with in New York in 1925 included Louis Armstrong and Joe Smith on cornet, Charlie Green on trombone, Buster Bailey and Don Redman on clarinet, Coleman Hawkins on sax, and Fletcher Henderson on piano; it was, in effect, the nucleus of the famous Fletcher Henderson jazz band. Armstrong's cornet playing was prominently featured in her definitive recording of "See See Rider Blues." Another group that backed her in some of her recording sessions featured Claude Hopkins on piano and Kid Ory on trombone. Ma Rainey also collaborated with the blues pianist and composer Thomas Dorsey on several recording dates that featured either Dorsey on solo piano, with an early city blues band called the Jug Washboard Band, or in a duo with blues guitar wizard Tampa Red. Other blues-oriented musicians with whom Rainey recorded were guitarist Blind Blake, the Puritt twins, who played banjo and guitar, and the legendary Papa Charlie Jackson. Rainey and Jackson recorded two vocal duets in 1928, and these proved to be her last recordings. Paramount terminated her contract shortly after, later claiming that her "downhome material had gone out of fashion." Ironically, she had gravitated toward her more "downhome" backup groups in the last years of her recording career, after having used jazz groups in its earlier stages.[106]

The remaining years of Ma Rainey's life were spent in relative ease and obscurity. She continued to tour on the African-American minstrel circuit in the South until 1935, when she retired as an entertainer and returned to Columbus, Georgia. In Columbus, she owned her own home and two local theaters, which she was involved in managing. She also became active in the Baptist church where her brother was a deacon. Ma Rainey never squandered her wealth while she was a minstrel star; hence she was relatively wealthy when she finally left show business, and she was able to live comfortably for the rest of her life. She died in Columbus in 1939. With her passed the era of the traveling black minstrel troupes, as well as one of the most compelling blues styles ever captured on record.

### Bessie Smith: "Tain't Nobody's Business If I Do"

While Ma Rainey was the archetypal "earth mother" of the classic blues, Bessie Smith was the high priestess. She was the undisputed "Empress" of the blues in the 1920s, with a strong following among the black masses. More than any other woman of her times, she came to symbolize the African Americans' resurgent militancy and racial pride. As a cultural leader by virtue of her mastery over the blues, Smith assumed a role comparable to that of Jack Johnson, the first black heavyweight champion of the world, whose defiance of white authority was legendary, and Marcus Garvey, the charismatic prophet of black nationalism. All three were highly visible in their advocacy of black pride and in their resistance to the unequal treatment and the inferior social status imposed on African Americans in the United States. They were three individual manifestations of the crucial changes taking place in American life; and as a direct consequence of their affirmation of a renewed black consciousness and identity, they were instrumental, each in his or her own way, in encouraging the ongoing resistance to white cultural hegemony by African Americans.

Bessie Smith's instinctive resistance against the music industry's tendency to appropriate and distort the music and performing arts of African Americans often put her in conflict with the status quo, even in her own community. Smith was an unabashed rebel, openly defiant of bourgeois conventions and the oppressive social relations between the races, between the sexes, and between the classes in American society. She never lost sight of her origins, just as she never faltered in her solidarity with her people in the South, whom she always referred to with great pride.

Bessie Smith was born in Chattanooga, Tennessee, on April 15, 1894. Her family was large, nine in all, and extremely poor. Her father, William Smith, was a Baptist preacher who operated a local mission; he died soon after Bessie was born. Death also took two brothers, Son and Bud, as well as her mother, Laura, before Bessie reached her teens. The oldest sister, Viola, took over as the nominal head of the household, and Bessie went to work on the city's street corners with her brother Andrew. She would sing for tips, while he accompanied her on guitar. During this period, Chattanooga was a rapidly growing yet rigidly segregated southern trade and transportation center; approximately half of the 30,000 inhabitants were black. They were crowded into the city's "Negro quarter," where unsanitary living conditions, disease, unemployment, poverty, and crime were common. Most of the jobs open to African Americans were for low-paid manual or domestic laborers, and there were not enough of these jobs to go around. The only other opportunity for employment, besides something illegal, was in the segregated entertainment business. This was to be Smith's avenue of escape from the Chattanooga slums.[107]

Bessie Smith broke into show business in her hometown at the age of eighteen, with the help of her older brother Clarence. He had earlier joined Moses Stokes's traveling minstrel troupe as a comedian, and when he returned to Chattanooga with the show in 1912, he arranged for his sister to audition for it. She was initially hired as a dancer, and she went out on the road with the troupe that same year. One of its members was Ma Rainey, at the time still married to Pa Rainey. Smith and Ma Rainey struck up a close friendship that lasted for the rest of their lives. Undoubtedly, Bessie Smith was influenced by the older "mother" of the blues; in fact, she later recorded two of Rainey's blues standards, "Moonshine Blues" and "Boll Weevil Blues." Suggestions that Smith was groomed for stardom by Ma Rainey, however, are exaggerated. She had been singing publicly, if not professionally, for close to ten years before meeting Ma Rainey, and she toured with her briefly on only two occasions. Bessie Smith developed her own singing style through years of hard work, mostly on her own, just as she persistently made her own way in the world of show business.[108]

In 1913, Smith relocated in Atlanta, where she soon became a fixture at Charles Bailey's 81 Theatre. Her starting salary was a mere ten dollars a week, but her evocative singing style brought in a deluge of tips to supplement her income. The song she was most remembered for during her years in Atlanta is "Weary Blues," a common folk blues first published by St. Louis ragtime pianist Artie Matthews in 1915. People who met Bessie Smith in this period remembered her as a raw and awkward performer. Yet they also acknowledged that she was already an exceptional blues singer with the ability to break up a show. Both Charles Bailey, Atlanta's TOBA kingpin, and Thomas Dorsey, who sold soft drinks at the 81 Theatre as a boy before launching his own career as a composer, concurred that she possessed a great vocal talent from the onset of her career. By 1918, Smith was a well-known headliner throughout the Deep South and as far north as Baltimore. Two years later she was the star of her own show on the TOBA circuit in the South and along the eastern seaboard.[109]

In the early 1920s, Bessie Smith moved to Philadelphia, where she performed regularly at the Standard and Dunbar theaters, as well as at Paradise Gardens, a popular nightclub in Atlantic City, New Jersey. Her initial attempts to break into the race recording industry proved to be frustrating. Her voice sounded coarse by Tin Pan Alley standards, and her mannerisms were defiantly plebeian; the combination won her very few adherents among the record producers. She apparently auditioned some material for the Emerson Record Company in 1921, but nothing was released under her name. She auditioned for Fred Hager at Okeh Records but was turned down because her voice was "too rough." Harry Pace of Black Swan Records rejected her on similar grounds, much to the later chagrin of his partner, W. C. Handy. Early in 1923, however, Smith was sought out by the head of Columbia Record's race catalogue, Frank Walker. He would later claim to have first heard her singing in a Selma, Alabama, gin mill in 1917, thereby implicitly taking credit for discovering her for the record industry. Actually, both Clarence Williams and Perry Bradford were active in attempting to negotiate a recording contract for Bessie Smith before Frank Walker showed any interest in her. In fact, Williams worked as Walker's assistant and served as the intermediary in locating her, which suggests that he may have had a hand in bringing her to Walker's attention. Williams took advantage of his friendship with Smith by talking her into taking him on as her manager and then inducing her to record material that he had copyrighted. When Smith discovered how much of her earnings from Columbia Records were earmarked for Clarence Williams's wallet, she terminated her contract with him and made new arrangements directly with Walker, who would handle her recording career from 1923 to 1931.[110]

Smith's earliest recording sessions for Columbia were in 1923. On February 11, her first session, she recorded ''Down Hearted Blues'' and ''Gulf Coast Blues''; the two would be her initial release on the Columbia label later in the year. Clarence Williams's piano accompaniment, even on the piece he had copyrighted as his own, ''Gulf Coast Blues,'' is stiff, mechanical, and uninspired. Smith's vocals, however, are quite the opposite, in spite of the primitive acoustic recording techniques then available. Her voice is both powerful and poignant, especially in her rendition of ''Down Hearted Blues,'' which had been recorded earlier by vocalist Alberta Hunter and pianist Lovie Austin.

Her next session produced no real blues numbers, but instead a string of well-known vaudeville songs, including ''Aggravatin' Pappa'' and ''Beale Street Mama,'' previously recorded by Harlem cabaret singer Lucille Hegamin, ''Oh Daddy,'' a vaudeville number popularized earlier by Ethel Waters, and Clarence Williams's song ''Baby, Won't You Please Come Home,'' which she gives a slower tempo and infuses with a blues intonation. Her undisputed masterpiece from this session is her rendition of Porter Grainger's saucy ''Tain't Nobody's Business If I Do.'' The opening verses were made to order for Smith's brazen personality, and the song became one of her signature pieces:

> There ain't nothing I can do or nothing I
>    can say,
> That folks don't criticize me,
> But I'm going to do just as I want to do
>    anyway,
> And I don't care if they despise me.
>
> If I should take a notion,
> To jump in the ocean,
> Tain't nobody's business if I do do do do.
>
> If I go to church on Sunday,
> Then just shimmy down on Monday,
> Tain't nobody's business if I do do do do.[111]

By the next session, Smith had switched piano players, dumping Clarence Williams for the youthful Fletcher Henderson, probably because of the revelation of Williams's scheme to swindle her out of half of her recording fees from

Columbia, but also because he was a mediocre pianist. Henderson had a shy and accommodating personal manner much better suited to Smith's fiery temperament; in addition, he was a better piano player. During this session, Smith returned to her tried and tested blues material, recording a version of "Weary Blues," the early favorite of her Atlanta audiences, which she renamed "Mama Got the Blues":

> Some people say that the weary blues
>     ain't bad,
> Some people say the weary blues ain't bad,
> But it's the worst ole feeling that I ever had.
>
> Woke up this morning with the jinks around
>     my bed,
> I woke up this morning with the jinks around
>     my bed,
> I didn't have no daddy to hold my aching head.
>
> Brownskin is deceitful, but a yellow man is
>     worse,
> Brownskin's deceitful, but a yellow man is
>     worse,
> I'm gonna get myself a black man and play it
>     safe at first.
>
> I got a man in Atlanta,
> Two in Alabama,
> Three in Chattanooga,
> Four in Cincinnati,
> Five in Mississippi,
> Six in Memphis, Tennessee,
> If you don't like my peaches, leave my orchard
>     be.[112]

The number had autobiographical overtones, given Smith's often stated preference for men with dark skin color and her penchant for a variety of sexual experiences and liaisons.

In June 1923, Bessie Smith returned to the Columbia studios in New York City, again accompanied by Fletcher Henderson on piano. A majority of the numbers she recorded were blues; among them the well-known "Jailhouse Blues," copyrighted by the ubiquitous Clarence Williams. The main verses to "Jailhouse Blues" had long been common knowledge among African Americans in the South, and they were obviously not Williams's sole creation. Folk-lorist Howard Odum had made a written transcription of them as early as 1908:

> I laid in jail, back turned to the wall,
> (I laid in jail, back turned to the wall),
> Told the jailer to put a new man in my stall.
>
> I don't mind being in jail,
> (I don't mind being in jail),
> If I didn't have to stay so long.[113]

The lyrics that Williams copyrighted went as follows:

> Thirty days in jail with my back turned to
> the wall,
> Thirty days in jail with my back turned to
> the wall,
> Look here mister jailkeeper, put another gal
> in my stall.
>
> I don't mind staying in jail, but I've got to
> stay there so long,
> I don't mind staying in jail, but I've got to
> stay there so long,
> When every friend I have is done shook hands
> and gone.
>
> Good morning blues, blues how do you do,
> Good morning blues, blues how do you do,
> Say, I just came to have a few words with you.[114]

The final verse was one of the more widespread folk blues lyrics in circulation. Smith's choice of certain of Williams's copyrighted songs, especially after their money dispute, suggests that she was familiar with their folk roots and their enormous popularity among much of the black population. Another of Williams's copyrighted numbers that she had recorded earlier, "Gulf Coast Blues," contained similar well-known floating verses from the public domain, such as the following:

> Some of you men sure do make me tired,
> Some of you men sure do make me tired,
> You got a handful of gimme and a mouthful of
> much obliged.[115]

Downhome folk lyrics of this caliber, coupled with Smith's compelling blues vocals, were bound to strike a responsive chord among the black record-buying public; her first release by Columbia Records in June 1923, "Down Hearted Blues" and "Gulf Coast Blues," sold approximately 780,000 copies by the end of the year. Throughout her career, she would return again and again to material drawn from the reservoir of the African-American oral tradition. It was a practice that helped to establish her strong personal bond with black audiences; she was the carrier of their cultural heritage.[116]

The release of Bessie Smith's first records gave her stage career a dramatic boost. During the rest of 1923, and well into the next year, she toured constantly. Her territory was no longer just in the South and along the Atlantic seaboard; she was now also in great demand in the northern and midwestern industrial belts. Cities that had attracted large numbers of African-American migrants during World War I—St. Louis, Detroit, Cleveland, Pittsburgh, Cincinnati, Indianapolis, Kansas City, and especially Chicago—were added to her touring schedule. Everywhere she appeared in front of overflow crowds of black admirers. They lined up around an entire city block waiting to hear her sing the blues, just as they waited in line to buy her latest record. In her southern homeland, she not only had a large and loyal following among African Americans but was also one of the few black performers of her era to stage shows for white audiences. Another indication of her increasing popularity was the fact that she was the first black woman to be broadcast live in concert on local radio stations in Atlanta and Memphis. Her fame and her influence as a creative artist were at a zenith.[117]

From the beginning, Smith's stage act included some dancing and an occasional husband and wife comedy routine with a male co-worker. Perry Bradford recalled that she was "a whopping good foot dancer" when he first saw her in Atlanta; at the time, she was working with a male comedian named Buzzin' Burton. But it was neither her dancing nor her humor that brought out the crowds; it was her vocal renditions of the blues. She sang them with a passionate conviction, and she had a stage presence that drew crowds of black people to her shows. Her voice was rich and resonant; she concentrated on her middle octave and center tones, although she had much greater range. Like other great black vocalists, Smith could bend, stretch, and slur notes to achieve a desired effect. She used her voice as a jazz instrument, like the growl of a trombone. Many musicians who worked with her commented on these vocal pyrotechnics and on her ability to hold an audience spellbound. New Orleans jazz guitarist Danny Barker once remarked:

> She could bring about mass hypnotism. When she was performing you could hear a pin drop. . . . When you went to see Bessie and she came out, that was it. If you had any church background, like people who

came from the South, like I did, you would recognize a similarity between what she was doing and what those preachers and evangelists from
there did, and how they moved people. . . . Bessie did the same thing
on stage.[118]

Perry Bradford also commented on the "spiritual touch" to her singing; and it
was the major inspiration for another New Orleans native, gospel queen Mahalia Jackson: "When I was a little girl I felt she [Smith] was having troubles
like me. That's why it was such a comfort for people of the South to hear her.
She expressed something they couldn't put into words."[119]

In 1924 and 1925, Smith was back in the recording studio for a series of
sessions that would prove to be, from a musical standpoint, the best of her
overall career. Through her association with Fletcher Henderson, she began to
use members of his New York–based dance orchestra as accompanists. They
happened to be some of the most talented jazzmen in the country, and their
participation in her recording sessions vastly improved the quality of her accompaniments. They included cornetist Joe Smith, trombone player Charlie
Green, clarinetist Buster Bailey, saxophonists Coleman Hawkins and Don Redman—as well as the era's premier jazz musician, Louis Armstrong. In addition, she found another pianist more to her liking, Fred Longshaw. These men
would be the key figures in Smith's best backup bands during the Columbia
recording sessions from 1924 until the end of the decade.

A memorable musical collaboration occurred in 1924, when Bessie Smith
teamed up with Charlie Green, and then Joe Smith, for the first in a series of
recordings they would make together. Both were seasoned black musicians
who had had previous experience playing instrumental blues in small jazz ensembles and accompanying other female blues singers. They knew the music
first hand and played it with a relaxed confidence, relying on head arrangements more than on published sheet music. They were both adept at answering
Smith's vocal lines with brief and innovative responses. Their laconic solos are
full-bodied in tone and are delivered in a "hot" New Orleans–influenced style.
At times, both of them employ mutes to bend or slur their tones to approximate blue notes or the vocal phrasing of a blues singer. On two of the 1924
recordings they made backing up Smith, "Weeping Willow Blues" and "The
Bye Bye Blues," they are featured together, and their endeavors produced an
exceptional record. They create a spontaneous interplay between the two horns
that embellish the accompaniment to the extent that even Smith's vocals sound
better than usual. The Empress was duly impressed; she would continue to
request Green and Smith as backup musicians in her recording sessions up
until the onset of the depression.

In 1925, Louis Armstrong backed up Bessie Smith in the recording studio on three separate occasions for a total of nine songs. At these sessions, Armstrong is at the height of his powers as a jazz instrumentalist. His tone is warm and full, even when playing in the higher registers; it is not necessarily overpowering, but its bell-like clarity makes it stand out. Armstrong's phrasing is also superb; he usually attacks the notes directly, giving them a razor-sharp edge. When he plays behind Smith's singing, he responds to each of her vocal lines with imagination and wit. His short solos, lasting only a chorus or two, sound as if he is holding a conversation with her, using his cornet instead of his voice; they give some indication of his uncanny ability to improvise with the melody of a song. The best titles they recorded were W. C. Handy's classic "St. Louis Blues," Ben Harney's satirical ragtime standard "You've Been a Good Old Wagon," and "Careless Love." Unfortunately, Armstrong and Smith never worked together after the 1925 recording sessions; hence, the nine Columbia releases produced in those sessions were the only collaborations of the decade's two most important black musicians.

The blues that Smith recorded in the mid- and late 1920s give equal attention to social and sexual themes. The social material she drew from the daily plight of the African-American masses, as she saw it; topics such as poverty, bootlegging, prisons and injustice, drinking and gambling, unemployment and hard times were all commonplace in her recordings. Some of her noteworthy early releases include "Rent House Blues," which focuses on an eviction notice Bessie had received from her landlord, and "Workhouse Blues," which finds her in a situation all too familiar to black people living in the South, men and women:

> Everybody's crying the workhouse blues all day,
>     oh lord, oh lord,
> The work is so hard, thirty days is so long,
>     oh lord, oh lord,
> I can't plow, I can't cook, if I run away would
>     that be good.
>
> 'Cause I'm goin' to the nation, I'm goin' to the
>     territor'
> Say I'm bound for the nation, I'm bound for the
>     territor',
> I got to leave here, I got to catch the next train
>     home.
>
> Workhouse sits on a long old lonesome road,
> The workhouse sits out on a long old lonesome road,
> I'm a hard luck gal, catch the devil everywhere I go.

Say, I wish I had me a heaven of my own,
Say, I wish I had me a heaven of my own,
I'd give all the poor girls a long old happy home.[120]

Other prison-related material that she recorded during the period includes
''Sing Sing Prison Blues,'' a grim reminder of the infamous New York State
penitentiary, and ''Woman's Trouble Blues,'' a story about the unjust incarceration of a young black woman.

Smith's biggest-selling blues number of the decade was ''Backwater
Blues,'' which she wrote herself after seeing a flood along the Ohio River. It
detailed the flood from the point of view of a female victim, who had to be
evacuated from her home before it was washed away by the raging flood waters. As if a prophecy, its release coincided with the worst flooding in the
known history of the Mississippi River, which may have accounted for some of
its extraordinary sales. Her accompanist and collaborator on ''Backwater
Blues'' was the outstanding stride piano virtuoso James P. Johnson. Theirs was
a brief but fruitful relationship, and Smith soon thereafter recorded one of his
compositions, ''Black Mountain Blues,'' a mischievous song about life in the
''Negro quarters'' of the South. ''Money Blues,'' ''Pickpocket Blues,'' and
''Dying Gambler's Blues'' deal with residents of the urban tenderloin;
''Foolish Man Blues'' is about homosexuality; and, ''Bedbug Blues'' and
''Washerwoman's Blues'' tell two satirical stories about city life for migrant
African Americans.

Smith's masterpiece of social protest is a song entitled ''Poor Man's
Blues'':

Mister rich man, rich man, open up your heart
    and mind,
Mister rich man, rich man, open up your heart
    and mind,
Give the poor man a chance, help stop these
    hard, hard times.

While you're living in your mansion, you don't
    know what hard times mean,
While you're living in your mansion, you don't
    know what hard times mean,
Poor working man's wife is starving, your wife
    is living like a queen.

Please listen to my pleadin', 'cause I can't
    stand these hard times long,

Please listen to my pleadin', 'cause I can't
   stand these hard times long,
They'll make an honest man do things that you
know is wrong.

Now the war is over, poor man must live the
same as you,
Now the war is over, poor man must live the
same as you,
If it wasn't for the poor man, mister rich man,
what would you do?[121]

There is much insight in the remark made by Smith's biographer, Chris Albert-son, that " 'Poor Man's Blues' was, in fact, 'Black Man's Blues.' " The im-plicit criticism of race relations in American Society is consistent with Smith's strong identification with her own people and her mistrust of white people in general. The class perspective is equally noteworthy. Here again, Smith iden-tifies with those who are victimized by the political economy of capitalism, that is, the poor and downtrodden. But poverty in American society has tradi-tionally cut across racial lines, and much of the country's working class lived below the poverty line during the 1920s. Hence it was a song that much of the population could identify with, regardless of whom Smith had in mind at the time she wrote it.[122]

Sex was one topic that Bessie Smith always dealt with candidly. At times, she could be risqué and employ blatantly sexual double entendres, as she does in her recording of "Kitchen Man" and the popular "Empty Bed Blues." When she turned to the subject of her personal relationships with men, how-ever, she tended to be more true to life. While she did record material of a traditional mold—for instance, "A Good Man Is Hard to Find," "My Man," and "Honey Man"—she also made several recordings that are critical of her male partners. In "Salt Water Blues," she boasts:

I may be crazy, but mama ain't nobody's fool,
I may be crazy, but mama ain't nobody's fool,
Before I'll take your doggin', I'll eat grass
like a Georgia mule.[123]

A verse from "Sinful Blues" warns her man:

Get your pistol, I've got mine,
I've been mistreated and I don't mind dyin',
That's why I'm sinful as can be.[124]

Coupled with this intolerance of male abuse, also evident in numbers like "I Ain't Gonna Play No Second Fiddle," "I've Been Mistreated and I Don't Like It," and "Hard Times Blues," there is a reciprocal sense of a newly acquired independence and freedom of choice. A more defiant message is evident in "Young Woman's Blues":

> I'm a young woman and ain't done runnin'
>    around,
> I'm a young woman and ain't done runnin'
>    around.
> Some people call me a hobo, some call me
>    a bum,
> Nobody knows my name, nobody knows what
>    I've done,
> I'm as good as any woman in your town.
>
> I ain't no high yellow, I'm deep yellow brown,
> I ain't gonna marry, ain't gonna settle down,
> I'm gonna drink good moonshine and run these
>    browns around.
> See that long lonesome road, don't you know
>    it's gotta end,
> And I'm a good woman and I can get plenty
>    of men.[125]

A similar attitude is voiced in "Reckless Blues":

> When I was young, nothing but a child,
> When I was young, nothing but a child,
> All you men tried to drive me wild.
>
> Now I'm growing old,
> Now I'm growing old,
> And I got what it takes to get all you
>    men's soul.
>
> My mama says I'm reckless, my daddy says
>    I'm wild,
> My mama says I'm reckless, my daddy says
>    I'm wild,
> I ain't good lookin', but I'm somebody's
>    angel child.[126]

Taken as a whole, the blues lyrics immortalized by Bessie Smith had two characteristics of great significance. First, they were drawn from the black oral tradition's repository of rural folk blues; hence, they were familiar to African Americans. For the most part, she was able to avoid the more commercialized material from the vaudeville stage or Tin Pan Alley, concentrating instead on verse that evoked deeply felt responses from her audiences. The second characteristic of the blues lyrics Smith used was that, although they often addressed far-reaching social issues and concerns, they expressed her own feelings and experiences as a black woman. Their individuality and emotional honesty appealed not only to African Americans but also to certain sectors of the white population. Smith's blues verses were poetry set to music; they were like all great art in that they expressed human emotions that were universal.

Bessie Smith's personal life was full of the excesses, conflicts, and rebelliousness that she sang about with such conviction. She was married twice, and not a stranger to heartbreak. Her first husband, Earl Love, died shortly after their marriage. When she moved to Philadelphia in 1922, she met and then married Jack Gee, a night watchman who claimed he was a policeman. They separated seven years later, after a stormy and exhausting marriage that often deteriorated into angry physical brawls. During this period of her life, Bessie also had numerous lovers, both male and female. Among her known male lovers were the musicians Sidney Bechet, Porter Grainger, and Lonnie Johnson, all of whom worked with her during the 1920s. Her longest-lasting, and perhaps steadiest, relationship with a man was with Richard Morgan, a Chicago-based bootlegger and patron of black music. Morgan got to know her in 1924, during her initial visits to Chicago; he remained close to her up until her death in 1935 and was, in fact, driving her car when the accident occurred that killed her. As for female lovers, Smith was open with other women about her bisexuality, but does not seem to have shared much of this information with the men in her life. The sexual liaisons she had with other women tended to be short lived and relegated to a twilight zone of female social activity carried out in relative secrecy. They most often occurred when Smith was on the road with a show and involved other women in the troupe. They lasted for the duration of the tour or as long as her husband did not discover her indiscretions.[127]

Bessie Smith indulged her appetites generally. She ate and drank with gusto and was especially fond of home-cooked southern food and moonshine. She was a binge drinker who often drank to forget her troubles. Alcohol sometimes brought out a volcanic rage in her, and her drinking sprees often ended in violence. To compound the problem, Smith had a penchant for the night life of the urban underworld. She made regular nocturnal ventures into tenderloin districts all over the country and was equally at home in Chattanooga, Atlanta, Harlem, and Chicago. Her cousin, Ruby, recalled one such venture in Cincinnati:

Did we have a ball! We went into every joint, and Bessie knew more joints. I don't know how that woman knew so many joints, but she could take you into more beat up places. And we just did everything we were big enough to do from one place to another, and when we walked in there was no telling when we'd walk out again. Bessie stayed drunk, and me right along with her.[128]

On another occasion, Ruby described a notorious "buffet flat" (that is, a nightclub in a private house that catered to Pullman porters and TOBA entertainers) that Smith frequented whenever she performed at Detroit's Koppin Theatre: "It was nothing but faggots and bulldykes, a real open house. Everything went on in that house—tongue baths, you name it. They called them buffet flats because buffet means everything, everything that's in life. Bessie was well known in that place."[129] This pattern of excess was part of Smith's chaotic lifestyle. To escape the pressures of fame, and perhaps also the painful memories of her childhood, she turned to drunken revelry, combined with sexual and culinary gratification. Whether she was attending a party in the sporting district where "the funk was flying," as she liked to put it, or holding court in the railroad car she toured the South in, the cycle of overindulgence hampered her development as a blues artist, not to mention damaging her health.

The extreme behavior for which Smith became notorious was an obvious manifestation of her unresolved conflicts with herself and the world around her. On the one hand, she could be fun loving and generous to a fault, lavishing gifts on her companions, picking up all their bar tabs, even sending them on paid vacations. But on several occasions she also walked out on a road show, leaving the cast and crew without the money to pay their bills, and she at times fired her employees gratuitously. She displayed remarkable courage in the face of danger. During one altercation she pursued a male attacker even after he had buried a knife in her side; another time she single-handedly repulsed a Ku Klux Klan raiding party with a barrage of scurrilous invective. But she could also be a merciless bully and beat her adversaries senseless or attack them with no provocation. Great strength of character, courage, love, and will power were contradicted by deep hurt, anger, and an unremitting rage toward the society she lived in. Little wonder that Smith's favorite saying was, "I ain't never heard of such shit!" Sidney Bechet remarked:

She had this trouble in her, this thing that wouldn't let her rest sometimes, a meanness that came and took her over. But what she had was alive; she'd been through the whole book. . . . Someways, you could almost have said beforehand that there was some kind of accident, some bad hurt, coming to her. It was like she had that hurt inside her all the time, and she was just bound to find it.[130]

With the onset of the depression, Smith's fortunes plummeted along with those of most black entertainers. The advent of talking motion pictures was the death blow to vaudeville in general, and to the TOBA in particular. The record industry also suffered serious setbacks. The sales of records dwindled considerably because of the overall economic decline and the gains made by radio in the entertainment business. Swing dance music, played by white orchestras, became the popular commercial music of the era, and interest in the blues waned. Bessie Smith's record contract with Columbia was terminated in 1931. She recorded once more in 1933 at a special session arranged and paid for by John Hammond, but other than that her career as a recording artist was over. During one of her final recording sessions for Columbia, Smith made a record that was destined to become both her personal epitaph and a depression-era classic; it was entitled "Nobody Knows You When You're Down and Out":

> Once I lived the life of a millionaire,
> Spending my money, I didn't care,
> I carried my friends out for a good time,
> Buyin' bootleg liquor, champagne and wine.
>
> When I began to fall so low,
> I didn't have a friend, and no place to go,
> So if I ever get my hands on a dollar again,
> I'm gonna hold on to it 'til them eagles grin.
>
> Nobody knows you when you're down and out,
> In my pocket, not one penny,
> And my friends, I haven't got any,
> But if I ever get on my feet again,
> Then I'll meet all my long lost friends.
>
> It's mighty strange, but without a doubt,
> Nobody knows you when you're down and out.[131]

If Bessie Smith's final years did not yield to her the prominence and financial rewards commensurate with her vocal artistry, they were at least less turbulent and less emotionally traumatic for her than the previous decade had been. She was better able to control the drinking binges, and her relationship with Richard Morgan deepened into a loving and supportive companionship. Smith seemed to have mellowed with age, learning from her past mistakes.

With the record contract gone, she found that even singing engagements in clubs were hard to come by; at times, she had to rely on Morgan for financial help. Still, Bessie persevered and even maintained her famous biting sense of humor. W. C. Handy recalled a story she told him in New York, late in her career, about the park that the mayor of Memphis had named after him:

Exclaimed Bessie, "Mr. Handy, you ain't seen that park since they cleaned it up, have you?"
"No," I replied.
"They sit out there and sleep day and night," she said.
"Is that so?"
"Yes," she concluded. "One fellow was sitting on a bench asleep when a passing policeman tapped him under the feet and said, 'Wake up and go home.' The lounger brushed his eyes, looked at the officer, and said, 'Y'll white folks ain't got nothin' to do with me sleepin' here. This is Handy's park!' "[132]

Smith continued to perform the blues up until her death, at the age of forty-three, in 1937. Her fatal automobile accident in Mississippi came at a time when her career and the nation's economy were on the rebound.

While Bessie Smith never received official recognition in her lifetime, her important contributions to the blues idiom were eventually acknowledged by American music historians and scholars. Within African-American culture, she will always be the greatest woman blues singer, a heroine of the race who sang the common people's music like no one else. Her influence on American culture in general is impressive. More than any other black performer in the 1920s and 1930s, she was responsible for introducing the blues into the mainstream of popular American music. If Columbia Records reaped the financial benefits of this profitable enterprise, Smith and her public at least enjoyed the cultural fruits of these endeavors. Her music was not to be a passing commercial fad; it was an enduring and permeating infusion into the fabric of American music that would change the course of the entire culture over the next fifty years.

## "Wild Women Don't Get the Blues"

Black women played an uneven role in the making of the blues. At the beginning, they were all but invisible in the rural blues cultures that developed in the Mississippi Delta, East Texas, and the Piedmont. There were exceptions:

Josie Bush, Louise Johnson, Lucille Davis, and Mattie Delaney in the Mississippi Delta; Bessie Tucker and Ida Mack in East Texas. But for the most part, African-American women were missing from the rural blues, and not without good reason. Black families tended to be large in the rural South; childbearing began early and ended late. Birth control was never a priority because more children meant more hands to pick cotton. Hence, African-American women not only raised large families; they also worked in the fields alongside the men. These never-ending tasks left little time for cultural activities like performing with a blues ensemble. Furthermore, black women in the South had less social mobility than black men; it was much more difficult for them to be independent of their families and constantly on the move because of both the physical dangers inherent in a transient life and the stigma that went along with the vocation. Female blues artists were likely branded as "fallen women," while male blues artists were being touted as "free men." In the male-dominated rural black community, what was good for the man was often the undoing of the woman, at least where the blues were concerned. This array of social barriers and constraints militated against black women's entering into local blues cultures as performers. They were more welcome as fans.

In the vaudeville blues milieu, however, the situation was reversed. Black women were in great demand as performers; they were the divas who packed the crowds into the TOBA theaters and sold millions of records to an adoring public. Black men were relegated to a supportive role in the social hierarchy; they were the backup musicians and the warmup acts—the extras. For the black women at center stage, the ascendency of vaudeville blues created a showcase for their talent and gave them a platform from which to proselytize their side of the African-American experience. Not that show business did not have limitations; the industry was male-oriented, and its commercial imperatives often conflicted with the artistic and social goals of the classic blues women. Nevertheless, their status as "stars" tended to enhance their visibility and communicative powers significantly. Ultimately, their commanding presence in the vaudeville blues enterprise enabled them to promulgate a renewed feminist discourse within the black oral tradition.

The classic blues women's feminist discourse grappled with the race, class, and sexual injustices they encountered living in urban America. They were outspoken opponents of racial discrimination in all guises, and hence critical of the dominant white social order—even while benefiting from it more than most of their peers. They identified with the struggles of the masses of black people, empathized with the plight of the downtrodden, and sang out for social change. Within the black community, the classic blues women were also critical of the way they were treated by men, challenging the sexual double standard. Concurrently, they reaffirmed and reclaimed their feminine powers—sexual and spiritual—to remake the world in their own image and to their own liking. This included freedom of choice across the social spectrum—from political to sexual resistance, from black nationalism to lesbianism. Like the first-generation rural blues troubadours, the classic blues women were cultural rebels, ahead of the times artistically and in the forefront of resistance to all the various forms of domination they encountered.

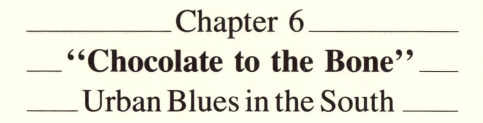

# Chapter 6
# "Chocolate to the Bone"
# Urban Blues in the South

The proximity of the cities of New Orleans, Atlanta, Birmingham, and Memphis to the cotton belt made them the first stops for black migrants fleeing the rural South. Legions of rural blues musicians merged their music with the styles and genres of African-American music already present in the cities. More often then not, the rural blues were the catalyst for the new blues styles that blossomed there. The scope of the music broadened. The piano became its premier solo instrument, while ensembles and vocalists experimented with interpretations of the blues song. A new urban blues tradition was in the making, and southern cities were its early breeding grounds.

## New Orleans: The Pleasure Capital of America

New Orleans was the oldest and most renowned city of leisure in the United States throughout the eighteenth and nineteenth centuries. Its French origins, coupled with Spanish, Creole, and African-American influences, set it far apart from the Anglo-American cultural norms that prevailed in the rest of the South. During the 1850s, New Orleans was the largest city in the South, with a total population of 125,000. It was famous for its elegant French opera house and its quadroon balls, at which beautiful young octoroon women were displayed for the city's white male aristocracy. Antebellum New Orleans was also renowned for the prevalence of prostitution. Early in the city's history, when men greatly outnumbered women, the French government sent prostitutes from Paris jails to New Orleans, where they established a strong presence that lasted many decades, and eventually became so prosperous that the city fathers attempted to license and tax them.[1]

The Civil War and its aftermath brought major changes to New Orleans and its red-light district. The city's slaveholding aristocracy lost much of their wealth and disintegrated as a social elite. A new order emerged in the tenderloin. Irish and Italian underworld elements now vied for control of the vice operations and their ascendancy dramatically altered the politics and culture of the red-light district.[2] The "uptown" section of New Orleans—also known as the "French Quarter"—became the center of the city's night life and vice operations. The French Quarter was traditionally populated by the "Creoles of color"—a "free" mulatto caste that had prospered in New Orleans before the war.[3] After the war, this mulatto population lost its special status and the mulattos' social and economic positions declined. They were subjected to the same Jim Crow restrictions imposed on the former slaves, and their neighborhoods degenerated into slums that were increasingly populated by the incoming foreign immigrants and black migrants.[4] By the 1880s, the French Quarter was poorer and more densely settled than any other section of the city. Sanitary conditions were deplorable. The water supply was often polluted; it came from local wells and needed to be boiled to make it suitable for drinking or cooking. There were no public sewage facilities; outdoor toilets were emptied into barrels, and the wastes were carried away on flatbed "aggravatin' wagons" to be dumped into the river. Leftover or spoiled food was customarily thrown into the streets for dog packs that roamed the neighborhood scavenging for edibles. The roads were not paved or even graveled; what sidewalks there were had been hastily constructed out of wooden planks. Combined with the humid climate and the heavy rainfall, these conditions transformed the French Quarter into a pungent cesspool. The filthy, muddy streets were sanctuaries for pestilent insects and breeding grounds for communicable diseases like smallpox and cholera. Mosquitoes, roaches, horseflies, and a distinctive malodor hovered over the area. Little wonder that the mortality rate in the Quarter was one of the highest in the South.[5]

The black population of New Orleans more than doubled between 1860 and 1880, rising from 25,425 to 57,017, according to the official census. For their own political advancement and protection, they organized clubs and benevolent societies, 226 of which were officially registered in the city between 1866 and 1880.[6] The clubs' social functions, rather than their political goals, involved more people and soon became their major concern. One of their most significant endeavors was the formation of marching brass bands.

New Orleans, because of its French heritage, always had a flair for marching bands and colorful parades. African Americans took over the tradition, then altered it to reflect and meet their own cultural needs. From the outset, the black marching bands of New Orleans were multifunctional; they played at political rallies, parades, picnics, lawn parties, fish fries, concerts, and funerals. Their music was an amalgam of European-American and African-American elements: the brass and reed instruments were European, but the rhythms were often traditional African ones. They played popular European and American martial music, but they also played spirituals and folk tunes. Furthermore, they tended to "rag" their marches, just as they did their own

music. This ubiquitous practice of separating the groundbeat from the melody
was inherited from their African homeland. These black marching bands were
the earliest training ground for many of the greatest first-generation New Orleans jazz musicians.[7]

During the final decades of the nineteenth century, New Orleans experienced both an economic upswing and heightening social tensions. The prosperity generated by the city's resurgence as a seaport and trade and transportation
center fueled business in the red-light district. The social tensions and violence
intensified with the continuing influx of Italian immigrants and black migrants. The native white population failed to distinguish between the two
groups; they subjected the newly arrived immigrants to the same discrimination and abuse that had always characterized their relations with African
Americans. A candid editorial in a New Orleans newspaper stated the common
position: "The Italians are corrupt and purchasable and according to the spirit
of our meaning when we speak of white man's government, they are as black
as the blackest Negro in existence."[8]

Among the city's working class, however, race relations were more amica-
ble. New Orleans was unique among southern cities in having some integrated
unions, and there was a history of solidarity between black and white workers
during strikes.[9] In the red-light district, Italians and African Americans also
forged good working relations. The peasant immigrants from southern Italy
and Sicily shared some important cultural traits with black migrants from the
rural South: they belonged to large extended families or clans, they were emotional and expressive people who liked to sing, dance, and socialize in an informal atmosphere, they were partial to improvised dance music played by
string bands, and they were attracted to the night life of the tenderloin. These
similarities were factors in the Italian gangsters' decision to hire black musicians to play in their saloons and cabarets, some of which also catered to an
African-American clientele.

While Italians were cementing their economic relations with African
Americans, local white hostility toward them reached a peak. In 1892, eleven
members of a Sicilian gang—the Matrangas clan—were lynched by a white
mob seeking revenge for the murder of an Irish policeman.[10] The tenderloin
then became the target of local reformers, who sought to constrain prostitution
through taxation and licensing. When that failed, they rallied behind an 1897
city ordinance that made it unlawful to engage in lewd dancing or sexual so-
licitation outside the thirty-eight-block area on the west side of the French
Quarter that contained the most prominent bordellos, and a small adjacent
neighborhood populated by black prostitutes. The former district was named
"Storyville" after Sidney Storey, the alderman who had authored the ordinance; the smaller one became known as "Black Storyville."[11]

With prostitution and its milieu thus restricted, Storyville soon became a compact haven for hedonism and vice. Inside the thirty-eight-block area a wide variety of amusements were available to the public. The cabarets catered to an exclusive clientele and featured expensive liquor and dancing with hostesses to the music of the house band. Champagne was the popular drink; the hostesses received a commission on every bottle they consumed with a customer. The most famous of the Storyville cabarets during this period were usually named for their proprietors: Billy Phillips', Eddie Grosheys', Pete Lala's, Rices', Hurtz and Nagels'. An exception was the Tuxedo Dance Hall, named after the formal dress of the house band; its proprietor was the notorious "Gyp the Blood." The honky-tonks were mostly neighborhood saloons that catered to a lower-class clientele. Liquor prices were half those of the cabarets. Liquor and beer were served out of barrels. Gambling was commonplace; frequently there was a pool table, and sometimes a piano. Like the cabarets, they were most often named for their owners. Honky-tonks were concentrated on Rampart and Perdido streets in the uptown area, where the black sporting crowd centered their activities. Arrest records for the neighborhood at the turn of the century list underworld characters with bizarre aliases like Drop o' Sack, Cinderella, Pudding Man, Willie the Pleaser, Ratty Kate, Diamond Dick, Lead Pencil, and Baggage Car Shorty. Other notable black underworld figures associated with the larger Storyville enclave were gamblers like Chicken Dick and the handsome ladies' man Chinee Morris; Bob Rowe, the district's leading sporting man, and his successor, Chuck Wade; Madame Papaloos, the reigning voodoo queen; and the district's most infamous outlaw, Aaron Harris.[12]

Violent shooting incidents were common in and around Storyville. Nearly everyone carried a handgun, since the ordinance prohibiting them was rarely enforced. In the summer of 1900, Robert Charles, a thirty-four-year-old black man, was drawn into a gunfight with a white policeman; both were wounded. Charles was pursued by the police, and there were further shootouts; by the time he was finally gunned down, he had shot twenty-seven white people, seven of whom died from their wounds. In retaliation, white vigilante gangs went on a rampage in the tenderloin, killing five African Americans and wounding and severely beating many more before order was restored by the state militia.[13] In the aftermath of another famous gunfight that took place in the tenderloin in 1913, the city's reform groups induced the municipal authorities to shut down Storyville for a while. A more effective shutdown on entertainment operations was ordered by the U.S. Navy in 1917 after a sailor on shore pass was killed within the boundaries of the district.[14] Storyville never overcame this closing. Many of its residents moved on to other urban tenderloins. The cycle of violence growing out of the district's social tensions had ultimately undermined its existence. Yet Storyville in its heyday was a haven for jazz and blues musicians.

## Early New Orleans Blues

New Orleans's fame as the birthplace of jazz tends to overshadow the city's early blues culture and the critical role that culture played in the birth of jazz. At the time there was little distinction between jazz and blues musicians. In particular, the piano "professors" in the tenderloin's brothels and saloons were comfortable with both traditions.

Before 1900, ragtime compositions and styles were in vogue among the piano players employed in the French Quarter. The evidence indicates, however, that by 1900, the rural blues were becoming as familiar to New Orleans piano players as were the ragtime favorites. A large contingent of piano players worked in the New Orleans tenderloin. Nowhere in the country (except possibly in St. Louis) was there a stronger African-American blues piano tradition during this period.

These musicians devised various means of producing blue notes on the piano—from special tuning schemes to playing major and minor keys simultaneously. The early piano blues numbers were referred to as "slow drags"; they were much slower paced than the ragtime "stomps" and were therefore ideal for erotic couple-dancing.

Two key figures in the marriage of the blues to the piano in New Orleans were Ferdinand "Jelly Roll" Morton and Tony Jackson. Both men were natives of New Orleans and rooted in its multifaceted musical culture. Jackson, born in 1876, and raised in the uptown area, learned to play in the local honky-tonks. He had an excellent ear and an excellent memory for melodies. He played the latest popular ragtime tunes in his own distinct single-handed ragged style and is remembered as having known as many as a thousand songs. New Orleans jazz musician Roy Carew described a Tony Jackson performance just after the turn of the century:

> It was the most remarkable playing and singing I had ever heard; the songs were just some of the popular songs of the day and time; but the beat of the bass and the embellished treble of the piano told me at once that there was something new to me in playing. And the singing was just as distinctive. It was a man's voice of very good quality which rang true on every tone; a vibrant voice that took each note with easy precision; a happy voice that had at times a sort of wild earnestness to it. High notes, low notes, fast or slow, the singer executed them all perfectly, blending them into a perfect performance with the remarkable piano style.[15]

After a 1904 road tour, Tony Jackson moved to Chicago, where he remained for the rest of his career.

Jelly Roll Morton recalled that the earliest blues he heard in New Orleans were performed by Mamie Desdoumes, a "hustlin' woman" who lived next door to him when he was a child. By the turn of the century, her blues singing was popular in New Orleans. Mamie played in the dance halls along Perdido Street, as well as at the exclusive bordellos of Lulu White and Hattie Rogers. Her blues signature piece was later recorded by Jelly Roll Morton as "Mamie's Blues":

> I stood on the corner, my feet was dripping wet,
> Stood on the corner, my feet was dripping wet,
> I asked every man I met:
>
> Can't give me a dollar, give me a lousy dime,
> You can't give me a dollar, give me a lousy dime,
> Just to feed that hungry man of mine.
>
> I got a husband and I got a kid man too,
> I got a husband, I got a kid man too,
> My husband can't do what my kid man can do.
>
> I like the way he cooks my cabbage for me,
> I like the way he cooks my cabbage for me,
> Looks like he sets my natural soul free.[16]

Game Kid, a "howler" and a hopeless alcoholic, was a prominent blues piano man in the district just after the turn of the century. According to Morton, he was best known for a blues number with the following lyrics:

> I could sit here and think a thousand miles
>     away,
> Yes, I could sit right here and think a
>     thousand miles away,
> I got the blues so bad I cannot remember the
>     day.[17]

Among Morton's better-known contemporaries were Albert Carroll, who also served as musical director for black minstrel troupes touring out of New Orleans; Alfred Wilson, a handsome mulatto hopelessly addicted to opium, yet talented enough to hold the "professor's" chair at Lulu White's Mahogany Hall until his death at the age of twenty-five; Buddy Carter, renowned for his honky-tonk blues and stomps; Sammie Davis, a coeval of Morton's who also idolized Tony Jackson; and Kid Ross, the best-known white pianist in New

Orleans to play "hot" music. These men formed the nucleus of the city's indigenous school of blues piano players.[18]

It was a fusion of elements from the ragtime and the blues traditions that produced New Orleans jazz: performers were not only "ragging" tunes but also using blue notes, blues song structures, and the "deep" blues tones and timbres associated with rural Delta blues. The breakthrough was made by the "uptown" black dance bands.

## New Orleans Dance Bands

The earliest dance bands evolved from either the marching bands or the older string bands. In the first category was the dance orchestra of John Robichoux, which had evolved out of the Excelsior Brass Band in 1893. Robichoux was a member of the New Orleans mulatto caste; his band was prominently featured at the outdoor dances held in Lincoln Park throughout the 1890s. The ensemble, which included small brass and reed sections, played the popular dance music of the era in a style that New Orleans jazzmen have described as "sweet." In the second category were the smaller string bands that played for the fish fries and lawn parties, which were the New Orleans version of the urban "rent party." Charles Galloway headed up one of the best-known string bands in the city. A native son, born in the French Quarter in 1869, Charles played guitar and also operated a small barbershop in the district; he booked his band out of his shop. Another local guitarist who grew up playing in a string band was Lonnie Johnson. Pops Foster recalls:

> Lonnie Johnson and his daddy and his brother used to go all over New Orleans playing on street corners. Lonnie played guitar, and his daddy and brother played violin. Lonnie was the only guy we had around New Orleans who could play jazz guitar. He was great on guitar.[19]

Johnson went on to become one of the most influential urban blues guitarists of the twentieth century, while Charles Galloway's band provided a forum for the founding father of New Orleans jazz, Charles "Buddy" Bolden.

Bolden was born in New Orleans on September 6, 1877, to a poor family that was active in a local Baptist church. He began to play the cornet when he was seventeen years old and shortly thereafter joined Charles Galloway's band. Bolden's natural talent soon garnered him a leadership position in the group, which quickly evolved into one of the most sought out musical groups in the local black community. Buddy Bolden did not imitate other local cornetists. He played by ear the music he heard around him, adapting it to his horn. This practice led to a new fusion of ragtime styles, marching-band music, black sacred music, and the rural blues. His small brass ensemble created a novel and exciting sound. In no time it had eclipsed the local string-band tradition. Bill Matthews, a contemporary of Bolden's, characterized his playing as follows:

> He was one of the sweetest trumpet players on waltzes and things like that and on those old slow blues, that boy could make the women jump out the window. On those old slow, low down blues, he had a moan in his cornet that went all through you, just like you were in church or something. Everybody was crazy about Bolden when he'd blow a waltz, schottische or old low down blues. He was the sweetest trumpet player in the world.[20]

Buddy Bolden's playing style has been described as "wide open," "tough," and, especially, "loud." Legend has it that his horn could be heard ten and even twelve miles from where it was being played. One local musician recalled that Bolden once "blew the turning slide out of his horn while playing a version of 'Ride on King.' " Many New Orleans natives remembered his famous musical battles with John Robichoux's band in the local parks. Hired to play at Johnson's Park when it opened for business next to Lincoln Park, where Robichoux's band was featured, Bolden's powerful cornet solos reputedly drew the crowd away from his rival, "callin' his chillun home."[21]

By the turn of the century, Bolden was the undisputed king of New Orleans black dance music. He and his band were making a living as musicians for the first time. In addition to the park concerts, they were hired to play in the local dance halls and for the private parties sponsored by the city's black social clubs. Their repertoire included spirituals such as "Ride on King," "Go Down Moses," "Nearer My God to Thee," and "What a Friend We Have in Jesus"—the last two were played for funeral marches. They also played the standard New Orleans marches, such as "Didn't He Ramble?" "Panama," and "Tiger Rag," as well as uptempo dance numbers such as "Don't Nobody Go Away," "If You Don't Shake It, You Don't Get No Cake," and "The House Got Ready." The blues were a major part of his repertoire. A Creole musician named Peter Bocage recalled that Bolden "had a good style in the blues and all that stuff. . . . He played everything in b-flat. He played a lot of blues, slow drag, not too many fast numbers."[22]

Bolden's band not only played the blues; they also sang them, often improvising their own lyrics for folk standards such as "Make Me a Pallet on the Floor" and "Careless Love." Their most famous vocal blues number was an improvisational tour de force that came to be called both "Funky Butt" and

"Buddy Bolden's Blues." The song was based on a secular black folksong, initially named "Emancipation Day," which was well known because of the following floating verses:

> I thought I hee'd Abe Lincoln shout,
> Rebels, close down them plantations and
>     let all them niggers out!
> I'm positively sure I hee'd Mr. Lincoln shout.
>
> I thought I hee'd Mr. Lincoln say,
> Rebels, close down them plantations and
>     let all them niggers out!
> You gonna lose your war, git on your knees
>     and pray!
> That's the words I hee'd Mr. Lincoln say.[23]

The lyrics were updated by Willie Cornish, a trombone player with Bolden's band, to commemorate a pungent odor released by a fellow band member at a local dance:

> I thought I heard Buddy Bolden say,
> Funky Butt, funky butt, take it away,
> You're nasty, you're dirty, take it away,
> I thought I heard old Bolden say.
>
> I thought I heard Buddy Bolden shout,
> Open up the window and let that bad air out,
> Open up the window and let that bad air out,
> I thought I heard old Bolden shout.[24]

This new version delighted Bolden's fans and soon became his signature piece; a local dance hall that often featured the band was renamed "Funky Butt Hall" by its patrons. Jelly Roll Morton included an additional verse in his recording of this New Orleans classic many years later:

> I thought I heard Judge Fogarty say,
> Thirty days in the market, take him away,
> Give him a broom, take the prisoner away
> I heard Judge Fogarty say.[25]

It is likely that this verse also came from Bolden's band, since the judge in question had sentenced a few of the band members to short terms in the municipal jail for various misdemeanors.[26]

The prominent role that vocals played in Buddy Bolden's band suggests that this new New Orleans dance music, which came to be called jazz, was far from being exclusively instrumental in its earliest manifestations. The band was renowned for "playing the dozens" (exchanging scatological barbs) just before their performances, most likely to warm up the audience. Trombonists Willie Cornish and Frankie Deusen and banjo player Lorenzo Staulz are remembered for their singing. Staulz was notorious for his bawdy verbal improvisations, especially when singing "Funky Butt." Bolden seems not to have handled any of the vocal chores himself, although he made up lyrics and his cornet playing was said to mimic a human voice, "moaning" on blues selections bent or slurred with a variety of mutes.

During Bolden's reign as the leading black musician of New Orleans, he lived as he played—with a reckless abandon. Always a heavy drinker, in 1907 he was declared insane and committed to a state mental institution, where he remained until his death in 1932. During that time, the musical style he had pioneered flourished, first in New Orleans and then wherever there was a black urban population.

Buddy Bolden's most significant musical innovation was to rearrange the New Orleans dance band to better accommodate the blues. By fusing elements from the string bands and the marching bands, he created a new kind of ensemble. The string instruments—bass fiddle, guitar, banjo—became the rhythm section, along with a drum. The front-line instruments were clarinets, trombones, and Bolden's cornet.[27] Bolden positioned the rural folk blues at the center of his musical experiments and thus paved the way for other musicians to develop original and experimental styles. Reminiscing about a newcomer to the New Orleans music scene, Mutt Carey recalled:

I remember once when Louis Armstrong came out to Lincoln Park in New Orleans to listen to the Kid Ory Band. . . . I let Louis sit in my chair. Now at that time I was the "Blues King" of New Orleans, and when Louis played that day he played more blues than I ever heard in my life. It never did strike my mind that blues could be interpreted so many different ways. Every time he played a chorus, it was different and you knew it was the blues. Yes, it was all blues what I mean.[28]

## Atlanta: Showcase of the New South

As the showcase of the "New South"—which relinquished the antebellum plantation system for a network of cotton mills and textile factories—Atlanta

became a major commerce and transportation center in the wake of Reconstruction, attracting large numbers of both black and white rural migrants. A
black ghetto sprang up in the western end of the city adjacent to a thriving
red-light district; by 1900 there were over thirty-five thousand African
Americans living in Atlanta, one-fourth of the total population.[29] Rapid
growth heightened social and racial tensions. The crime rate skyrocketed, and
by 1905 Atlanta's was the highest in the nation. Close to 90 percent of those
arrested (twenty-one thousand in 1900) were lower-class African Americans
who as a group were illiterate and chronically underemployed, and thus vulnerable to vagrancy laws.[30] (W. E. B. Du Bois, who taught at Atlanta University during this period, referred to this element of the black population as the
"submerged tenth.")[31] The city was rigidly segregated. Long-standing racial
antagonisms ignited a full-scale race riot in 1906 in which several people were
killed and scores injured.[32] Yet despite this racial violence and the rebirth of
the Ku Klux Klan in 1915 on Stone Mountain outside Atlanta, the city's black
population continued to increase. In 1910, the number of black residents was
fifty thousand; in 1920 it surpassed sixty thousand, and by 1930 it reached
ninety thousand—one-third of the city's total population.[33]

Decatur Street, the showcase of the night-life district, was lined with cabarets, theaters, saloons, restaurants, and barbershops. Charles Bailey's 81 Theatre was located on Decatur Street, as was Shorter's Barbershop—the favorite
hangout of the African-American sporting crowd. The saloons stayed open
around the clock, and the street was crowded day and night. The bordellos
were located on the adjacent Courtland Street. The most visible black gangsters
ran saloons: Joe Slocum, Walter Harrison, Henry Thomas, Lonnie Reid,
"Handsome Harry," and "Lucky Sambo." Perry Bradford, in his memoirs,
describes the fashionable apparel favored by Atlanta's more successful gangsters:

> The white and colored underworld characters could be spotted on sight,
> for they wouldn't wear anything but tailor-made Plymouth Rock suits.
> They had bell-bottom pants. The John T. Stetson-Miller block top pieces
> that these pimps wore were sold for ten semoleums, but they brought six
> needy bucks in the pawn shop.[34]

By the beginning of the 1920s, the night life subculture of Decatur Street rivaled that of Beale Street in Memphis and that of Storyville in its heyday; as
the lyrics from the popular "Atlanta Blues" put it:

> They got plenty good liquor,
> And everything for sale,
> If you get in trouble,
> You won't have to go to jail.

Step out in Atlanta,
Any time of night,
You'll get your lovin' on Decatur Street,
In Atlanta, down on Decatur Street.[35]

The piano was the first musical instrument to be associated with the blues in Atlanta. Piano players were in great demand in the tenderloin saloons and brothels even before World War I. Thomas Dorsey grew up in Atlanta during this period and was known as "Barrelhouse Tom" on Decatur Street. He vaguely recalled several fellow piano players who featured the blues in their repertoires. They included the polished and versatile house pianists at the 81 Theatre like Ed Butler and Eddie Heywood and bordello and barrelhouse musicians like Long Boy, Edgar Webb, Lark Lee, and James Hemingway.[36] Heywood moved on to a successful career as an accompanist, composer, and band leader in New York, while the mammoth Hemingway, reputed to weigh 375 pounds, was one of many Atlanta-based piano players to migrate north to Detroit and Chicago. Others included Dorsey himself, Charlie Spand, and Rufus "Speckled Red" Perryman, who made the first commercial recording of "The Dirty Dozen" in the 1920s. Perryman learned to play this barrelhouse blues number in the Atlanta red-light district.[37] Perry Bradford recalled that piano players Paul Turner and Frank Rachel were featured combatants at the "cakewalking" contests (dance and piano) that were the rage in the prewar years.[38] A popular blues lyric from this era expresses the credo of the Atlanta tenderloin and the important role of the piano in its night life:

Down in Atlanta, G.A.,
Under the viaduc everyday,
Drinking corn and hollering hooray,
Piano playing until the break of day.[39]

After World War I, piano players remained in the forefront of Atlanta blues—and of the city's popular black music in general. An elite group of African-American pianists continued to be key figures in the local entertainment business, while a more plebeian group played in the tenderloin saloons and brothels. The elite included Graham Jackson, who succeeded Eddie Heywood as house pianist at the 81 Theatre; Troy Snapp, who worked as Ma Rainey's accompanist and band leader while she was still based in Georgia; and T. Neal Montgomery and Harvey Quiggs, both of whom fronted bands at the Atlanta Roof Gardens—a fashionable white nightclub in downtown Atlanta. These black commercial dance bands played ragtime, early jazz, vaudeville tunes, and blues. Montgomery also worked as the session pianist on several vaudeville blues recordings cut in Atlanta by Okeh and Columbia in the 1920s.[40]

At the other end of the spectrum were the legions of migrant piano players playing and singing a rougher "barrelhouse" blues style in Atlanta's tenderloin district and the surrounding black enclaves. They included obscure legends with fanciful names such as Bell Street Slim and Soup Stick and youthful prodigies such as Big Maceo Merriweather and William "Piano Red" Perryman, younger brother of Speckled Red.

Merriweather's family moved to College Park, outside Atlanta, in 1920, when he was fifteen. Already a big-framed youth and a strong vocalist, he immediately took up piano, learning by watching others play the blues at local cafes and house parties. By the time he migrated north to Detroit in 1924, he had developed into a forceful piano player. Later in the decade, he emerged as one of the most important blues players in the Midwest.[41]

William "Piano Red" Perryman was born on the west side of the Atlanta tenderloin in 1911. He grew up with a piano in his house, where he first learned to play the blues with help from his older brother Rufus. While still in his teens, he graduated to playing for local rent parties. Fried fish, "white lightning," and "slow blues" were the staples at these weekend gatherings. As Piano Red recalled:

> You couldn't make a livin' playin' them rent parties, but you could have a good time. You could make a little something extra, eat and drink all you want, and hang around with the other musicians. There was a lot of piano players back then. Old Soup Stick was a good one, played that low-down type blues. Then there was them boys from Spartanburg I used to run around with—Ted Wright and Colfield West. Oh, there was a lot of them, but mostly they didn't have no names—just come and go.[42]

Unlike most of Atlanta's blues piano players, Piano Red remained based in Atlanta for his entire career, which spanned five decades. He made his first recordings with Blind Willie McTell in the mid 1930s; then in the postwar years he became "Dr. Feelgood," the popular host of a daily blues radio show broadcase on WERD.[43]

Throughout the 1920s, Atlanta was the major race recording site in the South and therefore attractive to migrant blues musicians. The two major race record labels active in Atlanta were Okeh and Columbia.

The man responsible for the Okeh recording sessions in the city was Polk Brockman, a white Atlanta native who got into the record business after taking over the phonograph department of his father's furniture store. Brockman had little interest in the blues, but when he realized that money could be made selling black secular and sacred recordings, he made a deal with Ralph Peer at Okeh Records. In essence, Polk Brockman became Peer's surrogate in Atlanta, and eventually in other southern cities like Birmingham, New Orleans, and Dallas. The best-known rural blues artists he signed for recording sessions included the Mississippi Sheiks and Blind Lemon Jefferson. On the local black music scene, he preferred the vaudeville performers who played at the 81 Theatre; it was there that he came across Eddie Heywood, and the famous comedy duo of Butterbeans and Susie and arranged recording sessions for them. His most prolific and profitable recording artist was a local preaching phenomenon, the Reverend J. M. Gates, who had a large following in Atlanta's black community.[44] Later in the decade, Brockman was joined by Frank Walker of Columbia Records, who made frequent trips to Atlanta to supervise recording sessions. Among those he recorded were Lillian Glinn and Blind Willie McTell.

## Atlanta Blues Legends

By the mid-1920s, blues guitar players were making their presence felt in Atlanta alongside the blues piano players. The guitarists came from the surrounding countryside, where the cotton economy was declining. Pegleg Howell and Blind Willie McTell were already fixtures on the Atlanta blues scene. They were joined by the Hicks brothers, Curley Weaver, and Buddy Moss—all of whom became key figures in the local blues culture. Charlie and Robert Hicks grew up in the small rural community of Walnut Grove in Walton County, about twenty-five miles east of Atlanta. Charlie was born there on March 11, 1900, and Robert on September 11, 1902. Neither got much schooling, and both worked long hours in the cotton fields while still boys. Charlie began to play a guitar around 1915 and Robert soon thereafter. Both developed an odd flailing style usually associated with the traditional claw-hammer banjo.[45] Charlie moved to Atlanta in 1923, and Robert followed a year later. Both tried a variety of working-class jobs and played music on the side. Robert Hicks was working as a cook at Tidwells' Barbecue, north of Atlanta, when he came to the attention of a Columbia record producer, Dan Hornsby. Besides recording Hicks, Hornsby also had him dress up in a white chef's outfit for publicity photos—and gave him the nickname ''Barbecue Bob.'' By this time, 1927, his standard instrument was a twelve-string guitar, just like Blind Willie McTell's. Hicks's blues releases proved to be extremely popular: his sales were well ahead of those of other local blues musicians, and he went on to record fifty-six songs in three years.[46] Those recordings include such standard folk blues as ''Po' Boy, Long Ways from Home,'' ''Honey, You Don't Know My Mind,'' and ''Motherless Chile Blues.''

> If I mistreat you, gal, I sure don't mean no harm,
> If I mistreat you, gal, I sure don't mean no harm,
> I'm just a motherless chile and I don't know
>     right from wrong.[47]

He also recorded gospel standards—"When the Saints Go Marching In" and "Jesus' Blood Can Make Me Whole"—and several partly original compositions. The best known was "Mississippi Heavy Water Blues," "Easy Rider, Don't You Deny My Name," "Dollar Down," and "Chocolate to the Bone."

> So glad I'm brownskin, so glad I'm brownskin,
> Chocolate to the bone,
> So glad I'm brownskin, chocolate to the bone,
> And I got what it takes to make a monkey man
>     leave his home.[48]

Robert Hicks's inventive lyrics in part accounted for his popularity; they were usually humorous, proverbial, and sometimes even playful, although he was also capable of writing social commentary, as evident in his 1930 comment on the Great Depression, "We Sure Got Hard Times Now." He embellished his strong voice with both growling and falsetto. His diction was clear and his singing style was as percussive as his guitar playing. He used a bottleneck regularly, while his right hand strummed out insistent rhythms and steadily snapped the bass string. It was an elemental style that relied on only one or two chord changes and an open Spanish tuning, more reminiscent of Charley Patton or even "Ragtime Texas" Henry Thomas than the Piedmont guitarists. From all indications, Hicks was a heavy drinker and a ladies' man with a penchant for fast living; his sudden popularity as a blues recording artist only heightened these tendencies. In October 1931, at the age of twenty-nine, he died from a combination of tuberculosis and pneumonia. His death so adversely affected his older brother Charlie that his marriage broke up and he became an embittered alcoholic, eventually dying in the state prison after being convicted of murder.[49]

Curley Weaver was a boyhood friend of the Hicks brothers; his mother, Savannah, most likely taught both the Hicks brothers and Curley how to play the guitar. Weaver was born into a musical family on March 25, 1904; he was playing a guitar at the age of ten. As a teenager he roamed about Walton County with a gifted young harmonica player named Eddie Mapp, seeking out the best local blues musicians. Weaver and Mapp eventually followed the Hicks brothers to Atlanta in 1925, where they joined their blues entourage. In 1928, Robert Hicks helped to arrange recording sessions with Columbia Records for Curley Weaver; the next year Weaver and Mapp recorded in New

York for a second label. Two years later Weaver was the lead guitarist for the
Georgia Cotton Pickers—which also featured Robert Hicks on second guitar
and a youthful Buddy Moss on harmonica. On all of these recordings Weaver
demonstrated his dexterity on the guitar. He could duplicate Robert Hicks's
archaic flailing style or he could emulate the subtle finger-picking style associated with the Piedmont blues tradition. Moreover, he was an inventive solo
guitarist and an excellent small ensemble player.

Weaver remained in Atlanta through the depression years. He teamed up
with various local bluesmen, including Blind Willie McTell, with whom he
would occasionally play for white audiences at the popular Pig 'n' Whistle
drive-in. In the 1930s he was also part of a well-known local blues trio along
with guitarist Jonas Brown and the legendary harmonica player ''Bo Weevil,''
who also played on the streets with Blind Willie McTell. Of the two harmonica players Weaver had associated with earlier in the decade, one was dead
and the other was in jail: Eddie Mapp was murdered in the Atlanta tenderloin
in 1930 when he was just twenty years old and embarking on a promising
career as a blues musician; Buddy Moss was looking forward to an equally
promising career when he was sentenced to prison in 1935.[50]

Eugene ''Buddy'' Moss was born in rural Hancock County southwest of
Atlanta on January 26, 1914. His family moved to Augusta when he was four
years old, and he moved to Atlanta in 1928. He was only fifteen, but he was
already a fluent blues harmonica player. Robert Hicks took him under his wing
and taught him how to play the guitar; he also learned from Curley Weaver
and from the recordings of Blind Blake. Moss's first opportunity to record
came in 1930 with the Georgia Cotton Pickers. His lively harmonica work on
this session was very similar to Eddie Mapp's playing. He recorded his first
solo in 1933. By that time he had mastered the Piedmont playing style epitomized by Blind Blake's guitar wizardry. In addition, he had developed into a
first-rate blues composer. His songs tended to be lean and unpretentious—in
''Hard Road Blues,'' he evoked a stark image of the effect of the depression
on those it displaced:

> Walkin' down the hard road done wore the soles off my shoes,
> Walkin' down the hard road done wore the soles off my shoes,
> My soles are ragged, I got those hard road blues.
>
> I lay down last night, a thousand things on my mind,
> I lay down last night, a thousand things on my mind,
> Goin' walk down these hard roads, just to cure my low down mind.[51]

At the time of his imprisonment in 1935, Buddy Moss was on the verge of
blues stardom. He was one of a mere handful of blues artists still being re-

corded at the height of the depression—not only in Atlanta but on the entire eastern seaboard. While Moss languished in prison, Blind Boy Fuller emerged as the East Coast's most formidable blues musician. Fuller sounded a lot like Moss, an irony that was no doubt noticed by the imprisoned bluesman. Roy Dunn, an Atlanta-based blues guitarist who was a friend of Moss's during this period, stated:

> Buddy Moss, he was still a young man when they throwed him in jail. About 20 or so I reckon. He was jus' then catchin' on, making records and all. Jus' bout to hit it big so when he went to prison it kinda broke his spirit. Couldn't do nothin' but watch it pass on by. Later on, some white record man got him paroled for his singing. He went to North Carolina and we didn't see him around here for a long spell.[52]

Pegleg Howell and His Gang and the Georgia Cotton Pickers were trios popular in the late 1920s. The Star Band, a loose ensemble of Atlanta blues musicians active in the 1930s, featured guitars, fiddles, washboards, harmonicas, jugs, and even brass and reed instruments. The Star Band was built around guitarists Jonas Brown and his brother Hollis, fiddler Ollie Griffin, multi-instrumentalist Charlie Rambo, and Cliff Lee. They never recorded as a unit, but their style has been described as closer to the Memphis and Louisville jug-band tradition than the rural African-American string-band tradition.[53] In retrospect, the ensemble blues of the Star Band can be seen as too little and too late. On the eve of World War II, the Atlanta blues scene was still suffering a long, slow decline. The depression put an end to the thriving night-life subculture along Decatur Street; abandoned buildings, pawn shops, and storefront churches replaced the saloons, theaters, and cafes.[54] In addition, the Atlanta blues community had lost too much talent. Robert Hicks, Eddie Anthony, and Eddie Mapp were dead; Charlie Hicks and Pegleg Howell were no longer active in local blues circles; Buddy Moss was in prison. In one way or another, they had all succumbed to the hedonism and violence endemic to the urban tenderloins and slums. The end of an era was at hand.

## Birmingham Blues

Birmingham's proximity to the coal fields in northern Alabama was the major factor in its development as one of the first industrial centers in the New South. In addition to the coal mines, there were numerous steel mills near the city and, later, factories that manufactured steel products. It was a working-class town with a strong labor movement organized into segregated local unions. However, the segregated unions had a history of cooperating with each other to prevent either group of workers from being used against the other as strikebreakers. Some of the larger industrial unions in the region, most notably the United Mine Workers and later the Congress of Industrial Organizations, even experimented with integrated unions, hoping to build more solidarity between black and white workers.[55]

Although lacking the kind of wide-open red-light district found in other urban centers that had rich blues traditions, Birmingham did have its share of honky-tonks, house parties, a segregated public park called East End Park where black musicians congregated, and a TOBA theater—the Frolic. In addition, it had a rapidly growing black population of rural migrants attracted by the upsurge of jobs in the mining and steel industries after the turn of the century.

Here too the piano was identified with the earliest blues recalled. Perry Bradford maintained that the piano player responsible for introducing the rolling left-handed bass figures associated with boogie woogie to Chicago pianists was a Birmingham native called "Lost John," who visited Chicago in 1908.[56] Cow Cow Davenport and Pinetop Smith did much to popularize the boogie-woogie fast blues style in the 1920s; both spent their formative years in Birmingham before moving on to national acclaim. Charles "Cow Cow" Davenport was the city's best-known blues pianist before World War I; Clarence "Pinetop" Smith held that distinction immediately after the war. Davenport relocated in Atlanta in 1915 and then moved north; Smith was a regular attraction at the East End Park before moving to Pittsburgh in 1920. In their wake, several younger piano players came to the forefront of Birmingham's blues circles, including Robert McCoy, John Bell, Mack Rineheart, and Walter Roland. McCoy grew up in the city and heard Cow Cow Davenport and Pinetop Smith play the blues at his father's house parties; he later went on to record in a piano-guitar duet in the 1930s, as did Rineheart. Roland played piano and guitar; he was popular enough to record on his own and back up Lucille Bogan, who was Birmingham's best-known female blues singer. Bogan was a long-time resident of the city who first recorded with the Okeh label in 1923; during the next fifteen years, she recorded many songs for several other companies, at times using the pseudonym Bessie Jackson. She recorded the initial versions of two numbers that went on to become urban blues standards: "Sloppy Drunk Blues" and "Black Angel Blues" (later called "Sweet Little Angel"). In addition, she made a number of blues recordings in which the subject of prostitution was approached realistically and from a woman's point of view: "Payroll Blues," "New Way Blues," "Coffee Grinding Blues," "Stew Meat Blues," "Tricks Ain't Walkin' No More" (the urban blues classic), and "B. D. Women Blues" (B. D. may be a reference to "bull dagger," the southern black term for lesbians):

Comin' a time B. D. women ain't going to
    need no men,
Comin' a time B. D. women ain't going to
    need no men,
Ah the way they treat us is a low-down
    and dirty sin.

B. D. women, they all done learnt their plan,
B. D. women, they all done learnt their plan,
They can lay their jive just like a not
    kind man.

B. D. women, B. D. women, you know they sure
    is rough,
B. D. women, B. D. women, you know they sure
    is rough,
They drink plenty of whiskey and they sure
    do strut their stuff.[57]

By the late 1920s, when mobile recording units began to make periodic visits to Birmingham, a group of blues musicians schooled in the rural folk traditions of Alabama's black belt moved into the forefront of the Birmingham blues scene. Foremost among them were two harmonica players, Burl "Jaybird" Coleman and George "Bullet" Williams. Coleman was born in 1896; his parents were sharecroppers near Gainesville, Alabama. He learned to play the harmonica by the time he was twelve. During World War I, he served in the army; afterward, he settled in the Birmingham-Bessemer region, where he remained based for the rest of his life. He picked up the nickname "Jaybird" while in the army; it referred to his independent personality and his habit of getting away from his military surroundings whenever he could manage it. When he was finally recorded in the late 1920s, his style and material revealed a lingering rural character. The numbers Coleman cut were all blues; their most noticeable quality was their indebtedness to the oral tradition of African Americans. He would follow his vocal lines with an instrumental response, and his lyrics were invariably a string of one-liners reminiscent of the phrases sung in field hollers or worksongs. The result was a call and response musical pattern with the vocal leading and the harmonica answering it. Jaybird's most acclaimed release was "Trunk Busted—Suitcase Full of Holes" and "Mean Old Trouble Blues"; the latter offers a good example of the musician's elementary arrangement of blues lyrics in free association:

> When a man gets in trouble, every woman
>   throws him down,
> I'm tired and worried, don't know what
>   to do,
> When a man gets in trouble, every woman
>   throws him down,
> I'm so worried, don't know what to do,
> I woke up this morning, mama, feeling sad
>   and blue,
> But the woman had done quit me, didn't
>   have nowhere to go,
> When I'm in my good whiskey, this the way
>   I sing the blues.[58]

George "Bullet" Williams also exhibited strong rural influences in his blues style. Like Coleman, he frequently used one-liners with responses from his harmonica. He recorded both a traditional train-imitation blues, "Frisco Leaving Birmingham," and a chase blues reminiscent of the worksong "The Escaped Convict." Williams grew up near Selma, Alabama, where he learned to play the harmonica. While still in his teens, he moved to Birmingham and stayed in the area for most of the 1920s. After a few recording sessions in Chicago, he ended up in the Mississippi Delta, where he played regularly with Big Joe Williams and Booker White until his death from alcoholism in the 1940s.

Bullet Williams and Jaybird Coleman had brief associations with the famous Birmingham Jug Band in the late twenties and early thirties. The group was closely identified with the Rabbit Foot Minstrels, with whom they toured during the same period. The personnel fluctuated from year to year. At one time or another, it included, besides Williams and Coleman, guitarists One-Armed Dave, Doctor Scott, Big Joe Williams, and Ben Covington, who also played the harmonica. The jug blower was called Honey Cup, the washboard player was New Orleans Slide. When not on the road, many of the members of the Birmingham Jug Band spent time in the city they were named after. The band made nine recordings for Okeh label in Atlanta in 1930; one was a rendition of "John Henry" called "Bill Wilson," in which the hero was a "wagon-driving man." Their music was popular enough in Birmingham to inspire the formation of Bogan's Birmingham Busters in the mid-thirties after the Birmingham Jug Band fell apart. The group was made up of musicians associated with Lucille Bogan, who, according to one member, was the group's manager. By the late 1920s, the guitar was the most popular instrument in Birmingham blues circles. The best-known local guitarists were Sonny

Scott, who backed up Lucille Bogan; R. D. Norwood, who made a few recordings accompanying Jaybird Coleman; and Bob Campbell and George To-
rey, who were both in Bogan's Birmingham Busters.

Jefferson County, which includes the cities of Birmingham and Bessemer,
was a hotbed of gospel quartet singing during the 1920s and the 1930s.
Groups like the Foster Singers and the Four Eagles were pioneers of the gospel
quartet style, and the popular Birmingham Jubilee Singers recorded more
titles than did all of the city's blues musicians put together. Thus, the gospel
tradition in the area appears to have overshadowed Birmingham's early blues
milieu.[59]

Birmingham, Atlanta, New Orleans, and Memphis were the first cities to
absorb significant numbers of rural black migrants. By the turn of the century,
these migrants had brought blues songs and styles into the cities, where the
new music was picked up by indigenous black musicians—tenderloin piano
players, vaudeville blues vocalists, and dance bands—and adapted to an urban
environment. The mix of blues and ragtime inspired the birth of jazz, while
the convergence of various African-American musical genres and styles resulted in a reformulation of the blues tradition. City-based black musicians
gave the blues the sounds of city life. This transition was nowhere more evident than in Memphis, Tennessee, where an urban blues culture established its
most important beachhead in the South.

## Memphis: Beale Street Melting Pot

The Memphis blues culture before World War II can be likened to a savory pot
of gumbo. The basic ingredients came from the rural blues hotbeds in northern
Mississippi and western Tennessee. The better known of these were located
just south of Memphis in the Mississippi Delta towns of Hernando, Clarksdale, and Drew. The hill country northeast of the Delta and southeast of Memphis, famous for its African-American fife-and-drum bands, also contributed
to the Memphis blues gumbo. But the most important country blues ingredients came from northeast of Memphis. The small towns in this region were the
home base for several blues musicians who were also well known on Beale
Street. In Ashport, Jim Guffin was the leader of a jug band almost a decade
before jug bands became fashionable in Memphis. Sleepy John Estes, Yank
Rachell, Hammie Nixon, and "Hambone" Willie Newbern all lived in
Brownsville for a while. Ashley Thompson and Noah Lewis lived in Ripley,
and John Lee "Sonny Boy" Williamson came from Jackson. These musicians
drew from a common reservoir of folk blues, which they refashioned into their

own songs. Their vocal style relied on subtlety and understatement with phrasing that was soft and flowing. Although they expressed a deep emotional involvement, their style seemed almost reserved when compared with the raw emotionalism of the Mississippi Delta's leading blues vocalists. The major guitar style of the Memphis blues tradition was based on an insistent strumming that accented the groundbeat on the lower strings with a thumb stroke and finger-picked single-note runs that sketched out themes or fragments of a melody—somewhat akin to the more traditional banjo-picking techniques that predated the rural blues.

Northern Mississippi, especially the northern Delta region, also contributed musicians, vocal and instrumental styles, and folk blues standards to the Memphis blues tradition. Gus Cannon, Frank Stokes, Jim Jackson, Robert Wilkins, Jab Jones, and many more moved to Memphis from towns like Hernando and Clarksdale. Stokes, Charlie Burse, and Jack Kelly all sang in a forceful, declamatory style associated with Delta bluesmen like Charley Patton and later Howling Wolf. Most of the better blues guitarists based in Memphis regularly used the Delta's famed bottleneck slide technique. Popular Delta folk blues classics like "Roll and Tumble," "Joe Turner," and "Po' Boy, Long Ways from Home" were also standards among Memphis blues singers.[60] These ingredients from the rural blues enclaves of northern Mississippi, combined with ingredients from the enclaves of western Tennessee, enhanced the rise of a distinctive blues idiom in Memphis. The convergence of these two rural blues cultures gave the small blues ensembles playing on the city streets and in the parks the special blend of African-American folk music—country dance tunes, city folksongs, and the rural blues—associated with the famous Memphis jug bands.

Homegrown musicians were very much involved in synthesizing the outside rural blues influences and incorporating other approaches and material into the music. Because Beale Street attracted African-American piano players, there was a long-standing blues piano presence in Memphis. Guitar duets were also popular in the city, as were the dance bands led by trained musicians like W. C. Handy. But in the prewar era, it was the jug bands that caught the imagination of the local blues musicians and their audiences. Native harmonica players like Will Shade, Jed Davenport, and Willie Borum played a vital role in shaping the jug bands' novel sound. Along with Noah Lewis, they made the harmonica into the leading solo instrument in these groups. The extensive use of the harmonica gave the Memphis jug bands their trademark and caused them to be oriented stylistically more toward the blues than were the traditional rural string bands and the jazz-oriented Louisville jug bands. The Memphis jug bands were in essence the first urban blues bands.

Memphis began as a riverport outpost on a high bluff just east of the Mississippi River—400 miles upstream from New Orleans. On the eve of the Civil

War, it was a bustling frontier town with a population of 8,900 and a local economy that revolved around the cotton trade and river transportation. A yellow fever epidemic devastated the city in the 1870s; over 50 percent of its residents—about 25,000 people—fled. Most of those who stayed were African Americans, and they were responsible for bringing prosperity and growth back to Memphis. By 1900 the population had reached 100,000, and white residents were once more in the majority. The local economy was again booming; besides the lucrative cotton commerce, there was also a flourishing lumber trade, and the city was beginning to attract industrial manufacturers. Moreover, its importance as a transportation hub was enhanced by an influx of railroad lines to complement the riverport.[61]

As a working-class trade and transportation center, Memphis was a stronghold of the Democratic party in the mid-South. The city's Democratic machine was in the hands of the ward political bosses, who controlled city hall, dispensed patronage to their cronies, and sanctioned the local underworld vice operations in return for votes and a percentage of the profits. In the early 1900s the ward-dominated political machine was ousted from city government by a progressive reform movement of dissident middle-class Democrats. One of the movement's leaders, Edward Hull Crump, a shrewd and ambitious political operator, used this victory as a springboard for his political career. Elected mayor in 1910, he quickly built up his own political machine through astute alliances with key constituencies in the city. In particular, he supported the saloon keepers and the large working-class population that frequented the saloons by ignoring the Prohibition laws. He also downplayed his pledge to clean up the red-light district after making a half-hearted effort to raid some of the brothels and to impose a midnight curfew on African Americans in the city. Neither effort proved successful, and Crump was soon doing just the reverse: instead of harassing the underworld entrepreneurs and their customers, he began to court them as a desirable constituency.[62]

The black community in Memphis became another major constituency in return for a token voice in local government. "Boss" Crump was a confirmed white supremacist, but he supported racial cooperation as long as the black people in Memphis stayed in their place. This was the best deal African Americans could get: most of the city's white political factions were openly hostile to their participation in local politics.

By 1920, African Americans made up 38 percent of the total population in Memphis, or approximately sixty thousand people. Employment opportunities were limited; most jobs were in the familiar categories of domestic work and unskilled labor. Black unemployment was invariably double white unemployment in Memphis, and often it soared even higher. Within the city's black community, an embryonic middle class operated small businesses, such as funeral homes, beauty salons, and barbershops or practiced their professions as teachers, ministers, lawyers, dentists, and doctors.

Working or living in the red-light district were black musicians and saloon attendants, bootleggers and prostitutes, and a growing army of unemployed fieldhands fleeing the Mississippi Delta's oppressive plantation economy. Although viewed with disdain by local white authorities, this underclass was nevertheless tolerated, in part because its members were constituents of Crump's machine and in part because they were easily exploited as a source of cheap labor.[63]

The Memphis tenderloin was much like its New Orleans counterpart because of their proximity to each other and because they attracted similar populations. Memphis was the next major port up the Mississippi River. Its dramatic growth in the post-Reconstruction era lured to the city jobless immigrants and underworld entrepreneurs who were familiar with the mobster enterprises in New Orleans and built up the same sort of vice operations on their own turf. Black migrants were an integral component of the red-light districts of both cities. They were seldom the owners of the tenderloin establishments and vice operations; mostly they were employees or customers. It was the black migrants, however, who provided much of the music for the red-light districts; they brought the rural blues with them and adapted the music's style and content to their new urban setting. The initial sphere of production for blues musicians in the southern cities appeared at the point where the tenderloin districts intersected with black people's segregated slum dwellings. This tied their identity and their fortunes to an outlaw subculture that happened to be at its zenith during this crucial early migratory period. The musical and cultural dynamics set in motion in the Storyville sector of New Orleans also resonated along Memphis's Beale Street, the legendary "home of the blues."

Beale Street was the major thoroughfare in the Memphis red-light district. It began at the bustling riverfront dock and open market area where roustabouts loaded and unloaded riverboat cargos of cotton, rice, manufactured goods, and domestic animals, while vendors hawked their goods from wagons—fruits, vegetables, clothing, jewelry, live chickens, barbecued chickens, fried fish, pigs feet, chitlins, and charms. The section of Beale Street closest to the river was lined with theaters, cabarets, brothels, pool halls, barbershops, saloons, cigar shops, clothing stores, and restaurants. As in New Orleans, these tenderloin businesses were usually owned by Italian or Jewish immigrants with underworld connections and a fascination for African-American music and dance. The inside story on Beale Street was that the Jews owned the pawn shops and grocery stores, the Greeks owned the restaurants, the Italians ran the saloons and the theaters, and the African Americans were the customers.[64]

John "Piano Red" Williams, a piano player who grew up in Memphis during this period, vividly recalled the people and saloons of Beale Street:

> There was all different kind of places on Beale. Them places I played, they was mostly just joints. To tell the truth, some of them was just real scalawag joints, like old man (Nellow) Grundy's and the Red Front. Folks go there, wear overalls, work in the coal yard, and go to the joints just after work. But there was places like the Monarch. It was the classiest; it was the town talk, the Monarch. Well, they're real dressed up, gambling men with diamond rings on and suits of clothes. And them pimps would go there—but Lord, they wasn't nothin' like these ragged fellows 'round here now sayin' they're pimps. Them men, you'd thought it was a preacher or lawyer, way they dressed then. Some of them would dress twice a day.[65]

The Monarch, known as the "castle of missing men," was owned by Jim Kinnane, the underworld "czar" of Beale Street, and run by "Bad Sam," a pistol-toting bouncer whom Jelly Roll Morton called "the toughest Negro in Memphis."[66]

Like New Orleans and Atlanta, Memphis had a long history of racial violence, much of which took place along the Beale Street corridor.[67] In 1908, Wild Bill Latra, a notorious white gangster, gunned down five black men after losing a card game; he was acquitted of murder by an all-white jury. "Two Gun" Charlie Pierce, a black desperado, became a local legend after killing two white policemen in a shootout:

> Two-gun Charlie is a mighty man,
> Mows down dem cops where ever he can,
> Got two pistols that sho' am fine,
> Gives 'dem bastards a hot old time.[68]

By the 1920s Memphis had been labeled the "murder capital of America."[69] Most of the killing occurred in the tenderloin, where the rule of the underworld was both permissive and vindictive.

Memphis's reputation as a southern haven for madams and their prostitutes was second only to that of New Orleans. Most of the brothels were registered as hotels and were located on the side streets adjacent to the Beale Street corridor. The city was also the home port for the most notorious floating brothel on the Mississippi River, the Katy Adams. Banjo player gus Cannon, leader of Cannon's Jug Stompers, described the operation as follows:

The Katy Adams, . . . all the sporting women would follow that
boat, . . . just pay fifty cents for cabin fare and ride that boat from
Memphis down to Rosedale, and that's the way they made their money,
go up and down the river. The boat was carrying Uncle Sam's mail so
all them women was protected.[70]

Moonshine liquor and marijuana were sold in the saloons and on the street
corners up and down Beale Street. Cocaine was sold in neighborhood drug-
stores; a small boxful cost five or ten cents before it was outlawed in 1906. Its
use as a stimulant had long been encouraged among black laborers by white
employers, and it was the most popular drug used by stevedores along the
Mississippi River. The Memphis police chief declared that his department was
"unable to cope with its ravages." It was estimated by the police at the turn of
the century that up to 80 percent of the black workforce in the city used cocaine. After it was classified as an illegal drug, its sale became more secretive
and its use diminished somewhat, though it was still obtainable at modest
prices well into the 1920s. By that time, cocaine was the subject of at least
two local blues folksongs. One is named after a major cocaine outlet at Fourth
and Union streets in Memphis, "Lehman's Drug Store":

> I went to Mr. Lehman 'bout half past nine,
> Said to Mr. Lehman, I've only got a dime,
> to get my habits on, to get my habits on.
>
> I went to Mr. Lehman 'bout half past ten,
> Said to Mr. Lehman, I'm back again,
> To get my habits, to get my habits on.
>
> I went to Mr. Lehman 'bout half past 'leben,
> Said to Mr. Lehman, I'll never get to heben,
> To get my habits, to get my habits on.
>
> I went to Mr. Lehman 'bout half past twelve,
> Said to Mr. Lehman, I'm gonna go to hell,
> To get my habits on, to get my habits on.[71]

A second is entitled "Cocaine Blues":

> Sniff my cocaine, sniff it by the grain,
> Doctor said it'd kill me but he didn't say when,
> Hey, hey, honey, take a whiff on me.

Buy my cocaine, put it in a box,
People say it's good for the old smallpox,
Hey, hey, honey, take a whiff on me.[72]

Prohibition was instituted as the state law in Tennessee in 1909, but it was pretty much ignored in Memphis until the federal Prohibition law went into effect in 1920. Soon afterward, pressure from federal authorities forced the sale of liquor underground; the Beale Street saloons were turned into "speakeasies" and "blind tigers." By the mid-1920s, the bootleggers were so well organized in Memphis that the federal agents considered the city to be the worst problem area in Tennessee, Mississippi, and Arkansas. Stills were built in remote hideouts along the Mississippi River; some were even concealed on barges that moved up and down the river. Special speed boats with oversized engines were used by the bootleggers to deliver the moonshine to the assigned points of distribution, and there was little fear of their being detected.[73] Like prostitution and gambling, the sale of illegal alcohol and drugs garnered huge profits for the Memphis underworld. As long as there was easy money to be made in these endeavors, the Beale Street tenderloin remained open for business around the clock. It was a powerful magnet attracting both thrill seekers and job seekers—not the least of which were the region's aspiring blues musicians.

The first major showcase for blues musicians in Memphis was Church Park. It was opened in 1899 at a six-acre site on the east end of Beale Street adjacent to a black residential neighborhood. Robert Church, a black millionaire and civic leader, built the park because there were no public parks in Memphis open to African Americans. It had everything from playgrounds to tame peacocks. The major attraction was an auditorium that could seat two thousand people. The park and auditorium became the hub of social life for African Americans living in the city. Vaudeville favorites like Billy Kersands, the Whiteman sisters, and pianist Blind Boone staged shows in the auditorium; local musicians engaged in jam sessions and cutting contests on the park's grounds.[74]

The ensemble music popular in Memphis in the years before 1900 was performed by either string bands or military brass bands. As in New Orleans, an instrumental fusion of the two occurred with the formation of African-American dance bands. They were already established when W. C. Handy moved to the city from Clarksdale, Mississippi, in 1909, after having been exposed to the early Delta folk blues. He began his musical career in Memphis directing a marching brass band, sponsored by a local barber, that played primarily for funerals. Later, Handy formed his own dance band and began to popularize some of the rural melodies and lyrics he had heard in Mississippi.

The end result was the publication of "Memphis Blues" (1912) and "St. Louis Blues" (1914)—the first commercial blues compositions to reach a national audience. W. C. Handy put together his first successful folk blues adaptation as a mock campaign song for E. H. Crump during the 1909 mayoral race:

> Mister Crump won't 'low no easy riders here,
> Mister Crump won't 'low no easy riders here,
> We don't care what Mister Crump don't 'low
> We gonna bar'lhouse anyhow,
> Mister Crump can go catch hisself some air.[75]

During the next decade, Beale Street became the major showplace for African-American blues and jazz in the mid-South. Vaudeville luminaries like Ma Rainey and Bessie Smith appeared at the Palace Theatre, which also employed a full-time orchestra of trained musicians. Black piano players were the mainstays of the Beale Street saloons and brothels. At first, Beale Street pianists were influenced by the ragtime tradition popular in the mid-South since the 1880s, but by the 1910s they were adapting the blues to the piano. Benny Frenchy was an early Beale Street standard-bearer on the piano who took up the blues during this period, although Jelly Roll Morton claims he learned it from his New Orleans rivals.[76] Peter Chatman, later known as "Memphis Slim," grew up in Memphis and began his career as a blues piano player and songwriter at the Midway Café on Beale Street in the late 1920s. His major influence initially was Roosevelt Sykes, whom he succeeded as the house pianist at the Midway for "a dollar and a half a night and two pints of whiskey." Memphis Slim's memories of Beale Street were fond ones, and he gave the piano more credit for the formation of a Memphis blues tradition than it has been given in the past:

> I don't think there was another street in America quite like Beale Street. A lot of musicians came here and this was it—this was like the crossroads. There was some great musicians here like Willie Bloom, Hatchett, Bad Nooks—all these piano players and they were fantastic.
> . . . In Memphis, there was much more pianos here than guitars because this was really a piano city. . . . That's why you got such great piano players here. . . . In most cities in the South it was guitars and harmonicas—in Memphis it was pianos because the Italians were running everything and they had all these little houses with a piano in there and a piano player.[77]

## The Memphis Jug Bands

The renowned Memphis jug bands did not coalesce as musical aggregations until the mid-1920s. They were inspired by the records of a Louisville jug band. The earliest groups in Louisville, which pre-dated the Memphis groups by at least a decade, were basically string bands—fiddle, guitar, banjo, or mandolin, and a jug in place of a bass fiddle; they played dance and popular show tunes from the minstrel tradition. By the time Louisville's leading jug bands were recorded in the early 1920s, however, they were sounding more like New Orleans jazz bands. They had added first a cornet and then another horn—a trombone or a saxophone. Even though some of their numbers were called blues, their music was increasingly jazz-oriented. The Memphis jug bands were primarily blues-oriented. They took on a different sound by show-casing the harmonica and sometimes a kazoo or a fiddle instead of a horn section. The most celebrated instrumental soloists in the major groups were harmonica players like Will Shade, Noah Lewis, Jed Davenport, Willie Borum, Sonny Boy Williamson, Walter Horton, and Hammie Nixon. The only jug-band fiddlers from Memphis noted for their prowess as instrumental solo- ists were Will Bates and Charlie Pierce.

Will Shade was also known as Son Brimmer because he was raised by his grandmother Annie Brimmer. He was born in Memphis on February 5, 1889, grew up on the fringes of the red-light district, and learned his music in the streets. His first mentor was a local blues musician called Tee Wee Blackman, who played guitar and sang for tips along Beale Street's sidewalks, or on the grounds of Church Park. Shade was taught to play the guitar by Blackman while he was still in his teens. The first blues he learned from the older street musician was entitled "Newport News Blues," a song about a black soldier leaving for France from Newport News, Virginia, during World War I. By the 1920s, Will Shade was alternating between playing in the joints along Beale Street and touring with one of the regional medicine shows based in Memphis. During his travels on the medicine show circuit, he learned to play the har- monica and may have gained some experience jamming in pick-up bands that included such makeshift instruments as the jug, the kazoo, the washboard, and the single-string washtub bass. Shade expressed a strong interest in setting up his own jug band when he heard the Dixieland Jug Blowers' early recordings. Later, at a spontaneous jam session in a Beale Street saloon with a group of musicians that included a jug blower named "Lionhouse," Shade was inspired to form his own jug band when the audience reacted by dancing jubilantly about and chanting, "Jug band! Jug band!" His original group featured him on harmonica and guitar, Ben Ramey on kazoo, "Lionhouse" on jug, and Will Weldon on guitar. He, Ramey, and Weldon sang as well. Shade was a determined leader. He rehearsed the group diligently, and their infectious playing style soon caught the attention of Charlie Williamson, the black manager of the Palace Theatre and a talent scout for the race recording industry. Williamson contacted Ralph Peer of the Victor Recording Company and made the necessary arrangements. After a successful audition for Peer, the group made their first commercial records at a Victor recording session held in Memphis during February 1927.[78]

Will Shade called his group the Memphis Jug Band on the initial releases. Over the next four years, they would record fifty-seven titles for the Victor Recording Company. The personnel in the band were in constant flux. As many as fifteen musicians contributed to its recordings, among them Tee Wee Blackman; Furry Lewis, the veteran Memphis bluesman; jug and piano virtuoso Jab Jones; blues singer Jenny Mae Clayton, who was the wife of Will Shade; Hattie Hart, another local female blues singer; and "Laughing" Charlie Burse, a country guitarist and storyteller who became Shade's closest friend. Burse had developed an extroverted performing style while working with a medicine show. His hip shaking and use of his guitar as a phallic symbol would much later be emulated by a young country singer named Elvis Presley.

The music the Memphis Jug Band recorded was a mixture of blues, dance tunes, and minstrel songs. Will Shade selected the songs and did most of the arranging for the group. At their initial recording session, he sang lead on "Newport News Blues," while Charlie Burse sang lead on "Memphis Jug Blues," a trademark number on which Shade and Weldon filled in vocal harmonies. The two other blues selections they recorded at this session were "Son Brimmer Blues" and "Stingy Woman Blues," with Weldon as lead vocalist. The jug work of Charlie Polk was monotonous and barely audible on these recordings; it contributed little to the overall sound. Luckily, the other instruments were clearly heard and well played. Shade's harmonica work was relaxed and almost wistful. He embroidered the texture of the band's blues numbers with poignant passages that provided a musical counterpoint to the lead vocal lines. There was a gentle and melodic quality to his sound reminiscent of quill players such as Henry "Ragtime Texas" Thomas. In sharp contrast was Pat Ramsey's kazoo playing. The sound and the style were molded after those of the cornet in small jazz ensembles. Weldon's guitar work was steady, and he played well in tandem with Shade when the latter switched over from harmonica to guitar on certain numbers.[79]

The quality of the material produced in the later recording sessions improved with the addition of Charlie Burse on guitar and Jab Jones on jug and keyboards. The slower-tempo selections had a relaxed fluidity sustained by the blending of instruments and a soft mournfulness created by the lilting vocal harmonies. Particularly haunting were "KC Moan," "Stealin'," and the folk classic "Hurry Down Sunshine, See What Tomorrow Brings." "KC Moan"

was a well-known worksong refashioned into a blues number by Tee Wee
Blackman; it contained an excellent duet between Shade on harmonica and
Ramsey on kazoo. "Stealin'" was a finely polished selection that featured
some exceptional harmonica passages in the upper registers performed by Will
Shade. The lyrics were recycled from the black oral tradition:

> Now put your arms around me, mama, like
>   the circle around the sun,
> I want you to love me, mama, like my easy
>   rider done,
> If you don't believe I love you, look what
>   a fool I've been,
> If you don't believe I'm sinking, look at
>   the hole I'm in,
> Stealin', stealin', pretty mama, don't tell
>   on me,
> I'm stealin' back to my old-time use-to-be.[80]

They also did a version of the traditional Beale Street folksong "Cocaine
Blues," which they retitled "Cocaine Habit Blues." Recorded in 1930, it
viewed the passing of the Memphis cocaine craze with mixed emotions:

> Cocaine habit is mighty bad, it's the worst
>   old habit I ever had,
> Hey, hey, honey, take a whiff on me.
> I went to Mr. Lehman in a lope, saw a sign in
>   the window, there's no more dope,
> Hey, hey, honey, take a whiff on me.
>
> . . .
>
> Since cocaine went out of style, you can catch
>   them shooting needles all the while,
> Hey, hey, honey, take a whiff on me.
> It takes a little coke to give me ease, you can
>   strut your stuff long as you please,
> Hey, hey, honey, take a whiff on me.[81]

The Memphis Jug Band's uptempo numbers were foot-stomping dance tunes
with whimsical lyrics drawn mostly from African-American folklore.
"Overseas Stomp" and "Whitewash Station" were typical of this category.
They both featured Ramsey's exuberant kazoo playing, Shade's exquisite har-

monica phrasing, and Jab Jones, who brought the jug more to the forefront in the band. Jones also handled the lead vocals on these songs with authority and vigor. The lyrics to "Overseas Stomp" juxtaposed African Americans' wartime experiences with the latest dance craze:

> Now, mama, don't you weep and moan,
> Uncle Sam got your man and gone,
> Now he's doing that Lindberg across the sea.[82]

"Whitewash Station" was a nonsense song toasting the band. It included a spoken blues fable set to verse:

> Now if you want to get to heaven, I'll tell you
>     what to do,
> You put on a sock, the foot in the shoe,
> You place a bottle of corn in your right hand,
> That will pass you over to the promised land,
> And if you meet the Devil, he asks you how you do,
> "I'm on my way to heaven, don't you want to come
>     too?
> Know there's a place, do just as well,
> It's called whitewash station, ten miles
>     from hell."
>
> Build a whitewash station, make it two miles
>     of floor so the jugband have a chance,
> Build a whitewash station, make it two miles
>     of floor so the jugband have a chance,
> Ain't got no stocking, ain't got no shoes,
> No, I got those Memphis Jug Band blues,
> Build a whitewash station, make it two miles
>     of floor so the jugband have a chance,
> I say, jugband have a chance.[83]

The band's commercial recordings enhanced their popularity in the surrounding region. They were in such demand that two groups were formed to handle the bookings, and an agent, Howard Yancey, was engaged to coordinate the business end of the enterprise. In addition to their routine gigs on Beale Street or in Church Park, Yancey got them hired for Crump's political rallies and for certain white social events. They also appeared regularly at the Mardi Gras in New Orleans. With the onset of the depression, however, the fortunes of the band were reversed. Their record contract with Victor was canceled, and although they recorded for other companies before disbanding, the sales of their records dropped off dramatically, never to return to their 1920s levels. Their engagements in Beale Street clubs and at nearby country dances were also curtailed. By the late 1930s, the Memphis Jug Band had ceased to exist. Will Shade and many of the other musicians in the band remained in Memphis for the rest of their lives, but the mainstream of popular music had passed them by.[84]

The second most renowned jug band in Memphis was called Cannon's Jug Stompers. The leader was Gus Cannon, who was born on a sharecropper plantation in the Mississippi Delta on September 12, 1883. His parents were former slaves who subsisted by farming cotton in the Delta. As a boy, Cannon also worked in the cotton fields, carrying water to the laborers. His family was large; he had nine brothers. It was his older brothers who introduced him to music. They often got together to sing folksongs and play traditional string-band tunes on the fiddle, guitar, and banjo. Gus Cannon's first instrument was a banjo he built out of an old guitar neck and a bread pan. To tighten the head of the instrument, he heated it over a fire. While he was a teenager, Cannon moved to Clarksdale, Mississippi, where he worked as an unskilled laborer and played music on the weekends. In Clarksdale, he came under the influence of two local musicians, fiddler Jim Turner and guitarist Alex Lee. Turner, featured in the dance band W. C. Handy had organized there, was considered the best fiddler in the Delta by his fellow musicians. His playing so impressed Gus Cannon that he decided to learn to play the fiddle in addition to the banjo. Alex Lee introduced Cannon to the blues and to the technique of using a knifeblade as a slide. Cannon adapted this technique to his banjo playing. He also learned his first folk blues, "Po' Boy, Long Ways from Home," from Lee.[85]

Cannon left Clarksdale around 1907. He worked as a roustabout on the Mississippi River for a while before moving to Ashport, Tennessee, a small riverport town not far from Memphis. There he played in his first jug band, which was led by Jim Guffin. Guffin was a talented instrumentalist who played guitar, fiddle, and a coal can he used as a jug. Just east of Ashport, in Ripley, Tennessee, Cannon met and began playing with Noah Lewis and Ashley Thompson, who both eventually became members of Cannon's Jug Stompers. Lewis, an extraordinary harmonica player, had been born in 1890 and raised in the vicinity of Ripley. As Cannon remembered him:

> Lord, he used to blow the hell outa that harp. He could play two harps at the same time . . . through his mouth and his nose—same key and same melody. Y' know he could curl his lips 'round the harp and his nose was just like a fist. Noah, he was full of cocaine all the time—I reckon that's why he could play so loud, and ahh he was good.[86]

Lewis carried a belt full of harmonicas, pitched in different keys. Before teaming up with Cannon, he had played in local string bands and even with brass bands, an honor that gives some indication of the strength and power of his playing. Lewis introduced Cannon to a young guitar player named Ashley Thompson. The three of them formed a group to play for weekend dances and parties. During this period, Cannon and Lewis also made occasional forays into Memphis to play along Beale Street. Cannon began touring on the regional medicine show circuit in 1914; he worked with four different shows over the next six years, from the spring to the fall of each year. Cannon adopted the stage name "Banjo Joe" on one of his early tours. He also met and played with Elijah Avery and Hosea Woods, who would later become important members of Cannon's Jug Stompers.[87]

While Gus Cannon was touring seasonally on the medicine show circuit, he moved his home base to Memphis. By the 1920s, he was a familiar figure on the local blues scene there, but he was not involved with any particular group. He continued to visit Ripley and play regularly with Noah Lewis and Ashley Thompson. Lewis also made regular trips to Memphis. When Will Shade's Memphis Jug Band became a hit in the mid-twenties, Cannon, who was familiar with the jug-band tradition, began playing a jug himself and quickly organized his own informal group. The commercial success of the jug-band recordings brought Ralph Peer back to Memphis looking for another band to record. Charlie Williamson seems to have recommended Cannon to Peer. Cannon was asked to put a jug band together for a Victor recording session in January 1928. He got together Thompson and Lewis for their first session, and they recorded four numbers, three blues and a ragtime tune. Local landmarks dominated the titles of three of these recordings. "Minglewood Blues," a favorite of Lewis's, refers to a lumber camp in the vicinity of Ripley that was renowned as a "good time spot"; Lewis had worked there in 1915. "Springdale Blues" refers to a street in a black neighborhood in northern Memphis where Cannon had lived after moving to the city. "Madison Rag" is named after a street four blocks away from Beale. Cannon had also recorded the piece three months earlier in Chicago during his only previous recording venture, which happened to be for Paramount Records. At that session, backed up by Blind Blake, Cannon recorded the rural blues standard "Po' Boy, Long Ways from Home" and a folksong he also learned from Alex Lee about Booker T. Washington's dinner with President Theodore Roosevelt in 1901. Entitled "Can You Blame the Colored Man?" it exemplifies the satirical edge often present in black folk music:

> Now Booker T. Washington left Tuskegee, to
> the White House he went one day,

He was going to call on the president in a
    quiet and sociable way,
He was in his car and was feeling fine, then
    he knocked on the president's door,
Now old Booker he began to grin and he almost
    changed his color,
When Roosevelt said, "Come in and we'll have
    some dinner in a little while."
Now can you blame the colored man for making
    them goo goo eyes?
And when he sat down at the president's table
    he began to smile,
Eating lamb, ham, chicken, roast chicken,
    turkey, bread or toast.
Now can you blame the colored man for making
    them goo goo eyes?
Now Booker was so delighted at the social words
    given to him,
Well, he hired him a horse and carriage, and he
    took the whole town in,
He's drunk on wine and was feeling fine.
Now can you blame the colored man for making
them goo goo eyes?[88]

The most successful recordings by Gus Cannon's Jug Stompers were made when Hosea Woods joined the group in the late 1920s. Woods played guitar, banjo, and kazoo, while also handling some of the vocal chores. An energetic musician with a good sense of showmanship, he often interjected shouts of encouragement during solos by Cannon and Lewis. During this period the band recorded "Walk Right In," a lighthearted nonsense song that Gus Cannon had used as his signature pieces since 1910, and two poignant blues numbers highlighted by Lewis's exquisite harmonica phrasing. "Prison Wall Blues" is a compilation of various floating verses from the black oral tradition focusing on pardons, bloodhounds, prison walls, and defiant dreams of escape:

When I leave these prison walls, I'll be running
    and dodging trees,
See the bottom of my feet so many times, you'll
    think I'm on my knees,
These prison wall blues keep rolling 'cross my
    mind.[89]

On "Viola Lee Blues," Lewis handled the lead vocal and played a melancholy harmonica solo. His tone control was superb. The lyrics tell a story that was all too familiar to the black population in Memphis:

> The judge he pleaded, the clerk he wrote it down,
>     clerk he wrote it down, indeedy,
> The judge he pleaded, clerk he wrote it down,
> If you get a jail sentence, you must be Nashville
>     bound.
>
> Some got six months, some got a solid, some got
>     one solid year, indeedy,
> Some got six month, some got one solid year,
> But me and my buddy got a lifetime here.[90]

Cannon's Jug Stompers made their last recording in November 1930. Then, like the Memphis Jug Band, the group faded out of existence. Woods died in the mid-1930s; Lewis returned to Ripley, where he lived out his life in obscurity. Cannon remained in Memphis and stayed active on the local music scene, but he was forced to make his living outside the music business until he was "rediscovered" in the 1960s.

Two other groups that figured prominently in the Memphis jug-band era were Jed Davenport's Beale Street Jug Band and Jack Kelly's Jug Busters, later known as the South Memphis Jug Band. Kelly's group was the only other jug band in Memphis that could rival Will Shade's group in popularity. His band was active for more than two decades. During that span, it featured Willie Borum on harmonica, Doc Higgs on jug, Ernest Motley on banjo, Kelly and Milton Robie on guitars, and Will Bates, the city's premier fiddler, who later acted as a co-leader of the group. Kelly was best remembered for his sonorous blues vocals—he was unrivaled as a jug-band vocalist on Beale Street. Other Memphis-based blues musicians who played with the Kelly/Bates group included harmonica player Walter Horton and the popular guitar duo of Frank Stokes and Dan Sane, who also recorded on their own as the Beale Street Sheiks. The recordings of the South Memphis Jug Band (made in New York City in 1933) were blues-based and strongly rhythmic. Their best efforts were "Policy Rag," a twelve-bar uptempo blues number, and "Doctor Medicine," named after Doc Higg's other vocation.

Jed Davenport, a native of Memphis, is best remembered for his powerful harmonica playing, even though he played an array of other musical instruments, including the trumpet. Davenport was a fixture along Beale Street in the 1920s, blowing his harmonica for tips. By 1930, he had formed the Beale Street Jug Band. It played locally and recorded with the noted blues guitar duet of Memphis Minnie Douglas and Kansas City Joe McCoy. On their own the band recorded an instrumental version of "The Dirty Dozen" and "Beale Street Breakdown"—the group's tour de force.[91]

## Memphis Blues Pioneers

Besides the jug-band musicians, many individual blues artists were active in Memphis in the 1920s and 1930s. The most prominent and influential were Jim Jackson, Frank Stokes, Furry Lewis, Sleepy John Estes, Memphis Minnie, and Rev. Robert Wilkins. Jim Jackson was a minstrel singer from Hernando, Mississippi, who was born in the 1880s; he played the banjo and the guitar. Jackson lived in Memphis in the 1920s and also toured with several famous minstrel shows, including the Rabbit Foot Minstrels and Silas Green's troupe. In 1927, Jackson recorded his trademark blues, "Goin' to Kansas City," for Vocalion Records in Chicago. The song became one of the most commercially successful race records of the decade, and Jackson went on to record a diverse repertoire of blues, as well as folksongs and standards from the minstrel tradition. These included his famous version of "Travelin' Man," his version of the folk classic "Old Dog Blues," and the comedy song "I Heard the Voice of a Porkchop." Next to his Kansas City sequence, Jackson's best-remembered blues recording was "Bootlegging Blues":

> The bootlegging man got his bottle in his hand,
> And all he needs is a little more speed,
> So he can outrun the revenue man.
>
> When the bootlegger goes to his still, gets ready
>     to make his stuff,
> He's got his concentrated lye, cocaine and his snuff,
> He'll fix you up a drink—just won't quit, it'll
>     make you bite a circle saw,
> Make you slap your lady down and make you pick a
>     fight with your boss.[92]

Frank Stokes was a mainstay of the Memphis blues scene from its beginning. He was born just outside the city in the late 1880s but was raised by a stepfather in Tutwiler, Mississippi. Returning to Memphis around the turn of the century, he worked regularly as a blacksmith but was also active as a street musician. Stokes's style was characterized by his strong, resonant voice and his rhythmic guitar accompaniments. The one song he was best known for lampooned E. H. Crump's politics and was called "Mister Crump Don't Like It." Its similarity to Handy's mock campaign song suggests that they may have come from the same source. Stokes's version goes, in part:

> Ah Mr. Crump don't like it, ain't gonna have
>     it here,
> Ah Mr. Crump don't like it, ain't gonna have
>     it here,
> Ah Mr. Crump don't like it, ain't gonna have
>     it here,
> No barrelhouse women startin' drinkin' no beer.[93]

The other verses satirized the church-going citizens of Memphis who supported Crump's reform candidacy.

In the early 1920s, Frank Stokes teamed up with another blues guitarist, Dan Sane. The duo was a popular attraction along Beale Street and among the black residents in the Memphis vicinity. They made a series of recordings in the late twenties for the Paramount and Victor labels, calling themselves the Beale Street Sheiks. Stokes handled the vocals and strummed his guitar forcefully, giving the songs a pulsating and danceable beat, while the nimble-fingered Sane embellished the melodies and the harmonies of the music with his more complex playing style. Much of the material they recorded together was either blues or from an even more traditional mold. "You Shall" was a comedy number that harshly burlesqued black preachers. Most of the verses were drawn from the black oral tradition and were well known throughout the South:

> Some folks said that a preacher wouldn't
>     steal,
> I caught about eleven in a watermelon field,
> Just a cuttin' and a slicin', got to tearin'
>     up vine,
> They was eatin' and talkin' most of the time,
> They was hungry.[94]

In the blues idiom, the duo also recorded standards like "Mistreating Blues," a version of a number dating to the 1890s that W. C. Handy had learned as "East St. Louis." "Tain't Nobody's Business" had been popularized by Bessie Smith in the early 1920s, but its folk origins were even earlier. The chorus used by Frank Stokes was a well-known Beale Street anthem:

It ain't nobody's business, honey,
How I spend my money,
It ain't nobody's business but mine,
It ain't nobody's business, honey,
Where in the world I get my money,
It ain't nobody's business but my own.[95]

Perhaps the duo's most accomplished blues recording was "Downtown Blues." It featured three extended instrumentals during which the interplay between the guitarists was perfectly synchronized, creating a fluid wave of sound that rose to its natural peak and then ebbed into the background of the next verse. The lyrics were in the standard three-line AAB stanzas.

And I'm goin' downtown, gonna stay around 'til
   dawn,
And I'm goin' downtown, gonna stay around there
   'til dawn,
I don't want no trouble, don't want to drive
   me on.[96]

Between 1927 and 1929 the Beale Street Sheiks recorded twenty-five titles, while Frank Stokes cut an additional eleven sides on his own or in tandem with other Memphis blues musicians. After their recording career was cut short by the depression, Stokes and Sane continued to perform locally, often teaming up with Jack Kelly and Will Bates of the South Memphis Jug Band. They remained active on the local blues scene until after World War II, but died, within a few years of each other, forgotten by all save a handful of close friends and family members.

Walter "Furry" Lewis and his family migrated to Memphis from Greenwood, Mississippi, in 1899. At that time, Lewis was six years old and his family consisted of his mother and two sisters; he never knew his father, who left the family before his birth. The Lewis family lived in a black neighborhood in a run-down section of northern Memphis. Furry Lewis learned to play the guitar on an instrument he constructed himself and soon thereafter picked up the harmonica. His real school was in the streets of the Memphis red-light district, where he learned most of his repertoire and gained invaluable experience playing informally with older street musicians. At the age of thirteen, Lewis ran off with a medicine show that featured his idol, Jim Jackson. The journey initiated a period of wanderlust. When not touring as a medicine show musician, he rode the rails through much of the South. In 1916 he lost a leg in a train accident; back in Memphis he was fitted with an artificial leg, which curtailed his travels for a while. Beale Street became his home ground and his major source of income.

Sometime before World War I, Lewis worked with a jug band in Memphis, an indication that the style was there long before the Memphis Jug Band was able to cash in on it. As Lewis recalled in an interview much later in his life:

> When I was twenty I had my own band and we all could play. Had a boy named Ham, played jug. Willie Polk played the fiddle and another boy, call him Shoefus, played the guitar, like I did. All of us North Memphis boys. We'd meet at my house and walk down Brinley to Poplar to Dunlap or maybe all the way down to Main. People would stop us in the streets and say, "Do you know so an so?" And we'd play it and they'd give us a little something. Sometimes we'd pick up fifteen or twenty dollars before we got to Beale.[97]

His description of the jug band's function—to provide people with the popular music of the day—illuminates the role folk musicians played in the preservation of popular black music before the coming of the phonograph record. They were, in a sense, the first urban juke boxes.

By the early 1920s, Lewis was a familiar figure on the Memphis music scene. He continued to work the streets for tips, but now he was also in demand in the Beale Street clubs, where he often played with Jim Jackson, Will Shade, and Gus Cannon. However, Lewis was still unable to support himself as a blues musician. In 1923 he took a job with the local sanitation department as a street cleaner and stayed with it off and on for forty years. Lewis's friend and mentor, Jim Jackson, was instrumental in getting him his first recording date in 1927, with Vocalion Records in Chicago. Lewis recorded two blues numbers during his first session. Over the next two years, he recorded twenty-one additional sides; four different record labels were involved. Most of his selections were standard blues well known among the Memphis bluesmen, but there were also three memorable folk ballads: "John Henry," "Casey Jones," and "Stacko 'lee." Lewis fashioned unique versions of each of these famous ballads. He treated "John Henry" and "Casey Jones" as tragedies and focused on the effect of the heroes' deaths and on the kin they left behind. "Stacko 'lee" was more of a morality tale; after each verse came the ominous refrain: "When you lose your money, learn to lose."

The other blues selections recorded by Lewis in the 1920s were out of the Memphis mold. The vocal style was introspective and subtle rather than forceful and outgoing, as were blues vocals in the Mississippi Delta. Lewis's voice was high-pitched, yet poignantly expressive within its own range. His versatility as a guitarist was quite evident in these recordings. He used a bottleneck slide regularly but sometimes switched over to a knifeblade. His light touch extended each note with a finesse that was uncommon among slide guitarists. His picking style owed something to both the banjo-picking styles prevalent on the medicine-show circuit and the more sophisticated approach of jazz-influenced guitar players like Lonnie Johnson. Lewis covered Johnson's big seller, "Mean Old Bedbug Blues," but his playing differed significantly from Johnson's. This suggests that Lewis was more of an innovator than an imitator in his guitar work.

Lewis's approach to composing blues lyrics was similar to his guitar style in that he fused folk material from the black oral tradition with his own experiences, while remaining within the established framework of the twelve-bar blues. As he put it:

> Well, one thing, when you write the blues and what you be thinking about, you be blue, and you ain't got nothin' hardly to think about, you just already blue and just goin' write . . . you just rhyme 'em up. See, the time when you just get a blues, what you call the blues sometimes you, you just haven't come out like you 'sposed to and it don't be right, you have to go all over again until you rhyme it. It got to be rhymed just like it is 'cause if you call yourself with the blues or anything else, if it ain't rhymed up it don't sound good to me or nobody else, do it?[98]

His recordings of such Memphis blues standards as "Judge Harsh Blues," his reworking of the old Memphis version of "Joe Turner Blues," and his rendition of the popular local blues number "Goin' to Brownsville" demonstrate his fidelity to the music of his hometown. Lewis also created his own songs, either by pulling together floating verses or by making up his own lyrics. A good example is "I Will Turn Your Money Green," which includes standard blues phrasing in the first two verses:

> When I was in Missouri, would not let me be,
> When I was in Missouri, would not let me be,
> Wouldn't rest content 'til I came to Tennessee.
>
> If you follow me, babe, I'll turn your money green,
> If you follow me, babe, I'll turn your money green,
> I'll show you more money than Rockefeller ever
>      seen.[99]

Furry Lewis's recording career was reminiscent of those of the other Memphis blues artists who recorded during this period. They made exceptional recordings for a few years and then slipped back into relative obscurity. Lewis made a little money from his recordings but then returned to working for the sanitation department. Eventually his music became more of a hobby than a vocation, and he ceased to play in public until the blues revival of the 1960s.

Sleepy John Estes actually spent very little time in Memphis—he often referred to the city as "the leader of evil doings in the world." Nevertheless, he was closely associated with the blues scene there in the late 1920s. Estes was born on a farm outside Ripley, Tennessee, on January 25, 1904. He was one of sixteen children. His father was a sharecropper who also played the guitar; while still a boy, Estes received his first guitar lessons from him. The family moved to the vicinity of Brownsville, Tennessee, about fifty miles west of Memphis, when Estes was eleven. Sometime during this period, he gained his nickname, Sleepy, and lost the sight in his right eye after being struck there by a rock. Estes labored in the cotton fields around Brownsville with his family, but he also began playing a homemade guitar and singing the blues at parties, picnics, and dances. His early guitar mentor was "Hambone" Willie Newbern, a resident of Brownsville whose signature piece was the Delta barrelhouse number "Roll and Tumble," which he was the first to record in the late twenties. At some point even before 1920, Sleepy John Estes teamed up with James "Yank" Rachell, a talented mandolin picker from the area who was four years younger than Estes. Later in the mid-1920s, they were joined by another blues musician, Hammie Nixon, who was the same age as Rachell; he played both the harmonica and a jug. The trio was in great demand around Brownsville, and they began to venture into Memphis, playing as a jug band in the streets, parks, and nightclubs. During their forays into Memphis, Estes and Rachell sometimes collaborated with the ubiquitous Jab Jones, calling themselves the Three J's Jug Band. They were regularly featured at the Blue Heaven Club on Beale Street; it was this exposure that eventually led to a recording date with Ralph Peer of Victor in 1929.

Sleepy John Estes, accompanied by Yank Rachell on mandolin and Jab Jones on piano, had four selections released by the Victor label as a result of that initial session. All were blues of exceptional quality. "Diving Duck Blues" was a standard folk blues with a random assortment of floating lyrics from the black oral tradition. The title verse was very popular among Memphis bluesmen:

> Now if the river was whiskey and I was a
> diving duck,
> Now if the river was whiskey and I was a
> diving duck,
> I would dive to the bottom, never would
> come up.

Another verse was the classic:

Now the sun gonna shine in my backdoor
    someday,
Now the sun gonna shine in my backdoor
    someday,
Now the wind's gonna rise, gonna blow my
    blues away.[100]

"Street Car Blues" refers to the electric street car system built in Memphis during the 1920s. "The Girl I Love, She Got Long Curly Hair" is Estes's version of the Memphis favorite, "Goin' to Brownsville"

Now I'm goin' to Brownsville, take the right-
    hand road,
Now I'm goin' to Brownsville, take that right-
    hand road,
Lord, I ain't gonna stop walkin' 'til I get in
    a sweet mama's door.[101]

The "right-hand road" was the local route from Memphis to Brownsville. Estes may have been responsible for the verse, since he identified more with Brownsville than with Memphis. However, the melody he used was also extremely popular in the Mississippi Delta. Charley Patton, among others, used it for a number called "Banty Rooster Blues." The final selection they recorded, "Milkcow Blues," was another traditional blues (also called "Sloppy Drunk Blues").

Now went upstairs to pack my leaving trunk,
I never saw no whiskey, the blues made me
    sloppy drunk,
Say I never saw no whiskey, blues done made
    me sloppy drunk,
Now I never saw no whiskey, blues made me
    sloppy drunk,
Now some says a dream, some says it was a
    dream,
But it's a slow consumption and it's killing
    you by degrees.[102]

Estes's vocals on these blues were some of the best recorded by a blues singer during this era. His piercing, high-pitched voice sounded like the wailing of a lost and lonely adolescent; his phrasing was economical and expressive. Estes's guitar playing was underdeveloped, but his associates more than made up for it. He would strum a steady rhythmical pattern, usually at twice the actual pace of the song. Jab Jones developed an interesting rhythmic counterpoint to Estes's insistent strumming by playing patterns of bass figures reminiscent of early boogie-woogie piano. In contrast to this bottom-heavy rhythm duet were the soaring madolin runs of Yank Rachell, which sometimes sounded like a banjo. He played lead in tandem with Estes's vocals, embellishing them exquisitely, while also providing some first-rate solos during vocal breaks.

Sleepy John Estes returned to Brownsville after the Victor recording session in 1930. Soon afterward he went out on the road with Hammie Nixon and ended up in Chicago the next year. Estes remained based in Chicago for most of the decade and recorded for labels owned by RCA Victor and Decca. His blues compositions from this period express more of his own experiences and his social concerns and observations. He had matured as a storyteller and a lyricist; his sense of narrative was heightened, and his verse became much more literal. One of his best-known blues of the 1930s, "Floating Bridge," tells the dramatic story of a car accident that nearly caused his death by drowning. One verse gives a vivid picture of its aftermath:

> They dried me off and they laid me in the bed,
> They dried me off and they laid me in the bed,
> Couldn't hear nothing but muddy water runnin'
>     through my head.[103]

Estes was equally adept at creating portraits of people who caught his fancy, and doing so with a minimum of words. A good example of this is "Lawyer Clark Blues":

> Now you know Mister Clark is a good lawyer,
>     good as I ever seen,
> He the first man prove water run upstream.
> That's the reason I like Mister Clark, boys, he
>     really is my friend,
> He say if I just stay out of the grave, poor
>     John, I'll see you won't go to the pen.[104]

His composition "Working Man Blues," recorded at the tail end of the depression, incisively criticizes the new industrial order from the perspective of those it was displacing:

Now you ought to cut off so many trucks and
     tractors, white folks,
You ought to work more mules and men,
Now you ought to cut off so many trucks and
     tractors, white folks,
You ought to work more mules and men,
Then you know that would make, ohh babe, money
     get thick again.

Now when a man gets together, you know he's
     turning his stocks into feed,
Now when a man gets together, you all know he's
     turning his stocks into feed,
He say he gonna sell all his corn and buy gas,
     o babe, pour it in his automobile.[105]

Before World War II had put an end to the depression, Sleepy John Estes returned to Brownsville. He lived there in relative obscurity. His eyesight slowly deteriorated, and by 1950 he was totally blind. His blindness left him helpless and poverty-stricken until the blues revival of the 1960s.

Robert Wilkins, like his early mentors Jim Jackson and Gus Cannon, grew up near Hernando, Mississippi, where he was born in 1896. His mother was part Cherokee, and they lived on a farm with Wilkins's stepfather, who taught him to play the guitar. The Hernando area had a lively blues culture and an abundance of homegrown musical talent and musical activities. As a teenager, Wilkins performed with Jackson, Cannon, Garfield Akers, and Buddy Taylor, among others. They worked the continuous round of fish fries, house parties, outdoor picnics, and country dances that took place in the area. Memphis, however, was still the urban mecca for Delta bluesmen, and Robert Wilkins moved there in 1915, following in the footsteps of his friends Jackson and Cannon. After serving in the army during World War I, he returned to Memphis, where he worked as a street musician and played with various jug-band combinations throughout the 1920s.

Wilkins was a versatile performer with a wide-ranging repertoire that allowed him to play for both black and white audiences. He was even popular with the local police: he performed for them at parties and occasionally dropped by the station to play their favorite songs. His guitar style was unusually subtle and fluid for a Delta-schooled blues musician. He regularly used a bottleneck slide and a light boom-chang strumming pattern in his blues accompaniments. His voice had a relaxed, lilting quality, which he embellished with a slight touch of vibrato. Wilkins was also a first-rate lyricist who wrote a number of successful blues. He employed unusual verse structures and based many of his songs on personal experiences or observations. One number, "Old Jim Canan's Blues," immortalized Beale Street's underworld kingpin Jim Kinnane. His best-known compositions were "That's No Way to Get Along" and "Rolling Stone." Wilkins made a series of recordings on the Victor, Brunswick, and Vocalion labels between 1928 and 1935. He then renounced the blues in favor of gospel songs and became an ordained minister in the Church of God in Christ Church, located in Memphis and renowned for its innovations in gospel music. He remained active in the church for the rest of his life.[106]

The city's most famous female blues artist was "Memphis" Minnie Douglas, an exciting performer who was in the forefront of the blues activity along Beale Street in its heyday. She was born on June 3, 1896, in Algiers, Louisiana, but her family moved to Walls, Mississippi, when she was seven. Walls was on Route 61, about fifteen miles southwest of Memphis. "Kid," as she was nicknamed by her parents because of her spunk and friskiness, demonstrated an early aptitude for music. She learned to play the banjo at the age of ten, and one year later she was also playing a guitar. When she was fourteen, she began to play and sing for tips in the streets and parks of Memphis and was soon a regular member of the local blues entourage there. Everybody called her Kid Douglas at first; later, she became known as Memphis Minnie. In the early 1920s, she teamed up with guitarist Will Weldon. They played together on Beale Street, lived together, and were eventually married. Weldon was an original member of Will Shade's Memphis Jug Band, and both he and Memphis Minnie were closely linked to the band during this period. Late in the decade, Memphis Minnie separated from Weldon and teamed up with another blues guitarist, Joe McCoy. He had been involved in the blues scene in Jackson, Mississippi, along with his brother Charlie McCoy, the Chatmon brothers, Tommy Johnson, and Ishman Bracey before relocating in Memphis. Joe McCoy and Memphis Minnie played regularly with Jed Davenport's Beale Street Jug Band in Memphis clubs and Church Park. They also played as a duo in a local barbershop that was a hangout for black musicians. A Columbia talent scout heard them there in 1929 and signed them up for a recording session in New York. They recorded six songs together. Five were blues that McCoy sang and the sixth was Memphis Minnie's signature piece, "Bumble Bee Blues."

Columbia Records, much to the firm's later chagrin, failed to release Memphis Minnie's number, preferring to go with McCoy's material. The two were polished guitarists, and they played together brilliantly, but McCoy's blues were fairly commonplace, and his technique as a vocalist was only adequate.

Mayo Williams, in Memphis scouting for talent for Vocalion Records, signed up the duo but paid much more attention to Memphis Minnie's talents as a blues singer. Their first release with Williams, "Bumble Bee Blues," went on to become one of the best-selling blues records of the year. It was a sexual blues that highlighted the duo's guitar playing and Memphis Minnie's strong vocal style. She sang the blues with great authority, economy, and toughness. Her voice was direct, almost blunt; she slightly slurred her words, giving them a bluesy intonation. The success of "Bumble Bee Blues" catapulted her into the limelight as a female blues recording artist. Williams returned to Memphis to record her again. This time she was the headliner, and she recorded not only with Joe McCoy but also with the Memphis Jug Band and even with one of her sisters. More important, Williams was able to lure her to Chicago with promises of more recording sessions and some club dates. She moved there in 1930, and remained in Chicago for the rest of her life.[107]

## The End of an Era

The onset of the depression in the 1930s brought hard times to Memphis, as it did to most industrial and commercial centers in the country. It was particularly devastating for the city's black inhabitants. Long breadlines were a common sight at the food distribution points set up by charity organizations and by government agencies. Ironically, the Beale Street vice corridor initially escaped the economic hardships of the depression years. The tenderloin business establishments continued to attract large crowds with money to spend, and one saloon keeper financed a free soup kitchen with the profits from liquor and games of chance. The policy operation, a long-shot numbers game run by Italian entrepreneurs, was extremely popular in urban black communities during hard times, since a winning number was a first-class ticket out of poverty, even though the odds were heavily weighted in favor of the saloon owners who controlled the game. Live music was still prominently featured in Beale Street saloons and parks, and therefore the locale remained a haven for African-American blues musicians.

In 1931, Boss Crump dedicated a park at the corner of Beale and Hernando streets to vaudeville blues pioneer W. C. Handy. Crump's motives were typically political—he hoped to stop black citizens' attempts to integrate the city's public facilities. In any event, the park became the daytime gathering place for itinerant blues musicians and the local jug bands and thus a new showcase for African-American music. Later in the decade, Mississippi bluesman Big Joe Williams passed through Memphis on his way north to St. Louis:

> Beale Street Park—back then they first called it that and then they named it Handy Park—that was the music center of Memphis. Even in the depression it was goin' strong. There were guitars, harps, bands,

everything out there in that park—right there on Beale and Hernando. I came in there and saw the Memphis Jug Band with tubs, fiddles, washboards—Will Shade was cuttin' up playing his harp, Jab Jones was huffin' on his jug. Oh boy, they were something. Gus Cannon and his band was there, so was Robert Johnson and Sonny Boy Williamson—everybody's in that park. They like to raise the devil with all them blues.[108]

Memphis blues in the prewar era documented the new urban experience of the incoming black migrant and charted the course for a transformation of the blues from a rural to an urban-based folk music. The blues texts produced in Memphis during this period provide a composite picture of city life as seen through the eyes of those at the bottom of the social order. The two overarching themes in their lyrics—living poor and being powerless—are expressed in complaints about money, mobility, work, floods, world wars, and especially the local criminal justice system. They seemed to dwell on jail sentences and prison terms, judges and lawyers, and omnipotent lawmen such as the infamous Joe Turner. Yet they also poked fun at civic leaders, black preachers, and even Booker T. Washington. Finally, they were ambivalent toward the local red-light district. On the one hand, they glorified Beale Street nightlife, bootleggers, white underworld czars, black desperados, and hedonism in general. But, on the other hand, they also cautioned about drug and alcohol addiction "killing you by degrees." Their composite picture was a reality-based continuation of the black oral tradition in a new social environment—a ghetto grapevine.

The sound of the blues was also transformed in Memphis. The solo instrumental styles associated with the rural blues gave way to ensemble playing, as practiced, in particular, by the Memphis jug bands. The jug was used as a primitive bass, much like the tuba in early New Orleans jazz. The harmonicas and kazoos were played more like jazz horns and less like field hollers or lonesome train whistles. When the bands played inside at night, a piano was added to the lineup, and maybe even some horns. The new blues sound was fuller and more rhythmically compelling than the old—a prefiguration of things to come all over the country.

# Chapter 7
## "Stormy Monday"
## Urban Blues in the Southwest

The surge in the number of African Americans migrating from rural to urban areas in the Deep South coincided with a similar surge in the Southwest. Between the two world wars, cities such as Dallas, Houston, and Kansas City recorded dramatic rises in their black populations. Many of the migrants came from small farming communities in northern Louisiana and eastern Texas, where a distinctive and widespread rural blues culture was already in the making. As in the Deep South, the cycle of urban transformation profoundly changed the blues. After World War II, the pattern was repeated in Los Angeles and Oakland. The blues moved west with the migratory flow of African Americans changing with each new influence along the way.

## Dallas Blues

Dallas was the first urban center of blues activity in the Southwest. After the turn of the century, itinerant East Texas rural bluesmen like "Ragtime Texas" Henry Thomas, Blind Lemon Jefferson, Leadbelly, and Texas Alexander began to filter into Dallas to play for tips and carouse in the tenderloin. At the turn of the century, the city had a black population of ten thousand; this number doubled in the next decade, and by 1930 the total was close to fifty thousand. The city was rigidly segregated but very prosperous because of the Texas oil boom and the city's importance as a major railroad terminal. The red-light district was along Central Avenue, or "Central Track" as it was known because of the abandoned railroad track that ran down the middle of the street. Elm Street, called "Deep Ellum," was the tenderloin's other major thoroughfare; it intersected with Central Avenue. Both were lined with theaters, cheap hotels, saloons, dance halls, cafes, pawnshops, and used-clothing stores. As in the South's other red-light districts, these establishments were usually owned by Jewish and Italian immigrants, and their clientele was mostly African Americans, although Mexicans as well as white gangsters and "cowboys" also frequented the area. A local black newspaper portrayed it as follows:

Down on Deep Ellum in Dallas, where Central Avenue empties into Elm Street and Ethiopia stretches forth her hands. It is the one spot in the city that needs no daylight saving time because there is no bedtime, and working hours have no limits. The only place recorded on earth where business, religion, hoodooism, gambling and stealing go on without friction.[1]

Piano players were the first blues musicians associated with the Deep Ellum tenderloin. In Dallas, Houston, and other cities of eastern Texas, the prevailing piano style for uptempo blues numbers was called "Fast Western" or "Fast Texas." An offshoot of boogie woogie, it probably came from the "Piney Woods" lumber and turpentine camps based in northwest Texas, northern Louisiana, and southern Arkansas. However, the style became a fixture in "Deep Ellum" after the turn of the century.

"Whistlin' " Alex Moore was born in Dallas on November 22, 1899. He grew up in the tenderloin, where he learned to play the blues by observing the city's more experienced piano players, among them some who were first-rate but in their prime too early to be recorded for posterity. Moore later recalled that these included Jesse Maloney, Mary Wright, Blind Bobby Bryant, Blind Benny, and a man called "Squad Low." These blues musicians played nightly in the saloons and brothels that honeycombed the Deep Ellum–Central Track area. During the day, they gathered at Ashman's Shine Parlor on Elm Street to swap songs and stories, as well as to find out about upcoming employment opportunities. They were the musical community that initiated an urban tradition in Dallas.[2]

Moore was a fixture in the "Deep Ellum" tenderloin all of his life. Like most of his fellow blues pianists, he was unable to make a living just playing the piano. Instead, he held a series of working-class jobs as a junkcart driver, hotel porter, and dishwasher. Moore modeled his celebrated whistling style after that of his sidekick, "Whistling" Billiken Johnson, a rotund, comic figure who was something of a legend in Deep Ellum before World War II. Johnson was a rambunctious blues singer noted for his imitations of train whistles and braying jackasses. Johnson, Moore, and a third compatriot named "Texas" Bill Day all recorded in the late 1920s. Moore was a talented composer who recorded his own unique blues numbers during his initial sessions; they included "West Texas Woman," "Heart Wrecked Blues," and the erotic "Blue Bloomer Blues," which goes in part:

She pulled off them blue bloomers, begin to whine and frown,
She pulled off her blue bloomers and begin to whine and frown,
I said, shush shush sweetie, let the deal go down.[3]

"Texas" Bill Day and Billiken Johnson teamed up to record the first of many "Elm Street Blues" in 1929. During the next decade, the song was so popular that two white Texas swing groups, the Lonesome Cowboys and the Dallas Jamboree Jug Band, recorded versions of it. Bill Neely, a white country singer and guitarist, heard many versions of "Deep Ellum Blues" when he visited the tenderloin during this period: "You'd hear it as a blues and a swing or hillbilly tune." Neely also recalled that local white gamblers and gangsters, including Baby Face Nelson and Bonnie and Clyde, were regular customers at Ma's Place, a nightclub in Deep Ellum that featured live music. He called it "the roughest place in town."[4] By that time, the blues had been an integral part of the tenderloin's night life for almost thirty years. Neely's own version of "Deep Ellum Blues" alluded to the mix of guns, gangsters, drugs, and blues that gave the district its notoriety:

When you go down on Deep Ellum you better tote a 44,
When you go down on Deep Ellum you better tote a 44,
'Cause when you get mixed up with gangsters,
You ain't comin' back to town no more.

Well it ain't nobody's business just what I'm goin' to do,
Well it ain't nobody's business just what I'm goin' to do,
I may stay right here and holler all night,
Long as I can sing the blues.

I'm gonna walk on down this road, get me one more fix and go to bed,
I'm gonna walk on down this road, get me one more fix and go to bed,
And when my baby finds me in the mornin',
Gonna find the best man she had was dead.[5]

Arron "T-Bone" Walker lived the early years of his life, from 1912 to 1935, in Dallas. Blind Lemon Jefferson was a friend of his family, and Walker associated with the famous blues bard from an early age:

I used to lead him around a lot. We'd go up and down Central Avenue. They had a railroad track there, and all the places were like clubs, beer joints, you know. They couldn't sell no whiskey no way. Beer joints and things like that, we used to play in them joints. Place upstairs called the Tip Top. We used to all play there.[6]

The musical versatility and inventiveness that characterized Walker's later career was nourished by the rich blend of blues, jazz, and gospel sounds he heard in Dallas during his youth. The black community there was saturated with musical genres available only in certain urban locales. Walker not only became a skilled guitarist, but also learned to play the violin, mandolin, banjo, ukulele, and piano. After his apprenticeship with Blind Lemon Jefferson, Walker played with a regional medicine show, Ida Cox's backup group, and a local dance band formed by his high school classmates—all before he reached his twentieth birthday. This mixture of musical experiences put him in touch with a wide range of African-American music, from the long-standing popular rural blues tradition grounded in East Texas to the newly emerging urban jazz bands found in cities like Dallas.

Walker's indebtedness to the older rural blues school was documented in the first record he made for Columbia in 1929. The two titles "Wichita Falls Blues" and "Trinity River Blues" were solo efforts clearly inspired by the style and material of Blind Lemon Jefferson. Yet the Lawson Brooks Band, in which Walker played guitar during this same period, was a sixteen-piece ensemble patterned after the popular "territory bands" of the day: Bennie Moton's group from Kansas City, Walter Page's Blue Devils from Oklahoma City, the Milton Larkin Band from Houston, Troy Floyd's band from San Antonio, Terrence T. Holder and his Clouds of Joy from Dallas, and the Alphonzo Trent Orchestra, also from Dallas. Because the Southwest remained relatively isolated from the influence of the commercial music industry and vaudeville, the territory bands were able to experiment more freely with fusing certain blues practices with jazz instrumentation. Most notably, blues vocal techniques were transferred to the musical instruments used in the brass and reed sections: in essence, the blues vocal became the blues instrumental. The guitar started out as part of the rhythm section, but it soon emerged as a solo instrument, especially when electric amplification was added. Two Dallas musicians, Eddie Durham and Charlie Christian, were in the forefront of the transition to electric guitar in the jazz world, while T-Bone Walker is credited with being the first blues musician to amplify his guitar. Walker first experimented with an electric guitar in the mid-1930s, soon after moving to Los Angeles from Dallas. He left his chair in the Lawson Brooks Band to Charlie Christian, a teenage musical prodigy destined to become the most highly acclaimed jazz guitarist of the era.[7]

Buster Smith was another jazz giant schooled in the Dallas tenderloin. He was born on August 26, 1904. His parents were sharecroppers who lived and worked in the cotton belt south of Dallas. Smith was still in his early teens when his father died. He had to quit school and go to work in the fields to help support his mother and the younger members of the family. The lure of city life and the slow decline of the cotton economy in East Texas eventually drew the family to Dallas in the early 1920s. A few months before the move, Smith had spotted a used clarinet in a pawnshop window and had picked cotton to earn $3.50 to buy it. In the city, Smith learned to play his clarinet as countless other first-generation urban black jazz artists did: by studying and imitating the musicians in the tenderloin:

> I just picked it up little by little by watching people who played the same instrument. I'd watch them and listen and pick up more and more. I used to hear a boy named Jesse Hooker, an awful good clarinet player who used to play down on Central Track at a place called the Tip Top Club. He couldn't read either. I'd go down there and listen to him until he moved on. This was in 1922. . . . About that time a little band come up from New Orleans and came in there at the Tip Top Club and hired me and another fellow 'cause they were two men short. Me and the other fellow made it five pieces. I played with them for a few weeks until they left and then I gigged around Dallas for a year or so with Voddie White—Voddie White played piano, I played clarinet and a drummer—I forgot his name. We played around town a few places and at Saturday night suppers. . . . We usually called our music barrelhouse or gut-bucket. It was considered rough music. We didn't use the word jazz very often.[8]

Buster Smith left Dallas with the Blue Devils in 1925 and went on to become an influential alto saxophonist in the Kansas City jazz bands of the 1930s. Had he never left the cotton belt for the city, he might have applied his talents to the rural blues, but it is unlikely that he would have been a jazz reed innovator. The early jazz groups were a dramatic departure from the traditional rural blues lineup of string instruments and homemade rhythm makers, even though they played a hybrid form of blues. They were an early manifestation of an urban blues ensemble style that developed in close proximity to the territory bands in the Southwest, incorporating jazz orchestration into its overall sound.

## Houston Blues

By the early 1900s, Houston was the site of the largest concentration of African Americans in Texas. There were close to thirty-five thousand black people living there in 1920; the number had risen past eighty-six thousand by 1940. This figure was about 22 percent of the city's total population. Houston had a bitter legacy of violent racial conflict dating to an 1866 white citizens' riot against black Union troops stationed near the city. Black federal troops were also involved in an armed conflict with local police in 1917, which left thirteen white citizens dead. Thirteen African-American soldiers were hanged for their role in this incident, and another forty-one were given life sentences.

In the late nineteenth century, Houston developed into a prosperous regional center for rail and water transportation; its railroad yards and docks handled huge cargoes of cotton and then oil. After the turn of the century, the yards and docks were also handling large shipments of lumber, textiles, and meat. Sawmills, textile factories, and meat-packing plants sprang up in the vicinity. Rural African Americans in East Texas, whose cotton economy was being ravaged by the boll weevil, were drawn into Houston to work as unskilled laborers and domestics, despite the racial violence, the Jim Crow laws, and the political disenfranchisement awaiting them. (It wasn't until the end of World War II that they finally won the right to vote in local elections.)[9]

African Americans living in Houston were confined to four segregated ghettos by the 1920s. The largest, and the earliest to be established, was the inner-city Fourth Ward, known as "Freedman's Town" in the post–Civil War era. The Fourth Ward was also the location of Houston's red-light district. It was centered in Dowling Street, with off-shoots along San Felipe Street and West Dallas Street. Dowling Street was the site of Houston's two TOBA theaters, the Lincoln and the Key, as well as the famous Eldorado Ballroom. The largest dance facility in the Fourth Ward was the Emancipation Park Dance Pavilion, where the traditional "Juneteenth" celebration—commemorating the freeing of the slaves in Texas—was held. Many of the tenderloin's saloons, restaurants, cabarets, and bordellos were clustered along San Felipe and West Dallas Streets.[10]

As in most southern cities, Houston's earliest blues artists were piano players. They were usually associated with the night life along West Dallas Street. These musicians were referred to as the "Santa Fe" group because some of them worked a circuit along the Santa Fe Railroad west of Houston, and because their "Fast Texas" style of boogie woogie owed much to the repetitive rhythms of train wheels on iron rails. The railroad also symbolized freedom and mobility to African-American migrants in the Southwest. Hence it is not surprising that this community of blues pianists had several train blues in their collective repertoire; some of the best known were "Santa Fe Train," "Rock Island Blues," "Mountain Jack," and "She Caught the L&N." Most of the older first-generation blues pianists associated with the West Dallas Street/Santa Fe network were never recorded and therefore exist only in the black oral tradition as collective memories evoked by such ancestral names as Black Shine, Pegleg Will, Pin Top Burks, Foster, Scanlin Smith, and Edgar Perry. Those who were recorded include the influential Thomas brothers, Rob Cooper, "Cowboy" Walter Washington, Andy Boy, and Buster Pickens.[11]

The older of the Thomas brothers, George Jr., was born in Houston in 1885; his father worked for the Southern Pacific Railroad. The entire family was musical. George Jr. was employed as a local TOBA piano player when he met Clarence Williams in 1911. At the time, his blues trademark was a boogie-woogie East Texas piece that he eventually entitled "New Orleans Hop Scop Blues." In 1914, he joined Clarence Williams in New Orleans and then moved on to Chicago, where he was recorded in the early 1920s. By then, he was employing walking bass progressions and leading his own band. George's younger brother Hersal was born in 1910 and proved to be the family's musical prodigy; he absorbed the music around him, and by the time he was a teenager, he was one of Houston's most promising blues pianists—already influencing older musicians in the West Dallas/Santa Fe network, including Rob Cooper and Andy Boy. Hersal joined his older brother in Chicago, where he recorded his trademark "Suitcase Blues" in 1924. It was a hit as a race record release and established Hersal as an up-and-coming blues pianist. Within a year, he was recording with jazz greats like King Oliver and Louis Armstrong and attracting the attention of Albert Ammons and Meade Lux Lewis, who were also immersed in the new boogie-woogie blues styles at the time. With a promising career on the horizon, Hersal died from food poisoning in Detroit at the age of sixteen. His sister, classic blues singer Sippie Wallace, remembered her brother with affection and awe:

> Baby brother Hersal was so precious, and he could play anything he heard. Play it right back when he was only a boy. Everybody took notice when he sat down at a piano. I went to Chicago after him 'cause they knew I liked to sing like Bessie Smith and them. I could play too and I could rhyme up songs. But Lord, my little Hersal, he was way up there and only a boy. Had them all crowding around him there in Chicago. They never heard nothing like him. He was so popular, only sixteen when he died . . . just a boy.[12]

Only a handful of other Houston-based blues piano players were recorded in the prewar era. Rob Cooper recorded his signature piece, "West Dallas Drag"; it was based on a pre-blues ragtime piano style with family ties to such numbers as "The Cows," "The Ma Grinder," and "The Dirty Dozen"—all well-known folksongs from the African-American underworld. "Cowboy" Walter Washington cut "West Dallas Woman," another rough-and-tumble tribute to the street their blues network was named after. There was also Andy Boy's "House Raid," chronicling a police raid on a Galveston nightclub. All of these songs in one way or another highlighted night life in the black urban tenderloin.

Andy Boy was originally from Galveston, where he was born in 1906, but he played often in Houston's Fourth Ward. When he was finally recorded there in the late 1930s, his original material contained some incisive blues lyrics that crystalized the perils of ghetto life:

> You can take my money, I know that's the thing you lack,
> You can take my money, I know that's the thing you lack,
> But please don't mistreat me just because I'm black.[13]

Robert Shaw and Buster Pickens were two blues pianists associated with the West Dallas/Santa Fe network who managed to survive into the postwar decades. Shaw was born in Houston in 1908 and learned his trade in the Fourth Ward honky-tonks in the 1920s. He recalled that most of the blues pianists playing in the tenderloin during that era had limited repertoires—a slow-tempo blues and a fast boogie woogie were all that was needed to keep the customers happy.[14] Buster Pickens was born just northwest of Houston in Hempstead, Texas, in 1916. He took to the rails as a teen during the depression and learned to play the blues by following the Santa Fe barrelhouse circuit in the region—saw mills, turpentine camps, oil boomtowns. Blues became his vocation and way of life:

> Back in the late 1920s and early 1930s . . . when blues touched a man's heart . . . whatever trouble he had, these blues solved his problems, . . . even these tears soon dried up behind these blues.[15]

Houston's black population was large enough by the 1920s to support several African-American marching and dance bands. City natives like Milt Larkin and Arnett Cobb learned to play their horns in local high school ensembles before moving on to become dance-band musicians. Larkin played both trumpet and valve trombone; he was also a gifted arranger and composer. Cobb modeled his tenor sax style after his idol, Coleman Hawkins, but like Buster Smith, he also had an authentic feel for the blues. He first teamed up with Milt Larkin in a local band that Milt organized in 1930, a territory dance band that played mostly blues. Larkin's group was featured at the fashionable Harlem Square Club and played its first "Juneteenth" celebration at the Emancipation Park Pavilion in 1931. Milt recalled their performance nostalgically:

> Juneteenth was our biggest celebration back then. It was special, . . . always drew the biggest crowd of the year. They'd fill up Emancipation Park. Never will forget when we first played for it—that was something for us because we were young and just coming up. Well, they loved us, especially our blues. You never seen such dancin' and carrying on. The whole town turned out to celebrate—it was wild. We never missed one

after that, made a point of being there even when we were touring some. . . . But then they stopped Juneteenth when the war came. Don't quite know why. Any country that don't have music gonna have wars.[16]

In its heyday in the 1930s, the Milt Larkin band featured a superb saxophone section; in addition to Arnett Cobb, it included Eddie "Cleanhead" Vinson and Illinois Jacquett. Vinson also developed into a first-rate blues vocalist—somewhat in the mold of the Kansas City blues "shouters." Another Houston-based blues singer popular during this period was Joe Pullen, who made a series of records and also broadcast live on KTLC, a local radio station. He had a sweet-sounding high falsetto voice. His backup piano player, Preston "Peachy" Chase, played a softer, more melodious style of blues than the West Dallas street group.[17] Their more sophisticated blues sound was similar to that of fellow Texans T-Bone Walker and Ivory Joe Hunter, whose music would eventually coalesce into a West Coast urban blues tradition in the postwar era.

Of all the younger musicians associated with the Houston blues scene before World War II, Sam "Lightnin' " Hopkins proved to be the most down-home, durable, and renowned for his folk wit, wisdom, and wily ways. He first came to Houston's Fourth Ward in the late 1920s as a teenager playing guitar behind his older cousin, East Texas blues great Alger "Texas" Alexander. Sam grew up on a farm outside Centerville in rural Texas. He came from a musical family; his father and older brothers introduced him to folk blues at an early age. As a youth, he learned to play blues guitar on a home-made instrument fashioned out of a cigar box. While still in his teens, he traveled with Blind Lemon Jefferson and then played guitar for Texas Alexander. These early influences and experiences shaped his approach to the blues tradition. Hopkins was a folksy country sage who used the blues to tell stories with moral messages the way an African-American preacher used the Scriptures:

You see, my songs are practically all true songs. They are about something real to my way of thinking. Like all that happened to me is liable to get into my songs. In my family they tell about my grandfather that was a slave that hung himself to escape bad treatment. Well, that's liable to be in one of my songs. Or that time I was out in Arizona—supposed to be picking cotton but I got to gambling and then I got to going over to Mexico and bringing back wine and bootlegging it to them Indians on that government reservation. That's liable to be in my songs. Or the time it was trouble up home, or when they got me on the country work gang, or had to say goodbye to some good girl, or be thinking of going to Galveston Beach—all that's liable to come up in my songs. Call 'em true songs.[18]

Toward the end of the depression, Hopkins served time on the Houston County prison farm. He had leg-iron scars on his ankles as a result of the ordeal. By the late 1930s, he was back in Houston working in several clubs with a small group of musicians that included Cleveland Chenier on washboard, his cousin Andrew "Smokey" Hogg playing backup guitar, and sometimes Buster Pickens on piano. In 1946, Hopkins made his first recordings for Aladdin Records in Los Angeles. At this juncture in his career, he was already using an amplified guitar, but his blues material was still folk poetry at its best. Hopkins was not reluctant to recycle the themes of racial mistreatment and estrangement that were central to the rural blues tradition in East Texas. In "Tim Moore's Farm" he sings:

> You know, they ain't but one thing this black man done wrong,
> Yes, folks, ain't but one thing this black man done wrong,
> Yes, you know I moved my wife and family down on
>     Tim Moore's farm.
>
> You know, I got a telegram this morning, it say, "Your wife
>     is dead,"
> I showed it to Mr. Moore, he said, "Go ahead, nigger, plow
>     that ridge,"
> White man say, "It's been rainin', yes sir, I'm way behind,
> I may let you bury that woman on your dinner time."[19]

The same persona is used in "Stranger Here":

> You know I'm a stranger here, so tell me if I'm wrong,
> I'm just a passing stranger, tell me if I'm wrong,
> If you don't got no food, baby, will you please do me a favor,
> Will you throw this old dog a bone?
>
> You know, they been raisin' sand, been raisin' sand, way
>     down in Alabama town,
> People keep on raisin' sand, they be raisin' sand down in
>     Alabama town (and Texas too, baby),
> You know, I don't stop no place that they fightin',
> That's the reason po' Lightnin' keeps scurryin' around.
>
> If they don't stop fightin', there's gonna be a war pretty soon,
> Yes, If they don't quit fightin', gonna be a war real soon,
> You know they already called me a low-down dirty dog,
> God knows I don't wanna be called a coon.[20]

Hopkins remained based in Houston for most of his career. He worked in the working-class honky-tonks and saloons that honeycombed the Fourth Ward's red-light district. His blues repertoire and style remained close to the folk roots of the music. He used four or five blues melodies with a minimal number of chord changes over and over again, simply refashioning each of them with a different set of lyrics. But even within this simple conceptual framework, he was able to create an aesthetic medium for converting the pain and anger in his life into a thing of beauty. Combined with his wry wit and his ability to laugh at himself, this rare talent made Sam ''Lightnin' '' Hopkins a giant among his peers.

Many Texas bluesmen moved to the West Coast during the last years of the depression and especially during the war years. Blues artists Ivory Joe Hunter, Amos Milburn, and Charles Brown moved from Houston to Los Angeles during this period. A similar pattern was evident in other cities in the Southwest. Roy Milton, a blues drummer and band leader, and Lowell Fulson, a blues guitarist and composer, both natives of Tulsa, had relocated in California by World War II. There they would help lay the groundwork for the postwar urban blues resurgence on the West Coast. Only Kansas City proved to be an exception among major cities in the Southwest during the depression era. In fact, the Texas blues and jazz musicians who did not move to the West Coast moved to Kansas City. There, a fusion of southwestern blues and jazz styles also helped to set the stage for the emergence of a new urban blues after World War II.

## Kansas City: The Last Tenderloin

The red-light district in Kansas City, Missouri, proved to be one of the few underworld strongholds in the country that survived and even flourished during the economic downturn in the 1930s. As a result, it remained a haven for migrant blues musicians throughout the depression. The town was founded in the early 1830s as a frontier outpost; by the turn of the century it had emerged as the commercial hub of the Southwest and the central plains states, famous for its malodorous stockyards and unrestricted night life. At the time, gambling seems to have been the tenderloins' most popular vice:

> The gambling industry attained a high state of development in Kansas City. . . . The faro banks at Marble Hall and No. 3 Missouri Avenue were famous throughout the West; . . . the citizens exercised their financial genius at chuck-a-luck, faro, three card monte, roulette, high five,

keno, poker and occasionally, craps. They bet on horseraces, dog fights, free for alls with rats, cock fights.[21]

Kansas City's working-class ghettos—the Irish West Bottoms and the Italian North End, later called "Little Italy"—were controlled by a Democratic political machine under the leadership of Jim Pendergast, a politician who also happened to be in the wholesale liquor and hotel businesses. The machine he organized was tied to the local liquor, gambling, and prostitution interests operating in the city. In exchange for protection from the police, the vice operators provided Pendergast with money and votes. In 1910, Jim Pendergast passed on his position as the political boss of the ward to his younger brother, Tom Pendergast, who was elected to the city council a year later. From that vantage point, Tom Pendergast was able to consolidate his power until he was the undisputed boss of Kansas City politics. Like his brother, he was a shrewd businessman. He took over management of the family's liquor business and the Jefferson Hotel in downtown Kansas City. He turned the hotel into both his political headquarters and an exclusive pleasure palace catering to the city's political and underworld elite, with gambling, prostitution, freely flowing liquor, a cabaret in the basement, and no closing time. When Prohibition was passed, Pendergast entrusted his liquor operations to his childhood pal from the Italian section of the First Ward, Johnny Lazia. Before the end of the decade, Lazia was the reigning mobster chieftain of the city's vice operations and the political boss of "Little Italy."[22]

The team of Pendergast and Lazia brought unprecedented profits and notoriety to the city's red-light district, which gained a reputation as the vice capital of middle America. "If you want to see some sin, forget about Paris and go to Kansas City" were the words Edward R. Murrow used to sum up his impressions of the city in the thirties. Even the repeal of federal Prohibition failed to put a damper on its fabled underworld amusements; Kansas City remained an oasis for racketeers and pleasure seekers, while the other urban hotspots around the country went into a slow decline. Only the murder of Johnny Lazia in 1934 and the conviction of Tom Pendergast along with many of his associates on income tax evasion in 1938 brought an end to the city's formidable mobster syndicate and its tenderloin stronghold. In the wake of Pendergast's lengthy administration, Kansas City found that it had a deficit of $20 million, and that three thousand individuals on the city payroll did no work for their monthly paychecks. It was also learned that Tom Pendergast had gambled away $6 million between 1925 and 1935.[23]

Before the decline of Kansas City's red-light district, however, fifteen years of "Pendergast prosperity" had attracted a flood of African-American migrants to the city. By 1930, they made up about 15 percent of its half-million inhabitants. The black tenderloin was centered in a six-block area between

12th and 18th streets near the railyards and stockyards in the North End. It contained the usual assortment of barbershops; shoeshine parlors; saloons and cabarets, many featuring live music; and numerous restaurants specializing in chili, barbecued chicken, pigsfeet, spare ribs, crawdads, and brain sandwiches. Most of the larger, more lucrative nightclubs were owned by gangsters who operated them as legitimate businesses. Two of these gangsters, Felix Payne and "Papa" Sol Epstein, were key members of the Pendergast-Lazia syndicate. Payne was the owner of a string of well-known local cabarets, including the Twin Cities club, the Sunset Club, and the Subway Club. The Twin Cities Club was built on the Kansas-Missouri border in a ploy calculated to discourage and confuse the police from both states. The Subway Club and the Sunset Club were famous for their blues and jazz. Boogie-woogie pianist Pete Johnson and blues shouter Joe Turner began their musical careers at the Sunset Club. Felix Payne's nightclubs in the black tenderloin district were managed by Piney Brown, a legendary figure among territory musicians. Brown always featured live music in the clubs he ran and regularly provided food and shelter to needy musicians. These clubs were famous for sensational jam sessions, which attracted the best jazz performers in town. Blues scholar and poet Sterling A. Brown met Piney Brown in Kansas City in 1927:

> Piney was over six feet tall, a handsome man, attractive to the ladies. We played some tennis together, and he proved to be pretty good, even though he was still learning to play. He was a successful gambler and nightclub operator who ran with a rough crowd, but he was always a gentlemen and also a race man, proud of his heritage. He loved music and he was very sociable; everybody liked and respected him, especially the musicians in Kansas City. Piney was generous with his time and a marvelous storyteller; he could make anyone in his presence feel right at home.[24]

The jewel of the Kansas City cabarets was Epstein's Reno Club. It was a segregated club with a divider down the middle to separate the black customers from the white customers; each side had its own bar, dance floor, and tables. Prostitutes worked out of bedrooms on the second floor of the club. Marijuana imported from Mexico was sold in the vacant lot in back and smoked in the club's balcony. Rolled marijuana cigarettes, called "reefers" or "sticks of shit," cost ten cents or three for a quarter. The food and drinks were also inexpensive, but the real drawing card was the music. There was usually a floor show with TOBA talent, and the house band featured the hottest musicians in town. The wages for these black entertainers were low, but there was free food and drink and a "kitty" for tips. The musicians had the freedom to play their own styles of dance music, and the club was known for its exciting after-hours jam sessions. These musical battles allowed visiting musicians and the city's aspiring young performers to test their skills and ideas in competition with seasoned local players. The highlight of the week at the Reno club was the "spook breakfast," a special jam session held early on Sunday morning. It attracted the cream of the Kansas City sporting crowd and the best musicians in the region.

The other popular cabarets noted for showcasing blues and jazz musicians were Eddie Spitz's College Inn, Joe Barone's Boulevard Lounge, Milton Morris' Novelty Club, and Chief Ellis Burton's Yellow Front Saloon. Burton was as avid a patron of black musicians as was Piney Brown, with a policy of providing food, drink, and shelter when needed. His saloon was a modest establishment, as was the Novelty Club, where Milton Morris used bales of hay and wine caskets for chairs and tables, and an old wagon for a bandstand. At its zenith in the 1930s, the Kansas City red-light district had a higher concentration of nightclubs presenting live music than any comparable tenderloin district in the country. The local crime syndicate netted millions in gambling, drug sales, prostitution, and the operation of cabarets. This financial windfall supported the city's celebrated musical milieu at its peak period, making Kansas City the liveliest blues and jazz center in the nation during the depression.[25]

## Kansas City's Blues-Jazz Fusion

Marching brass bands, ragtime piano, and vaudeville blues had more of a presence in Kansas City than in Texas during the first decades of the twentieth century. Arthur Pryor's brass band, the pride of the Midwest, often performed in the city before large, enthusiastic audiences. His musical style and material drew much more from such traditional African-American sources as cakewalks and ragtime compositions than did those of his chief rival, John Philip Sousa. The most famous black marching brass band in the region was the Queen City Concert Band, led by cornetist Ed Gravitt. The twelve-piece group was based in Sedalia, but routinely traveled to Kansas City's black ward to challenge the local bands there. The city's African-American high school, Lincoln High, and several local black social organizations had their own marching bands. These volunteer ensembles marched in the city's annual parades and played the summer concerts in the parks. They proved to be an important training ground for younger musicians who would eventually join the smaller dance bands playing in the city's burgeoning entertainment district. Although these early Kansas City groups featured horn players, they were most often led by piano players schooled in the prevailing ragtime style and able to read sheet music.

The best-known black rag-time musicians associated with Kansas City were Otis Saunders and James Scott. Saunder's sobriquet "Crackerjack" alluded to his dapper dress and good looks. He was a close friend of Scott Joplin's. The two were based in Sedalia during the 1890s and made frequent trips together to other hotbeds of ragtime piano. Saunders then moved on to the Oklahoma Territory and eventually drifted into Kansas City where he stayed until just before World War I. James Scott was born in Neasho, in the southwest corner of Missouri, in 1886 and grew up in nearby Carthage, where he began his career as a ragtime pianist and composer. He moved to Kansas City in 1914, about the same time Saunders left for Chicago, and remained there for the rest of his life. He was known affectionately as the "Little Professor," and next to Scott Joplin, he was the leading ragtime composer of the era. James Scott taught piano and composition in Kansas City, while also playing organ and arranging music for the house bands he organized for the local vaudeville theaters. He started to work for the Panama Theatre in 1916, then went on to the Lincoln and finally the Eblon in the late twenties.

This was black vaudeville's golden age, and Kansas City was a major stop on the TOBA circuit. It was the western turnaround point for the shows and rated just below Chicago as the city that the musicians and performers most liked to visit. Scott was instrumental in launching the career of his cousin, classic blues singer Ada Brown, who as a singer with the famous Bennie Moton Band made the first record associated with the Kansas City blues and jazz blend, "Evil Mama Blues," in 1923. Three other well-known classic blues singers from Kansas City were Mary Bradford who also recorded with Bennie Moton's group; Julia Lee, the sister of band leader George Lee; and Lottie Beamon, later known as Lottie Kimbrough. These women all sang the blues with Kansas City dance bands, and toured occasionally on the TOBA circuit. Their music reflected the increasing influence of vaudeville blues styles on Kansas City jazz bands by the 1920s.[26]

By the time Kansas City's seasoned jazz bands reached their height of creativity in the depression years, they were playing a basic blues-infused dance music. The earlier groups, however, had been more ragtime and vaudeville-oriented. Bennie Moton and George Lee, Kansas City natives, organized the first successful local bands. Lee, a ballad singer who also played saxophone, teamed up with his sister, singer and pianist Julia Lee. Their band, made up of a small horn section, piano, and drums, was modeled on the ensembles that played behind the classic blues singers on the TOBA circuit. Moton, on the other hand, was a student of ragtime; after starting his musical training in a marching brass band playing a baritone horn, he studied piano with two of Scott Joplin's former pupils. His earliest group was a trio, which he soon abandoned in favor of a six-piece band in 1921. Their music was initially an instrumental style of ragtime, but by the time the band made its first series of recordings for the Okeh label in 1923, they were also backing up classic blues singers Ada Brown and Mary Bradford. As a result, close to three-quarters of the songs they recorded during these initial sessions were blues numbers. Moton's band would continue to explore and develop a fusion of blues and jazz elements in their material well into the 1930s; they would greatly benefit from the influx of such Texas musicians as Eddie Durham, Oran "Hot Lips" Page, Ben Webster, and Buster Smith. The demise of the legendary Blue Devils from Oklahoma City also contributed some key musicians to Bennie Moton's growing jazz band, including bassist Walter Page, trombone player Jap Allen, tenor saxophone player Lester Young, pianist Bill "Count" Basie, and blues vocalist Jimmy Rushing. Basie took over the leadership of the band in 1935 when Moton died during minor surgery.[27]

## The Kansas City Blues Shouters

Jimmy Rushing was born into a musical family in Oklahoma City; his parents were musicians, and his uncle, Wesley Manning, was the most celebrated honky-tonk pianist in the town. Rushing's mother encouraged him to play the violin at an early age; while he was in his teens, his uncle taught him to play the piano and introduced him to the blues. He went on to study music in high school and college before moving to Los Angeles, where he worked as a piano player and vocalist. In Los Angeles, he occasionally sang with Jelly Roll Morton's band. Jimmy Rushing returned to Oklahoma City in 1926 and started singing in his father's cafe with members of the Blue Devil's talented entourage. He joined the group as the band vocalist and stayed in it until 1932, when he moved on to the Bennie Moton organization in Kansas City; for the next two decades, he was an integral part of the Moton-Basie jazz band. Early in his career, his small stature and portly midsection earned him his famous stage name, "Mr. Five by Five." Rushing was the first of the urban blues "shouters." He was a powerful singer with a tonal range from baritone to tenor, which enabled him to project his voice even in a big-band setting. He sang with a touch of vibrato and a buoyancy that allowed his voice to soar above the hefty horn and reed sections playing behind him. His best numbers were simply charted blues compositions, sometimes combined with components of popular songs. The lyrics focused on male-female relationships, and, like the lyrics of most jazz-band vocalists during the "swing" era, they were more indebted to the romantic lyricism of the popular ballad than to the realistic lyricism of the rural blues. Above all, Jimmy Rushing was one of a new breed of male blues singers able to hold their own in the most renowned jazz bands in the country. His collaborator, "Count" Basie, stated that Rushing "never had an equal" as a blues vocalist.[28]

Jimmy Rushing's chief rival in Kansas City music circles was another native of the city, an authoritative blues shouter with a sonorous voice known as Big Joe Turner, born in 1911. As a youth, he worked as a guide for a blind street musician and sang with a quartet in the local parks. He and his boyhood friends also hung around his uncle's club at night listening to the music and watching the musicians through the windows; at the time, they were too young to go in as paying customers. While still in his early teens, Turner launched his singing career as a vocalist in honky-tonks such as the Kingfish Club, Backbiters, the Hole in the Wall, and the Cherry Blossom. He soon moved on to team up with Pete Johnson, who was working as the house pianist at Piney Brown's Sunset Club. Johnson was seven years older than Turner and already established as the city's finest boogie-woogie piano player. He was famous for his powerful left-hand playing technique and his ability to sound like an entire rhythm section. Turner was hired as a bartender at the Sunset Club, but he also became the resident blues shouter. Kansas City pianist Mary Lou Williams frequented the club during this period. She remembered their performances vividly:

> While Joe was serving drinks, he would suddenly pick up a tune for a blues and sing it right where he stood, with Pete playing piano for him. I don't think I'll ever forget the thrill of listening to Big Joe Turner shouting and sending everybody while mixing drinks.[29]

To take advantage of Turner's booming voice, Brown hooked up a loudspeaker over the front door of the club so that his bartender could be heard up and down the street. Turner later had fond memories of the evenings he spent in the club:

> All the working people came in early to the Sunset and got high and had a ball. Then things would quiet down and finally there wouldn't be nobody in there except the bartender, waiter, and the boss, and we'd start playing about three o'clock in the morning. People used to say they could hear me hollerin' five blocks away. It would be in the still of the morning and the bossman would set up pitchers of corn liquor and we'd rock. Just about the time we'd be starting to have a good time, here would come the high hats and we'd set the joint on fire then and really have a ball till ten or eleven o'clock in the day. Sleep? Who wants to sleep with all that blues jumping around.[30]

In the long after-hours jam sessions, some of the blues numbers became very long:

> I'd sing three, four hours and never sing the same verse. I'd keep all those things in my head, and they didn't know how I'd do it. But all the time I'd be writing that stuff as I go along. Once I get started into a good blues song, I could carry on for hours. And I'd get the people all stirred up, just like the preacher. Stir 'em up.[31]

Early Saturday morning was the prime time for the Sunset Club jam sessions during the decade that Turner and Johnson worked there; musicians from the Moton-Basie band sat in whenever they could. Johnson also had his own band—featuring him on piano, a rhythm section, a few horns, and Turner on vocals; they would play around town at breakfast parties and dances organized by Kansas City's black social clubs, which numbered in the hundreds before World War II.

It was out of this constant round of paid gigs and after-hours jam sessions that a distinct Kansas City style emerged, a synthesis of blues and jazz. The vehicle for accomplishing this synthesis was a musical innovation called the "riff"; it was a thirty-two-bar song formula with an AABA structure. As jazz historian Ross Russell has pointed out:

> The bare bones character of the riff may be likened to the simple twelve bar form and three chord system chosen by the blues singers of the Southwest. The twelve bar blues and the Kansas City riff are both solutions to the problems of form within which individual improvisation may proceed by methods in keeping with the Afro-American tradition.[32]

The improvisational soloing for which Kansas City's black musicians were famous borrowed from the techniques used by blues vocalists. Effects such as vibrato, pitch variation, tremolo, and slurring and sliding notes were all commonplace among the city's horn players. The riff, these instrumental blues, and a swinging rhythm section were the defining characteristics of Kansas City jazz in its heyday during the depression.

The free-flowing jam sessions also created a laboratory for experimenting with new musical techniques and ideas, and a school for training young players in the fundamentals of the new style. The city supported as many as eight territory bands. The number of black musicians living and playing in the red-light district numbered in the hundreds. An annual band competition sponsored by the local black musicians' union always drew six to eight bands and close to one hundred musicians. It was held in the El Paso Ballroom. Huge crowds came out to see the musical pyrotechnics of the town's leading ensembles, headed up by Bennie Moton, Count Basie, George Lee, Jesse Stone, Harlan Leonard, and Andy Kirk. This battle of the bands was the musical event of the year for the members of these groups, and an indication of the vitality of their style of music.

The sudden collapse of Pendergast prosperity closed down much of the red-light district in Kansas City. The black workforce, including the musicians, lost their jobs and began to disperse. New York City became the new jazz mecca of the country, attracting many of Kansas City's more established and talented musicians. The Basie band played extended engagements in New York and held most of its recording sessions there. Charlie Christian and Charlie Parker became leading figures in the bebop revolution in jazz, centered in Harlem in the early 1940s. Even Big Joe Turner and Pete Johnson moved to New York, where they appeared at the Café Society and cut their first big recording in 1938 for the Vocalion label—"Roll 'em Pete" and "Cherry Red." "Roll 'em Pete" was a rambling boogie woogie with Turner contributing sets of random blues lyrics: "Roll 'em boy, we gonna jump for joy." "Cherry Red" was a sexually assertive blues number in praise of erotic love:

> Now you can take me, pretty mama, and dump
>  me in your Hollywood bed,
> And boogie my woogie 'til my face turns cherry
>  red.[33]

Two years later, the death of Piney Brown dealt a final blow to the Kansas City music scene. His close friends Johnson and Turner paid tribute to their former patron that same year when they released "Piney Brown Blues," improvised in a recording studio after they learned that he had died:

> Yes, I dreamed last night, I was standing on
>  the corner of 18th and Vine,
> Yes, I dreamed last night, I was standing on
>  the corner of 18th and Vine,
> I shook hands with Piney Brown and could
>  hardly keep from cryin'.[34]

On the eve of World War II, blues culture reached a watershed in the urban Southwest. Earlier in the century, the mass migration into cities like Dallas, Houston, and Kansas City had completely transformed the style and sound of secular black music. When rural blues troubadours played their guitars and sang their cautionary laments on tenderloin street corners, piano players in the nearby bordellos and barrelhouses picked up this new folk music, adapting it to their instruments and clientele—as did the local black dance bands. Gunther Schuller notes:

> Before the 1920s the blues existed at a separate social-cultural-musical level from that occupied by orchestras playing in hotels and dance halls. Once the blues had broken through into the middle class urban realm, however, the larger Southwestern orchestras quickly adopted the form and used it more consistently than bands anywhere else.[35]

Perhaps more important, the blues continued to be the most popular style of music among the new black urban proletariat, but not without going through some significant changes. Manufactured instruments such as pianos, drums, and horns (including saxophone, trumpet, and trombone) replaced the home-made variety used in rural blues bands; the guitar and harmonica remained, but they were amplified. What emerged was a unique urban blues ensemble style and repertoire flavored by regional characteristics. Yet just as a new urban blues culture was taking root in the Southwest, the tenderloins that had nurtured it went into a decline. Much of the economic infrastructure supporting the music collapsed, leaving the fate of the blues in the region blowing in the winds of war and further westward migration.

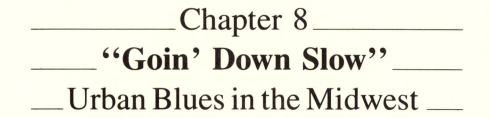

# Chapter 8
## "Goin' Down Slow"
## Urban Blues in the Midwest

### St. Louis: Trouble in River City

St. Louis was the third riverport on the Mississippi River to become a major center of urban blues activity, and, as in Memphis and New Orleans, the blues culture was entangled in the local red-light district. The city was founded by French fur traders in the eighteenth century; during the next century it became a bustling trade and transportation center, "the Gateway to the West." Because of its access to both railroad and river transportation, St. Louis was an ideal location for industrial development after the Civil War. By the turn of the century, it had a prosperous manufacturing base and was the nation's fourth largest city. Politically, St. Louis was a Democratic stronghold with a ward system of government based on the ethnic composition of the large working-class population. The German immigrants were the largest ethnic enclave in the city, but there were also Irish, Italian, Polish, and African-American neighborhoods. In 1876, the city voters chose to secede from the territory of Missouri rather than pay taxes to extend municipal services to homesteaders living outside the city boundaries. The decision later prevented the city from annexing land around it when it needed to expand. This would prove to be crucial when the nineteenth-century transportation system, dominated by street cars, railroads, and steamships, gave way to the twentieth-century system of subways, automobiles, and airplanes. St. Louis was unable to adapt effectively to the changes that were generated by rapid industrialization, and as a result an unruly industrial slum grew up across the river in East St. Louis, Illinois.[1]

Throughout the nineteenth century, St. Louis was a northern stronghold of southern-style de jure segregation: parks, schools, churches, theaters, libraries, restaurants, and public transportation and housing were all segregated. The only place in the city that allowed some contact between the races was the red-light district located along Market, Chestnut, and Targee streets. This area was a magnet for the St. Louis sporting crowd even before the turn of the century. When W. C. Handy visited the area in 1892, he worked for a while in a factory in East St. Louis, where he was cheated out of his wages by a labor contractor. This was not uncommon treatment for black migrants. In his memoirs, Handy recalled being swindled, and he recalled the harsh punishment vagrants like himself received from St. Louis police officers, notorious for their expert and unrestrained use of the yard-long nightstick. Yet Handy remembered the city's sporting district fondly:

> I have tried to forget that first sojourn in Saint Louis, but I wouldn't want to forget Targee Street as it was then. I don't think I'd want to forget the high roller Stetson hats of the men or the diamonds the girls wear in their ears. Then there were those who set for company in little plush parlors under gaslights. The prettiest women I've ever seen I saw while I was down and out in Saint Louis.[2]

Targee Street was the scene of a famous underworld shooting in 1899. Frankie Baker, a black prostitute, shot her boyfriend/pimp, Allen "Johnny" Britt, in a fit of jealous rage. Britt's dying words were reputedly: "Bye-bye, babe, I was your man, but I done you wrong," They became the chorus refrain for the immortal black folk ballad "Frankie and Johnny," which sprang from local sources immediately after the shooting. The song was the signature piece of Mammy Lou, the legendary "African-looking" woman who sang spirituals, blues, field songs, and folk ballads during this period at a club on Market Street that catered to free-spending white customers. The song's now-famous refrain clearly illustrates how the addition of a traditional African choral device to the Anglo-American ballad form heightens its dramatic tension:

> Frankie and Johnny were lovers, oh lawdy how
>     they could love,
> Swore to be true to each other, true as the
>     stars above,
> He was her man, but he done her wrong.
>
> . . .
>
> Eleven macks aridin' to the graveyard all in
>     a rubber-tired hack,
> Eleven macks aridin' to the graveyard, but only
>     ten acomin' back,
> He was her man, but he done her wrong.[3]

## Early Ragtime Pianists

St. Louis was an early hotbed of ragtime piano activity. At the center of this enterprise were the Rosebud Café on Market Street and Tom Turpin, its proprietor. Thomas Milton Turpin was born in 1873 in Savannah, Georgia, but moved to St. Louis with his family in the early 1880s. His father, known as "Old Man Jack," became a successful entrepreneur there. He owned the Silver Dollar Saloon, a livery stable, and a string of race horses. Tom Turpin opened up his own saloon in the sporting district in 1895. The Rosebud featured liquor, gambling, and live music. A bar and tables occupied the large front room downstairs; an upright piano and a dance floor were in the rear "wine room." Access to the wine room, reserved for musicians and other special clientele, was through secret "family" doors behind the bar and on the side of the building. Upstairs were several smaller "hotel" rooms for gambling and prostitution. Turpin was one of a select group of African Americans who managed and controlled vice operations in St. Louis. But, more important, this self-taught piano player was both a pioneer practitioner and a patron of ragtime piano. Piano players from all over the region flocked to the Rosebud Café to hear the latest music and the best talent in the Midwest. Among the great ragtime pianists closely associated with Turpin and the Rosebud Café were Scott Joplin and Louis Chauvin.

Scott Joplin, also a self-taught musician, was a native of Texas and led a nomadic life as an itinerant piano player before joining Turpin's entourage in St. Louis late in the 1890s. Joplin was at the height of his creativity as a ragtime innovator and composer during that decade. He no longer needed to hustle for money in the sporting houses after the successful publication of "Maple Leaf Rag." Although he preferred being secluded with a piano to participating in the around-the-clock piano duels at the Rosebud Café, he was always willing to share his knowledge and skills with younger, upcoming ragtime pianists and composers and was a major influence on the music and musicians in St. Louis during the eight years he lived there. He and Turpin grew to be close friends and exchanged ideas about their music. Joplin also maintained close contact with the city's other major ragtime figures. When he moved to New York City in 1906, he was sorely missed by St. Louis musicians.

In many respects, Louis Chauvin was the opposite of Scott Joplin, even though both were gifted ragtime musicians and close friends. Whereas Joplin chose to dissociate himself from the red-light district and eventually moved beyond ragtime composition to writing operas, Chauvin put his creative energy into playing the piano and became the darling of the red-light district while still in his teens. He was a native of St. Louis and a mulatto; his mother was African American and his father was Mexican. Although he published only a few ragtime compositions, he was well remembered as both a brilliant piano player and an engaging performer.

In his youth, Chauvin quit school to go on the road for a while with a traveling minstrel troupe for which he sang, danced, and did comedy routines. Back in St. Louis he played the piano non-stop, dividing his time between Madam Betty Rae's fashionable bordello and the Rosebud Café. From all accounts, he was an amusing innovator who constantly came up with novel ragtime strains, but he failed to develop his musical ideas into finished entities and completed only three compositions. To those who knew him around St. Louis, his technical brilliance, his startling keyboard inventiveness, and the emotional depth of his playing were unsurpassed. An alcoholic while still a teenager and an opium addict later in life, he was physically frail. All too soon, Louis Chauvin burned himself out; he was only twenty-seven when he died of "complications" in a Chicago hospital.[4]

Many other talented piano players contributed to the reputation of St. Louis as the keyboard capital of ragtime. The well-known and successful black concert pianist Blind Boone lived in St. Louis in the 1890s, and on occasion visited the tenderloin dives to play the latest ragtime favorites. Scott Hayden and Arthur Marshall were young protégés of Joplin who followed him to St. Louis from Sedalia. Sam Patterson was a native of the city and Louis Chauvin's best friend. By the second decade of the twentieth century, most of these first-generation ragtime musicians had moved on. They were soon replaced by a second wave of piano players who were more blues-oriented, and a fusion of the two musical genres began. Artie Matthews was in the forefront of these blues experiments. He was the first composer to use the term in a published composition and the legal author of the famous "Weary Blues," which was Bessie Smith's early signature piece. Matthews and most of his colleagues abruptly left St. Louis in 1916 when the red-light district was closed down in support of the nation's war effort.

## East St. Louis: The Making of a Ghetto

Much of the local action moved to East St. Louis or Lovejoy, a small black town that had no restrictions on merrymaking just north of East St. Louis. Lovejoy was the location of "Aunt Kate's," a honky-tonk renowned for its proprietor, Kate Gruder, and its house pianists, Rob Hampton and Charles Thompson. Both were leaders, along with Artie Matthews, in the extension of the local ragtime tradition and its interaction with the emerging blues culture.

Hampton was also a composer who had published numerous ragtime compositions and a few blues titles; like the others, he was a transitional figure in the evolution from ragtime piano to piano blues.[5]

The major industries in East St. Louis were aluminum, chemicals, meatpacking, and slaughterhouses. At the height of World War I, its population of 75,000 included African Americans, and their numbers were increasing rapidly. The town was controlled by large industrial companies with little civic pride or concern for the well-being of the people they employed. It was run by a notoriously corrupt city government that provided very few municipal services. The town's politicians were in league with local gangsters who lorded over a wide-open red-light district where over 350 saloons were in operation and gambling, prostitution, and drug trafficking were commonplace. The police department numbered fewer than fifty men, and only five of them were black. The police were totally inept at controlling the rampant crime in the city and merely ignored the vice operations. The sudden influx of workers during World War I caused a severe housing shortage. The existing dwellings were overcrowded and without sewers, toilets, and running water. Local manufacturers even resorted to housing newly recruited black workers in railroad box cars. The housing shortage, the lack of proper municipal services, and competition for jobs created a rising level of racial tension in East St. Louis. The situation was further exacerbated when the city's major industrial employers began recruiting African Americans as strikebreakers. The local unions contributed to the problem by maintaining a lily-white membership policy.[6]

In the summer of 1917, a shooting incident brought all the simmering frustrations and animosity to a head, and a race war erupted. Four white men drove through the black neighborhood in a car, shooting randomly at houses and people. It was not the first time that such an incident had taken place, and the black population had no reason to believe that the police would protect them or catch the culprits. In fact, most East St. Louis African Americans suspected that the police were behind it. After the shooting, a group of about two hundred armed black citizens marched on city hall. They were met by four plainclothes policemen in an unmarked police car. There was an argument and then an exchange of gunfire during which two of the police officers were killed. Over the next thirty-six hours, bands of armed white vigilantes terrorized the black community in East St. Louis while the police and later the state militia stood by. Thirty-nine African Americans were murdered, many burned alive in their homes; over a hundred others were treated for wounds or beatings they received from the white mob. The property damage was estimated at $3 million. Over three hundred houses and apartment buildings were burned to the ground, leaving close to six thousand African Americans homeless. Eight whites were killed by defenders of the black neighborhoods.[7]

Josephine Baker, the internationally acclaimed queen of the Folies Bergère in Paris, lived through the harrowing East St. Louis race riot and later gave an eyewitness account. She lived with her mother in the boxcar town within the city limits. On the first night of violence, she was attending an outdoor dance in the boxcar enclave when white vigilantes descended on the festive and unsuspecting gathering from all sides. They beat and shot black people and then burned down their houses. Baker and her mother fled to their railroad car and then, when the white mob put torches to it, they escaped to a nearby woods. Josephine saw her friend Jimmy clubbed to death and her idol, Madam Billie, the owner of a notorious St. Louis brothel, burned alive in her Packard automobile.[8]

The East St. Louis massacre set off a wave of protest throughout the country. In New York City, fifteen thousand African Americans marched to show solidarity with its victims, and an editorial in the *Saint Louis Post Dispatch* compared the white vigilantes to the German army. Still, there were few changes in the festering social conditions of East St. Louis as a result of either the riot or the congressional investigation into its causes. Life in this industrial ghetto soon returned to business as usual.[9]

Across the river, the St. Louis municipal government responded to the sudden influx of African Americans during the war years by instituting legal segregation in the city. The law was ruled unconstitutional by the U.S. Supreme Court in 1917, but the effect of the ruling was negligible. By the 1920s, the St. Louis red-light district had been revitalized, even though the city itself was already showing signs of urban decay. The center of the tenderloin's night life had shifted to Morgan Street, where there was a large black tenement complex. The most prestigious underworld nightclubs in "Deep Morgan" were the Chauffeurs' Club, the Deluxe Club, the Jazzland Club, the Cardinal's Nest, and the Modern Horseshoe.

The Chauffeurs' Club was the home of the city's finest jazz band, led by trumpeter Charlie Creath. The Modern Horseshoe was owned by Ollie Jackson, the most notorious black gambler and underworld figure in St. Louis. The home base for blues activity was the Deluxe Club, owned by Jesse and Edith Johnson, who also operated a local record store with the same name. Jesse Johnson was a talent scout for various race record labels; Edith Johnson was one of the city's finest female blues singers. Market Street remained competitive with Morgan Street largely because of the efforts of the indefatigable Charles Turpin, who built and operated the first black theater on Market, which he named after Booker T. Washington. He also took over the Rosebud Café after his brother Tom's death and renamed it the Jazzland Club.

When federal Prohibition went into effect in the twenties, the tenderloin went into the speakeasy business. The speakeasies were plentiful and ingeniously disguised as shoeshine parlors, barbershops, and funeral parlors. Over in East St. Louis, the Third Avenue sporting district, known as the "Valley," had been rebuilt in the wake of the race riot. The center for blues was a honky-tonk called Katy Red's, which attracted many of the same musicians who played at the Deluxe Club across the river. Both red-light districts were the sites of numerous rent parties that regularly featured blues musicians. Despite the economic and social erosion increasingly evident in St. Louis and East St. Louis during the 1920s, their respective blues circles, nourished by the revived tenderloins, managed to survive and even flourish.[10]

## St. Louis Blues Pianists

The rich piano tradition centered in St. Louis accounts in large part for its domination of the region's early blues culture. The evidence also suggests that the rural folk blues were initially adopted to the piano in red-light districts like those in the St. Louis area and points farther south. Jesse Johnson's brother, James "Stump" Johnson, was born in St. Louis in 1905; while still a youngster he learned to play the blues on a piano under the tutelage of an older musician named Son Long. Johnson claimed that Long originated "boogie woogie" while playing in the Deep Morgan honky-tonks. Boogie woogie, however, was a well-known style even before World War I. It employed recurring bass figures, usually eighth notes, played with the left hand. This ground-beat was complemented by right-hand single-note runs that sketched out fragments of a melody, or more repetitive figures that produced startling cross-rhythms that sometimes imitated the sound of moving trains. Blue notes were created by striking a black minor key and the white major key in front of it simultaneously. In effect, boogie woogie was a simple variation on the standard twelve-bar blues, which had repetitive quarter notes as a bass line. The earliest blues piano style was most likely a straight adaptation of a guitar or banjo accompaniment by a rural bluesman. However, piano blues tended to be more percussive. Boogie-woogie bass figures were fairly standard. The emphasis was on patterns of complex rhythms that built up tensions rather than on simple melodies calculated to resolve them. Whereas ragtime pianists had taken European dances and song forms, along with their harmonic structure, and fused them with African-influenced rhythms, the blues pianists did almost the opposite. They took the rural blues in their most rudimentary forms and adapted them as faithfully as possible to the piano. But in the process, they also injected them with a new rhythmic sensibility that would be the heartbeat of the emerging urban sound. Ragtime piano was an instrumental music that synthesized European harmony and African rhythms. Blues piano, on the other hand, was a return to the basic function and form of the African-American folk music indigenous to the South. It was both a vocal music that aided in the continuation of the black oral tradition, and a dance music that employed African rhythms to create a communal experience for the participants.[11]

There were enough first-rate blues pianists based in St. Louis in the 1920s to constitute a distinct school of players. Henry Brown was representative of this group. He was born in Troy, Tennessee, in 1906, but moved to St. Louis in 1918. Like Stump Johnson, Brown learned to play the piano from the "professors" of Deep Morgan. One of them went by the name of "Blackmouth." As Brown remembered him, "he was a real old time blues player and he'd stomp 'em down to the bricks." (The phrase "stomp 'em down" suggests a percussive playing style that provided a groundbeat for dancing.) Henry Brown also learned from Tom Cross, another Deep Morgan proponent of the early St. Louis piano blues. Brown's own playing style was lean and forceful. It relied on regularly accented left-hand bass figures that were either highly repetitive or followed a simple chord progression. Brown's trademark number, "Deep Morgan Blues," which he recorded for Paramount in 1929, documented the traits he had learned from the older bluesmen, especially in his use of standard boogie-woogie bass figures.[12]

Lee Green also played a key role in St. Louis blues circles during the 1920s. His background is somewhat obscure. According to Little Brother Montgomery, Green came from Vicksburg, where he worked as a tailor and played the piano on the side. Montgomery taught him to play his version of "Vicksburg Blues." Green renamed it "44 Blues" when he moved to St. Louis, and it became his signature piece. A cadre of younger piano players gathered around Green in the mid-twenties, among them Roosevelt Sykes, Walter Davis, and "St. Louis" Jimmy Odem.

Sykes, Green's earliest protégé was born in West Helena, Arkansas, in 1906. Three years later, his family moved to St. Louis. His father and his three older brothers were musicians. Sykes's first musical experience was playing the organ in a local church. But while still in his teens, he found the music and the night life in the red-light districts more to his liking. It was during this period that he acquired the nickname "Honeydripper," a tribute to his notoriety as a ladies' man. In the St. Louis tenderloin, Lee Green was his chief mentor, but he also learned from "Red Eye" Jesse Bell, an old-time blues pianist who had vanished by the late twenties. The onset of the depression coincided with an acceleration of Sykes's recording career. He moved to Chicago in the early thirties to better coordinate his careers as a race recording artist, a touring blues pianist, a studio musician, and a talent scout for two Chicago-based record labels.[13]

Walter Davis was born on a cotton farm near Grenada, Mississippi, on March 1, 1910. He learned the rudiments of blues piano in Delta juke joints before joining Green and Sykes in St. Louis in the mid-1920s. Davis was the best singer of the three. He had a rich resonant voice that was as emotional and expressive as the best of the Delta blues vocalists. The warmth and poignancy of his singing, rather than his piano playing, highlighted his best-known recording—a moving rendition of the train blues standard "Sunnyland Blues," released in 1931. Walter Davis's recording career spanned twenty-three years, from 1930 to 1953, during which he recorded over 150 blues sides. He also maintained his St. Louis residency and played regularly with local blues musicians such as Henry Townsend and J. D. Short at the Deluxe Club, or across the river in the "Valley" at the J. C. Nightclub. Davis's blues releases sold well enough to warrant a steady series of recording dates. He remained active in St. Louis blues circles until an illness forced his retirement in the early 1950s.[14]

James Odem was born in Nashville on June 26, 1903, and grew up there. His parents died while he was still young, leaving him as a ward of the city until he ran off to St. Louis at the age of fourteen. He acquired the nickname "St. Louis Jimmy" in the sporting district, where he began hanging out with Lee Green, Roosevelt Sykes, and later, Walter Davis. Odem was active on the local blues scene until 1933, when like Sykes, he moved to Chicago. Although not an exceptionally strong piano player or vocalist, Odem excelled as a composer of urban blues. His much copied "Patience Like Job," written with Sunnyland Slim, was a masterful and subversive application of biblical metaphors to the blues idiom. Its final verse gives an indication of his ironic sense of humor:

> Adam and Eve made sin, what more can we do?
> Adam and Eve made sin, Lord, what more can
>     we do?
> How can we live in this old world and say
>     that we live true?[15]

Odem's undisputed masterpiece "Goin' Down Slow" was to become an urban blues classic. Its loosely constructed narrative of a dying man's last testimony captures the plight of black migrants caught up in fast city living:

> I've had my fun if I don't get well no more,
> Said, I've had my fun if I don't get well no
>     more,
> My health is failing me and I'm goin' down slow.
>
> Somebody please write my mother and tell her
>     the shape I'm in,

Somebody please write my mother and tell her
    the shape I'm in,
Tell her to pray for me and forgive me for my
    sins.

Don't send for no doctor, you see the doctor
    can't do me no good,
Don't send for no doctor, you see the doctor
    can't do me no good,
I've been a sinful man and I didn't do the
    things I should.

On the first train south, you can look for my
    clothes back home,
On the first train south, you can look for my
    clothes back home,
And if you don't see my body, all you can do
    is mourn.[16]

The song would become a mainstay in the repertoires of the major urban blues
artists of the postwar era.

## St. Louis Guitar Players

The most influential musician in St. Louis blues circles during the 1920s was
Lonnie Johnson, the string-instrument virtuoso from New Orleans. Johnson
had left New Orleans after Storyville was shut down. When most of his family
was wiped out in an influenza epidemic soon after his departure, he was too
grief-stricken to return. His association with St. Louis began in 1920, when he
and his only remaining brother, James "Steady Roll" Johnson, signed on as
violinists in Charlie Creath's band, the Jazz-O-Maniacs. They played on the
SS *St. Paul*, a riverboat docked in St. Louis. The Johnson brothers liked the
city enough to settle down there. By 1925, they were regulars at Katy Red's
honky-tonk in East St. Louis, and Lonnie Johnson married a local blues singer
named Mary Williams. That same year, he won a blues contest staged at the
Booker T. Washington Theatre by blues promoter Jesse Johnson. The prize
was a recording contract with Okeh Records.

Over the next seven years, Lonnie Johnson would record some 130 selections, more than any other bluesman of the period. These recordings document

both his versatility on string instruments, which allowed him to play the violin, guitar, mandolin, banjo, and piano in a variety of musical settings, and his role as an innovator in the development of an urban blues guitar style. He recorded not only with many of his fellow blues artists, including Texas Alexander and Victoria Spivey, but also with the two greatest jazzmen of his generation, Louis Armstrong and Duke Ellington. Johnson's solo work on Armstrong's "Savoy Blues" and Ellington's "Misty Morning" was technically ahead of its time and played with a sensitive touch. Also unique were his recordings with the white jazz guitarist Eddie Lang; their musicianship was unrivaled in the 1920s. It is unclear whether it was Johnson or Lang who first used a flat-pick to intensify his single-string guitar solos. It is clear, however, that Johnson introduced the flat-picking technique to other urban blues guitarists, and that Lang did the same thing for jazz. Lonnie Johnson's guitar style set the standard for urban blues guitarists for decades to come. The one-string vibrato he mastered with his picking technique created a high-pitched wailing sound easily used to approximate the human voice. It was a style that would become even more appropriate when bluesmen began experimenting with amplified guitars in the late 1930s.[17]

Johnson was also a gifted composer of urban blues who used the medium to depict the new social conditions confronting the black populace in the cities. Songs such as "Working Man Blues," "Fine Booze and Heavy Dues," "Roamin' Rambler," and his tribute to the depression, "Hard Times Ain't Gone Nowhere," dealt with the perils and hardships of life for lower-class blacks in the city. One of the perils was that the criminal justice system often worked against poor African Americans—an issue addressed in "There Is No Justice":

> Boy's it's a pity, but I sure can't understand,
> They say the judge is for justice,
> But he still framed an innocent man.[18]

But the underworld vice lords also exploited black urban migrants, as depicted in "Racketeers' Blues":

> When they demand your money, you got to give
>     it up with a smile,
> When they demand your money, you got to give
>     it up with a smile,
> And if you refuse, they'll read about you in a
>     short little while.

When the gang is out to get you, it don't do
   no good to run,
When the gang is out to get you, it don't do
   no good to run,
It's true you can dodge the law, but you can't dodge the slugs
   out of a submachine gun.[19]

"Helena Blues" is an excellent example of the integration of social concerns and personal experiences in a portrayal of the plight of uprooted black farm workers being conscripted into labor gangs:

I want to go back to Helena, but the high
   water got me barred,
I want to go back to Helena, but the high
   water got me barred,
I woke up early this morning, it wandered
   all in my back yard.

They want me to work on the levee, I had
   to leave my home,
They want me to work on the levee, I had
   to leave my home,
I was so scared the levee would break, lord,
   and I might drown.

The police run me from Cairo all through
   Arkansas,
The police run me from Cairo all through
   Arkansas,
They put me in jail behind those cold iron
   bars.

The police say, "Work or go to jail," I say, "I
   ain't totin' no sack,"
The police say, "Work or go to jail," I say, "I
   ain't totin' no sack,"
I ain't drillin' no levee, the planks is
   all down and I ain't drivin' no nails.[20]

Because floods, forced labor, judges, jails, and police were part of the everyday lives of black people during this migratory period, blues like this struck a responsive chord. Johnson also excelled at capturing the nuances of male-female love relationships in his lyrics. Unlike the Tin Pan Alley song-writers, whose approach was sentimental and adolescent, Johnson focused on the real contradictions in sexual relationships, and he did so from various points of view. In his "Why Women Go Wrong," he puts the blame on men:

> The reason why so many good women's done
>   gone wrong,
> The reason why so many good women's done
>   gone wrong,
> Just trying to find the love and happiness
>   that they don't get at home.[21]

"When You Fall for Someone That's Not Your Own" depicts the conflicts that beset a man in love with a married woman, while "When I Was Lovin' Changed My Mind Blues" depicts the unpredictableness of a relationship:

> You didn't want me baby when I was being
>   lovin' and kind,
> You didn't want me baby when I was lovin'
>   and kind,
> Now you want me but I have changed my mind.[22]

Other compositions, such as "Another Night to Cry," "I Don't Hurt Any-more," and "Too Late to Cry" seized upon the vulnerability and pain of un-requited love. The success of the new urban bluesmen depended to a large extent on their ability to evoke these emotional themes in their music, and nobody knew this better than Johnson himself. In an interview later in his life, he stated:

> I sing blues. My blues is built on human beings on land. See how they live, see their heartaches and the shifts they go through with love affairs and things like that—that's what I write about and that's the way I make my living. It's understanding others, and that's the best I can tell you. My style of singing has nothing to do with the part of the country I comes from. It comes from my soul within. The heartaches and the things that have happened in my life—that's what makes a good blues singer.[23]

Lonnie Johnson had many heartaches. Although he and Mary Williams had six children and they became the most famous blues couple in St. Louis, their marriage ended with a great deal of bitterness. Both wrote, and even recorded, vindictive blues numbers about the breakup. Meanwhile, Johnson had severed his connection with the St. Louis blues scene. He lived in New York City for about a year in the late 1920s and hosted what may have been the first regular radio blues show to feature a black man. He toured with Bessie Smith's TOBA show in 1929 and then moved to Chicago in the early 1930s, but a dispute with Lester Melrose, the city's race record czar, about his material and his playing style ended his record contract.[24] He left Chicago soon afterward and never returned. For the next five years, Johnson worked outside music circles; he returned to the fold in the late thirties, but he never regained the success and popularity he had achieved in the 1920s.

Guitar and piano duets became fashionable in St. Louis blues circles in the late twenties, in part because of the influence of the decade's most successful blues duet—guitarist Scrapper Blackwell and pianist Leroy Carr. Although based in Indianapolis, the two made frequent trips to St. Louis to play in clubs like the Jazzland, where they were greatly admired and then emulated by the city's most talented blues musicians. The most prominent piano-guitar duo based in the St. Louis area during this period were Charley Jordan and Peetie Wheatstraw. Jordan was born in the small rural town of Mabelville, Arkansas, in 1890. He spent his youth working with his family in the cotton fields but left home while still in his teens, hoping to make a living as an itinerant blues guitarist. After a brief stint in the army, he returned to rambling and traveled through the Delta region, visiting Memphis and even Kansas City. By 1925, he had settled in East St. Louis, where he established a profitable bootlegging operation and played the blues on the side in the local clubs. He teamed up with Peetie Wheatstraw in 1930 and worked sporadically with him for the next decade. In addition, he worked as a local talent scout for both the Vocalion and Decca record labels. For a time in the late thirties, he even owned a share of a St. Louis blues club along with Peetie Wheatstraw and Big Joe Williams.

Jordan's longtime friend and collaborator, Peetie Wheatstraw, was born William Bunch in 1902 in Ripley, Tennessee. His family moved to Cotton Plant, Arkansas, a small farming community near Little Rock, while he was still a boy. He grew up on a farm there, working in the field. He had little formal schooling, but he managed to learn both the piano and the guitar. Bunch left home in his teens to hobo around the South and eventually settled in East St. Louis in 1929. During this period, he decided to change his name to Peetie Wheatstraw—a black folk figure—and he began to build up his public image as a street-wise, self-confident, jive-talking blues rebel. His signature piece, "The Peetie Wheatstraw Stomp," was a boisterous bit of self-aggrandizement that aligned him with the supernatural forces of the Christian underworld. It includes the following verses:

Everybody hollering, "Here come that Peetie
    Wheatstraw,"
Everybody hollering, "Here come that Peetie
    Wheatstraw,
Now he's better known as the Devil's son-in-law.

Don't tell all those girls what that Peetie
    Wheatstraw can do,
Oh well, well, well, what that Peetie Wheatstraw
    can do,
That will cause them suspicion and you know
    they will try him too.

If you want to see the women and men clown
If you want to see the women and men clown,
Just get that Peetie Wheatstraw to come into
    your town.

I am Peetie Wheatstraw, the high sheriff of hell,
I am Peetie Wheatstraw, the high sheriff of hell,
The way I strut my stuff, well you never can tell.[25]

A similar tone is evident in "Mister Livingood" ("I had a butler just to fetch
my gin"),[26] while "Confidence Man" promulgates a subversive work ethic
that friends said was Wheatstraw's own:

Now work was made for two things, that was a
    fool and a mule,
Now work was made for two things, that was a
    fool and a mule,
I couldn't start to work, oh well, well, well,
    because I didn't go to school.[27]

Wheatstraw celebrated sex in "I Want Some Seafood" and "Block and
Tackle."[28] In the ribald "The First Shall Be Last and the Last Shall Be First,"
he pokes fun at sexual inhibitions:

Well, the first woman I ever had, she made me
    get down on my knees,
Well, the first woman I ever had, she made me
    get down on my knees,
And she had the nerve to ask me, oh well, well,
    well, if I liked limburger cheese.[29]

Sex, work, play—whatever the subject, the persona of Peetie Wheatstraw opposed bourgeois attitudes and social practices. He was a self-indulgent anti-hero and a fun-loving raconteur—a braggart and a sage.

Another dimension of the Peetie Wheatstraw persona was stoical resilience in the face of hardship, an attitude common to many black heroes in the oral tradition. Wheatstraw had lived as a vagabond; his song "Road Tramp Blues" depicts feelings shared by many African Americans during the depression:

> I have walked the lonesome road 'til my feet
>   was too sore to walk,
> I have walked the lonesome road 'til my feet
>   was too sore to walk,
> I have begged the people for scraps 'til my
>   tongue was too stiff to speak.
>
> Anybody can tell you people, oh well, that I ain't no lazy man,
> Anybody can tell you people, oh well, well, that I ain't no lazy man,
> But I guess I'll have to go to the poorhouse and do the best I can.[30]

The playing style of Peetie Wheatstraw and Charley Jordan was loosely modeled on the style established by the Carr-Blackwell team (see "Indianapolis Blues" in this chapter). Wheatstraw's piano carried the bass line in a manner reminiscent of the city's long tradition of blues pianists, while Jordan's single-string finger picking was concentrated on the upper frets of the treble strings. Wheatstraw's piano playing fell off when he was singing, but his strength as a singer more than compensated for this deficiency. He sang in a forceful, declamatory style popularized by Delta blues giant Charley Patton and, like Patton, he had a tendency to slur his words and to interject utterances of encouragement. His emotional range, however, was far greater than Patton's, and his timing was much more developed. Furthermore, there was often a provocative humor in his voice, as if he were laughing at the world and its follies. Numbers such as "Bring Me Flowers When I'm Living," "Don't Hang My Clothes on No Barb Wire Fence," and "Throw Me in the Alley" all rippled with the wit of an irascible raconteur. Peetie Wheatstraw liked to assume the posture of an infidel bluesman defiantly in league with the Devil. A revealing portrait of the character he created can be found in Ralph Ellison's novel *The Invisible Man*. Ellison spent time in St. Louis and got to know Peetie Wheatstraw. The character in his book is a fast-talking Harlem bluesman roaming the streets and singing:

> She's got feet like a monkey, legs like
>   a frog, lawd, lawd,

But when she starts to lovin' me, I holler,
   whoo God-dog 'cause I love my baby, better
   than I do myself.[31]

In 1941 Peetie Wheatstraw was killed in an automobile accident in St. Louis. He left a host of imitators who tried to cash in on his popular hellion image by recording under sobriquets like Peetie Wheatstraw's Buddy, the Devil's Daddy-in-Law, and Peetie Wheatstraw's Brother. None of them, however, was able to match the raw vitality of the original.


## Depression Blues


The Great Depression was particularly devastating for large cities with a traditional and inflexible industrial base like St. Louis. Symbolic of this plight was the atrophy of the city's famous waterfront district. In the 1880s, the riverport operation was a bustling enterprise that contributed jobs and tax monies to the city. Fifty years later, the large warehouses were in such a state of disrepair that many of them were fire hazards. The granite levees were deserted and strewn with garbage, as were the narrow waterfront streets, where the windows of the business offices were boarded up. The riverport had come to a virtual standstill as a center of commerce and was deteriorating rapidly as a residential neighborhood.

Unemployment in St. Louis was twice the national level, and close to half of the workforce was without jobs. The city had one of the largest "Hooverville" settlements in the nation. It was located on the shore of the Mississippi River, just south of a major railroad yard with a complex network of tracks. It began just beyond the city limits and stretched out along the river for over a mile. Thousands of itinerant and unemployed migrants made their home there, living in flimsy huts made from scraps of lumber and tar paper, and eating catfish caught in the river and rations from the federal relief agencies. Most of the population at the St. Louis Hooverville was black. A blues recorded in 1933 by J. D. Short, who was a resident of St. Louis, makes a reference to the city's "Hooverville" and the bleak job outlook. It was aptly entitled, "It's Hard Time":

I went down to the factory where I worked
   for years,
I went down to the factory where I worked
   for years ago,

And the boss man tol' me that I ain't comin'
   here no mo'.

And we have a little city that they call
   down in Hooverville,
Now we have a little city that they call
   down in Hooverville,
Times have got so hard people, they ain't
   got no place to live.[32]

The hard times brought on by the depression put a damper on night life in the red-light districts. Only a handful of clubs continued to feature blues artists, but the slack was taken up to some extent by rent parties and revelry at the after-hours buffet flats. St. Louis remained an active blues center in which hardship only made the music more relevant and more in demand. Big Joe Williams recalled blues activity even in the city's Hooverville:

Lotta blues happenin' out there along the river back then, right there in them tents and shacks. Oh yea, see they'd have a honky-tonk right out there with the hobos and po' peoples . . . have moonshine and maybe some folks be gamblin'. . . . Always be blues musicians out there driftin' in and out, . . . they'd always be hangin' around playin' in them honky-tonks. Big crowds, too. Wasn't no work, nothin' to do but hunt for food and firewood. So lots a peoples be out there in those barrel-houses singin' and dancin' and carryin' on—rough joints too—be fights and cuttin' going on. Everyone like to crowd around us bluesmen, maybe drink a taste if they had any spare change or something to trade. You see blues used to make the peoples feel happy for a little while anyway . . . consolin' them 'cause those were real hard times back then before the war. No jobs around . . . nobody got homes . . . livin' took some doin'.[33]

Although the race recording industry had shrunk, the blues scene in the city continued to mature and evolve in new directions. By the 1930s, blues guitarists had moved toward the forefront of the new developments in the music, sharing the spotlight with the piano players. In addition to Lonnie Johnson and Charley Jordan, the other important blues guitar players active in St. Louis from the 1920s until World War II were Teddy Darby, Hi Henry Brown, Clifford Gibson, Henry Townsend, J. D. Short, and Big Joe Williams.

Teddy Darby was born in Henderson, Kentucky, in 1902. His family moved to St. Louis while he was still a child. His mother taught him to play the guitar, but he was more inclined toward bootlegging. He spent a year in a reformatory and later another year in the city workhouse—both sentences were for selling moonshine. In 1926, Darby lost his eyesight because of glaucoma. Soon after going blind, he took up the guitar again. By the late twenties, he was a mainstay of the local blues scene. He moved to East St. Louis and began a longtime association with Peetie Wheatstraw, backing him on guitar when Charley Johnson was unavailable. He was a competent musician whose guitar work sounded very much like Jordan's.

Darby participated in several recording sessions for St. Louis bluesmen in the 1930s, backing others and recording a few of his own blues compositions. Among his own pieces were a vaguely autobiographical blues, "Bootleggin' Ain't No Good No More," and a gambler's forlorn testimony, "Pitty Pat Blues":

> I lost my last dime tryin' to play pitty pat
> My watch and ring, coat and Stetson hat.[34]

Darby renounced the blues for the church in the late 1930s. He remained in East St. Louis and became an ordained deacon at the King Solomon Holy House of Prayer.

Lonnie Johnson's impeccable musicianship was the major influence on the guitar styles of Henry Townsend and Clifford Gibson. They often visited the Katy Red, Lonnie's favorite hangout in East St. Louis in the mid-twenties, in order to watch his fingerwork. Gibson grew up in Louisville and in his early twenties, moved to St. Louis, where he met Townsend, as well as pianists Henry Brown and Roosevelt Sykes. He recorded with both blues piano players in the 1930s. Henry Townsend's family were migrants from Mississippi who settled in Future City, near Cairo, Illinois, when he was a boy. Violent clashes with his stern, abusive father compelled him to leave his family when he was only nine years old. He hoboed his way to St. Louis, where he found work as a shoeshine boy in the sporting district; the parlor he worked in was a front for a speakeasy operation. He took up the guitar in his early teens under the tutelage of "Dudlow Joe," one of the city's best blues guitarists. Dudlow Joe was sent to the state penitentiary in the mid-twenties for killing two men in retaliation for a beating they gave him. He never saw the streets of St. Louis again.

Townsend continued to play locally, often in the company of two older bluesmen from the area, Son Ryan and Henry Spaulding. Both were guitarists in a more traditional blues mode, and before long Townsend was drawn to the more contemporary guitar work of Lonnie Johnson and Scrapper Blackwell. Building on the foundations he borrowed from the old-timers, he adopted Johnson's picking technique and Blackwell's string-popping effect, evolving a style consistent with the prevailing trend in St. Louis blues circles. By the late twenties, Townsend had acquired the nickname "Mule" because of his sturdy character and physique. During this period, he began to work in tandem with pianist Walter Davis. Throughout the next decade, Townsend was Davis's favorite guitar accompanist, and they frequently recorded together. After Charley Jordan and Peetie Wheatstraw, they were the area's most recorded blues duet.[35]

For a time in the 1920s, Townsend worked with J. D. Short, who migrated to the city from Mississippi in 1923 at the age of twenty-one. Short was raised on sharecropping plantations in the Delta; his father played guitar and was a friend of Charley Patton's, who occasionally visited the Short household. Before migrating to St. Louis, Short spent eleven years living in Clarksdale, Mississippi, where he came to be regarded as an up-and-coming young bluesman. By the time he reached St. Louis, Short's singing and guitar style were firmly entrenched in the Delta blues tradition. He worked as an unskilled laborer in a brass foundry, playing nights and weekends at small clubs and yard parties. By the early thirties, he had established himself on the St. Louis blues scene and was a regular in the Davis-Sykes entourage.

In 1931, Short made his first record, backed up by Sykes on piano and Clifford Gibson on guitar. Entitled "She Got Jordan River in Her Hips," it was a priceless example of the blues tradition's continuing subversion of Christian symbols. The simple refrain went as follows:

> You got Jordan River in your hips, mama,
> Daddy's screaming to be baptized.[36]

Short's strongest musical asset was his voice. Its tense emotional tone was well suited to the Delta blues he specialized in. His guitar playing was an unspectacular copy of the rural Delta style practiced by Charley Patton; he also played harmonica, clarinet, and piano.

Short was joined in St. Louis by his cousin, Big Joe Williams, during the depression. Williams was also schooled in the Delta blues tradition and was a faithful disciple of its folk standards and practices. He was born near Crawford, Mississippi, in 1903. His father, John "Redbone" Williams, was a Cherokee Indian, and his mother, Cora Lee, was of African descent. It was his grandfather, Bert Logan, who first kindled his interest in music. He played the accordion and sang folksongs, including an early version of "Candy Man." An older cousin, Jesse Logan, taught Williams the rudiments of playing the Delta blues on a homemade guitar. Jesse Logan was considered one of the finest guitarists in the region, but he was never to have an opportunity to record. He died at an early age from head injuries sustained in a beating by unknown assailants while he was doing time on Parchman Farm, Mississippi's infamous penal colony. The prison authorities listed the cause of death as a heart attack. This grim example of southern injustice left an indelible imprint on Williams. While still in his late teens, Williams joined the jug band touring with the Rabbit Foot Minstrels when the show stopped in his hometown. The next decade found him roaming all over the South as an itinerant blues musician and from time to time recording with his fellow band members as the Birmingham Jug Band (See Chapter 6).[37]

In the early thirties, Williams was based in St. Louis and active in the local blues scene. His expressive, highly-pitched Delta vocal style, which often relied on falsetto phrasing borrowed from Tommy Johnson, and his large repertoire of traditional material from the wellspring of Delta's blues culture, caught the attention of Charley Jordan and, through him, Lester Melrose, who arranged for his first solo recordings in 1935. Over the next six years, Williams cut several solo records. In addition to his versions of standard folk blues—"Highway 49," "Stack o' Dollars," "Crawling Kingsnake"—he recorded many of his own pieces, some of which were remarkable for their originality and insight. "Providence Help the Poor People" is a caustic indictment of Christianity and of the federal government. It goes in part:

> Well, Mister Roosevelt told me there not
>    gonna be hard time no more,
> He's gonna let the poor people go and play
>    if they want to go.
> I told him yes, Providence ain't gonna help
>    no more,
> Well, well, it may be tomorrow, Lord, I won't
>    be back no more.[38]

On these recordings, Williams played a unique nine-string guitar—one he adapted from a six-string model by simply adding three strings. With it he was able to maintain a resonating groundbeat by strumming the doubled bass strings while simultaneously playing single-string treble notes. He played this way only as a solo performer; when he recorded with a group, he left the bass groundbeat to a second guitarist.

In the mid-thirties, Williams began to play regularly with Robert Nighthawk and Sonny Boy Williamson. Nighthawk was born Robert Lee McCullum on November 30, 1909, near Helena, Arkansas. He learned to play the blues on guitar and harmonica as an itinerant laborer and musician in the Deep South before migrating to St. Louis in 1935. One of his earliest recordings, "Prowlin' Nighthawk," became his signature piece and provided his nickname. Harmonica ace John Lee "Sonny Boy" Williamson was schooled in rural western Tennessee and Memphis before moving on to St. Louis at the age of twenty-two in 1936. All three musicians recorded a series of blues together for the RCA Bluebird label in 1937. Each sang the lead vocal on some of his favorite blues numbers while the others backed him up. Williamson recorded his early standards, "Bluebird Blues" and "Jackson Blues," named after his hometown. Nighthawk cut his classic "Prowlin' Nighthawk." William's numbers included "Brother James" and "I Know You're Gonna Miss Me."

The three followed a standard procedure in all of these selections. Nighthawk flat-picked a single-string bass line, sometimes walking it and sometimes rocking it. Williamson played his harmonica non-stop throughout each number, sometimes soloing in juxtaposition to the vocal line and sometimes answering the vocals with short, innovative refrains. Williams capoed farther up the neck of his guitar than most bluesmen in order to play in a higher key. He also picked single-string runs that were more rhythmic than melodic. At their best, they complemented Nighthawk's bass line nicely; sometimes, however, they clashed with it.

The importance of these trio recordings is twofold. They were the first to display the prodigious talents of Williamson and Nighthawk, who would move on to play an important role in Chicago blues circles. In addition, the trio lineup of bass guitar, guitar, and harmonica prefigured the urban blues bands that would determine the direction of the music in the 1940s and 1950s.[39]

Although the lure of the record companies in New York and Chicago had caused the departure of Lonnie Johnson, St. Louis Jimmy Odem, and Roosevelt Sykes, Peetie Wheatstraw, Charley Jordan, Lee Green, Walter Davis, Henry Townsend, J. D. Short, and Big Joe Williams stayed on. They were joined by the likes of Robert Nighthawk, Sonny Boy Williamson, and even the mercurial Robert Johnson for a short time in the mid-1930s. Henry Townsend maintains that this period was one of the most creative and fruitful in St. Louis blues history. There were ongoing jam sessions at local clubs and rent parties that allowed musicians to experiment and stretch out with their music. As Townsend recalled:

It was a whole lotta fun. A whole lotta fun. You didn't find a dead place in town. You always got to have good live sounds. Sometimes we'd just get together as a group and just do jamming, you know. And Charley Jordan's was one of the places we'd go to—just go there and do our thing. Get it all together and cook up a roomful of blues. Sometimes the jam sessions would last four or five hours. And they included jazz horn players like Ike Rogers—he and others would come and sit in. Henry Brown would show up, Peetie Wheatstraw, Robert Johnson was there for a while, and of course Robert Nighthawk, Big Joe Williams and my main man, Sonny Boy. St. Louis was a hot town for blues in those days, just like Chicago.[40]

If there was not much money to go around, the blues musicians shared what they had in the way of food, clothing, and shelter. The hard times seemed to bring people closer together in the black community. But, ultimately, most of St. Louis's better blues musicians left town. Robert Nighthawk and Sonny Boy Williamson departed for Chicago; Big Joe Williams moved back to Mississippi; Henry Townsend and J. D. Short were drafted into the army soon after Pearl Harbor was bombed by the Japanese; Charley Jordan was gunned down in the streets of his adopted city. The St. Louis tenderloins withered—"goin' down slow"; only the ghettos remained. The infrastructure of clubs, dance halls, theaters, bordellos, and buffet flats that had supported all the blues activity from the turn of the century into the 1930s no longer existed. The most productive era of urban blues in St. Louis had passed.

## Louisville Blues

The riverport town of Louisville on the Ohio River enjoyed a long-standing reputation as a haven for gambling, horse racing, and African-American music. The site of the Kentucky Derby, the city's prestigious racetrack regularly attracted a large sporting crowd. Black jockeys dominated the Derby's winner's circle with fourteen victories between 1875 and 1902. African-American string-band musicians were a ubiquitous part of the racetrack's gala atmosphere, and by 1905, the more percussive and bluesy jug bands had made their debut there. The city's red-light district attracted a full stable of talented ragtime piano players, who worked in the saloons, dance halls, and bordellos. The most reputable nightclubs featuring live music during this period were the Cosmopolitan, Tom Pryor's Club, Jimmy Boyd's Club, and the Ben Brush, named after a famous race horse. The tenderloin's two most fashionable bordellos were named after their proprietresses, Annette Winters and Madam Leo Belle.[41]

The Louisville ragtime tradition dates back to the 1880s. Scott Joplin occasionally visited the city to play engagements, and Ben Harney, the famous ragtime pianist and composer began his career playing in a saloon in Louisville. His closest collaborator during this period was a black ragtime piano player named Henry Green. In 1896 Harney and Green became the first musicians to publish ragtime compositions. Their initial pieces, "Mr. Johnson, Turn Me Loose" and "You've Been a Good Old Wagon but You Done Broke Down," were eventually credited exclusively to Harney, who went on to popularize them on New York's vaudeville stages. Both contained elements of the twelve-bar blues structure and floating verses, commonly used in the black oral tradition, suggesting that the early folk blues may have reached Louisville before 1900. By the turn of the century, Louisville's best-known pianists were George Talbot, Jimmy Clark, Pete Givens, Mike Jackson, Glover Compton, and "Piano" Price Davis. Givens, a relative of Scott Joplin, often played with local dance bands because he could read music. Jackson grew up in Louisville but later moved to St. Louis. Glover Compton was a close friend of Tony Jackson, who stayed with him in Louisville for a while to play some engagements. Compton also sat in for "Piano" Price Davis when the latter was unable to meet his commitments because of his obsession with gambling. Davis was the undisputed king of ragtime piano in Louisville during this period; his best-known number, "Piano Price Rag," was always a showstopper. He had a raw talent with great potential, but he was also drawn to the underworld of gambling and pimping, which eventually overshadowed his musical career.[42]

After the turn of the century, there was a steady flow of black migrants from Alabama and Tennessee into Louisville; by 1914, a third of Kentucky's black population lived in the city. In an attempt then to preserve the existing all-white neighborhoods and stem the influx of rural African Americans, the city legalized segregated housing. The largest of Louisville's three black neighborhoods was centered in the local red-light district. It was seven blocks wide and ran from 4th Street down to 27th Street; up to twenty thousand African Americans lived there during World War I. The main thoroughfare of the tenderloin was Walnut Street. It was the location of the leading cabaret, called the Top Hat Club; the Lincoln Theatre, which was a major TOBA outlet; and numerous saloons, barbershops, clothing stores, pawn shops, and pool halls. The annual Kentucky Derby was always a peak period for the Louisville red-light district. The race attracted a unique array of big spenders from the scions of the southern gentry to the underworld elite. It was also something of a musical convention, attracting musicians from as far north as Chicago, and as far south as New Orleans.[43] A veteran of the Louisville jug bands, Henry Miles, remembered the Derby in the 1920s:

They had a lot of clubs, all they way from 6th on down to 25th, before they tore down Walnut Street. Some guys come in from different places that played harps and like that. Hang out, hit right there to 6th and Walnut. That was the headquarters. Poolrooms and them things, and they'd hit right through there, some would get jobs. They'd stay here maybe about one or two days and then jump up and go somewheres else. Like the Derby was one reason they come. See, they made good money. They'd make good tips. The Derby. That's where people from everywheres come to Louisville. White and colored. It's a money town.[44]

The Louisville blues culture was rich and varied during its golden era—the 1920s. At one end of the musical spectrum were the vaudeville entertainers who included the blues in their stage acts. These performers, drawn from throughout the South, more often than not, were trained musicians and considered themselves to be show-business professionals. At the other end of the spectrum were the rural jug band musicians playing their spirited music in the streets and parks, in the nightclubs, and especially at the racetrack. The African Americans in this group came mostly from the states of Alabama, Tennessee, and Kentucky, and therefore their blues numbers and dance tunes were influenced by regional folk traditions. Both groups intermingled freely, however, and often became indistinguishable from one another. Louisville was the home of classic blues singers Sara Martin and Edith Wilson. Guitarist Sylvester Weaver was also a native of the city; he was the first black man to make a solo instrumental recording: "Guitar Rag," released in 1920. Weaver did solo work, played with a local string band, and accompanied Sara Martin on a few of her recording dates; his other major solo effort was "Guitar Blues," recorded in 1923. Other popular guitarists included Cal Smith, a nephew of Clifford Hayes, and Clifford Gibson, who commuted between St. Louis and Louisville. The red-light district was still fertile ground for piano players. Fats Jefferson, a resident keyboard bluesman, remembered it as a "hot spot" in the twenties. Leroy Carr spent time there, as did Peetie Wheatstraw. The best-known local blues pianists, in addition to Jefferson, were Johnny Gatewood, a blind child prodigy who eventually moved on to Chicago, and Dan Briscoe, also a reputed underworld figure.[45]

The pride of the Louisville blues scene during this period was undoubtedly its pioneer corps of jug bands, which had been playing marches, ragtime numbers, spirituals, dance tunes, and the blues for the sporting crowds at the racetrack or in the tenderloin since the early 1900s. These jug bands were small ensembles with unorthodox combinations of folk and European musical instruments; they played all kinds of whistles, kazoos, combs, washboards, spoons and jugs, as well as saxophones, flutes, clarinets, cornets, violins, and even (in some recording sessions) pianos. The groups were invariably identified with their leaders. Walter Taylor led a local jug band that featured him on washboard and jug, John Boyd on twelve-string guitar, and a mandolin player who doubled on the kazoo. Emmett Phillips was the leader of a band that sometimes featured only him on jug or kazoo, and his longtime sidekick Hooks Tilford on saxophone or flute. A black man known only as Whistler led a group that comprised Willie Love, a local musician, on mandolin and Jess Foster on saxophone or jug. Whistler played a guitar and a whistle simultaneously. As a fellow musician described it: "He blowed one of them real long nose whistles, sounded just like a horn."

The two most prominent Louisville jug bands were led by Clifford Hayes and Earl McDonald. Hayes was born into a family of musicians and grew up in the area; by the time he was twenty, he played the piano, violin, and saxophone. His earliest group, called the Old Southern Jug Band, recorded for the Vocalion label in the early 1920s. The group had a string-band orientation and featured Hayes on violin, two banjo players, a guitarist, and a youthful Earl McDonald playing the jug. Clifford Hayes named his second recording group the Louisville Jug Band to avoid contract problems with another record label; it was basically the same unit minus a banjo player. The band recorded a session of rollicking blues material for Okeh Records in 1924; included were "Louisville Bluezees" and "Struttin' the Blues," two uptempo dance tunes. Hayes's next session group, the Dixieland Jug Blowers on the Victor label, marked the beginning of his transformation into a jazz-band leader. He kept his jug blower in the group, but he also featured Johnny Dodds, the renowned New Orleans clarinetist. The transition from blues to jazz was complete with the formation of Clifford's Louisville Stompers in the late twenties. The jug was abandoned in favor of a string bass, and upcoming young jazz musicians like Earl Hines were brought into the band.[46]

The man who single-handedly brought the jug into prominence in the race record industry was Earl McDonald, a Louisville native. Jugs had been used as folk instruments in rural string bands even before the turn of the century; later, they became novelty instruments in vaudeville blues performances. McDonald transformed a novelty item into a front-line musical instrument by developing a sound that was much like that of the trombone in New Orleans jazz bands. Once his innovative playing style was recorded, it was widely imitated. In particular, it sparked the jug-band craze in Memphis during the 1920s.

In addition to recording with two of Clifford Hayes's bands, McDonald did some sessions for Columbia Records as the leader of his own group, the Original Louisville Jug Band, which produced versions of two ribald nonsense songs, "Monkey and the Baboon" and "Beedle-ee-bum." McDonald also was active in several jug bands promoted by local commercial enterprises: the Old Grand Dad Jug Band, Sells Floyd Circus Jug Band, and the Ballad Chefs, who performed regularly on a Louisville radio station, WHAS, under the sponsorship of the Ballad Flour Company. Whatever the name or guise, McDonald played with the same basic group of black musicians: Fred Smith on banjo, Curtis Hayes on banjo and guitar, Henry Miles on fiddle, and James Hardy on the spoons. Their music was indebted to the rural southern string-board tradition, except that its rhythms were much more percussive and complex. McDonald's group was all-purpose: they played all kinds of music for all kinds of occasions. In his later years, fiddler Henry Miles recalled:

We played blues, swing tunes, marches. All kinds of songs. "My Old Kentucky Home," that was their theme song. The whole band sung. Earl could sing this blues—jug players they kept up with blues stuff. Earl played piano, played drums, played bass too. We'd have rehearsals three times a week—Monday, Wednesday, and Friday, jobs or no jobs.[47]

Miles's description of McDonald's affinity for the blues, and his versatility lends credence to his reputation as Louisville's foremost bluesman and jugband leader. So does the fact that he was in great demand as a session musician, recording with Clifford Hayes, classic blues singer Sara Martin, and even Jimmie Rodgers, the legendary "blue yodeler." McDonald continued to lead his jug band into the 1940s, as did Clifford Hayes, but the heyday for their music had passed. What was original in the twenties was passé by the war years. Thus the Louisville jug bands, like those based in Memphis, became relics of an early urban blues tradition, while the city's once-promising blues culture slowly diminished in size and importance.


## Cincinnati Blues


Cincinnati was a riverport town on the Ohio River with an early reputation for vice and hedonism. Writing in a local newspaper in 1876, Lafcadio Hearn observed that the city's levee district teemed with roustabouts, travelers of all classes and races, riverboat gamblers, prostitutes, and male pleasure-seekers. In a working-class saloon at Sixth and Culver, located in Cincinnati's only integrated neighborhood, Hearn heard two African-American musicians play and sing a folksong for a receptive audience of dancers and revelers who laughed, shouted, and stamped their feet in approval.[48]

After the turn of the century, the West End neighborhood evolved into the city's only black district, and a lively blues scene slowly emerged along the Sixth Street corridor. The Roosevelt Theatre, built after World War I, was the local TOBA outlet. It was famous for its weekly "Midnight Rambles." The theater's management put local performers on the bill with the major touring vaudeville acts for these special shows, which customarily drew an overflow audience from Cincinnati's black ghetto. The most popular out-of-town blues performer was Bessie Smith, who regularly appeared before capacity crowds during the 1920s. The only other theater showcasing black performers was the Keith, where Deford Bailey, the diminutive black harmonica player with the all-white "Grand Ole Opry," was a major attraction in his heyday. The Cotton Club, located in the basement of the Sterling Hotel at Sixth and

Mamie Smith with band

Gertrude "Ma" Rainey

Ida Cox

Bessie Smith, 1923

Sippie Wallace

Gus Cannon and his Jug Stompers

Gus Cannon

"Memphis" Minnie Douglas

Peetie Wheatstraw

Leroy Carr and Scrapper Blackwell

Lonnie Johnson

Pete Johnson

Hudson Woodbridge ("Tampa Red")

Robert Brown ("Washboard Sam")

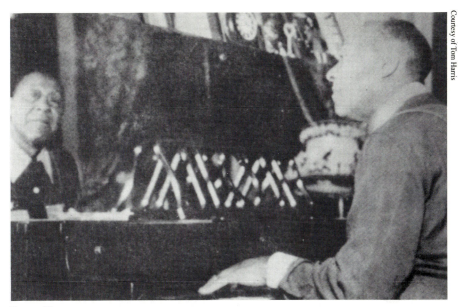

Jimmy Yancy

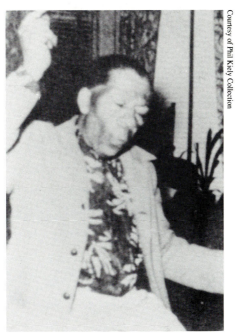

"Cripple" Clarence Lofton

Jimmy Rushing ("Mr. Five by Five")

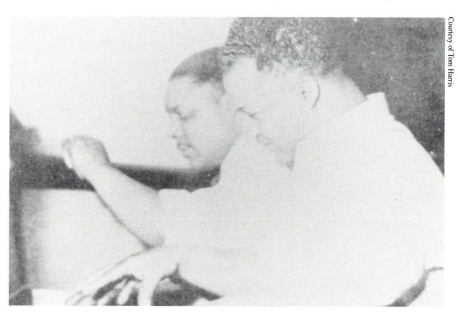

Mead Lux Lewis and Albert Ammons

Big Joe Turner and Pete Johnson

John Lee "Sonny Boy" Williamson [l] and William Lee Conley "Big Bill" Broonzy [r]

"Sleepy" John Estes

Rice Miller and James "Peck" Curtis

Chester "Howling Wolf" Burnett

Arron "T-Bone" Walker

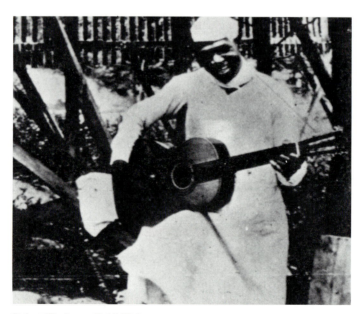

Robert "Barbecue Bob" Hicks

Mound, also booked black musicians of national stature like Fats Waller and Leroy Carr. Waller was based in Cincinnati during much of 1933, while he hosted a weekly live-music program, "Fats Waller's Rhythm Club" on WLW, a high-powered radio station located there. Several smaller West End clubs and saloons featuring resident bluesmen had names like Mom's, Bucket of Blood, and Vet's Inn. The blues were also played on the levee, then still a vital part of the city's commerce, and on the busy streets of the tenderloin. Cincinnati had its share of all-purpose jug bands and street musicians living off the tips they collected for playing in public. It was these musicians who first made the blues a part of the city life.[49]

Although historical data on Cincinnati's blues musicians are fragmentary, a series of disks were recorded by local bluesmen in the 1920s and the 1930s. The earliest of these was by Sam Jones, also known as Stovepipe Number 1, who made recordings for the Columbia and Gennett labels in 1924. Jones was remembered as a tall, imposing man with a stovepipe top hat who played guitar along with a harmonica fastened onto a rack around his neck. He was an older street musician, schooled in black minstrelsy, who often worked on the streets of the West End with a comb player. His recordings include a selection of blues commemorating popular city locales ("Sixth Street Blues" and "Lockland Blues"), gospel songs ("I've Got Salvation in My Heart" and "Lord, Don't You Know I Have No Friend Like You?"), and traditional folk tunes ("Turkey in the Straw," "Lonesome John," "Cripple Creek," and "Sourwood Mountain"). Sam Jones also recorded with King David's Jug Band, a local group led by the elusive guitarist David Crockett.

Local themes were present in the recordings of other Cincinnati blues artists after the mid-twenties. Kid Cole cut "Sixth Street Moan" in June 1928. Bob Coleman, who recorded "Cincinnati Underworld Woman" in January 1929, also led the popular Cincinnati Jug Band, which made its first recording, "George Street Stomp," during the same session. Finally, Walter Coleman, who probably made his first records using the alias Kid Cole, recorded "I'm Going to Cincinnati," in 1936.

> Because I'm going to Cincinnati, the times
>     is good,
> I'm going to Cincinnati, where they eat
>     fried food,
> And I'm going to Cincinnati, boys, where
>     hitting the bottle is good.
>
> Now I'm goin' to Cincinnati, I'm going to
>     spread the news,

The fan foots in Chicago sure don't wear
    no shoes.

Now when you come to Cincinnati, don't you
    get too full,
You're liable to meet a cop that they call
    Stargel Bull.

Now when you come to Cincinnati, stop on Sixth
    and Main,
That's where the good huggin' women get
    the good cocaine.

Now when you come to Cincinnati, stop by
    Hog Head Joe's,
Where you get your turnip greens and your
    good hog jowls.

Now the meanest man I ever saw,
A judge in Cincinnati called Judge Landshaw.

I got a bone in my throat, I can't hardly
    swallow,
There's a place in Cincinnati called Lockland
    Hollow.[50]

The recollections of senior members of Cincinnati's blues community have helped round out the picture of the blues culture there. James Miles was a native of Georgia who moved to Cincinnati with his family in the mid-twenties at the age of twelve. His uncle had already taught him how to play the blues on a harmonica, and soon after his arrival he was playing with the other street musicians based in the West End. Miles recalled that Cincinnati blues musicians usually worked together in small groups and routinely engaged in cutting contests in the streets or at house parties. His earliest rival was Stovepipe Number 1: "We run upon one another lots of times. They would come to parties where we would be playing and they would play a piece to show us up. He'd play things like 'M & O Blues.' I believe he played that 'Mama Blues,' too."[51]

James "Pigmeat" Jarrett was a blues pianist who grew up in Cincinnati. He remained there throughout his life, and for a time during Prohibition operated a still at the famous Lockland sanctuary. Jarrett learned to play by duplicating the styles he heard at the West End saloons and rent parties:

Blind Ted, a blues pianist. Blackjack too, a dirty blues pianist. Psychy Willie he brought out the boogie woogie in the 1920s. Jesse James played only blues. Older than Stovepipe, about 85 today. His brother Willie played sentimental tunes on the piano. Lots of guitar and harps. Baby Ruth, a one-man band; he could beat Stovepipe. The best harp player around, he went to Florida.[52]

Blues singer Cleveland Green was another longtime observer of the Cincinnati blues scene, and a friend of Pigmeat Jarrett. He remembered blues pianist Blind Ted as Blind Pimp, an underworld figure with a stable of hookers who escorted him wherever he went. The "Midnight Rambles" often relied on local vaudeville blues performers like Peg Leg Bates and Blackjack—whose playing styles resembled that of Fats Waller, according to Green. Boogie-woogie specialist Joe Duskin moved to Cincinnati in the 1930s from his hometown of Birmingham. In that decade, he recalled jug bands were still playing and even dancing on West End streets, but the center of musical activity had moved from Sixth Street to the nearby Central Avenue. There were a few good blues pianists playing in the bars and also an exceptional local trumpet player, but generally things were bleak for Cincinnati's blues musicians; many, like Duskin himself, were forced to move on. As had been true in the other major riverport blues centers, the early manifestations of an urban blues culture were not sustained. The overall decline of river commerce, social strife and stagnation in the inner-city tenderloins, the economic hardships of the depression, and the advent of the juke box and World War II caused a lull in Cincinnati's blues activities from the mid-thirties until after the war years.[53]

## Indianapolis Blues

Indianapolis was a key migration center in the Midwest for African Americans moving north from Alabama, Tennessee, and Kentucky. It had major railroad links to the south, as well as to Cincinnati to the southeast and St. Louis to the southwest. The early black community in the city was small, conservative, and middle class. Many of its members owned their own houses in the Douglass Park suburb. The city's first black newspaper, the *Indianapolis Freeman*, was a staunch proponent of the teachings of Booker T. Washington. A sudden influx of southern migrants during World War I to work in the war industries increased the city's black population 59 percent (to 22,385) by 1920. A segregated ghetto in the inner city, first called "Bucktown," grew up during this period. Segregation of the school system followed.

The ghetto, which soon became known as "Naptown," had two major commercial and entertainment corridors located along Indiana Avenue and Tenth Street. The classy Golden West Cabaret and the rougher Paradise Club (both on Indiana Avenue) were the best-known blues clubs in the 1920s. The Cotton Club held that distinction in the 1930s and 1940s. Tenth Street was the heart of the city's red-light district. Live blues could also be heard in neighborhood taverns along Bright Street and two nightclubs on Northwestern Avenue named after their proprietors, Ron Butler and Phil Bolton.[54]

Even before the 1920s, the city's tenderloin attracted African-American piano players, who were the first musicians to play the blues in Naptown's clubs or at its ubiquitous rent parties. Montana Taylor, who moved to Indianapolis in 1920 at the age of eighteen, recalled old timers like "Funky Five," "Slick" Jimmy Collins, and Tom and Phil Harding. These men were the best blues pianists in town, but by the end of the decade they had passed from the scene. None was ever recorded by the race labels. They were replaced by a new generation of blues keyboard artists, including Montana Taylor and Leroy Carr.

Taylor was raised in Butte, Montana, where his father ran the Silver City Club. His first job after moving to Indianapolis was playing the piano for two dollars a night at Goosie Lee's Rock House. Later in the decade, Taylor also worked at the Golden West Café and then the Hole in the Wall, located on the corner of Indiana Avenue and Rag Alley in the sporting district. In addition, he was a regular at the rent parties on Senate Avenue and Blake Street. Taylor had a brief recording career with the Vocalion label. In 1928 he cut his trademark number, "Montana Blues," and his tribute to Naptown's liveliest night strip, "Indiana Avenue Stomp," under the supervision of Lester Melrose, Chicago's race record czar. However, Taylor became disillusioned with the music business upon discovering that he had unknowingly signed away his royalties, and by 1930 he had stopped playing in public altogether.[55]

Leroy Carr enjoyed a more successful career as a blues recording artist. Born in Nashville on March 27, 1906, he grew up in Indianapolis, where he learned to play the piano. While still a teenager, he ran off with a traveling circus, embarking on a ten-year odyssey that included a stint in the army, a year on a state farm for bootlegging, a broken marriage, and countless nights playing the piano and singing the blues in honky-tonks around Louisville, St. Louis, and Indianapolis. In the late 1920s he was introduced to Scrapper Blackwell, the most talented guitarist in Naptown blues circles.

Blackwell and his family, which numbered eighteen in all, moved to Indianapolis in 1906 when he was three years old. His father played the violin, one brother played the guitar, another played the drums, and a sister played the piano. Blackwell himself, who was given the nickname "Scrapper" by his grandmother, learned to play his first chords on a guitar he built from the neck of an old mandolin and a wooden cigar box. With the onset of Prohibition in

1920, Blackwell went into the moonshine liquor business. He avoided being recorded at first but gigged around Naptown.

Carr and Blackwell proved to be an ideal blues match. Carr's forte was the blues vocal. His style was urbane, introspective, and understated; the mood of his most moving vocals was one of wistful melancholy and resignation. Blackwell's strengths were his guitar playing and the poetic blues compositions he claimed to have written for the duo with his sister, Mae Malone. Authorship is still disputed because the blues numbers he recorded with Leroy Carr were copyrighted in Carr's name. There was no mistaking his guitar playing, however; it was his own creation, although he always used the traditional twelve-bar blues form. The intricate single-note runs he finger-picked anticipated the tendency to standardize instrumental breaks between verses. He also had the habit of simultaneously strumming a bass figure and plucking the treble strings to produce a dissonant but snappy groundbeat. Playing together, Blackwell and Carr created a textured tension with their diverse sounds. Carr's piano style, while never very advanced, had nonetheless a soft, lilting quality that paralleled his vocal style; it was never as percussive as the St. Louis blues piano style. In sharp contrast to Carr's mellow, introspective playing and singing was Blackwell's polished, biting, and intensely rhythmic guitar style. By giving Carr the responsibility for the bass line, Blackwell was able to concentrate his finger work on the treble strings. The overall result was a balanced and compelling piano-guitar partnership.[56]

Their first release in 1928, "How Long, How Long Blues," was an instant commercial hit, and they went on to record three more versions of it over the next five years because the master kept wearing out. It was one of the biggest-selling race records of the 1920s, and also one of the most beautifully composed blues poems of the era. It goes, in part:

> How long, how long has the evening train been
>   gone,
> How long, how long, baby, how long?
>
> I can hear the whistle blow, but I cannot see
>   the train,
> For deep down in my heart, baby, I have an
>   aching pain.
> For how long, how long, baby, how long?
>
> My mind gets to rambling, I feel so bad,
> Thinking about the bad luck that I have had.
> 'Cause how long, how long, baby, how long?[57]

Another composition notable for its delicate poetic phrasing was "Blues Before Sunrise," which Blackwell maintained that he wrote with his sister; it too blended traditional lyrics with freshly conceived ones. Two of the verses, the first traditional and the second original, are as follows:

> Hurry down, sunshine, see what tomorrow brings,
> Hurry down, sunshine, see what tomorrow brings,
> It may bring happiness, then again it may bring
>     pain.
>
> I got the blues before sunrise with tears
>     startin' in my eyes,
> I got the blues before sunrise with tears
>     startin' in my eyes,
> It's such a miserable feeling, a feeling I do
>     despise.[58]

Two other Carr-Blackwell releases that did well commercially were "Shady Lane Blues," which refers to an alley in Naptown, and "Prison Bound," the forlorn lament of a recently incarcerated black man. Even in the depths of the depression, the duet's popularity continued to rise, making them the most influential recording team of the times. Yet constant club engagements, drinking binges, and after-hours parties took their toll on Carr's health; he died in 1935 at the age of thirty from alcohol abuse. Thousands of mourners turned out to pay their last respects when he was buried in Indianapolis. Blackwell was so distraught over the loss of his partner that he gave up his blues career, took a job as a manual laborer, and faded into obscurity. Twenty-six years later, he died in the streets of his hometown in a shooting incident.[59]

While Carr and Blackwell were still active in Indianapolis, they attracted a number of aspiring young blues musicians into their entourage. Shirley Griffith, a native of the Mississippi Delta, was a pupil of Tommy Johnson and Ishman Bracey in Jackson, Mississippi, before moving north to Indianapolis in 1928. He played guitar regularly with Blackwell and Carr in local nightclubs. After Carr died, Griffith dropped out of music and went to work on an assembly line in a Chevrolet body plant.

In the early 1930s Champion Jack Dupree moved to Naptown from New Orleans, where, like Louis Armstrong, he had grown up in an orphan's home and played in its brass band. Young Dupree learned to play blues piano in New Orleans from Willie Hill—better known as "Drive 'em Down." In Indianapolis, Dupree played with Blackwell and Carr at the Lincoln Theatre (a TOBA outlet) and the Cotton Club. Others active in Naptown blues circles during the depression included Honey Hill, Wilson Swain, Little Bill Gaither, and a band

called "Socks." In 1940, Dupree and some of the city's top bluesmen recorded for Lester Melrose. The most notable cuts released from these sessions
on the Okeh label were Dupree's "Cabbage Greens" and "Angola Blues," the
former a rollicking New Orleans barrelhouse number. "Angola Blues" was
about the notorious Angola prison farm in Louisiana. Of all the blues musicians active in Indianapolis before World War II, only Dupree went on to gain
national and even international fame as a blues artist. Yet he never lost touch
with the source of his music: "Blues was built on ill treatment, everyday hardships and politics. Today it's the same as it was back in slavery times and as
long as black people live it will always be the same."[60]

## Detroit Blues

Detroit was second only to Chicago in the Midwest as a center for urban blues
activity. The city began to attract large numbers of migrant black workers with
the onset of World War I: in 1910 it had 6,000 black residents, in 1920 there
were 42,000. African-American migrants found work in service industries,
such as hotels, restaurants, and laundries, and made slow inroads into the automobile industry. Automobile manufacturers hired 17 African Americans in
1910; by 1920, 3,780 were employed in the industry.[61] Residential segregation
was the order of the day in Detroit as in other large metropolises. A 1919
government-sponsored report described Detroit's black neighborhoods:

> There is not a single vacant house or tenement in the several Negro sec-
> tions of the city. The majority of Negroes are living under such crowded
> conditions that three or four families in an apartment is the rule rather
> than the exception. Seventy-five percent of the Negro homes have so
> many lodgers that they are really hotels. Stables, garages and cellars
> have been converted into homes for Negroes. The pool rooms and gam-
> bling clubs are beginning to charge for the privilege of sleeping on the
> pool tables overnight.[62]

Yet the 1920s were prosperous years for Detroit, and some of that wealth
trickled down to the black community, concentrated for the most part on the
east side of the city. Hastings Street, which ran through the heart of the
African-American district, was lined with saloons, poolrooms, barbershops,
clothing stores, and restaurants. The best-known blues clubs were Henry's
Swing Club, the Crystal Bar, and Brown's Bar. Private house parties were also
a source of employment for blues musicians. The Koppin Theatre was the major TOBA outlet in the city. Bessie Smith was on good terms with a madam

who ran a notorious buffet flat in the tenderloin district. Whenever Smith was in town for an engagement at the Koppin Theatre, she would visit her friend's after-hours business establishment with some select members of her road-show cast for a night of revelry.[63]

Piano players who had moved up from Georgia dominated the Detroit blues scene in the 1920s. Two of the earliest to make commercial recordings were Will Ezell and Charlie Spand. Big Maceo Merriweather moved to Detroit in 1924 to join other members of his family; he married a local woman who hosted a regular blues house party, and eventually he became the main attraction at Brown's Bar. Rufus Perryman, better known as "Speckled Red" because of his light, freckled complexion, spent his youth in Detroit. He fondly recalled the old-time blues pianists who played in the city even before the 1920s and were never recorded: Paul Seminole, Tupelo Slim, and a man known only as Fishtail. Seminole taught Speckled Red to play the blues on a piano in Butch's Club on Hastings Street. It was one of the earliest places to feature live music regularly. In the 1920s, Speckled Red gained attention as a blues pianist and singer in local clubs and at house parties; for a short time, he also worked with a band called the Wolverine Nighthawks. His signature piece was "The Dirty Dozen," a traditional game of insults that had been transformed into a scatological underworld folksong. The term originally referred to the flawed or handicapped members of the African-American slave population, who were sold by the dozen instead of individually like the more prized physical specimens of their race. After the Civil War, "the dozens" was maintained in the black oral tradition as a verbal battle in which the intent was to humiliate one's opponent through derogatory comments about his or her genealogy. By the time Speckled Red learned the number from Seminole, the insult game had also became the topic of a popular barrelhouse classic. When Speckled Red finally recorded it much later in his career, he had to change the lyrics; as he explained:

> They was real bad words you see. I was playing in one of them tenderloin jukes where it didn't matter. Anything I said there was alright in there. . . . I had to clean it up for the record, but it meaned the same thing. . . . In those days and in them places you could say some of them smelly words and don't think nothing of it, but it's a whole lots different now.[64]

Speckled Red's sanitized version goes, in part:

> Well, I want all you women folks to fall in
>     line,
> Shake your shimmy like I'm shaking mine,

Shake your shimmy and shake it fast,
You can't shake your shimmy, shake your yes
    yes yes.

Now you's a dirty mistreater,
A robber and a cheater,
Slip you in the dozens,
Your pappy is your cousin,
Your mama do's the lawdy lawd.[65]

Wartime industrial expansion set off a second large wave of black migration to Detroit in the 1940s. The influx triggered white vigilante violence. In the winter of 1943, white mobs attacked African Americans moving into the federal government's Sojourner Truth Housing Project. In the summer, an altercation at the Belle Isle recreation area sparked a full-scale race riot. White mobs again invaded black neighborhoods and attacked residents indiscriminately. Ignoring the white lawbreakers, the police concentrated on black "looters" along Hastings Street, arresting and even shooting some of them, and searching and disarming any African Americans encountered on the streets. Thirty-four people died in the riot; twenty-five were black and of these seventeen were killed by the police. The situation provoked a young lawyer, Thurgood Marshall, to compare Detroit's law enforcement officers to the Nazi Gestapo.[66]

The black migration to Detroit during the war years dramatically altered the blues heard there. Georgia piano players gave way to a new generation of Delta-schooled blues guitarists, working with small combos behind them. These groups were modeled after the urban blues bands formed in Memphis, St. Louis, and Chicago. They featured a second guitar, harmonica, drums, sometimes a piano, and a bass. The best known of the urban blues guitarists in Detroit were John Lee Hooker, Bobo Jenkins, Baby Boy Warren, and Little Eddie Kirkland. Their backgrounds were similar, although only Hooker achieved national success as a blues artist. He was born in 1917 and grew up on a sharecroppers farm near Clarksdale in the Mississippi Delta; his early mentor was his stepfather, Will Moore, who in turn learned his blues style and repertoire from the great Charley Patton. While still in his teens, Hooker was playing in juke joints and at house parties in the Delta region; his associates included Tommy McClennan and Tony Hollins. After moving to Detroit in 1943, he got a factory job and began to play in local clubs on the weekends. He eventually formed his own band and recorded a commercially successful rhythm and blues hit, "Boogie Chillum," in the late 1940s. The hit record allowed Hooker to quit his factory job and begin a career as a full-time blues musician. He went on to become one of the most recorded urban blues artists of the postwar decades, composing an impressive number of his own blues. In discussing his music, John Lee Hooker recently stated:

> Now, where do I get my songs from? I write songs about life in the present day and in the past. That's where the blues come from: life, people, how they're living and how some of them are suffering. It hits everybody in the audience because they know it's the real thing, . . . it's the truth about things. . . . I don't get my songs from books, they come from the way I feel down here.[67]

Perhaps more typical of Detroit's urban blues musicians was Bobo Jenkins. His established material was more likely to refer specifically to life in the "Motor City," where he worked in a Chrysler plant for twenty-six years. One of the numbers he sang contains the following verse:

> Please, Mister Foreman, slow down that assembly
> line,
> Will you please, Mister Foreman, slow down that
> assembly line,
> I don't mind workin', but I do mind dying.[68]

Jenkins moved to Detroit in the 1940s; unlike Hooker, he never had a hit record, and therefore never made it beyond the local blues scene. Yet he remained a creative and productive blues artist even while working on an automobile assembly line. One of his favorite blues, "24 Years on the Wrong Road," goes in part:

> Cut my gas, baby, stole my speed,
> I said they cut my gas, baby, stole my speed,
> Now I'm paying double for everything I need.[69]

Jenkins's description of how he wrote his songs captured the new mood and drive of Detroit's urban blues: "That whirlin' machinery gives me the beat," he said. "It's like hearin' a band playing all day long. Every song I ever wrote that's any good has come to me standin' on that line.[70]

The blues tradition reached a highwater mark in the Midwest during the prewar years, successfully negotiating the transition from a rural to an urban culture. In St. Louis, Louisville, Cincinnati, Indianapolis, and Detroit, the blues became the collective voice of the black migrants, extending and deepening the black oral tradition's discourse on race and class relations in urban America. Nowhere was this more evident than in Chicago, where blues culture reached its zenith in density and longevity.

# Chapter 9
## "Looking Up at Down"
### Chicago Blues

The central role that Chicago played in the formation of an urban blues culture stemmed from three major factors. First, the city was a key refuge for black migrants, especially from the densely populated Mississippi Delta, where the blues were deeply rooted in the rural culture. By 1920, only Harlem was larger and more famous than Chicago's black community. Second, the city was also an underworld stronghold with well-entrenched mobster operations organized along ethnic lines, and a sizable red-light district that had been in existence even before the Civil War. As in other American cities with large black populations, segregation confined African Americans to an area that overlapped with the red-light district. And third, the city was surpassed only by New York as a center for show business during the first decades of the twentieth century. Thus, Chicago was able to provide black entertainers and musicians with rare employment and recording opportunities. The interaction of these three factors—the black community, the sporting district, and the entertainment industry—in time generated the cultural formation out of which a new urban blues tradition would emerge.

## Toddlin' Town

Chicago was founded in 1790 by a French-speaking black pioneer (Jean Baptiste Pointe Du Sable) but was soon taken over by white settlers; by the 1840s, the frontier outpost had been transformed into a booming trade and transportation center. During the pre–Civil War period, the city had only a small African-American population, but it was a key northern station for the "underground railroad" that smuggled runaway slaves out of the South and into Canada. Although it was disdainfully referred to as a "nigger-loving town" by the southern press and their racist sympathizers in the North in the 1850s, black residents of Chicago never accounted for more than 1 percent of the city's total population until after the Civil War. During the Reconstruction era,

Chicago was the fastest-growing city in the country, absorbing a huge influx of foreign immigrants and putting them to work in the mills, factories, and stockyards. In the 1890 census, Chicago's population exceeded one million; in that year, approximately 75 percent of its inhabitants were either foreign-born or the children of immigrants.[1]

The first significant wave of black migration to Chicago occurred between the 1890s, when the African-American population was still under fifteen thousand, and 1915, when it reached fifty thousand. The collapse of Reconstruction in the South and the stultifying economic servitude that ensnared most black farm workers were general "push" factors that contributed to this trend. However, there were also some significant "pull" factors that were particular to Chicago. One was the active recruiting of African Americans by industrial employers. The wages in Chicago were always higher than those African Americans could earn in the South; but in many instances the black workers were brought in as strikebreakers, as happened during the stockyards strike of 1904–5. Later in 1905, the same tactic was used by the city's merchants against a teamsters strike. In this case, however, the importation of the black strikebreakers precipitated a series of violent and indiscriminate attacks on African Americans that nearly resulted in a full-scale race riot.[2]

Robert Abbott's *Chicago Defender,* the town's leading black newspaper, was another pull factor. The *Defender* served as a beacon for the African-American migration to Chicago. Abbott had started his weekly paper in 1905 on a shoestring budget and with an initial press run of 300 copies. The paper's first years were lean ones until 1910, when Abbott hired J. Huckley Smiley as his assistant editor. Smiley revamped the *Defender,* borrowing freely from the bag of tricks developed by famous yellow journalists like Joseph Pulitzer and William Randolph Hearst. To the paper's format he added banner headlines, often printed in red; sensational stories, many about atrocities committed against African Americans in the South; and a large entertainment section; but he maintained Abbott's focus on racial issues and his commitment to racial militancy. When the paper's circulation began to climb, Abbott and Smiley started a "national" edition, directed primarily at black people in the South, and launched "The Great Northern Drive," a public relations campaign to encourage black migration north. The paper listed job openings and printed articles, letters, cartoons, and poems that compared the migration to an "exodus," a "flight out of Egypt," to end bondage. Abbott ingeniously recruited railroad porters and entertainers who traveled regularly to haul bundles of the latest *Defender* to drop-off points farther south. Despite efforts by southern authorities to suppress the *Defender,* its circulation jumped from a few thousand in 1910 to 282,571 by 1920, at which point two-thirds of the readers were outside Chicago. Since the *Defender* was passed from hand to hand, millions saw it regularly. It was by far the most important black publication in the country, and its influence on the northward migration of black people would be hard to overestimate.[3]

African Americans had traditionally settled on the city's Southside. Segregation, overcrowding, and the lack of adequate public facilities and services created slum conditions; proximity to the red-light districts compounded the problem, as did the segregated job market that kept black unemployment rates twice and three times those of white workers. African Americans were forced to rely on their own resources: self-help institutions like churches, fraternal orders, civic action groups, and women's social clubs, and the black politicians who had begun to work themselves into positions of authority in the wards heavily populated by black people but controlled by the city's Republican machine.

Chicago mayor "Big Bill" Thompson presided over one of the most notoriously corrupt big-city political machines of the era, using extensive job patronage and a lucrative alliance with the Chicago underworld to bolster his power. Thompson garnered 80 percent of the black vote in the mayoral race of 1915 by promising employment opportunities and a wide-open town. "I'll give your people jobs, and any of you want to shoot craps go ahead and do it," he pledged in a Southside campaign speech. The mayor delivered on his promises; he fraternized with African Americans on the Southside, and he placed black politicians in positions of importance within the precinct organizations in their own wards. By the early 1920s, black Republican politicians allied with Thompson's Republican machine had more political clout than did black politicians anywhere else in the country, including Harlem. Yet despite having a friendly mayor, a cut of the job patronage, and a modicum of political power, Chicago's black community remained hemmed into a physical ghetto. Even those who could afford it were unable to live anywhere other than in the clearly delineated black neighborhoods. As a consequence, Chicago's Southside became a "city within a city," a "black metropolis" surrounded by the larger white metropolis.[4]

The second great wave of black migrants came to Chicago during World War I. Between 1916 and 1920, the African-American population more than doubled (from 50,000 to 109,000) as a result of the opening of the industrial job market to black workers and the *Defender*'s "Great Northern Drive." On the Southside, the more enterprising slumlords began to divide conventional apartments into "kitchenettes." Units that originally sheltered one family were now occupied by three or four. Friction soon developed along the perimeters of the Southside between African Americans and the Poles and the Irish living on the other side. Beginning in 1917, black Chicagoans experienced an increasing number of random physical assaults as well as bombings of their homes and businesses. Open racial warfare erupted in the summer of 1919. In five days of fighting, thirty-eight people were killed and millions of dollars' worth of property was destroyed. A study of the underlying causes of the race riot blamed the pervasive pattern of discrimination against African Americans in the city and even recommended actions to remedy the problems, but it was ignored by the local power structure, and business continued as usual in Chicago.[5]

## The Chicago Underworld

In the city's tenderloin, business as usual meant the traditional around-the-clock vice activities—gambling, prostitution, and liquor and drug trafficking. They operated in tandem with the honky-tonks, cabarets, and dance halls offering live entertainment. The early vice corridor was located in downtown Chicago and dominated by the Irish. When it burned down in 1871, the tenderloin residents moved to a Southside location called "The Levee." By 1900, there were over two hundred bordellos, two thousand saloons, and approximately five thousand prostitutes in the area. The local authorities did little more than attempt to contain prostitution within the red-light district. The more successful Irish underworld entrepreneurs began to relocate their own clubs and saloons along the downtown Chicago "Loop" or on the Northside after the turn of the century. They were replaced by Sicilian and Jewish racketeers, who, like their counterparts in New Orleans and Memphis, opened dance halls and cabarets that featured black musicians and performers. In Chicago, these night-life establishments were first called "black and whites" because they featured black artists but catered to white customers. The Italian and Jewish mobsters were quick to align themselves with the Thompson political machine. In exchange for immunity from local vice laws, they turned over a cut of the profits, and plenty of votes on election day.[6]

A list of local gangsters who owned nightclubs during the first three decades of the century reads like a who's who of the Chicago underworld. The list includes the Mangano clan and the Capone brothers. Larry Mangano played guitar and sang popular blues numbers in his cabaret, and all three Capone brothers—Al, Ralph, and Mitzi—who controlled a string of nightclubs in and out of Chicago, were patrons of the music and on friendly terms with many of the local black musicians. Al Capone was known to lavish tips on musicians he favored.[7] Jug-band musician Hammie Nixon recalled:

They had the dope and the liquor hustles—the Italian gangsters, or head knockers we called them. They had barns all over where the gang members hung out at and we'd go there to play for them 'cause they liked our music. Al Capone used to be at the barn. Come up in one of those fancy cars with chauffeurs. He'd come in and drop some money on you, maybe twenty dollars at a time. As he left, he was liable to throw another twenty at you. Oh, he was crazy about that music now. You got to cut up and act a fool. I always acted the fool with them jugs—yeah they went for that.[8]

State Street was at the center of the vice corridor on the Southside. Vaudeville blues composer Perry Bradford visited a State Street saloon during World War I. In his autobiography, he writes:

I was short of money in Chicago and old "Mojo" seemed to whisper in my ear, "sing and play your blues." The first one I sung did it. I saw all the pimps and their gals and I remembered this verse of the blues I started with:

> My gal walked in the street in the rain and wet,
> This is what she said to every man she met,
> I don't want your nickel just give me a lousy dime,
> So I can feed this hungry pimp of mine.

The house roared and yelled for more, more, more. For the next twenty minutes, I sang every blues I could think of, and they still yelled for more.[9]

The most popular night spots were the Casino Gardens, the Sunset Café, the Dreamland dance hall, the Lincoln Gardens—a club with seating for a thousand—Friar's Inn, the Panama Club, the Deluxe Café, the Royal Gardens, and the elegant Grand Terrace. In 1922, the number of nightclubs and saloons operating in Chicago was estimated to be twelve thousand; by 1928 that estimate had risen to twenty-five thousand.[10] Jazz pianist Earl Hines summed up the relationship between these gangland operations and African-American music in one sentence: "Mobsters found the music a swell front for their backroom rackets that included everything from gambling to dope peddling to prostitution."[11]

African-American underworld entrepreneurs, like their Italian and Jewish counterparts, established lucrative vice operations on the Southside and were economically supportive of black musicians and entertainers. John "Mushmouth" Johnson, the first black man to own and operate a State Street gambling house, amassed a fortune before he died in 1907. Robert T. Motts, having become a wealthy man through his illegal business ventures, then became a noted civic leader and in 1905 opened the Perkins Theatre. Henry "Teenan" Jones, who owned two State Street nightclubs called the Elite #1 and the Elite #2, made generous contributions to various causes in the black community. Dan Jackson, a college graduate, used his funeral parlors as fronts for his gambling and "policy" operations; later, he became the leader of a Southside syndicate involved in gambling, bootlegging, policy games, prostitution, and nightclubs. In 1927, he was appointed to a ward committee seat on the city council by Mayor Thompson.[12] Another African-American gambler and bootlegger noted for his successful business ventures was Richard Morgan, longtime intimate of Bessie Smith. Morgan's Southside home was the scene of constant parties and jam sessions in the 1920s. As Bessie Smith's biographer described it:

> The music, always in ample supply, was provided by guests from just about every bandstand and stage in town. It was, for instance, not unusual to find Ma Rainey there, singing to the accompaniment of pianist Jelly Roll Morton, or Louis Armstrong cutting through the smoke-filled air in royal battle with violinist Eddie South, while the rest of Jimmy Wade's Syncopators—who were almost nightly guests, joined in.[13]

Richard Morgan's after-hours parties were a microcosm of night life on the Southside, which reached its zenith in the years following World War I. Poet Langston Hughes found State Street in 1918 to be "a teeming Negro street with crowded theatres, cabarets and restaurants and excitement from noon to noon. Midnight was like day."[14] More than any other African-American ghetto in the country, with the possible exception of Harlem, Chicago's Southside underworld stronghold came to symbolize the carefree hedonism, the gaiety, and the rebellious excesses of the "Roaring Twenties." Blues were a catalyst for the cultural insurgency.

## Race Records in Chicago

As the only major recording center outside New York in the 1920s, Chicago attracted many of the most talented blues artists in the South. They made the city their new home base and collectively produced much of the best blues material recorded in the entire country between 1924 and 1941. With the help of full-page advertisements in the *Chicago Defender*'s national edition, Chicago blues releases reached a nationwide black audience. This exposure, in turn, brought the music more to the forefront of the recording industry, especially when it became obvious that African Americans in the North and the South would buy blues disks if they were made available to them. At the height of their sales in the 1920s, race records accounted for at least 5 percent of all records sold in the United States, or $40 million worth of merchandise.

The commercial blues releases initially recorded in Chicago during the twenties were an eclectic potpourri of rural and regional styles overlaid with the influences of vaudeville blues, and to some extent, Tin Pan Alley lyrics. By the 1930s, however, record sales were off 80 percent; only blues artists with established reputations were given the opportunity to record. Under these depressed conditions, the industry's endless appetite for hit records was often translated into a search for a song formula based on previous hits. This tendency was encouraged by the technical demands of the record manufacturers (all songs put on wax during this period had to be three minutes long), as well as by the belief of most record company executives that standardized musical arrangements and lyrics would appeal to a wider audience. These conservative restraints helped to shape a more conventional Chicago blues sound. As a result, some of the unique regional styles and themes that had been brought to Chicago from the rural South began to disappear. The price often paid for the commercial success of the blues was separation from their folk roots. The ongoing flow of black migrants grounded in rural folk blues traditions tended to offset the commercial and technical constraints of the race recording industry, and the dialectic between these two forces, created an urban blues synthesis unique to the city's Southside ghetto.

The Chicago record industry was still dominated by three major labels—Okeh, Paramount, and Brunswick/Vocalion. Okeh was an early leader in the recording of vaudeville and country blues singers nationwide because of the efforts of Ralph Peer; most of Okeh's recording sessions still took place in New York, but some were held in Chicago. Texas vocalists Victoria Spivey and Sippie Wallace recorded for Okeh in the city, as did the versatile Lonnie Johnson. During the summer of 1926, the company sponsored the Okeh Race Records Ball in Chicago amid much fanfare. In addition to Wallace, Spivey, and Johnson, the dance concert featured Alberta Hunter and the jazz bands of King Oliver and Louis Armstrong. It was the black social event of the year, and its sponsorship by Okeh indicates that the company recognized the significance of Chicago's blues market.[15]

By the mid-twenties, however, Chicago's premier race recording company was Paramount. After a lackluster beginning in the race record market, the company hired J. Mayo "Ink" Williams in 1924 to manage its race artists series. Williams, an aggressive and energetic black promoter, was responsible for recording many of the greatest blues artists of the decade. In 1924, he signed up Ma Rainey and Papa Charlie Jackson, and a year later he recorded Ida Cox, Blind Lemon Jefferson, and Blind Blake. When his own venture, Black Patti, folded in 1927, he took a job with Brunswick/Vocalion as talent scout for its race series. Once again, he signed many quality blues artists, who

recorded some of the most successful blues numbers of the decade. He lured
Jim Jackson, Joe McCoy, and Memphis Minnie Douglas away from Memphis.
Leroy Carr and Scrapper Blackwell's "How Long, How Long Blues" and
Tampa Red and Thomas Dorsey's "It's Tight Like That" were recorded by
Vocalion in 1928. With the onset of the depression, Brunswick/Vocalion re-
duced the price of its records but sales remained low throughout the thirties.[16]

## Chicago Blues Pianists

The thriving red-light district on the Southside and Chicago's fledgling race
recording industry attracted black musicians in droves through the 1920s. The
first generation of pianists who played the blues were born early enough—the
1880s and 1890s—to be familiar with the older ragtime piano tradition.
Among the most notable who lived in Chicago at some point after the turn of
the century were Tony Jackson and Jelly Roll Morton from New Orleans, Eddie Heywood and Thomas Dorsey from Atlanta, "Cripple" Clarence Lofton
from Tennessee, "Cow Cow" Davenport from Alabama, and Doug Suggs and
Roosevelt Sykes from St. Louis, as well as Chicago-born Jimmy Yancy,
Jimmy Blythe, and Lovie Austin. These musicians were not exclusively blues
pianists; they also worked in jazz bands and vaudeville revues, playing the
popular show tunes and jazz numbers of the period.
    Typical of the group was "Cripple" Clarence Lofton, who was born in
Kingsport, Tennessee, on March 28, 1887. A birth defect had left Lofton partially disabled. He grew up in Kingsport, learned to play the piano on his
own, traveled briefly with a medicine show, and landed in Chicago in 1917.
Besides being a piano player, Lofton was an entertainer from the old school, a
one-man minstrel show. He was a skilled dancer, even though partially lame;
he was an accomplished percussionist who would often drum solos on the lid
of the piano with a pair of drumsticks. He could whistle like a bird, he wrote
his own music, and he even played the piano with his hands behind his back.
Lofton's signature piece was "Strut That Thing," a rollicking barrelhouse
number with playfully aggressive lyrics:

>            Gettin' sick and tired of the way you do,
>            'Time mama gonna poison you,
>            Sprinkle goffer dust 'round your bed,
>            Wake up some morning find your own self
>                dead.
>            'Cause you shouldn't, ah,
>            Shouldn't do what, darlin'?

I don't know, I don't know,
I don't know, I don't know,
I'm tellin' you, lover,
How to strut that thing night and day.

Shake it and break it, girls, you can hang
    it on the wall,
Pitch it out the window, catch it before it
    fall,
Stop a while, shimmy if it's all night long,
Sometime the thing's got your habits on.[17]

(Goffer dust refers to a magic potion common in black Folklore.) Clarence Lofton was a mainstay of the Chicago blues scene for over two decades, and during that time he developed a following among younger blues artists, who borrowed from his style and repertoire. Like many of the city's early bluesmen, he supported himself by taking a regular working-class job—for him it was polishing automobiles. Later, he was able to open his own small club on South State Street; he named it the Big Apple and performed there every night. Jazz historian William Russell visited Lofton there in the thirties and made the following observations:

No one can complain of Clarence's lack of variety or versatility. When he really gets going, he's a three ring circus. During one number he plays, sings, whistles a chorus, and snaps his fingers with the technique of a Spanish dancer to give further percussive accompaniment to his blues. At times he turns sideways, almost with his back to the piano as he keeps pounding away at the keyboard and stomping his feet, meanwhile continuing to sing and shout at his audience or his drummer. Suddenly in the middle of a number he jumps up, his hands clasped in front of him, and walks around the piano stool, and then, unexpectedly, out booms a vocal break in a bass voice from somewhere. One second later, he has turned and is back at the keyboard, both hands flying at lightning like pace. His actions and facial expressions are as intensely dramatic and exciting as his music. Clarence likes to work with a drummer. Last winter one night he had two of them and was trying his best to keep at least one sober. Clarence's place is no high class place; beer and sandwiches are five cents, other drinks ten. There's no checkroom; you park your coat and hat on top of the piano, or leave them on, and pull up a chair beside the piano and get your ear full of the crudest and the most honest to goodness piano playing you ever heard.[18]

Another blues pianist who moved to Chicago during World War I, and became a fixture on the local blues scene in the 1920s was Thomas Dorsey, also
known as "Barrelhouse Tom" and "Georgia Tom." Dorsey was raised in a
small rural Goergia town, Villa Rica, where he was born on July 1, 1899. His
father was a Baptist preacher and his mother was the church organist. When
the family moved to Atlanta in 1910, Dorsey began singing in a local church
choir and selling soft drinks at the 81 Theatre. In the orchestra pit of the
theater he learned to play the piano and to read music from touring TOBA
pianists. Dorsey moved to Chicago in 1916, and found work in an automobile
tire factory. He played piano in the wine rooms located in the back of the
saloons on the Southside, or in music stores along State Street. In the early
twenties, he played with a few local jazz bands and gained the attention of
Mayo Williams, who helped him get a job backing Ma Rainey. Dorsey worked
with Ma Rainey off and on for almost five years before teaming up with guitarist Tampa Red in the late 1920s.

During this period, Dorsey became interested in a new development in sacred singing. He coined the term "gospel songs" to describe the new black
religious music emanating from urban churches. He formed his own gospel
music publishing company in 1930 and two years later took over as choral
director of the Pilgrim Baptist Church. From that point on, his blues career
was a thing of the past, and he devoted himself exclusively to gospel music,
composing classics like "Precious Lord" and "Peace in the Valley."[19]

Although most of Chicago's early blues pianists were migrants from the
South, a few natives of the city were active by the 1920s, the most notable
being Jimmy Yancy, born in 1898. His father was a vaudeville performer, and
while still a youngster, Jimmy toured with him as a singer and buck dancer.
(The two took part in a command performance for the king and queen of England at Buckingham Palace in 1913.) Jimmy Yancy began to play the piano
under the instruction of his older brother Alonzo. For the next few years,
Yancy played the clubs on the Southside, including the Beartrap Inn and the
Cabaret Moonlight Inn. He specialized in the blues. During this same period,
he played baseball for a black semi-professional team—the Chicago All-
Americans. In the mid-twenties, Yancy went to work as a groundskeeper for
the Chicago White Sox at Cominsky Park. One of his fellow workers was a
much-admired blues pianist from St. Louis named Doug Suggs, whose signature piece, "Mr. Freddie Blues," was well known among Southside piano
players. Both Suggs and Yancy used the hypnotic boogie-woogie bass figures
popular in the South; they also used habanera (Cuban) rhythms, found in
W. C. Handy's "St. Louis Blues" and associated with Jelly Roll Morton's
playing. Jimmy Yancy married a blues singer, Estella Harris, and settled permanently on the Southside. He and his wife were active in blues circles from
the 1920s until he died in the early fifties.[20]

Perhaps the most influencial member of the first wave of pianists associated with the blues in Chicago in the 1920s was Charles Davenport. He was the product of a religious family from Anniston, Alabama, where his father was a local preacher and his mother the church organist. He was born on April 23, 1894, spent his childhood in Anniston, and entered the Alabama Theological Seminary at Selma, Alabama, in the fall of 1910. After a year there, he was expelled for ragging a tune while playing the piano at a social gathering. He spent the next few years gaining playing experience on the honky-tonk piano circuits in Birmingham, Atlanta, and New Orleans. By the early twenties, he had teamed up with Dora Carr to tour as a TOBA vaudeville act; later in the decade he teamed up with Ivy Smith, a snake charmer.

Davenport settled in Chicago in the mid-twenties and, much to his later regret, got tied into a business deal with Ink Williams. He was brought over from the Okeh label to Paramount in 1927 and moved on with Williams to the Brunswick/Vocalion label in 1928, working as a songwriter and arranger for Williams much as Thomas Dorsey had done earlier in the decade. Davenport sold "Mama Don't Allow" and "I'll Be Glad When You're Dead, You Rascal You" to Williams for a flat fee; he received no royalties or credit as the composer. His signature piece was "Cow Cow Blues," a rambling boogie-woogie instrumental number inspired by the locomotion of a railroad engine; it had long been his nickname when he finally recorded it in 1928. Davenport also mastered a variety of styles including ragtime and fast and slow blues; he liked to use repetitive bass figures or walking bass figures for his groundbeat in the blues numbers. The lyrics to his songs were fairly conventional, though he could vividly express the feelings of first-generation black migrants like him:

> I'm tired of this Jim Crow, gonna leave this
>    Jim Crow town,
> Doggone my black soul, I'm sweet Chicago bound,
> Yes I'm leavin' here from this ole Jim Crow
>    town.
>
> I'm goin' up north where they say money grows
>    on trees,
> I don't give a doggone if my black soul leaves,
> I'm goin' where I don't need no BVDs.[21]

Cow Cow Davenport remained active in Southside blues circles until 1930, when he moved to Cleveland and opened a record shop. He never returned to Chicago.[22]

In the mid-twenties, while still based on the Southside, Davenport came across Clarence "Pinetop" Smith in a club in Pittsburgh. He was impressed with the younger pianist's "mean boogie woogie" and encouraged him to come to Chicago. Smith and his wife moved there soon after and settled in a rooming house on Prairie Street in a crowded Southside neighborhood.

Clarence Smith was born on January 11, 1904, in Troy, Alabama. He acquired the nickname "Pinetop" because of his lankiness and a love for pine trees. After teaching himself to play the piano, he left for Birmingham, where he was based for a few years before touring on the TOBA circuit in the early 1920s. During his vaudeville stint, Pinetop moved north to Pittsburgh and was living there when he met Davenport. Once he arrived in Chicago and began to play on the Southside, Pinetop Smith was quickly recognized as an exciting new blues talent. His trademark number, "Pinetop's Boogie Woogie" launched a boogie woogie craze among Chicago's bluesmen. It was destined to become the most imitated piano blues of the era.

Smith was a transitional figure in the development of blues piano. Although closely identified with the newer boogie-woogie piano blues style, he was also fluent in vaudeville standards and the conventional jazz of the day, much like the older first-generation blues pianists. In a record of one of his favorite numbers, "I'm Sober Now," Smith begins with a boogie-woogie riff and then suddenly switches over to a more standardized groundbeat based on quarter notes, which he embellishes with a Tin Pan Alley melody. His audience complains about the change, and, in response, Pinetop complains that nobody has brought him a drink—"I'm sober now," he explains. After being set up with a drink, he goes back to his original boogie-woogie riff amid shouts of approval from the audience.

The recording offers a glimpse of Smith's carefree personality. He was fond of sleeping all day and playing all night. He would start with his regular gig at the Forestville Tavern and then move from saloon to saloon on the Southside until they all closed. From there he would seek out the after-hours buffet flats or perhaps descend at dawn on a sleeping friend who happened to own a piano so he could continue with the music and merrymaking. Nor did Smith limit his carousing to Chicago's Southside; he made frequent trips to the red-light districts in St. Louis and Omaha, Nebraska. This unrelenting quest for excitement and new musical challenges was often reckless and ended tragically. On March 15, 1929, he was caught in a crossfire between two feuding customers at a late-night dance in Chicago and died soon after. He was only twenty-five.[23]

The death of Pinetop Smith did not mean the end of boogie woogie. Several younger Chicago blues pianists were well schooled in the infectious style and continued to play it with religious fervor. Albert Ammons and Meade Lux Lewis were two such disciples; they had been tenants with Smith in the same apartment building on the Southside. Since Lewis was the only one in the building who had a piano, his room was the scene of frequent jam sessions involving the three.

Albert Ammons was a Chicago native. Both his parents played piano, and he learned to play at an early age; he also played drums in a drum-and-bugle marching band. In the mid-twenties, Ammons went to work for a local taxicab company, where he met Meade Lux Lewis, a fellow driver. Lewis was born in Louisville, Kentucky, in 1904, and moved to Chicago after World War I. His father was a Pullman porter who also sang and played the guitar. Lewis learned to play the piano in the Southside clubs watching the Yancy brothers, Clarence Lofton, and Jimmy Blythe. He recorded his trademark boogie-woogie number, "Honky Tonk Train Blues," in 1927 for Paramount; it was from the same mold as "Pinetop's Boogie Woogie," recorded a year later for Vocalion. Smith's recording was released before Lewis's because Paramount failed to put "Honky Tonk Train Blues" on the market until 1929. After Smith died, Ammons and Lewis became the foremost exponents of boogie-woogie piano in the city, carrying on their friend's legacy. Ammons had learned "Pinetop's Boogie Woogie" note for note and steadfastly featured it in his nightclub sets after Smith's death. Lewis developed his "Honky Tonk Train Blues" into a boogie-woogie tour de force. He was known to improve on its musical themes for up to half an hour when he played it in Southside clubs and saloons. Ammons and Lewis remained active on the local blues scene but lived in relative obscurity. Times were hard; Lewis even took a job at a car wash to make ends meet and later went on relief. Luckily, the careers of both piano men were revived in the late thirties through the efforts of Columbia talent scout John Hammond.[24]

By the late twenties, the piano players dominated the blues culture in Chicago. Younger men, born after the turn of the century, were coming to the forefront; they were strictly bluesmen and strongly influenced by the boogie-woogie boom. Among the better known was Romeo Nelson, who grew up in East St. Louis but moved to the Southside between the two world wars to play in the clubs or at the popular rent parties. Nelson recorded his trademark number, "Head Rag Hop," for Vocalion in 1929; it was a powerful boogie-woogie blues reminiscent of Pinetop Smith's classic. Other blues pianists active in the city during this period included Charles Avery, Will Ezell, Romeo Briggs, Freddie Shyne, and Alex Channey. They were regularly featured in Southside clubs like Bill Lewis's Mineral Café, Charlie Letts' Café, Henry "Teeman" Jones' Elite Café #1 at Thirty-first and State streets, the Fiume Club, the Panama Club, and Bud Sneeze's Forest Inn Café, where Pinetop Smith played. In general, the club scene for blues was thriving up until the depression. Southside music stores and theaters like the Big Grand, the Vendome, and the Lincoln, as well as the ubiquitous Chicago rent parties, kept the city's blues piano players busy.

## Early Chicago Blues Guitarists

At the height of the blues boom in the late 1920s, the Chicago record companies showed a new preference for piano and guitar blues duets, hoping to duplicate the success of Leroy Carr and Scrapper Blackwell's "How Long, How
Long Blues." The best-known blues duo to emerge from Chicago were Thomas
Dorsey and Tampa Red; Big Bill Broonzy's pairing with pianists Black Bob or
Josh Altheimer was a close second. Broonzy and Tampa Red were important
additions to Chicago's small circle of recorded blues musicians because they
were the first guitar players to have a significant impact on the development of
an urban blues style on the Southside. Within two decades of their recording
debuts in the late 1920s, the guitar would totally eclipse the piano as the lead
instrument in Chicago Blues.[25]

### Big Bill Broonzy: "Key to the Highway"

William Lee Conley Broonzy was the venerable father figure of the Southside
blues community. A generous, warm-hearted man with strong convictions and
unwavering dignity, he stood out among his peers. He was a beacon for the
city's transient blues musicians, and he was the male archetype of Chicago-
style blues from the late 1920s until the advent of Muddy Waters and Howling
Wolf in the postwar era. The Delta blues he learned as a child (see Chapter
2) became the foundation of Broonzy's blues repertoire; in his later years he
featured it in his concerts and on his recordings.

The first group of musicians Broonzy worked with was a small country
string band that played for dances and picnics around Scott, Mississippi; he
performed with them until he moved across the state line to Arkansas in 1912.
There he began preaching the gospel and singing church songs, and put the
blues aside for a while. He worked as a plowhand and later as a coal miner
after a drought destroyed the cotton crop in the region. He served in the army
for the duration of World War I, returned to the South briefly, and then embarked on his journey to Chicago.[26]

Once he had found a job with the Pullman Company, Broonzy began to
frequent the Saturday-night blues parties on the Southside. He described them
to his biographer as follows:

> In 1920, I came to Chicago and the people asked me to come to their
> house. Some of them had known me at home and they knew I could play
> and sing the blues. So I went to their houses and they had fried chicken
> and pig feet and chittlins for seventy-five cents a plate, and if you could
> play and sing you got all the eats and drinks free. . . .

. . . All of them was from some part of the South and had come to Chicago to better their living. And these people started to give parties and some Saturday nights they would make enough money to pay the rent, and so they started to call them house rent parties because they sold chicken, pig feet, home brew, chittlins and moonshine whiskey.[27]

On the Southside's rent-party circuit, Broonzy got to know many of the most renowned bluesmen living in the city at that time—Blind Lemon Jefferson, Sleepy John Estes, and Papa Charlie Jackson, who helped him develop his guitar style. These contacts led him into a frustrating series of recording dates with Ink Williams in the late twenties. The commercial failure of these solo efforts led Broonzy's record producers to record him with a variety of small ensembles over the next decade. They were called "hokum bands" in Chicago, and were made up of guitars, piano, bass, drums, trumpet, saxophone, and occasionally a washboard. They produced an upbeat, happy-go-lucky sound, closer to the black minstrel and vaudeville musical tradition than to the rural Delta blues that Broonzy had grown up on. Most of the recordings he made during this period were influenced by the hokum music craze, which was centered in Chicago.

Despite this temporary drift toward a more commercialized musical product, Broonzy developed into a first-rate blues composer capable of telling a compelling story in a few succinct verses. He copyrighted over three hundred songs in his lifetime. Many of them were adaptations of traditional folk numbers, but others were strikingly original blues drawn from his own experiences. "When Will I Get to Be Called a Man?" written in 1928, was inspired by a childhood acquaintance. As he explained it:

There was a man that I knew when I was ten years old, that the white people called "boy." He was about thirty then. When I went to the Army and came back in 1919, well he was an old man then and the white people was calling him Uncle Mackray. So he never got to be called a man, from "boy" to Uncle Mackray.[28]

The lyrics read:

When I was born in this world, this was what
    happened to me,
I was never called a man and now I'm fifty-three.
I wonder when will I be called a man,
Or do I have to wait until I get ninety-three?

When I got back from overseas, that night we had
   a ball,
I met the boss the next day, he told me "Boy, get
   you some overall."
I wonder when will I be called a man,
Or do I have to wait until I get ninety-three?

I worked on a levee camp and a chain gang too,
A black man is a boy to a white, don't care what
   he can do.
I wonder when will I be called a man,
Or do I have to wait until I get ninety-three?

They said I was undereducated, my clothes dirty
   and torn,
Now I got a little education, but I'm a boy
   right on.
I wonder when will I be called a man,
Or do I have to wait until I get ninety-three?[29]

Another blues with an overt social protest theme was "Black, Brown and
White," which Broonzy wrote later in his life. Many of the verses were again
drawn from the wellspring of his own experience, while the chorus refrain was
taken from a popular black street saying. Some of the lyrics are as follows:

This little song that I'm singing about, people,
   you know it's true,
If you're black and got to work for a living, this
   is what they say to you.

They say if you's white, you's alright,
If you's brown, stick around,
But if you're black, mmm brother, get back, get
   back, get back.

I was in a place one night, they was all having
   fun,
They was all buying beer and wine, but they
   would not sell me none.

Me and a white man was working side by side, this is
   what it meant,

They was paying him a dollar an hour, and they
    was payin' me fifty cents.

I went to the employment office, got a number
    and I got in line,
They called everybody's number, but they never
    did call mine.

I helped win sweet victory with my little
    plough and hoe,
Now I want you to tell me brother, what you
    gonna do 'bout the old Jim Crow.[30]

This outspoken condemnation of racism is atypical only to the extent that his protest is direct and overt. Thus, although his verses occupy the radical end of the blues continuum, they are still at the center of the black oral tradition. Within that tradition, protest, like resistance, operates overtly and covertly, directly and indirectly. Broonzy was unique as a blues composer in that he wrote from the many vantage points he had experienced in his own rural-to-urban migration. For example, some of the more subtle expressions of protest and resistance found in his blues lyrics focus on the degradation of black labor in the southern workplace. In "Stump Blues" he laments:

Yeah, you never get to do me like you did my buddy Shine,
Now you'll never get to do me like you did my buddy Shine,
You know you worked him down on the levee until he went
    real stone blind.[31]

Likewise, "Plowhand Blues" evokes the black migrants' bitter memories of sharecropping and tenant farming:

I ain't gonna raise no more cotton 'n' I declare I ain't
    gonna raise no corn,
I ain't gonna raise no more cotton 'n' I declare I ain't
    gonna raise no corn,
Now if a mule started runnin' away with the world,
Lord, I declare I'm gonna let him go on ahead.[32]

Broonzy also wrote migration blues celebrating social mobility and freedom. The most famous was his signature piece, "Key to the Highway":

> I got the key to the highway, yes I'm billed out and bound to go,
> I'm gonna leave here runnin', 'cause walkin' mos' too slow.[33]

Finally, there was his subversive blues humor in the face of adversity, poking fun at himself:

> Everything I get ahold of, baby, it goes away like snow in June,
> If I get a chance again, baby, I'm going up to the moon,
> Yeah now, baby, gal, I believe I'll change towns,
> Yeah, poor me's down so low, baby, Big Bill is lookin' up at down.[34]

Broonzy's greatest triumphs as a bluesman came later in his life when he toured Europe as a solo performer. His reception there far surpassed the attention he was given in the United States, where the blues were seldom considered a serious art form with important social implications. Almost the opposite was true of Europe, where jazz and then the blues received a good deal of critical acclaim. Broonzy made frequent trips to Europe after his initial tour; he made several recordings there, and he was even the subject of two documentary films. By the time of his death from cancer in 1957, his life and music had been well documented, and he had received some long-overdue recognition.

## Tampa Red: "Tight Like That"

It was something of an irony that Mississippian Big Bill Broonzy encountered his first slide guitarist on the Southside in the person of Tampa Red, a migrant bluesman who grew up in Florida. Tampa Red was the originator of Chicago's single-string bottleneck guitar style; from all accounts he developed it before moving to the city from Florida in the mid-twenties. He was born Hudson Woodbridge sometime between 1900 and 1904 in Smithsville, Georgia, but was forced to move to Tampa, Florida, at an early age to live with his grandmother after his parents died. His older brother, Eddie, played guitar and entertained locally in Tampa, and he eagerly followed in his brother's footsteps. He was especially inspired by an old singer and street musician called Piccolo Pete, who showed him how to play his first blues licks on a guitar. By the time he ventured to Chicago, the young guitarist had already perfected his silky slide technique, and he soon became a popular Southside street musician. It was during this period that he was nicknamed Tampa Red by his admirers, a reference to his hometown and his red hair.

Ink Williams teamed him with Thomas Dorsey for a recording session in 1928, sponsored by Paramount. The second number they recorded, "Tight Like That," proved to be a windfall for them. Dorsey recalled the song's origin:

"Tight Like That" wasn't no original tune. It was just something that popped up at the right time, to make some money. . . . Tampa and, oh, it was a bunch of us, somewhere one night. And there used to be a phrase they used around town, you know, folks started saying, "Ah, it's tight like that! Tight like that!" So we said, "Well, that oughta work." So we picked out a song. Tampa and I got the guitar sitting around the house one night at the dinner table after dinner, and J. Mayo Williams heard it and he said, "Oh man, we gonna record that! We gonna record that right away! Hold it right like that!" And so we did, and that thing actually was a money maker.[35]

Tampa Red confirmed the banal character of the number, saying that it was "just a little old jive song, but they really went for it." Many of his subsequent recording ventures were in the hokum style—he and Dorsey even called themselves the "Hokum Boys" at first—but Tampa Red was both a gifted guitar player and a sensitive blues composer. Eventually, these dimensions of his artistry came to the forefront, even on his commercial recordings. He made popular versions of such urban blues classics as "Love Her with a Feeling," "It Hurts Me, Too," and "Sweet Little Angel"; moreover, his unique single-string bottleneck style was a major influence on other leading Chicago blues guitarists like Big Bill Broonzy and Robert Nighthawk.

During his recording career, Tampa Red cut more disks than any other pre-war blues artist. He was also popular with his fellow musicians, and his Southside flat was the scene of frequent blues jams throughout the depression and the war years. As pianist Blind John Davis described it, "The house went all the way from the front to the alley. He had a big rehearsal room and he had two rooms for the different artists that came in from out of town to record. [RCA Victor Bluebird record producer] Melrose'd pay him for the lodging and Mrs. Tampa would cook for 'em."[36] The advent of the electric guitar eclipsed his style during the 1940s, however, and after that Tampa Red's stature as the Southside "guitar wizard" diminished considerably. His decline was hastened by a drinking problem, which eventually left him virtually incapacitated.

## Chicago Blues During the Depression

The black community in Chicago was hard hit by the depression of the 1930s. The economic foothold they had managed to secure for themselves during World War I and the Jazz Age gave way to an unescapable downward cycle of unemployment and poverty. The optimism of the recently arrived African-

American migrants was replaced by dismay, and then by angry resolve to survive. Eviction struggles became common occurrences in front of the Southside's dilapidated tenements. Landlords, backed by the police, attempted to expel families unable to pay the rent, while neighborhood "unemployment councils" physically resisted these forced removals. Industrial employment came to a standstill, domestic and service jobs dried up, and the black labor force became even more marginal to the stagnant economy. Only the policy games of the Southside underworld continued to do a thriving business. At the height of the depression, the interracial underworld syndicate controlling the racket employed up to 5,000 people and collected $18 million annually.

By the mid-thirties, the Roosevelt administration, with the aid of a revived Democratic city machine, had turned Chicago into a New Deal showcase and succeeded in luring the African-American vote away from the Republicans. Over half of the impoverished black population signed up for welfare or unemployment stipends, and many others were employed by New Deal public works programs. Although the hard times persisted, the advent of the New Deal and later the retooling of America's war industries encouraged a steady flow of African-American migrants from the South. The Southside absorbed another 50,000 African Americans during the thirties, and their numbers reached 277,731 by the 1940 census. Black people now constituted almost 9 percent of the city's total population.[37]

Meanwhile, the first years of the depression had devastated Chicago's commercial music industry, forcing many theaters, nightclubs, and record companies out of business. Only two Chicago-based record operations, Brunswick/Vocalion and Victor (now owned by RCA), continued to make local blues recordings. The former, as we have seen, slashed disk prices. RCA Victor launched its "Bluebird" race record label in 1934, under the direction of Lester Melrose. He recorded many of the new urban blues groups based in Chicago, as well as some blues musicians still playing in a more traditional rural style. Small bands made up of guitars, pianos, harmonicas, drums, washboards, and bass were the most popular category. They involved guitarists like Big Bill Broonzy, Tampa Red, Memphis Minnie Douglas, and Bumble Bee Slim; pianists Roosevelt Sykes, Josh Altheimer, and Blind John Davis; harmonica players Sonny Boy Williamson and Jazz Gillum; drummer Fred Williams; and bass player Ransome Knowling. The most successful country blues musicians Melrose recorded in the thirties were Tommy McClennan, Bukka White, Big Joe Williams, and Arthur "Big Boy" Crudup. All four were raised in Mississippi and performed within the parameters of the Delta blues tradition.

Melrose was so anxious to sign Tommy McClennan to a record contract that he drove from Chicago to Mississippi to locate him in the late thirties, in spite of Broonzy's warning that he would not be welcomed by the white plantation owners. The warning proved to be well founded; Melrose was branded a "yankee" and run off the plantation where McClennan worked, so fast that he left his car behind. It was his first and last trip to Mississippi as a talent scout.[38]

Tommy McClennan was a native of Yazoo County in the Delta, born April 8, 1908. He grew up on the J. F. Sligh plantation and began working in the cotton fields at an early age. In his youth, he started to play the guitar and sing on the streets in the small Delta towns of Yazoo City, Itta Bena, and Greenwood. Tommy's vocals were highly reminiscent of those of Charley Patton, whom he no doubt observed in the Delta while growing up. He was a small, intense man who sang in a harsh, declamatory manner; he often shouted out the lyrics, interjected spoken comments, and pounded on his steel-bodied National guitar. The guitar had a built-in resonator, which gave it more volume than wooden guitars. His playing style also resembled Patton's; he flailed his instrument rhythmically while following a simple chord progression. As Big Bill Broonzy curtly described it:

> Tommy McClennan had a different style of playing guitar. You just make the chords E, A or B and just rake your fingers across all strings and sing the blues, and change from E to A to B just when you feel like changing. Any time will do. You don't have to be in no hurry. Jus' close your eyes.[39]

McClennan moved to Chicago in the late 1930s to record for Melrose on the Bluebird label. A few of his recordings were relatively popular. His best numbers were "I'm a Guitar King," "Goodbye, Baby," "Deep Blue Sea Blues," and his signature piece, "Bottle Up and Go"; the last two songs were his renditions of well-known Delta folk blues. McClennan loved to drink and party as much as physically possible. Big Bill Broonzy recalled that he also got into fights because he repeatedly used a verse from "Bottle Up and Go" that he knew would offend African Americans in Chicago. On one such occasion, after McClennan had insisted on singing the inflammatory verse, he had his guitar broken around his neck, and he and Broonzy had to leave the party abruptly through a window. The verse goes as follows:

> The nigger and the white man playing seven up,
> The nigger beats the white man and was scared
>     to pick it up,
> He had to bottle up and go, he had to bottle up and go.

As Broonzy explained: "In Mississippi we didn't mind being called nigger, because we called one another nigger and all the people called us that way. In Chicago and New York, they didn't use that word."[40]

Although Southside residents hated that verse, McClennan's stark Delta blues style was in great demand because there were by now in Chicago more black migrants from Mississippi than from any other southern state.

Arthur "Big Boy" Crudup was another transplanted Delta bluesman who made several popular recordings during the late thirties and the war years. He was from Forest, Mississippi, where he was born on August 25, 1905, and was raised by his father, a farm worker who played the guitar. In his youth, Arthur was attracted to black church music; he started to sing in a local church choir at the age of ten. He was also drawn to the blues of a folk musician named Papa Harvey. However, it was not until much later in his life that he learned to play the guitar and became a bluesman. In the interim, he grew over six feet tall. His height and weight (in excess of two hundred pounds) earned him the sobriquet "Big Boy." He worked as a farm hand, a logger, and a common laborer on the Mississippi levees before moving to Silver City in the Delta, where he set up a bootlegging operation.

Big Boy Crudup did not reach Chicago until 1939. At that time, he was traveling and singing with a gospel quartet called the Harmonizing Four. He left the gospel group there and, for a time, literally lived in the streets, playing for spare change and sleeping in a shanty-town crate. Melrose happened to hear him, and he liked Crudup's rough Delta sound; he booked him into a Southside club and set up a Bluebird recording date for the migrant bluesman. At his first session in 1941, Crudup recorded "If I Get Lucky," his rendition of the Little Brother Montgomery classic "Vicksburg Blues," which had been popular in the Delta since the 1920s. It did well enough when it was released to warrant another session in the spring of 1942. At this session, Crudup switched from a steel National guitar to an electric guitar to record a version of a Delta train blues, which he called "Mean Old Frisco." It was a commercial hit, and he soon after adopted it as a signature piece. This was the first Chicago blues recording that featured an electric guitar. (T-Bone Walker had pioneered its use in the blues on the West Coast in 1940, following the lead of black jazz guitarists Eddie Durham and Charlie Christian.) Crudup's elementary time-keeping accompaniments, strummed in the key of E, were ideal for electric amplification, and his recordings heralded the postwar electric guitar boom in Chicago blues circles.

Crudup sang in an impassioned, high-pitched voice reminiscent of Delta blues great Son House; his vocal style also owed something to the traditional southern field hollers. He recorded for Melrose for seven years, releasing a number of blues hits such as "Rock Me, Mama," and "That's Alright." "Rock Me, Mama" was soon to be a favorite of such postwar blues giants as

Riley B. King, Bobby Blue Bland, and Willa Mae "Big Mama" Thornton. "That's Alright" would become the first black cover record released by Elvis Presley for Sun Records in the mid-1950s.

During this period, Crudup divided his attention between his recording career in Chicago and his bootlegging business in Silver City, Mississippi. He broke with Melrose in 1947, after finally realizing that he was being swindled out of his royalties. Crudup then left Chicago permanently and returned to Mississippi. "The reason I quit playing is that gradually I realized I was making everybody rich, and here I was poor," Crudup told an interviewer in the last years of his life; later he added, "I was born poor, I live poor, and I'm going to die poor." True to his word, Arthur "Big Boy" Crudup died in poverty after legal attempts to regain his royalty monies from Melrose's estate and the publishing company handling Presley both failed.[41]

The New Deal slowly revived Chicago's dormant music business. Federal jobs and welfare checks revitalized the cash flow on the Southside, pumping new life into the clubs, theaters, and record companies. As early as 1934, Lester Melrose observed nightclubs and saloons reopening in Chicago's black neighborhoods. However, in lieu of presenting live music, they were installing juke boxes that featured the popular race records of the day. This turn of events curtailed the job market for blues musicians while opening up a new and promising market for record companies such as RCA Victor, Columbia, and Brunswick/Vocalion, all of which were still involved in manufacturing blues disks during this period. They were joined by a new label, Decca Records, which hired Ink Williams in 1935 to supervise its race record operations in Chicago. Williams hired a studio band to back up vocalists and to make some recordings on their own. The band recorded under the name "The Harlem Hamfats." The group's veteran leader was Joe McCoy; he was apparently responsible for combining string-band instruments with a New Orleans–style jazz band organized by trumpeter Herb "Kid" Morand. The reconstructed group featured Joe McCoy on guitar, his brother Charlie on mandolin, John Lindsey on string bass, Morand on trumpet, Odell Rand on clarinet, Horace Malcom on piano, and Fred Flynn or Pearlis Williams on drums. Decca released seventy-five of their disks over a three-year period; many of them were rough-and-tumble blues numbers associated with the urban underworld. Jack Kapp, who was responsible for Decca's race catalogues, arranged for the group's live appearances. Most of the bookings were at clubs in Italian neighborhoods, owned by Sicilian gangsters, where they were expected to play Italian dance music. The Harlem Hamfats were an early prototype of postwar urban blues combos. They disbanded in 1940.[42]

Williams's marketing strategy was to find and record undiscovered country blues artists. Decca's discovery was James "Kokomo" Arnold, a talented left-handed slide guitarist. Arnold was originally from Georgia, where he grew up in a small town just south of Atlanta. His older cousin was a local musician who taught him to play the guitar. While still in his teens, Arnold moved north to Buffalo, New York; he worked there as an unskilled laborer, playing the blues on weekends.

This was the beginning of a fast-moving urban and industrial odyssey for Arnold. He worked in the steel mills of Pittsburgh and Gary, Indiana, played a few gigs with Peetie Wheatstraw in the Midwest, made some obscure recordings in Memphis using the alias "Gitfiddle Jim," and eventually settled in Chicago, where he set up a successful bootlegging operation on the Southside. Joe McCoy heard Arnold in a club and immediately offered to get him a recording session with Decca. He was reluctant to record at first, fearing that the publicity would jeopardize his bootlegging business. Luckily for Williams, however, he later relented, signing with Decca in 1934. Late that year, the company released his first two songs, "Milk Cow Blues" and "Old Original Kokomo Blues," which was later transformed into the blues classic "Sweet Home Chicago." The record was something of a sensation and it helped push the Decca label into the forefront of the blues recording business. Arnold became an instant Chicago blues celebrity and acquired the nickname "Kokomo" from the blues standard he named after a popular regional brand of coffee.

Arnold's guitar style was highly original. He used a slide along with a finger-picking technique to produce a fusillade of extended notes in rapid succession; his playing sounded like the high-pitched wailing of a human voice. He sang with a falsetto intonation and sometimes hummed along with his guitar solos or shouted words of encouragement to himself. Kokomo Arnold recorded for Decca until 1938 and was a featured performer at the 33rd Street Club and Club Claremount on the Southside. He returned to work in the steel mills during World War II and never revived his blues career afterward.[43]

As the job opportunities in Chicago diminished in the aftermath of the depression, so did the commercial pressures to make the blues conform more to conventional pop standards. Left more and more to their own devices, Southside blues artists gravitated toward the traditional sources of musical inspiration in their own culture, and the Delta blues tradition became more deeply rooted in Chicago soil than anywhere else in the country outside its Mississippi homeland. Blues artists in the city increasingly relied on the local black community for support and sustenance. They played mostly for their friends and neighbors at rent parties, at never-ending jam sessions on the sidewalks of State Street, or in their own homes. In these settings, the blues were not a commodified form of commercial entertainment but a living cultural tradition nourishing an ethnic group hard pressed by poverty and discrimination. As the collective voice of the black masses, the blues reaffirmed their historic quest for equality, prosperity, and freedom in the United States.

The blues that gradually came to the forefront during the depression years captured the mood and the momentum of the times and thus enabled the blues artists to play a critical role in the cultural resistance of their people. In Chicago, even before the stock market crashed, there was an emerging consciousness that all was not well, economically and socially, for the black urban migrants. Itinerant blues bard Blind Lemon Jefferson moved to the city in the late twenties to record ominous prophecies of the impending disaster, such as "Tin Cup Blues":

> Baby, times is so hard, I almost call it tough,
> Baby, times is so hard, I almost call it tough,
> I can't earn no money to buy no bread, and I
>     can't buy my stuff.[44]

Blind Blake predicted hard times in "No Dough Blues," and in 1928 Big Bill Broonzy contributed "Starvation Blues":

> Starvation in my kitchen, rent signs on my door,
> Starvation in my kitchen, rent signs on my door,
> Times is so hard, I can't find work no more.[45]

Once the depression hit, a constant flow of Chicago blues releases depicted its impact on African Americans with grim realism. At the time, race records were still the principal cultural products purchased in the black community, but their message was in sharp contrast to the full-scale retreat into fantasy that characterized much of the major networks' radio programming during the depression years. In 1931, Tampa Red cut "Depression Blues":

> If I could tell you my troubles, it would
>     give my poor mind ease,
> Said if I could tell my troubles, it would
>     give poor Tampa ease,
> But Depression has got me, somebody help me
>     please.[46]

Later in the decade, Sleepy John Estes recorded his blues recollection of Chicago's "Hooverville" encampment, entitled "Hobo Jungle Blues":

> Now when I came in on the Mae West, I put
>     down at Chicago Heights,
> Now when I came in on the Mae West, I put
>     down all at Chicago Heights,

> Now you know the hobo jungle and that's where
>     I stayed all night.
>
> Now if you hobo and if you brown, you better
>     not be sleepin' out,
> Now if you hobo, if you brown, you better not
>     be sleepin' out,
> Now Mr. Wynn will get you and Mr. Callahan will
>     wear you out.[47]

When the New Deal was launched by the Roosevelt administration amid much fanfare, Chicago residents' hope was tempered by their dire situation. Carl Martin's "Let's Have a New Deal" comments:

> Now I'm gettin' tired of sittin' around,
> I ain't makin' a dime, just wearin' my shoe
>     soles down,
> Now everybody's cryin' let's have a new deal,
> 'Cause I've got to make a living if I have to
>     rob and steal.[48]

Compounding this skepticism was the federal government's history of neglect and even betrayal in its dealings with black people. Sonny Boy Williamson's "Welfare Store" was an adaptation of "Red Cross Blues," which depicts the violation of African Americans' civil rights in Red Cross relief camps during the 1927 Mississippi River flood. The updated version expresses a deep reluctance to become a ward of the federal government again:

> Now me and my baby talked last night, and we
>     talked for nearly an hour,
> She wanted me to go down to that welfare store
>     for a sack of that welfare flour.
>
> But I told her, no baby, I sure don't want to go,
> I'll do anything in the world for you,
> But I don't want to go down to the welfare store.
>
> Now you need to go get you some real white man,
> You know, to sign your little note,
> They give you a pair of them keen toed shoes,
> And one of them old pinch-back soldier coats.

President Roosevelt said them welfare people,
   they gonna treat everybody right,
Said they give you a can of them beans and a
   can or two of them old tripe.[49]

African Americans who applied for relief were often frustrated in their attempts to secure it; Floyd Council's "Don't Want No Hungry Woman" detailed this experience:

Hey the welfare didn't answer, the government
   paid me no mind,
Hey the government didn't answer, welfare paid
   me no mind,
Hey boy, if you think we goin' help you, swear
   you better change your mind.

I done phoned the welfare, wrote to the government too,
I done phoned to the welfare, wrote to the
   government too,
And asked them to help me get my woman a pair of
   shoes.[50]

One of the most popular topical blues of the thirties was Casey Bill Weldon's "WPA Blues." It told a story about a "WPA wrecking crew" that went around tearing down dilapidated housing still occupied by poverty-stricken African Americans. Rather than accept government handouts, unemployed black people living in northern industrial cities like Chicago sometimes chose to return to the rural South. This possibility is the topic of Jazz Gillum's "Down South Blues":

It's a sign on the building, yes I mean hear
   me sing,
There's a sign on the building, we all gotta
   move right away,
I ain't got no money, no rent that I can pay.

It will soon be cold, you hear me sing, yes I
   mean,
It will soon be cold, I ain't got no place to
   go,
I'm goin' back down South where the chilly winds
   don't blow.[51]

In "Creole Queen," Little Bill Gaither has a similar lament:

> I used to live near New Orleans, it's been a
>     good many years ago,
> I used to live near New Orleans, it's been a
>     good many years ago,
> But since I been up North, I been sleepin' on
>     the barroom floor.
>
> I been on relief in Chicago and soup lines in
>     Kokomo,
> I been on relief in Chicago and soup lines in
>     Kokomo,
> But I'm goin' back down South where I won't
>     be driven from door to door.[52]

By the end of the decade, a handful of relatively new Chicago residents had emerged as major blues talents on the Southside. They included guitarists Amos Easton, Johnny Temple, Robert Nighthawk, and Memphis Minnie Douglas; piano players Big Maceo Merriweather and Memphis Slim; harmonica players Jazz Gillum and Sonny Boy Williamson; and blues composer and vocalist Robert Brown ("Washboard Sam"). Brown was born and raised in Arkansas; he migrated to Chicago in the early 1930s just after turning twenty-one. As a young man, he also lived in Memphis, where he played a washboard for a jug band that featured Sleepy John Estes and Hammie Nixon. Once he moved to the Southside, Robert Brown became closely associated with Big Bill Broonzy, his half-brother, and Jazz Gillum; he wrote several blues numbers for them, and they often played together. Brown also recorded over 150 disks of his own as Washboard Sam and was a popular performer in Chicago blues circles. His voice was his best musical asset; it was loud and rough, and he used a pronounced vibrato in his singing style. It was well suited to his pulsating washboard accompaniments, and the hard sense of urgency or oppression in his lyrics—for example, "I'm on My Way":

> I was standing on the corner and I was wringing
>     my hands,
> I was standing on the corner and I was wringing
>     my hands,
> And up comes a copper and said he was a plain
>     clothes man.

> He carried me to the station and put me in a cell,
> He carried me to the station and put me in a cell,
> He said you'll stay there partner until about
>     twelve.[53]

and "I Been Treated Wrong":

> I been treated like an orphan and been worked
>     like a slave,
> I been treated like an orphan and been worked
>     like a slave,
> And if I never get my revenge, this will carry
>     me to my grave.
>
> Now I been having trouble ever since I been grown,
> Now I been having trouble ever since I been grown,
> I'm too old for the orphanage and too young for
>     the old folks home.[54]

Jazz Gillum was the featured harmonica player with Washboard Sam and Big Bill Broonzy on many of their Bluebird releases in the 1930s; the three were also a popular attraction in local clubs. Gillum was a native of the Mississippi Delta, where he had learned to play the harmonica before he moved to Chicago. He did not write much of his own material, but he had a fine expressive voice and he recorded excellent versions of blues compositions by Broonzy and Washboard Sam.

The two piano players most closely associated with Tampa Red, Big Bill Broonzy, and their entourage of musicians in the late thirties and the war years were Big Maceo Merriweather and Memphis Slim. Merriweather moved to Chicago in 1941, after being befriended by Tampa Red, and recorded his biggest commercial hit, "Worried Life Blues" that same year. Merriweather was six feet four inches tall and weighed over 250 pounds; he had a raw, emotional vocal style that contrasted nicely with his powerful left-hand-oriented piano playing. His undisputed masterpiece was a boogie-woogie number, "Chicago Breakdown" famous for its pyrotechnics.

Memphis Slim left Memphis in the early thirties, spent a few years on the road, and eventually settled in Chicago in 1937. He teamed up with Big Bill Broonzy and friends to form a small blues combo that performed in Southside clubs like Ruby's Tavern, Cozy Corner, 1410 Club, the Bee Hive, and the Ran Club. Memphis Slim made his initial recordings with Big Bill Broonzy on the Bluebird label and later moved on to establish his own blues ensemble, which was eventually recorded after World War II. The Houserockers, his seven-piece band, were unique to Chicago blues circles; their instrumentation was well ahead of the times, even though the music was strictly blues. As he recalled:

> Didn't want no harp players in my band because I already had a sax section—two tenors and an alto. You can get a much fuller sound with the sax—more suited for city folks. All the band members were from Memphis then; . . . we had saxophones, guitar, bass, drums and me on piano; . . . [we] played together as a unit and they knowed my music and way of playin' from back in my Beale Street days. We played around Chicago during the war tryin' to stay out of the Army. We played at the Bee Hive, Ruby's—places like that. We were the only blues band on the Southside with a sax section; . . . [we] had a big fat sound, swingin' tempo and here we was still playin' some downhome blues. The people in Chicago couldn't get enough of our music. . . . The Houserockers were the gospel truth in those days. Yes sir, we had it goin' back then.[55]

Memphis Slim was also a gifted blues composer; during this period with the Houserockers he wrote some of his best material—urban blues classics like "Messin' Around," "Blue and Lonesome," "Angel Child," "Mother Earth," and "Everyday I Have the Blues."[56]

Among the blues guitarists who came to the forefront during the depression, Amos "Bumble Bee Slim" Easton was the most prolific as a recording artist, but he had the least impact on Chicago's blues culture, in part because, though he did most of his recordings in Chicago, he never lived there for long. He originally came from Georgia and, after a decade of travel, returned to live in Atlanta in the mid-1930s. He was primarily influenced by the blues of Leroy Carr and Scrapper Blackwell. He emulated Carr's voice on the recordings he made after his mentor's death, and he modeled his guitar work after Blackwell's, but it was never as polished and precise. He also played the piano on occasion. This identification with the blues of Blackwell and Carr contributed to Bumble Bee Slim's popularity and enabled him to record for Decca, Bluebird, and Paramount during the depression years. In many respects he took up where Carr had left off as a city blues idol.

Johnny Temple was more typical of the many Chicago blues guitarists who were active in the thirties. For one thing, he was a native of the Mississippi Delta. He had also lived in Jackson, Mississippi, before migrating north and there came under the influence of Tommy Johnson and Skip James. Despite the rural blues cast to his guitar style, he made many of his recordings backed up by the Harlem Hamfats. This incongruity probably contributed to his lack of success as a recording artist. However, he was an admired figure on the

Southside blues scene and certainly made an important contribution to its vitality during the 1930s.

The most innovative blues guitarist of this period and group proved to be Robert Nighthawk. He played with Will Shade's Memphis Jug Band in the late twenties and early thirties before moving on to St. Louis, where he teamed up with Big Joe Williams and Sonny Boy Williamson to make their historic 1937 recordings for the Bluebird label. His success there prompted him to relocate in Chicago, where he became a studio musician for Lester Melrose. He also developed a unique guitar style; it was modeled somewhat on Tampa Red's playing techniques, especially his use of a bottleneck slide, but Nighthawk transformed Tampa Red's style through his experiments with an electrically amplified guitar. He was a forerunner of the modern urban blues guitar stylists.

Memphis Minnie Douglas, another early convert to the electric guitar, was using one in her club appearances by 1942. Since her success with "Bumble Bee Blues" and her subsequent move to Chicago in 1930, she had established herself as the Southside's premier female blues artist through her recordings and performances in the clubs—especially the famous "Blue Monday" jam sessions she hosted at Ruby's Tavern. Langston Hughes, who wrote a regular column in the *Chicago Defender* during the war years, wrote the following account of her blues performance on a New Year's Eve in a small Southside club.

> Then through the smoke and racket of the noisy Chicago bar float Louisiana bayous, muddy old swamps, Mississippi dust and sun, cotton fields, lonesome roads, train whistles in the night, mosquitoes at dawn and the Rural Free Delivery that never brings the right letter. All these things cry through the strings on Memphis Minnie's electric guitar—amplified to machine proportions—a musical version of electric welders plus a rolling mill. Big rough old Delta cities float in the smoke too. Also border cities, Northern cities, Relief, WPA, Muscle Shoals, the jooks. "Has Anyone Seen My Pigmeat on the Line," "See See Rider," Saint Louis, Antoine Street, Willow Run, folks on the move who leave and don't care. The hand with the dice-ring picks out music like this. Music with so much in it folks remember that sometimes it makes them holler out loud.[57]

While living in Chicago, Memphis Minnie remarried, but her fiery temperament remained as volatile as ever. One of her contemporaries, Johnny Shines, remembered her as a woman who could hold her own against any man in the rough Southside blues clubs:

Any men that fool with her, she'd go for them right away. She didn't
take no foolishness from them. Guitar, pocketknife, pistol, anything she
get her hand on she'd use it; y'know Memphis Minnie used to be a hell
cat. Y'know her and Son Joe (her third husband) and Roosevelt Sykes
used to work together—Boy! They'd have some of the terriblest rows
but Memphis Minnie be the winner everytime—she'd have it her way or
else![58]

With such a reputation, it is understandable why Memphis Minnie Douglas felt
at home in Chicago's blues milieu and was a dominant figure on the local club
circuit for so many years.


## Sonny Boy Williamson: ''Stop Breakin' Down''


John Lee "Sonny Boy" Williamson was the heart and soul of Chicago's
emerging urban blues culture during his eleven years in the city. A gifted musician with boyish charm, a playful sense of humor, and a generous personality, Williamson was an immediate sensation among Southside blues people
when he arrived there from St. Louis in 1937. He had come originally from
Jackson, Tennessee, where he was born on March 30, 1914. Williamson was
drawn to the blues at an early age; his favorite instrument from the start was
the harmonica, which he learned to play as a teenager. Given the premier role
of the harmonica in the string and jug bands popular throughout the region and
the abundance of first-rate harmonica players in and around Memphis, it was
quite natural that a young blues lover like Sonny Boy Williamson would
choose to play it. Had he lived in or near New Orleans during this same period, his choice of instruments would most likely have been a cornet or a
trumpet. Williamson's earliest mentors were Sleepy John Estes, Yank Rachell,
and Hammie Nixon, whom he joined in 1929 along with his boyhood friend
John "Homesick James" Williamson. They traveled together in western Tennessee, playing at clubs and picnics in Jackson, Brownsville, Sommerville,
Pleasant Grove, Mason, and other small towns. The next year, Williamson
began to frequent Memphis; so he must also have been familiar with the harmonica playing of Will Shade, Noah Lewis, and Big Walter Horton. After a
brief stay in St. Louis working with Big Joe Williams and Robert Nighthawk,
he returned to Jackson to marry Lacey Belle, his boyhood girlfriend; they
moved to Chicago in 1937 and settled there permanently. By this time,
Williamson had totally mastered the harmonica techniques and shadings associated with the Memphis region. Moreover, he had developed an engaging vo-

cal delivery that took advantage of his slight stutter; he slurred his words, mumbled, and sometimes talked his own particular brand of jive talk in double time. His voice was earnest and expressive; it sounded fresh, youthful, and even innocent. These diverse talents as a blues musician, combined with his affable character, made Williamson a natural leader of local blues combos and a leading force in the evolution of the music during what would prove to be a critical time of change.

Williamson was drawn to Chicago in part by Lester Melrose's Bluebird label; he stayed with Melrose and Bluebird for ten years. His overall output during this period, playing with a progression of small blues bands, illustrates the evolution of a traditional country blues sound into its modern urban counterpart. Williamson's earliest recording groups were modeled after the vintage rural Tennessee string bands he grew up with and played in as a teenager. Big Joe Williams's traditional Delta bottleneck guitar style was showcased in the 1937–38 session bands, as were Robert Nighthawk's flat-picked bass lines. Mandolin virtuoso Yank Rachell even joined the group for at least one of the 1938 recording dates. Yet despite this traditionalist mold, Williamson's sessions with these musicians proved to be a success commercially and artistically. For one thing his sharp and incisive playing was accented like a vocal line, and this novelty was underlined by his handling of the lead vocals. The intricate interplay between his voice and the harmonica was highly unusual for the times and propelled the harmonica into the forefront as a lead instrument in Chicago blues bands. The early material he recorded included some of his best-loved numbers, especially "Good Morning, School Girl" and "Sugar Mama"—both destined to become urban blues classics.

By 1938, however, Williamson was moving away from the rural blues tradition. That was the year he first recorded with a piano player. The piano strengthened his rhythm section, while also filling in with a solo from time to time; it was a mainstay of his session bands from 1938 on. By 1940, he was further expanding his rhythm section with the addition of Fred Williams on drums and then Ransome Knowling on bass. These changes did not come without a good deal of experimentation. Williamson was slow to abandon the customary role of the acoustic guitar in his recording groups. After Big Joe Williams and Robert Nighthawk, he used Big Bill Broonzy or Charles McCoy in the sessions he did from 1939 to 1942. The major change in these recording sessions was the establishment of a much more forceful groundbeat by drummer Fred Williams, who was called upon to play his washboard, and bass players Ransome Knowling and Alfred Elkins.

A two-year hiatus in the recording industry followed because of wartime shellac rationing and the ban on commercial recordings by J. C. Petrillo, president of the American Federation of Musicians. When Williamson returned to the Bluebird studios in 1944 after the two-year layoff, his groups included a house pianist (Blind John Davis or Big Maceo Merriweather), a guitarist (Tampa Red or Ted Summitt), and a drummer (Armand "Jump" Jackson or Charles Saunders). The guitarists were still from the old school, however, and he resisted the inclusion of an electric guitar player in his lineup until Willie Lacey joined the group in 1946, even though the electric guitar had been a part of the Chicago blues scene since the early 1940s. Finally, in 1947, all of the essential components of the modern Chicago urban blues band were in place: Williamson on harmonica and lead vocals, the youthful Eddie Boyd on piano, Willie Lacey on electric guitar, Ransome Knowling on bass, and Judge Riley on drums. Appropriately, they recorded the rousing and popular "Wonderful World"; this upbeat blues number featured a thunderous rhythm section, bluesy harmonica playing, a vibrant electric guitar solo, and Williamson's jubilant vocals. The transition from an acoustic rural blues to an electric urban blues was complete.[59]

The blues titles that Sonny Boy Williamson recorded were a composite of older material drawn from the black oral tradition, popular and more current numbers shared among Chicago musicians, and original blues he composed with his wife, Lacey Belle. In the first two categories were his rendition of the standard "Sitting on Top of the World," which he entitled "G M & O Blues," and two renditions of a number associated with both Sleepy John Estes ("Someday Baby") and Big Maceo Merriweather ("Worried Life Blues"), which Williamson retitled "Shady Grove Blues" and then "Springtime Blues." The third category contained an interesting cross-section of material dealing with all aspects of black life and culture in Chicago, often from the perspective of a newcomer from down South. A consciousness of the economic hard times is revealed through lyrical realism in "Insurance Man Blues":

> I said you know how times is nowadays, can't no
>     man find no job,
> I say I can't even take care of my wife and baby,
> And I might near to let my own family starve.[60]

and "Collector Man":

> Now go to the door, here come that collector man,
> Go open the door, here come that collector man,
> Well, you can tell him I said come back tomorrow
> Because Sonny Boy ain't got a doggone thing.
>
> Tell him that I ain't got no money now, and he know
>     how times is nowadays,

Tell him that I ain't got no money, and he knows how
   times is nowadays,
Well then tell him if a man ain't got no money,
He can't hardly find a place to stay.[61]

Most of the blues numbers credited to Sonny Boy Williamson and his wife
convey real-life situations. Some focus on social ills afflicting the black urban
population, such as alcohol abuse or the high crime rate in the ghetto. In
"Sloppy Drunk Blues," Williamson, himself a heavy drinker, makes a plug
for alcoholic euphoria, but he also wrote and sang two blues numbers that
speak frankly about the ravages of alcoholism in his own life—"Moonshine":

Now moonshine will make you shot dice, make
   you want to fight,
Now when you go home and you can't treat your
   wife right,
You been drinking moonshine, moonshine have
   harmed many men,
Now that is the reason why I believe I'll make
   a change.[62]

and "Alcohol Blues":

My baby tell me, papa, papa, she say, Sonny Boy,
   you know you ain't no good at all,
My baby tell me, papa, papa, she say, Sonny Boy,
   you know you ain't no good at all,
She said, the reason you don't make me happy,
'Cause you drink too much of this old alcohol.

I said, but baby won't you go riding, can I take
   you riding with me in my car?
I said, but baby won't you go riding, can I take
   you riding with me in my car?
She said, but I'm scared you'll get drunk on
   alcohol,
Said, Sonny Boy, we wouldn't ride very far.[63]

A personal connection to tragedy is again used effectively in "Bad Luck
Blues," a forlorn account of the murder of one of his cousins:

Baby, did you hear about the bad luck, the bad
    luck that happened six months ago?
Now did you hear about the bad luck, the bad
    luck that happened six months ago?
My cousin Marshall got shot down just as he was
    walking out the door.[64]

The candor and relevance of Williamson's best material also encouraged spontaneity; blues lyrics were often fashioned at the recording session or just a few days before. Four days after the bombing of Pearl Harbor, Williamson and some friends were in the studio recording "I Have Got to Go":

Now I want you to gather around boys, we've all
    got to go,
I want you to gather around boys, we all got
    to go,
Now ain't no use to you a worrying, you won't
    see your baby no more.

Now you got to wear a uniform, man you got to
    be in style,
Now you got to wear Uncle Sam's uniform so you
    can be in style,
Now you got to walk straight and tote a rifle,
Uncle Sam want to use you awhile.[65]

Williamson wrote other blues numbers that were supportive of the war effort, including "Checkin' Up on My Baby" (1944) and "Win the War Blues" (1944).

Sonny Boy and Lacey Belle Williamson often used satire and humor to embellish a story or make a point, as in "Christmas Morning Blues":

Now Santa Claus, Santa Claus, now can I get you
    to understand?
Santa Claus, Santa Claus, can I get you to
    understand?
I want you to bring my baby one of those radios,
And two or three of those electric fans.[66]

In "Elevator Woman," one of the marvels of urban living was transformed into a double entendre:

> Now elevate me, mama, now mama take me five or
>     six floors down,
> Elevate me, mama, five or six floors down,
> You know everybody tells me you must be the
>     elevatingest woman in town.[67]

Nor did love relationships escape the barbs. The chorus refrain from "Stop Breaking Down" implores mockingly:

> Stop breaking down, baby, please stop breaking
>     down,
> Stop breaking down, baby, please stop breaking
>     down,
> I don't believe you really really love me,
> I think you just like the way my music sound.[68]

In Williamson's recording of "Hoodoo Hoodoo," which was destined to become his most famous urban blues standard, the joke is on him:

> I used to have a way with women,
> Make plenty of money and everything,
> But my woman don't love me no more,
> She say someone done hoodooed the hoodoo man.[69]

It was the fun-loving nature of Williamson's lyrics and music that gave them their mass appeal. This material tended to overshadow his more poignant material and captured the more optimistic spirit of urban blues in the postwar decade.

On June 1, 1948, in the early morning hours, Sonny Boy Williamson was murdered while on his way home from performing at the Plantation Club, a Southside blues cabaret. He was mugged for his wallet, wristwatch, and three harmonicas. His death underscored the dangers still inherent in the urban ghettos, which were now the home and workplace of more and more blues musicians. Chicago's black community had lost one of its most gifted musical talents in the prime of his life. The leader of a series of highly acclaimed blues combos, the teacher to many of the city's younger harmonica players, a pioneer of modern urban blues, was dead at thirty-four—another casualty of the wanton violence endemic to the red-light districts. Williamson's closest friends fondly remembered him as a gentle man and generous to a fault. According to Sunnyland Slim: "Thing about Sonny Boy was he worked so hard and then give it all away. He'd . . . spend all his money on others all the time. That was Sonny Boy's problem."[70] Another side of Williamson's character was his overindulgence in alcohol and the consequent belligerent behavior and black-outs. These extremes mirror some of the contradictions in the blues culture of the urban black population. Sonny Boy Williamson was no different from many others who lived and died in similar circumstances, except that the music he made on his harmonica inspired many of the major Chicago blues ensembles in the postwar era and established him as a founding father of modern urban blues.

At the conclusion of World War II, Chicago was the undisputed capital of urban blues in the United States—a position it would not relinquish in the coming decades. A second and larger tidal wave of black migrants from the Deep South had swept into the city during the war years, once again to work in the war industries. The influx led to the formation of a second black ghetto in Chicago on the west side of town. Blues clubs began to spring up there to entertain the newly arriving migrants. The Maxwell Street area, traditionally used by Jewish merchants and vendors, also became a focal point for outdoor blues jam sessions. Back over on the Southside, the blues culture was also experiencing a period of unprecedented growth and vitality. The music had been collectively transformed from a rough and realistic rural folk blues into a hard-driving, electric urban folk blues, without losing its critical quality. It was played and enjoyed by large numbers of African Americans on both the Westside and the Southside. It had survived the depression and managed to avoid the many pitfalls of commercialized music. As a result, Chicago's urban blues culture would enter an era of unsurpassed creativity and innovation.

# Conclusion

## The Blues Line: Resistance
## and Diffusion in the Heartland

The blues tradition fifty years after its birth on the cotton plantations of the South was a mature and familiar touchstone within urban black culture. Over the years, it had again and again made important contributions to the oral tradition and had consequently remained on the cutting edge of African-American cultural resistance to white domination.

The components of that resistance were fourfold. At a primary level, there was the blues sound, or, perhaps more appropriately, the blues soundscape— all those "weird," "visceral," "suggestive," "dirty" sounds, "out of tune" and "off key" if judged by European musical standards. The use of blue notes was at the heart of the blues sound; they gave it its subversive character, a dissonance instantly recognizable in both vocal and instrumental renderings. In addition, the blues sound relied heavily on the use of tonic chords, which provided immediate release from musical tensions. They were, in effect, a wellspring of instant gratification. The release of pleasurable energy was also encouraged by the use of polyrhythms, which exploded tensions by stacking different rhythms on top of each other, thereby adding a dense, repetitive, and fluid locomotion to the overall blues sound. Finally, there were the wide variety of vocal techniques, like falsetto, melisma, slurring, and moaning, used to embellish the songs. These were based on affective pitch tones that masked the blues voice in order to evoke tonal memories. The "deep" blues sounds of pioneers such as Charley Patton, Blind Lemon Jefferson, Ma Rainey, and Bessie Smith were resurrected in the vocals of Muddy Waters, Howling Wolf, Billie Holiday, and Dinah Washington.

The blues texts were also bulwarks of cultural resistance, providing a composite view of American society from the bottom. They were not linear narratives, but were circular and indirect in their discourse, in keeping with African custom. They focused on the everyday lives of the black masses—their working conditions, living conditions, prison experiences, travels, and sexual relationships. The texts fall into two broad categories: cautionary folktales— lessons on how to survive in a hostile social environment—and prideful songs of self-assertion. While the former caution the listener through example to be ever vigilant against misfortune, the latter tend to urge on artist and audience alike to greater heights of emotion, endurance, pleasure, and even ecstasy.

Blues texts, sung in the vernacular of the black masses, were the "true songs" or "reals" of hope, despair, humor, and struggle, which documented from within the epic African-American exodus out of the rural South and into the industrial centers of urban America during the first half of the twentieth century. In the words of St. Louis bluesman Henry Townsend:

> Although they call it the blues today, the original name given to this kind of music was "reals." And it was real because it made the truth available to the people in the songs—if you wanted to tell the truth. Most good blues is about telling the truth about things. Just as gospel music is songs about people in biblical times, the blues is songs about black folks today—and these songs are dedicated to the truth. I'm telling stories that were told to me or events that happened to me—just like all blues singers. The blues is one of the few things that was born here in America by black people. It's our music.[1]

The blues sound and text were transformed into a third component of African-American cultural resistance and renewal in performance. Blues performance was an important manifestation of African-American "orature." Molefi Kete Asante, in *The Afrocentric Idea,* defines "orature" as "the comprehensive body of oral discourse on every subject and in every genre of expression produced by people of African descent. It includes sermons, lectures, raps, the dozen, poetry and humor."[2] Blues performers meshed orature and music by engaging in instrumental, voice, and visual styling. They affected certain mannerisms and sang their songs in ways calculated to enhance their ability to communicate with their audience intimately and profoundly. Blues performers often played musical instruments and danced, but it was in singing the blues lyrics that they evoked the spoken word, the "nommo" of traditional African philosophy, in order to unleash its magical powers to heal and transform. They used the word as a catalyst for claiming and shaping their own culture. Performance was the true test of the blues artists; it was the medium through which they honed their skills and perfected their calling as communicators of black cultural resistance and renewal.

Improvisation was the centerpiece of the blues performers' aesthetic approach to their medium. It was based on a traditional African-American reverence for spontaneity in communication. According to Asante:

> In oratory, as in music, the individualistic, the improvisational, is the soul of performance. . . . Just as with jazz . . . the improvised voice, with spontaneity and variety, is the voice of African-American oratory. . . . The Afrocentric presentation forms are related to music, particularly the epic styles of blues and jazz. The forms also may be

seen further back, in the work songs, which predate the blues, spirituals, and jazz. In these folk-forms one finds call-and-response, improvisation, and rhythm.[3]

Because of the transitory nature of black musical improvisation, it was a communal reflex always in flux, always responding to the constraining social reality of black people in the United States. This improvisational tendency was historically connected to African Americans' understanding of freedom as social mobility and cultural autonomy. To improvise, then, was an individual affirmation of freedom in a group setting—a lyrical response to the vicissitudes of life that linked artist and audience in a communication process at the center of the African-American cultural experience.

Audience participation made blues performance a communal art form. Call and response between artist and audience was common, while kinetic exchanges took place through handclapping and dancing. The immediate purpose of these interactions was to achieve emotional release, catharsis, euphoria, transcendence, a healing of body and soul, and social harmony. In the long run, the collective memories that emerged from these cultural rituals promoted solidarity and cohesion. As Asante points out:

> In any good blues or jazz club you can get the same soulful sound as you get in the African-American church. Christianity claims the experience, but the motif, the rhythm, the feeling, the transcendence occurs anywhere the conditions present themselves. That is to say, it does not depend on icons of faith but on the incessant collective drive of a people for harmony with self, fellow earthlings, and nature.[4]

A final component of cultural resistance was manifested in the blues praxis of the artists and, to a lesser extent, their fans. The blues praxis included the radical lifestyles of these cultural rebels, the images they cultivated of themselves and their art, and their way of seeing the world around them—in short, their blues sensibilities. As cultural rebels, the blues artists adopted any number of personas, depending on their circumstances and sex. The blues men were vagabonds, tricksters, ladies' men, hellions, hoodoo doctors, honeydrippers, clowns or the Devil's disciples, while the blues women were voodoo queens, matriarchs, wild women, lesbians, high priestesses, or earthshakers. These masks enabled blues performers to act out their fantasies, experiment with their images, and stretch their collective imaginations. Blues personas achieved mythical stature in the black community, constituting a black pantheon separate from—and in many ways antithetical to—the white heroes and heroines of middle-class America. As folk iconoclasts, they stood in sharp contrast to the one-dimensional, docile black stereotypes created by and for the dominant white culture. Ultimately, they were the key products of blues praxis—its legacy, along with the music, to future generations of Americans.

## Blues After World War II

The postwar years proved to be the golden age of urban blues—especially in Chicago. In the 1940s, 150,000 rural black migrants flooded into the city, half of them from Mississippi. They crowded first into the constrained Southside ghetto and then increasingly into the Westside. The Southside was honey-combed with small neighborhood bars that sold liquor and featured live enter-tainment on the weekends. It was in these clubs that the itinerant Mississippi Delta blues musicians, playing their downhome style of blues for fellow mi-grants, found a receptive audience. The bars had names like the Gatewood Tavern, the White Elephant, the High Life Inn, the Boogie Woogie Inn, the Triangle Inn, and the Flame Club. On the Westside, the open-air Maxwell Street Market became an important focal point of blues activity. Founded by Jewish merchants in 1912, it grew into a four-block-long street bazaar that offered just about anything anyone wanted—legal or illegal. By that time, the Jewish immigrants who had initially inhabited the Westside neighborhood sur-rounding the market area had moved on and been replaced by incoming black and Hispanic migrants. Beginning in the 1930s, transient blues musicians could be found playing in small groups along Maxwell Street, while the buy-ing, selling, and trading swirled around them.[5]

After World War II, amplification of vocals and instrumentals became a standard practice in Chicago's burgeoning blues scene, both in the bars and on the streets. The city's blues sound grew louder, more intense, and percussive. This was compounded by a steady infusion of Mississippi Delta blues—now also amplified. Moreover, the new Chicago-flavored urban blues was not only being played live in the clubs or on Maxwell Street; it was also beginning to be recorded on disks and played on the local airways. "Race records" were being played on a few Chicago radio stations as early as the 1930s and were the centerpiece of the pioneering black radio shows hosted by Jack L. Cooper. However, Cooper and his protégés were decidedly jazz oriented in their musi-cal tastes as befitted their middle-class aspirations as businessmen and broad-casters. The blues were the music of the black working class, recently arrived from the rural South. It was not until Al Benson, "de ole Swingmaster," broke into Chicago radio in 1946 that the blues were played on the airways with any regularity.[6]

Al Benson was a native of Mississippi who moved to Chicago in the 1930s. After working in local black vaudeville shows, he started a radio show on a local commercial outlet, WGES. Benson was immediately popular with the newer southern migrants because he was the first disk jockey who spoke their language and played the blues on the radio. By 1948, he was doing shows on three Chicago stations and training apprentice disk jockeys. During the 1950s, Benson became a cultural magnate in Chicago's black community; in addition to his radio shows, he also did a weekly television show, produced blues concerts at the Regal Theatre, and launched his own record labels. In the process, he became a millionaire and an early civil rights leader. But more important, his successful mixture of street talk and huckstering with local and national blues disks established a new beachhead in commercial radio that opened the door to an influx of downhome blues disk jockeys including Sam Evans, Big Bill Hill, McKie Fitzhugh, and Purvis Spann. Collectively, they kept the Chicago airways saturated with homegrown blues throughout the 1950s and well into the 1960s.[7]

This upsurge in commercial blues shows was economically linked to the rise of several local blues record labels during the same period. As early as 1945, Charley Glenn, the owner of the Rhumboogie Café, an upscale jazz and blues nightclub on the Southside, founded the Rhumboogie label to record his star attraction, T-Bone Walker. Al Benson started his Swingmaster label in 1949 to record local bluesmen like Floyd Jones and Snooky Pryor; a few years later he tried again with Parrot Records, which released J. B. Lenoir's memorable "Eisenhower Blues" in 1953. Lenoir was also featured on Joe Brown's J.O.B. label, which put out its first releases in 1949. Other local bluesmen to record on J.O.B. included Sunnyland Slim, St. Louis Jimmy Odem, Johnny Shines, and Eddie Boyd—who gave Brown his only hit with "Five Long Years" in 1952.[8]

Chicago's most famous blues label during the postwar years—one that played a pivotal rôle in winning the city's urban blues a national and even international audience—was founded by the Chess brothers. Leonard and Phil Chess were Polish Jews who immigrated to Chicago in 1928; during the depression they operated a string of Southside bars under the protection of Al Capone. Their record business grew out of the connections they developed booking African-American musicians into their clubs. They also operated a record store on the Southside; thus they knew the preferences of black record buyers. In 1947, the brothers launched Aristocrat Records, which was renamed Chess Records three years later; their first local hit record was the 1948 release "I Can't Be Satisfied," by a Mississippi Delta guitarist called Muddy Waters. His real name was McKinley Morganfield, and he was born in Rolling Fork, Mississippi in 1915. He was first recorded for the Library of Congress by folklorist Alan Lomax during a fieldtrip to the Delta in 1941. A few years later, the young sharecropper moved north to Chicago; his subsequent rise to fame and fortune along with the Chess brothers was the success story of the city's postwar blues boom.

The Chess label was able to sign the best blues songwriter of the era, Willie Dixon, and then to record an impressive roster of urban blues musicians with a good deal of commercial and artistic success. Besides Muddy Waters, the roster included Howling Wolf, Little Walter Jacobs, Sonny Boy William-son II, J. B. Lenoir, Little Milton Campbell, Chuck Berry, and Bo Diddley. But in the end, it was the Muddy Waters band that set the standards for Chi-cago in the postwar years. Through it passed the cream of the city's blues talent: harmonica players Little Walter Jacobs, Junior Wells, James Cotton, Big Walter Horton, Mojo Buford, George Smith, and Carey Bell; pianists Sun-nyland Slim, Johnny Jones, Otis Spann, Pinetop Perkins, and Lovey Lee; gui-tarists Jimmy Rogers, Pat Hare, Matt Murphy, Buddy Guy, Luther Johnson, Luther Tucker, and Earl Hooker. Along with the formidable Howling Wolf, Muddy Waters put Chicago at the center of the urban blues universe, gaining national and international recognition and acclaim. It is a distinction that the city holds to this day.[9]

There were other hotbeds of urban blues activity during the postwar years. The Hasting Street night-life strip in nearby Detroit was home base for many blues musicians, some of whom, like John Lee Hooker, Bobo Jenkins, Eddie Kirkland, and Baby Boy Warren, led their own small club bands. But, unlike Chicago, Detroit lacked an economic infrastructure that encouraged indigenous blues-oriented record labels, radio outlets, and live music venues; thus only John Lee Hooker managed to reach a national audience and subsequently make a career out of his music. The Memphis blues scene, on the other hand, not only supported live entertainment, local recording endeavors, and radio air-play, but was itself bolstered by two satellite blues centers: one across the river in West Memphis, and the other downriver in Helena, Arkansas. Helena's KFFA aired the first live blues show in the mid-South; beginning in late 1941, the legendary "King Biscuit Time" was broadcast by the station daily. The featured attraction was Rice Miller, a veteran Delta blues musician born in Glendora, Mississippi, in the late 1890s; he played harmonica and wrote and sang some of the most memorable blues compositions of the era. Miller called himself "Sonny Boy Williamson" for his radio broadcasts; it was the name made famous in blues circles by the recently deceased Chicago blues legend John Lee "Sonny Boy" Williamson.

The initial "King Biscuit Time" backup band included Robert Jr. Lock-wood and Willie Joe Wilkins on guitar, Robert Dudlow Taylor on piano, and James "Peck" Curtis on drums. It was the first electric blues band heard on the airways anywhere in the country inasmuch as both Lockwood and Miller were already amplifying their instruments by 1941. The commercial success of "King Biscuit Time" enabled other blues musicians like Robert Nighthawk to broadcast regularly on KFFA; it also catapulted Sonny Boy Williamson II into the limelight as a major blues talent in the mid-South. Throughout the decade, African Americans listened to him religiously on KFFA. Being the first black personality from the Delta to be heard regularly on the airways enhanced his status as a popular blues raconteur and a local folk hero. In the late 1940s, Sonny Boy Williamson grew restless and moved upriver to West Memphis, where he hosted another live radio show on KWEM before moving on to Chicago to record for the Chess brothers in the 1950s.[10]

Another blues veteran based in West Memphis and broadcasting on KWEM was Chester Burnett, also known as Howling Wolf. Like Rice Miller, Howling Wolf was a native of the Delta. Born in Rueville, Mississippi, in 1910, he became a student of Charley Patton's in the late 1920s. During the depression years he played on weekends with Rice Miller and Robert Johnson. After serving in the armed forces during World War II, he formed his first blues band in West Memphis in the late 1940s. The personnel over the next few years included guitarists Matt Murphy, Pat Hare, Willie Johnson, and Hubert Sumlin, with Willie Steele on drums, "Destruction" on piano, and occasionally Junior Parker on harmonica. Like Muddy Waters's band in Chicago, Howling Wolf's West Memphis band electrified the Delta blues. Its loud and abrasive style crackled and thundered with voltage, while Wolf prowled out front, microphone in hand, moaning and groaning and growling his unique vocal interpretations of traditional Delta blues standards. No other performer of the postwar era could act out the blues with such ferocious intensity. Howling Wolf and his band were first recorded by Sam Phillips, a young white freelance record producer from Memphis who also ran his own recording studio. Phillips immediately recognized in the six-foot-four, 270-pound bluesman an unusual talent. But so did the Chess brothers, who bought some of the early Howling Wolf material from Phillips to release on their new label. By 1952, they were able to entice Wolf to Chicago with promises of steady club work and a custom-tailored record contract. He never returned to the South.[11]

Sam Phillips recorded a number of other Memphis-based bluesmen during this period, the most notable being Junior Parker, Big Walter Horton, and B. B. King. Their recordings were released on the Modern/RPM labels owned by the Bahari brothers, who were based in Los Angeles. B. B. King's records were an early springboard for his long and illustrious career as America's premier blues virtuoso; over the years, his distinctive electric guitar style has become the centerpiece of modern urban blues. Riley "Blues Boy" King also grew up in the Delta, but he first won recognition as a blues artist at the Palace Theatre talent contests on Beale Street in downtown Memphis. Consequently, he was hired at WDIA, where he worked as a disk jockey and did occasional live performances on his own show. WDIA was the mid-South's first black-oriented radio station; beginning in 1949, it featured the music of local and national blues and gospel artists. Although owned and managed by white businessmen, WDIA was programmed and for the most part staffed by African Americans, thanks to the tireless efforts of Nat D. Williams, who had created the station's unique format. From the beginning, the blues were an integral part of WDIA's air sound; the station was soon a magnet for blues fans within the range of its signal. In addition to Nat D. Williams and B. B. King, Rufus Thomas, Maurice "Hot Rod" Hulbert, Willie Nix, and A. C. "Mohah" Williams hosted blues shows; regular visitors to the WDIA broadcast studios included Johnny Ace, Bobby Blue Bland, Roscoe Gordon, and Junior Parker—known collectively along with B. B. King as the "Beale Street Blues Boys."

The Memphis blues resurgence, at its zenith in the early 1950s, generated a proliferation of new radio shows and recording ventures to highlight regional blues talent. In addition to WDIA and KWEM, WLOK and WHBQ adopted a new urban black music format. Significantly, WHBQ's appeal was based on the popularity of high-profile disk jockeys like the pioneering "Jitterbug" Johnny Poorhall and his successors, Dewey Phillips and Bill Gordon; they played the latest and the "hottest" blues and jazz releases. Phillips, Gordon, and Poorhall were all white and very likely some of their listeners were also white; they were in effect crossing the color line in commercial radio. Moreover, there was a similar interracial collaboration afoot in some of the local recording ventures. Sam Phillips founded Sun Records in 1952 and recorded James Cotton, Big Walter Horton, Little Milton Campbell, and Junior Parker—all black blues musicians. Competition came from the youngest of the Bahari brothers—Lester—who opened a recording studio in Memphis and started the Meteor label. Simultaneously, James Mattis and Bill Fitzgerald launched the Duke label to record Bobby Blue Bland, Junior Parker, Johnny Ace, and Roscoe Gordon. But the Memphis blues renaissance proved to be short lived. The Duke label was soon thereafter sold to Don Robey, owner of Peacock Records, who was based in Houston. Neither the Meteor nor the Sun label approached the level of commercial success that Chess enjoyed in Chicago. By the mid-1950s, Sam Phillips had switched from recording black blues artists to recording white rockabilly performers like Elvis Presley and Carl Perkins. By then, many of the most prominent Memphis blues figures—B. B. King, Howling Wolf, Sonny Boy Williams II, Bobby Blue Bland—had already left the region. Chicago—not Memphis—was the blues mecca in the post war years.[12]

Houston, too, benefited from the exodus of Memphis blues talent. Indigenous blues recording ventures began there in 1946 when a white entrepreneur named Bill Quinn established the Gold Star label to record Sam "Lightnin' "

Hopkins and others. The city's most important and successful recording operation was the Duke/Peacock enterprise owned by Don Robey, a black businessman with links to the underworld. Robey was a reputed numbers boss who also ran Houston's most celebrated black nightclub, the Bronze Peacock. He began his career in the record business recording popular gospel quartets like the Mighty Clouds of Joy, the Dixie Hummingbirds, and the Five Blind Boys of Mississippi on the Peacock label; then he expanded his operation with the purchase of Duke Records to include the new urban blues of former Memphis blues artists Johnny Ace, Bobby Blue Bland, and Junior Parker, as well as Willa Mae "Big Mama" Thornton, the blues belter who recorded Robey's first commercial hit, "Hound Dog" in 1953. The Duke/Peacock urban blues sound featured jazz big-band arrangements with electric guitar solos and squalling brass riffs. Joe Scott was the arranger and producer most responsible for the labels' musical trademarks. Other blues musicians who were featured on Duke/Peacock included Clarence "Gatemouth" Brown, Little Richard Penniman (just before his meteoric rise to fame as a rock-and-roller) and Johnny Otis, who also worked as a West Coast talent scout for Robey.[13]

California attracted many African Americans from Texas and the Southwest during the climax of the rural to urban black migration. In 1930, 80,000 African Americans lived in the state; the number reached 460,000 in 1950. Most of the black migrants settled in Los Angeles or the Bay Area in northern California, where they worked in the oil refineries and the shipbuilding yards. By the end of World War II, Los Angeles was the major blues hotspot on the West Coast. Black musicians from the Southwest played in the nightclubs and bars along Central Avenue in the Watts ghetto, in places called the Club Alabam, Swanee Club, Ivy Anderson's Chicken Shack, and the Club Alimony. Most prominent were the "soft" or "sepia" urban blues vocalists who invariably accompanied themselves on piano—Cecil Grant, Charles Brown, Ivory Joe Hunter, Amos Milburn, and Mel Walker. Other blues musicians who played an important role in Los Angeles music circles during this period included T-Bone Walker, Roy Milton, Joe Liggins, Wynonie Harris, Johnny Otis, Big Mama Thornton, and Little Esther Phillips.

Los Angeles was also the base of operations for several independent record companies with an interest in urban blues: Eddie and Leo Mesner's Aladdin Records, which recorded Lightnin' Hopkins and Amos Milburn; Leon and Otis Rene's Exclusive/Excelsior labels, which recorded Joe Liggins and Jimmy Rushing; the Bahari brothers' Modern label, which recorded B. B. King and Jimmy Witherspoon; Art Rupe's Specialty label, which recorded Roy Milton and Percy Mayfield. Other local record labels involved in blues recording ventures included Black and White Records and 4 Star Records; as in the prewar race record era, these companies were owned and operated by white entrepreneurs, many of whom were Jewish. A similar crossover was also evident in

Los Angeles radio, where white disk jockeys such as Dick "Huggie Boy" Hugg on KRKD and Hunter Hancock on KPOP and KFVD were the first to play recorded blues and jazz on the airways; this was also true in San Francisco. There were some exceptions: Joe Adams was the first black disk jockey in Los Angeles, and Bob Geddins, a black record producer based in Oakland, was responsible for the initial blues releases of Lowell Fulson and Jimmy McCracklin. In general, however, the West Coast pattern followed the national trend: urban blues, when aggressively marketed by independent white entrepreneurs, continued to make inroads in the music industry, and not without unexpected results.[14]

## The Postwar Blues Diffusion

On June 25, 1949, the music industry's official trade publication, *Billboard,* at the urging of a young staff writer named Jerry Wexler, reclassified "Race Music" as "Rhythm and Blues" (R&B) in its pages. The name change was a reflection of the changes taking place in both the making and the marketing of black music. "Rhythm and blues" was already a familiar term, commonly used to characterize the popular new styles of black music that incorporated elements of urban blues, jazz, and gospel. Dinah Washington and Louis Jordan were the two most important R&B pioneers in the 1940s. Washington was a talented and versatile singer. She was born and grew up in the Chicago Southside ghetto, where her initial musical apprenticeship was with the famous gospel singer Sallie Martin. While still in her teens, Washington left the world of gospel music to sing the blues in Southside clubs and bars, where she could make more money than on the gospel circuit. She was discovered there in the early 1940s and invited to join Lionel Hampton's jazz band as lead vocalist—a position that helped her to secure a record contract with the Apollo label in 1945. Her early releases were almost exclusively blues numbers with jazz-band arrangements; later, when she moved on to Mercury Records, she sang more jazz and pop ballads. Her voice combined poignancy with a silky softness; its lush blue-velvet sonority, coupled with her ability to convey intensity, depth of feeling, and a broad range of emotions made her the uncontested "Queen of the Blues" in the postwar era and the major inspiration for upcoming female R&B vocalists.[15]

Louis Jordan, in contrast, was born in rural Arkansas and received his musical training on the black vaudeville circuit. By 1940, he was a seasoned vocalist and saxophonist, having worked with the Rabbit Foot Minstrels in the South in the early 1930s and then later in the decade with Chick Webb's

Harlem-based jazz band. Jordan formed his own group—the Tympany Five—just before the outbreak of World War II; the band featured a riffing horn section, a boogie-woogie piano player, and a jazz-schooled rhythm section. To this mix he added his "dirty"—that is, gritty-sounding—alto sax solos, and a declamatory, almost conversational vocal delivery. Jordan performed mostly uptempo numbers, sometimes called "jump blues" ("I made the blues jump!" he proclaimed in an interview later in his life). His landmark recordings—"Caldonia" and "Saturday Night Fish Fry"—are humorous novelty items with a danceable beat. Jordan inserted hipster argot into his lyrics and repartee with band members and audience. Years on the black vaudeville circuit had honed his craft not only as a musician and singer but also as a showman and standup comedian. Throughout the 1940s and well into the fifties, Louis Jordan and his jump blues combo influenced a whole generation of younger musicians as diverse as B. B. King, Chuck Berry, and Bill Haley.[16]

The rhythm and blues boom paralleled the resurgence of urban blues in that its impetus came from independent record labels and disk jockeys. The new musical synthesis that characterized R&B had been simmering in urban black communities for some time before being discovered by the music industry and subsequently mass produced and marketed nationally. Most of the more commercially successful independent labels were clustered in and around New York and Los Angeles, the two centers of the music industry, the major exceptions being the Chess label in Chicago, the King label in Cincinnati, and the Duke and Peacock labels in Houston.

In the New York City area, four key independent labels fostered the rise of R&B—Apollo, Savoy, National, and Atlantic. Apollo was launched in 1942 under the guidance of Ike and Bess Berman, who owned a record store. The label specialized in gospel and R&B; its best-known artists were Mahalia Jackson, Roberta Martin, and the Dixie Hummingbirds in the gospel category; and Dinah Washington, the Five Royales, and Wynonie Harris in R&B. Savoy was owned and operated by Herman Lubinsky, who started the label in Newark, New Jersey. Lubinsky, a former record-store owner and, reputedly, a cut-throat businessman, recorded jazz artist Charlie Parker, gospel singer James Cleveland, and R&B artists Big Maybelle, Nappy Brown, and Wilbert Harrison. National Records was founded in 1945 in New York City by Al Green—another rough-and-tumble entrepreneur on the fringes of the music industry. The label recorded Big Joe Turner with Pete Johnson, Billy Eckstine's big band, and the Ravens, a pioneering R&B vocal group. But it was Atlantic Records, established in 1947 by the Ertegun brothers and Herb Abramson, that had the greatest impact of all the New York–based independent record companies. With much help from the arranger/songwriter Jesse Stone, who first charted the uptempo bass patterns for the label's studio sessions, the producer Jerry Wexler, who later also became a partner in the company, and the composers

Jerry Leiber and Mike Stroller, Atlantic was in the forefront of R&B from the label's inception. The company assembled the decade's most successful roster of black musical acts: LaVerne Baker, Ruth Brown, the Clovers, the Coasters, the Drifters, the Platters, Clyde McPhatter, Chuck Willis, Big Joe Turner, and Ray Charles. With these acts, the company produced 19 number-one records and 126 top-ten hits on the fifties' R&B charts. It was with Atlantic that Ray Charles first recorded his secular renditions of traditional gospel standards, which revolutionized rhythm and blues song structures and vocal techniques. Typically, Charles viewed his breakthrough as a modest accomplishment; as he put it in his autobiography: "Now I'd been singing spirituals since I was three, and I'd been hearing blues just as long. So what could be more natural than to combine them?"[17]

Atlantic producers first heard Ray Charles playing with a studio band in New Orleans, a city that proved to be a vital source of new music and talent for independent R&B labels after World War II. Three of the top Los Angeles companies—Imperial, Aladdin, and Specialty—regularly recorded New Orleans–based artists like Guitar Slim, Roy Brown, Little Richard, and Fats Domino in Cosimo Matussa's J&M studios. These sessions featured the city's most gifted R&B musicians, including bandleader and arranger Dave Bartholomew, tenor saxophone virtuoso Lee Allen, and master drummer Earl Palmer. Little Richard and Fats Domino were in the forefront of the new black recording stars who were making a dramatic impression on young white listeners in the early 1950s and paving the way for the rise of rock and roll. New Orleans deserves credit not only for being the birthplace of jazz but also for putting the infectious big beat in rock and roll and giving the music its basic dance rhythms. Rock and roll was a black musical innovation, but it also expressed a new urban sensibility that was attractive to both black and white youths. Given the proliferation of R&B through independent record labels and disk jockeys in the postwar era, little wonder that young white musicians like Elvis Presley, Bill Haley, Jerry Lee Lewis, and Buddy Holly began to copy the new black musical styles they heard all around them. And, given the segregation built into the music industry, little wonder that their cover versions of popular black numbers received preferential treatment. All too soon rock and roll became big business; the music was bought up by the major record labels, while the independents fell by the wayside. Presley signed a lucrative contract with RCA Victor, and Sun Records passed into oblivion. Within the radio industry, the payola scandals of the late 1950s reversed the fortunes of the independent disk jockeys, black and white; their power to play records of their own choosing was drastically curtailed by the subsequent rise of the "top-forty" format. Allen Freed was only the most visible casualty. Top-forty radio institutionalized management control of the records played on the air, which tended to reinforce the music industry's corporate hegemony over rock and roll. By the end of the decade, the primal "roots" rock and roll of Little Richard, Fats Domino, Chuck Berry, Bo Diddley, Elvis Presley, and Jerry Lee Lewis was being replaced by the sanitized "schlock rock" of Fabian, Paul Anka, and Frankie Avalon—or the clean-cut, white-buck cover versions of Pat Boone. Yet along the way, rock and roll, especially in its early years, helped to radically alter the sensibilities of a new generation drawn to its pulsating beat and rebellious spirit. In the process, a teenage revolt against the conformity and the placidity of the dominant culture of the 1950s was set in motion.[18]

The blues diffusion continued to be a vital component of both black and white popular musical styles in the 1960s and 1970s, challenging the homogeneity of the music industry. The major R&B innovators during this period were still inclined to experiment with combinations of blues, jazz, and gospel, but new commercial and technological considerations were coming to the forefront. Barry Gordy's success with Motown Records in Detroit epitomizes the later tendencies in black popular music, which often negated its blues roots. He turned the tables on the music industry by mass-producing a uniquely appealing sound and image calculated to recapture the white teenage market for his roster of young black recording artists. He was successful, made millions of dollars, and built up a black entertainment empire (it eventually relocated to Los Angeles). In beating the major labels at their own game, Motown became something of a parody of its white corporate competition, which was the antithesis of the urban blues and gospel traditions. Yet in its later years Motown conceded to its major artists the freedom that enabled Stevie Wonder, Marvin Gaye, Smokey Robinson, and others to experiment and mature as musicians and songwriters.[19]

At the other extreme of the R&B continuum was the downhome "soul" music produced for the most part by independent record labels and studios based in the South. Southern R&B borrowed freely from the blues, jazz, and gospel traditions, but it was above all a vocal art form. Like the blues, it had a social message—an extension and an updating of the black oral tradition. However, the emotional fervor of the vocal line in southern R&B was its definitive characteristic, and that was taken from the gospel tradition, in which singing and preaching were merged with performance and ritual. Secular love and salvation superseded the sacred thematic in these gospel songs, but the song structures and the rhythms remained the same. The vocal line was then further embellished with a jazz-influenced horn section, often playing call and response riffs. A rhythm section rounded out the sound by standardizing the beat and the bass patterns; it usually consisted of drums, electric bass, rhythm guitar, and sometimes an electric piano or organ. The result was a compelling mix of propulsive rhythms, sonorous instrumental solos or fills, and heart-wrenching vocals that alternated between inspired despair and sensual optimism.

The two major recording centers for southern R&B were Memphis, Tennessee, and Muscle Shoals, Alabama. In Memphis, much of the activity was associated with the Stax/Volt enterprise, which from 1963 to 1975 went through one of the most spectacular boom-and-bust cycles in the history of the American music industry. The venture began as a neighborhood recording studio in the black ghetto, which engaged a handful of young local musicians to produce records for a few prospective customers. It quickly mushroomed into a multimillion-dollar operation with close to one hundred acts on its roster; at its zenith in the late 1960s, Stax was bringing in $14 million annually, rivaling Motown as the country's most successful black music enterprise. The label's list of artists included local talent like Rufus and Carla Thomas, Booker T. and the MGs, Isaac Hayes, and David Porter. But it was the out-of-town talent that Stax attracted—in particular, Otis Redding and Sam, and Dave—that made the greatest impact on the overall style and direction of R&B. In 1967, Redding's death at the height of his success signaled the end of prosperity for the label. Although Stax had some continued success recording bluesman Albert King and gospel renegade Johnny Taylor, rumors of mismanagement and dissension among the principal executives became persistent. Even Isaac Hayes's blockbuster *Hot Buttered Soul* album and the movie *Wattstax* could not save the enterprise. In 1973, the Internal Revenue Service initiated an investigation of the firm's finances; two years later, Stax failed to meet its payroll and filed for bankruptcy. The cycle was complete.

Memphis's loss was Muscle Shoals' gain. As in the early days at Stax, the Fame recording studio—first located in Florence, Alabama, and then moved next door to Muscle Shoals—was a cooperative venture undertaken by a group of young, aspiring local musicians and songwriters. Unlike the racially mixed Stax crew, however, the Muscle Shoals core group (Rick Hall, Dan Penn, Donnie Frits, Spooner Oldham, Jimmy Johnson, Chips Moman, Roger Hawkins) were all white. But they had all grown up listening to R&B nightly on WLAC—the 100,000-watt clear channel AM station in Nashville, Tennessee, which blanketed the Deep South with its signal. By the time the group coalesced around the Fame studio enterprise in 1963, all of them were longtime R&B students and devotees. Significantly, they scored their greatest triumphs recording black vocalists—a few of whom, like Percy Sledge, were local, but most of whom, like Joe Tex, were brought in by outside agents. The success of Sledge's "When a Man Loves a Woman" in 1966 attracted the attention of Jerry Wexler, who brought Wilson Pickett to the Fame studios soon thereafter. Aretha Franklin came to Atlantic around this time after an unsatisfactory stint with Columbia Records, where producer John Hammond had attempted to groom her as a blues singer in the Dinah Washington/Billie Holiday mold. With Atlantic and at Muscle Shoals, Aretha Franklin returned to her gospel roots. The result was the beginning of a remarkable series of recordings that would make her the most popular and successful female R&B vocalist of the decade.

Aretha Franklin's male counterpart during this era was the Augusta Georgia, soul brother, James Brown—southern R&B's hardest-working showman. Like Franklin, James Brown started his career as a gospel singer. This background helps to account for his fervent vocal style and performance rituals. Brown's live shows, featuring a twenty-piece orchestra, dancers, backup singers, and master of ceremonies, became legendary on the "chitlin" circuit and made him into something of a folk hero in America's black urban ghettos. In 1962 an album of his stage show—"Live at the Apollo"—crossed over onto the pop charts, sold in the millions, and became one of the most acclaimed albums of the decade. Brown was at the center of two critical musical innovations. One was to extend the rhythmic dimensions of a song until they totally dominated it; as a result, the bass lines and patterns came to the forefront of the music and the rhythm section became, in effect, the lead instrument. In this respect Brown was a precursor of the black funk bands of the 1970s. Brown's second innovation was to engage the audience in sermonlike dramatizations of a song telling a story or advancing a point of view with layers of meaning. Some of Brown's songs anticipated the advent of rap music by more than a decade. The song "Say It Loud, I'm Black and I'm Proud" was indicative of this sermonizing tendency. Along with Aretha Franklin's rendition of "Respect," "Say It Loud" became the clarion call for black pride and militancy in the 1960s.[20]

The influence of the blues diffusion on the popular musical styles of white youth during the 1960s and thereafter was twofold. There was a rediscovery of the rural and vaudeville blues traditions within the folk music revival already under way in the early sixties, and a parallel discovery of the urban blues by legions of aspiring young white rock musicians. Both blues taproots would enrich the musical synthesis that followed. Young white folk musicians and fans began to listen to old blues recordings from the prewar era. Before long, not only were they performing this traditional material in coffeehouses and on college campuses, but a group of novice field researchers had gone out and located some of the early blues recording artists. Racial and generational barriers fell as the blues elders, drawn out of obscurity and urged on by their ardent new disciples, took to the stage at the prestigious Newport Folk Festival and other folk music showcases for one final collective encore. Representing the Piedmont blues tradition were Blind Gary Davis, Sonny Terry, and Brownie McGhee, Mississippi John Hurt, Pegleg Howell, and Pink Anderson; from the Delta came Son House, Skip James, Bukka White, Big Boy Crudup, Mississippi Fred McDowell, and Sam Chatmon; and from East Texas came

Sam "Lightnin' " Hopkins, Mance Lipscomb, Alex Moore, and Robert Shaw. The classic blues women who made comebacks were Ida Cox, Victoria Spivey, Sippie Wallace, and Alberta Hunter. These blues elders, along with a handful of other survivors, were able to pass on their vintage musical and oral traditions to a younger generation of white musicians and fans who had little, if any, previous exposure to the roots of black music. This process generated a new audience and long-overdue recognition for the standard-bearers of traditional blues, while also invigorating the folk revival of the era by providing a reservoir of African-American folk material for it to draw upon.

The second wellspring of blues diffusion into the pop mainstream during this period emanated from the remaining urban blues enclaves in Chicago, New Orleans, Houston, Los Angeles, San Francisco, and other less prominent cities. The blues culture that continued to prosper in these cities was uncovered, studied, emulated, and finally absorbed by young white musicians on both sides of the Atlantic Ocean. The major English rock bands that cultivated an American audience in the 1960s were all influenced by postwar R&B. Some groups, such as the Beatles, moved well beyond the urban blues spectrum as they matured along with their music. Others, such as John Mayall and the Blues Breakers, stayed well within the basic urban blues format. Between these two extremes were bands like the Rolling Stones, who adopted a ''dirty'' blues sound and a rebellious blues profile but soon abandoned the basic blues form for more experimental song structures.

In America a lingering urban blues culture fused with the emerging white rock counterculture. Cities like Chicago and New Orleans, which continued to be black music strongholds, also began to produce and attract young white musicians raised on R&B. Legions of white musicians played in bands led by African-American bluesmen such as Muddy Waters, Sonny Boy Williamson II, Robert Jr. Lockwood, and Sunnyland Slim. Thus, even as the blues were slowly becoming marginal to the music of African Americans, they were being absorbed into the mainstream of rock music. The lag time in this cross-cultural phenomenon created a mushrooming young white blues audience at the same time that the black blues audience was both aging and dwindling in numbers.

## The Blues Today

During the last two decades, the blues have become institutionalized as an international and interracial musical culture involving thousands of people all over the planet. Chicago remains at the center of the blues universe, but now there are outposts in Canada, Great Britain, Europe, and Japan. The blues culture is built up around the musicians who continue to play the music for a living. They are supported in turn by an institutional infrastructure consisting of record companies, radio shows, management firms, booking agencies, nightclubs, festival organizations, publications, and blues societies and foundations. In addition, long-overdue public recognition of the blues as an American cultural treasure has led to increased scholarly interest in, and even some government financial support for, the music. The academic interest has generated a substantial body of literature on the blues, as well as numerous course offerings and some media productions. Public monies have been used to help fund blues musicians, museums, archives, festivals, forums, performance series, educational programs, films, radio series, and international tours. All of this has helped to shore up the infrastructure that brings cohesiveness to the blues culture. Unfortunately, this support comes at a time when the blues tradition is past its prime. The music and message are no longer on the cutting edge of the black oral tradition. Nonetheless, the blues continue to be an important component of popular American music, in part through the influence of the music's new-found white devotees.

The Blues-oriented record companies that have managed to stay afloat during the last decade have prospered over the long run while supporting the music. Alligator Records, based in Chicago, is the prototypical blues label success story of the 1980s. It was launched in 1973 as a labor of love by a young white blues enthusiast named Bruce Iglauer. For the first decade he operated on a shoestring budget out of his house in a Northside neighborhood. Showcasing the best of Chicago's blues talent, the Alligator catalogue is a virtual who's who of Chicago blues over the past fifteen years: Son Seals, Koko Taylor, Hound Dog Taylor, Lonnie Brooks, Fenton Robinson, Magic Slim, James Cotton, Big Twist, Buddy Guy, and others. But for every Alligator there are five other labels with equally noble aspirations that went under because of financial difficulties. Delmark Records was also based in Chicago and even preceded Alligator in recording some of the city's most talented blues artists, including Otis Rush, Magic Sam, Jimmy Dawkins, J. B. Hutto, and Junior Wells. But Delmark was not able to distribute its product at a volume that insured a steady profit, and therefore, a label that had shown great promise in the 1960s all but withered away in the next decade. Yet despite such setbacks, which were and still are quite common, the number and quality of blues-oriented record companies that have survived and prospered in the 1970s and 1980s are impressive. The most successful to date other than Alligator are Rounder Records in Boston; Flying Fish Records in Ann Arbor, Michigan; Malaco Records, located just outside of Jackson, Mississippi; Ichiban Records, in Atlanta; King Snake Records in Sanford, Florida; Waylo Records in Memphis; Antone's Records in Austin, Texas; Hightone Records in Oakland, California; and Blind Pig Records in San Francisco. The geographic

spread of these labels and their commitment to indigenous blues artists help
to ensure that a wide range of contemporary blues styles are being recorded
for posterity. Moreover, the success of these record companies paved the way
for the development of blues-oriented booking agencies and management
firms, both of which were virtually nonexistent even during the golden era of
R&B. Some of the most established examples of this institutionalizing tendency are the Scott Cameron Agency, which managed Muddy Waters's career
before he died, and now does the same for Willie Dixon and Eddie Shaw;
Sidney Sidenburg and Associates, who manage the career of B. B. King; Bon
Ton West, a California-based agency specializing in Louisiana R&B; and the
Rosebud Agency, which handles John Lee Hooker and the Robert Cray Band,
among others.

The making of the present-day blues culture is also facilitated by the blues
nightclub and concert circuits. The marginal status of the blues in the music
industry constrains the choice of the site, the size of the audience, the price of
the tickets, and other such details. It is still difficult to showcase blues artists
and make a profit. Nevertheless, the commercial blues club and concert circuits continue somehow to hold together and even to flourish in cities like
Chicago, where the music is still in great demand. Moreover, the private-
sector blues venues are being supplemented by a growing number of public-
sector venues in the form of blues festivals and concert series. There are now
dozens of yearly festivals held all over the United States. The biggest takes
place in Chicago for three days in June and is sponsored by the city government; in 1988 there were over a half-million people in attendance. The oldest
existing festival has been staged in San Francisco every September since 1973.
Other major blues festivals include the Delta Blues Festival in Greenville, Mississippi; the Juneteenth Blues Festival in Houston; and the Long Beach Blues
Festival in California. Many blues societies produce local blues shows and festivals. Finally, colleges and universities have been more receptive to including
blues artists in their concert series and special cultural programs. The net result of these developments is that there are now more wage-paying venues for
every variety of blues act than ever before, and hence the blues audience has a
wider variety of blues traditions and styles to enjoy.

Radio stations facilitate communication and the exchange of information
within the subculture. The two principal sources of radio airplay for the blues
are black-owned and black-oriented commercial radio outlets and public radio
outlets, particularly noncommercial college and community stations. Within
black commercial radio there still exists an old guard of R&B disk jockeys
who continue to feature the blues on their shows as a matter of pride and
habit. Prominent members of this group include Vernon Winslow, the first
black disk jockey ("Dr. Daddy O") on the airways in New Orleans in the
1950s, who has recently revived his show there on WYLD; Sonny Paine, who

continues to host an updated version of "King Biscuit Time" on KFFA in Helena, Arkansas; Hoss Allen, a pioneering white R&B disk jockey on WLAC in Nashville, who also recently returned to the airways on his old station; Jayne Mitchell, who does a weekend blues show on WDIA in Memphis; King Ro, a regular on WRDW in Augusta, Georgia; Pervis Spann, a former Chicago disk jockey now running WXFS in Memphis, where he hosts a blues show, as does Dick King Cole, Big Bill Collins on WNIB and Tom Marker on WXRT, both in Chicago; and Martha Jean "the Queen" Steinburg on WCHB in Detroit. These seasoned R&B disk jockeys on commercial outlets have been complemented by a growing number of blues disk jockeys on noncommercial radio stations. Those on the black-oriented public stations often resemble their counterparts in black commercial radio. Whether it is "Captain Pete's Blues Cruise" on WEVL in Memphis or Uncle Jack's drive time blues show, aired every weekday afternoon on WMPR in Jackson, Mississippi, or Jerry Washington's "The Bama Hours" on WPFW in Washington, or Ernie K. Doe ("Burn KDoe Burn!") on WWOZ in New Orleans, the common denominator for all of these shows is a strong and folksy reverence for the blues of a bygone era. Among the white blues disk jockeys, a few continue to emulate the jive-talking black R&B disk jockeys of the 1950s; Ice Cube Slim's "Down at the Greasy Spoon" on KUSP in Santa Cruz, California, is an example of this style of program, but it is declining in popularity. For the most part, the white blues programmers are straight-talking and knowledgeable musicians, producers, researchers, and fans: Johnny Otis, probably the first white musician to become involved in postwar R&B, still does a blues show on KPFK in Los Angeles; blues researcher and record producer Chris Strachwitz has a long-running blues program on KPFA in Berkeley, California; blues festival producers Janice Lafloon (Arkansas River Blues Festival), Bernie Pearl (Long Beach Blues Festival), Tom Massolini (San Francisco Blues Festival) all organized their respective blues festivals as outgrowths of their local blues radio shows. Scholars who do blues radio programming as an extension of their academic work include Bill Ferris (University of Mississippi), Russell J. Linneman (University of Tennessee), and the author (Howard University). In addition to a weekend show on Mississippi Public Radio, Ferris also does a weekly blues program for the Armed Forces Radio Network. What all of this adds up to is that the blues can now be heard somewhere on the AM or FM radio bands all over the country; most blues airplay, however, is still concentrated in black population centers, metropolitan areas, and college communities.

The international dimension of the contemporary blues culture has an infrastructure similar to that found in the United States. First introduced to foreign audiences after World War II, the music quickly gained a following in Great Britain, France, West Germany, Italy, the Netherlands, the Scandinavian countries, and eventually Japan as more and more blues artists toured overseas.

Their reception was generally so favorable that some of these musicians, like many of their jazz counterparts, remained abroad. The best-known post-war blues expatriates were Memphis Slim, Willie Maborn, Eddie Boyd, Champion Jack Dupree, Billy Boy Arnold, and Mickey Baker. More recently, they have been joined by younger blues musicians from the United States, including Louisiana Red, Luther Allison, Luther Tucker, Johnny Mars, and Billy "The Kid" Emerson. Young musicians in other countries, once exposed to the blues, were captivated. They worked as apprentices in backup bands for touring blues musicians or formed their own groups and tried to emulate their idols. Foreign record companies tend to specialize in reissuing vintage blues material that is well researched and documented. Blues journals are published in many European countries: *Blues Unlimited* and *Juke Blues* in England; *Blues Life* in West Germany; *I Blues* in Italy; *Block* in the Netherlands; *Jefferson* in Scandinavia; and *Black Music* in Japan. In general, foreign research into blues history and discography has been a bit ahead of such research in the United States. The first surveys of blues history to be published were written by Englishmen Paul Oliver and Giles Oakley; two Englishmen were also responsible for compiling the first comprehensive blues discographies.[21] Only in the last decade has blues scholarship in the United States surged to the forefront.

American scholars have approached the blues from three different perspectives: blues as folklore, blues as oral literature, and blues as cultural history. The folklorists were the first to look at the blues as a music worthy of scholarly inquiry; they documented the existence of rural blues traditions in the Mississippi Delta (Charles Peabody, Howard Odum, E. C. Perrow), Texas (Gates Thomas, Will Thomas, Prescott Webb), and the Piedmont (Howard Odum, Guy Johnson) well before 1920. John Lomax and his son Alan were the most visible of the folklorists doing blues field research and recordings in the 1930s and 1940s, but Zora Neale Hurston, John W. Work Jr., and others also made significant contributions to the investigation of the music and its subculture during this period. More recently, a new generation of folklorists and ethnomusicologists have come into their own as blues scholars. Bruce Bastin, David Evans, Bill Ferris, Charles Keil, Barry Lee Pearson, and Jeff Titon have all published impressive studies based on their extensive field research.[22]

The study of the blues as an oral literature originated in the work of Sterling A. Brown during the 1930s; he was the first scholar to characterize the blues as an African-American genre of folk poetry, and the first poet to incorporate blues cadences, metaphors, and archetypes into his poems. Langston Hughes and Richard Wright also wrote blues-inspired poetry; it was their way of championing the folklore and wisdom of African Americans, described by Hughes as the "common people." In the postwar era, during the civil rights movement, the emphasis was on the social dimensions of the blues, particularly the role they played in the ongoing struggle for freedom and equality in the aftermath of slavery. Amiri Imamu Baraka, then known as LeRoi Jones, elaborated on this perspective in *Blues People*. More recently, such literary scholars as Stephen Henderson, Albert Murray, and Houston Baker Jr. have approached the blues as a folk discourse on the epic African-American odyssey. Murray views the "blues idiom style" as a purified folk expression of black life—a distillation of the collective experiences of Africans on the North American continent. The "blues heroes" he venerates in his literary essays and his fiction are mythical black social rebels who transcend history and symbolize cultural resistance in the tradition of Stagolee and Railroad Bill. Houston Baker Jr. in *Blues, Ideology and Afro-American Literature* goes just as far in his assessment of the importance of the music to black culture, and like Murray, argues that the blues are a collective response to the oppression and racism encountered in a foreign land; in effect, they constitute a cultural "matrix":

> The blues are a synthesis (albeit one always synthesizing rather than one already hypostatized) combining worksongs, group seculars, field harmonies, sacred harmonies, proverbial wisdom, folk philosophy, political commentary, ribald humor, elegiac lament, and much more. They constitute an amalgam that seems to have always been in motion in America—always becoming, shaping, transforming, displacing the peculiar experiences of Africans in the New World.[23]

In contrast, the cultural historians have labored to establish the specificity of the blues tradition, hoping to pinpoint and fully describe its origins, patterns of growth, pinnacles of artistic innovation, and declining influence. Many of the major contributions in this area are biographies of such major blues figures as Charley Patton, Ma Rainey, Robert Johnson, Bessie Smith, T-Bone Walker, Dinah Washington, and B. B. King. Other publications have focused on specific regions or cities, such as the Mississippi Delta or Chicago, specific periods of blues development, such as the prewar or postwar eras, or some combination of both. Many of these blues histories were written by music journalists (e.g., Robert Palmer and Peter Guralnick) or freelance writers and producers (e.g., Sam Charters). University-based cultural historians like Lawrence Levine, on the other hand, write about the blues as part of the larger black oral tradition.[24] Overall, blues scholarship—after a prolonged infancy—has caught up and kept pace with the blues tradition, especially over the past two decades. In so doing, it has helped to legitimate the music as a valuable expression of African-American culture—a communal voice from its heartland.

An unusual cross-section of people are currently engaged in blues culture. Their race, class, and generational differences have made it one of those rare, eclectic, and in many ways utopian social experiments that can take place only on the fringes of the dominant culture. In mainstream American society, integration on the job and in the schools is mandated by law, but social space remains color- and class-coded. That is, people work together and share public accommodations and services, but spend their leisure time in separate communities according to race and social class, in that order. The blues culture runs contrary to this sort of social stratification, especially where color is concerned. What began as a black proletarian cultural formation a hundred years ago has been transformed by succeeding generations of blues people into a novel interracial melting pot. In particular, the postwar transference of the blues tradition from an older black working-class generation to a younger white middle-class generation has sent ripples of unconventional social relations throughout the society.

The magnitude of this cultural exchange is unprecedented in the history of race relations in the United States. Not that all is peace, harmony, sisterhood, and brotherhood in the blues community. The historical legacy of racism must still be overcome, and there are class, generational, and gender differences that need to be breached. But at least there exists the possibility of some cross-cultural communication and even conflict resolution, if only because people are already bound together by their common love and respect for the music. This proclivity to break down cultural barriers and to refashion race and social relations along more egalitarian lines gives the blues culture its utopian potential and positions it as a radical alternative to the color-coded, hierarchical dominant culture.

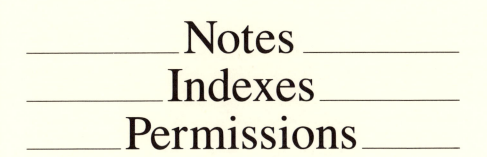

Notes
Indexes
Permissions

# Notes

## Before the Blues

1. Eugene Genovese, *Roll Jordan Roll: The World the Slaves Made* (New York: Pantheon, 1972), p. xv. Further discussion of the dynamics of cultural resistance in slave communities can be found in John W. Blassingame, *The Slave Community: Plantation Life in the Antebellum South* (New York: Oxford University Press, 1972), and George P. Rawick, *From Sundown to Sunup: The Making of the Black Community* (Westport, Conn.: Greenwood, 1972).

2. Dena J. Epstein, *Sinful Tunes and Spirituals: Black Folk Music to the Civil War* (Urbana: University of Illinois Press, 1974); John Lovell Jr., *Black Song: The Forge and the Flame* (New York: Macmillan, 1972). Also see Wyatt Tee Walker, *Somebody's Calling My Name* (Valley Forge, Pa.: Judson, 1979), for an interesting discussion of "double" or "coded" meaning in the spirituals.

3. Lawrence Levine, *Black Culture and Black Consciousness: Afro-American Folk Thought from Slavery to Freedom* (New York: Oxford University Press, 1977), p. 296.

4. Jesse Lemisch, "The American Revolution Seen from the Bottom Up," in Jesse Lemisch, ed., *The Reinterpretation of American History* (New York: Doubleday, 1972), p. 6.

5. Charles Wolfe, "Where the Blues Is At: A Survey of Recent Research," *Popular Music and Society* 1 (1971–72):153.

## Introduction to Part I: Rural Blues

1. Lawrence Levine, *Black Culture and Black Consciousness: Afro-American Folk Thought from Slavery to Freedom* (New York: Oxford University Press, 1977), p. 204.

2. Sam "Lightnin' " Hopkins, *Lightnin' Hopkins: My Life in the Blues*, Prestige PR 7370.

3. For more detailed information on the African-American workforce during this period, see John Hope Franklin, *From Slavery to Freedom: A History of Negro Americans* (New York: Alfred A. Knopf, 1947), pp. 397–402, 436; Florette Henri, *Black Migration: Movement North, 1900–1920* (New York: Anchor/Doubleday, 1976), pp. 26–34, 133–60; Phillip S. Foner, *Organized Labor and the Black Worker, 1619–1981* (New York: International Publishers, 1982), pp. 64–136.

4. For more information on African musical practices, see J. H. Kwabena Nketia, *The Music of Africa* (New York: Norton, 1974); John Miller Chernoff, *African Rhythm and African Sensibility* (Chicago: University of Chicago Press, 1979). Also see Paul

Oliver, *Savannah Syncopators: African Retentions in the Blues* (London: Studio Vista, 1970), for a discussion of the relationship between the blues and West African musical practices.

5. John W. Work Jr., *American Negro Songs* (New York: Howell, Suskin, 1940), p. 28.

6. The term "cautionary folktales" was first brought to my attention by Lorenzo Thomas during a blues seminar at the University of Mississippi in July 1988.

7. For recent scholarship on rural blues pioneers see Bruce Bastin, *Red River Blues: The Blues Tradition in the Southeast* (Urbana: University of Illinois Press, 1986); David Evans, *Big Road Blues: Tradition and Creativity in the Folk Blues* (Berkeley: University of California Press, 1982); David Evans, "Charley Patton: Conscience of the Delta," in *The Voice of the Delta: Charley Patton*, ed. Robert Sacre (Liege, Belgium: Presses Universitaires, 1987), pp. 111–220; Alan Govenar, *Living Texas Blues* (Dallas: Dallas Museum of Art, 1985); Mack McCormick, "Biography of Henry Thomas: Our Deepest Look at Roots," notes to *Henry Thomas: Ragtime Texas*, Herwin 209; Paul Oliver, *Blues off the Record* (London: Baton, 1984); Robert Palmer, *Deep Blues* (New York: Viking, 1981).

## Chapter 1: "I Been 'Buked and I Been Scorned": The Folk Roots of the Blues

1. Some blues scholars place the origins of the blues earlier, in the 1870s or in the 1880s; see William Ferris, *Blues from the Delta* (New York: Doubleday, 1978), p. 31. However, most evidence points to the early 1890s as the beginning of the blues as a specific black musical genre. See Jeff Titon, *Early Downhome Blues* (Urbana: University of Illinois Press, 1976), p. 25, and David Evans, "Africa and the Blues," *Living Blues* 10 (Autumn 1972):27–29.

2. Maurice Dela Fasse, *The Negro in Africa* (New York: International Publishers, 1978), p. 271. Also see John Miller Chernoff, *African Rhythm and African Sensibility* (Chicago: University of Chicago Press, 1979), and Paul Oliver, *Savannah Syncopators: African Retentions in the Blues* (London: Studio Vista, 1970), for more detailed descriptions of West African griots.

3. Interview with Nat D. Williams by Ron Walters, Memphis, Sept. 1976. Interview in archives at Smithsonian Institution, Washington, D.C.

4. See Albert Murray, *Stomping the Blues* (New York: McGraw-Hill, 1976), pp. 63–65, and Paul Oliver, *The Meaning of the Blues* (New York: Collier, 1963), p. 333.

5. The earliest written reference to the blues in a song title is "Black Alfalfa's Jailhouse Shouting Blues" sung by Ophelia Simpson. It was recorded by folklorist John Jacob Niles in 1898. See John J. Niles, "Shout Coon Shout," *Musical Quarterly* 16 (October 1930):519–21.

6. Thomas Wentworth Higginson, *Army Life in a Black Regiment* (Boston, 1865; rpt. Boston: Beacon, 1962), p. 197.

7. James Miller McKim, "Negro Songs," in *The Social Implications of Early Negro Music in the United States*, ed. Bernard Katz (New York: Arno, 1965), p. 2.

8. See W. E. B. Du Bois, *The Souls of Black Folk: Essays and Sketches* (New York: McClury, 1902; rpt. New York: Fawcett, 1964).

9. Theodore Seward, *Jubilee Songs: As Sung by the Jubilee Singers of Fisk University, Nashville, Tenn. Under the Auspices of the American Missionary Association* (New York: Biglow & Main, 1872), p. 48.

10. See Keith Warner, *Kaiso! the Trinidad Calypso: A Study of the Calypso as Oral Literature* (Washington, D.C.: Three Continents, 1982).

11. Dena J. Epstein, *Sinful Tunes and Spirituals: Black Folk Music to the Civil War* (Urbana: University of Illinois Press, 1974), p. 180.

12. Eugene Genovese, *Roll Jordan Roll: The World the Slaves Made* (New York: Pantheon, 1972), p. 606.

13. Solomon Northup, *Twelve Years a Slave* (New York: Derby & Miller, 1853), p. 337.

14. William Francis Allen, Charles Pickard Ware, and Lucy McKim Garrison, *Slave Songs of the United States* (New York: Simpson, 1867), p. 28.

15. B. A. Botkin, ed., *Lay My Burden Down: A Folk History of Slavery* (Chicago: University of Chicago Press, 1945), p. 3.

16. William Wells Brown, *Clotel; or, The President's Daughter* (Boston: Marsh, 1852), p. 138. Also see Lawrence Levine, *Black Culture and Black Consciousness: Afro-American Folk Thought from Slavery to Freedom* (New York: Oxford University Press, 1977), p. 249, for an example of the evolution of this folk verse.

17. Frederick Douglass, *Life and Times of Frederick Douglass, Written by Himself* (New York: Pathway, 1941), pp. 146–47.

18. Levine, *Black Culture*, p. 10.

19. Ibid., p. 247.

20. See Epstein, *Sinful Tunes*, pp. 161–84, for a discussion of the omnipresence of the worksong in the lives of the slaves.

21. Frederick Douglass, *My Bondage and My Freedom* (New York: Miller, Orton & Mulligan, 1855), p. 97.

22. Higginson, *Army Life in a Black Regiment*, p. 219.

23. Quoted in J. Kinnard Jr., "Who Are Our National Poets?" *Knickerbocker Magazine* 26 (Oct. 1845):331–41.

24. Lafcadio Hearn, "American Sketches," *Selected Writings of Lafcadio Hearn* (Boston: Little, Brown, 1952), p. 224.

25. See Zora Neale Hurston, "High John de Conqueror," *American Mercury* 57 (1943):450–58; Harry Oster, "John and Old Marster," *Journal of the Folklore Institute* (1968):42–57; John Q. Anderson, "Old John and the Master," *Southern Folk Quarterly* 25 (1961):195–97; Richard M. Dorson, *Afro-American Folktales* (Bloomington: Indiana University Press, 1958), pp. 124–70, for discussions of this important African-American folksong cycle.

26. This version of the folksong was recorded by Gates Thomas, in *Publications of the Texas Folklore Society* 5 (1926):172.

27. *Afro-American Blues and Game Songs*, ed. Alan Lomax, Library of Congress Recording AFS L4.

28. *Negro Prison Camp Songs*, Ethnic Folkways Library FE 4475.

29. Frances Ann Kemble, *Journal of a Resident on a Georgia Plantation in 1838–1839* (New York: Harper, 1863), p. 128. Also see Harold Courlander, *Negro Folk Music in the U.S.A.* (New York: Columbia University Press, 1963), pp. 81–85, and Epstein, *Sinful Tunes*, pp. 161–83, for discussions of cries, calls, and hollers during slavery.

30. Son House, quoted in Samuel Charters, *The Bluesmen* (New York: Oak, 1967), p. 7.

31. Interview with Sam "Lightnin' " Hopkins by Samuel Charters, *My Life in the Blues*, Prestige PR 7370.

32. Interview with Sonny Terry by the author, Washington, D.C., Mar. 1982.

33. Translation quoted in Harold Courlander, *Negro Folk Music*, p. 169.

34. Henry Spalding, ed., *Encyclopedia of Black Folklore and Humor* (Middle Village, N.Y.: Jonathan David, 1972), pp. 236–37.

35. Richard Dorson, "The Career of John Henry," *Western Folklore* 24 (1965): 155–63.

36. See Levine, *Black Culture*, pp. 410–11.

37. Reprinted in Genovese, *Roll Jordan Roll*, p. 626. Also see H. C. Bearly, "Ba-ad Nigger," *South Atlantic Quarterly* 38 (Jan. 1939):75. See Bearly's discussion of this folk type, pp. 71–81.

38. See Eric Hobsbawn, *Primitive Rebels* (New York: Dell, 1960) and *Bandits* (New York: Dell, 1969), for a discussion of social banditry.

39. See John A. Lomax and Alan Lomax, *American Ballads and Folksongs* (New York: Macmillan, 1941), pp. 112–17, for examples of this ballad.

40. W. C. Handy, *Father of the Blues: An Autobiography* (New York: Macmillan, 1942), p. 79.

41. John Lomax and Alan Lomax, *Negro Songs as Sung by Leadbelly* (New York: Macmillan, 1940), pp. 108–10.

42. Alan Lomax, notes to 15A, "The Gray Goose," *Afro-American Spirituals, Worksongs, and Ballads*, Library of Congress Recording AAFS L3.

## Chapter 2: "Everyday Seems Like Murder Here": Mississippi Delta Blues

1. See Charles Johnson, "The Negro Migration: An Economic Interpretation," *Modern Quarterly* 14 (1934):314–25. Also see Florette Henri, *Black Migration: Movement North, 1900–1920* (New York: Anchor/Doubleday, 1976), pp. 20–34, for a discussion and for specific figures on the migration of the black population during this period.

2. Richard A. Easterlin, "Regional Income Trends, 1840–1950," in Jesse Lemisch, ed., *The Reinterpretation of American History* (New York: Doubleday, 1972), p. 140.

3. See Charles Johnson, *Shadow of the Plantation* (Chicago: University of Chicago

Press, 1934); John Ray Skates, *Mississippi: A History* (New York: Norton, 1979); and Harry Ashmore, *Arkansas: A History* (New York: Norton, 1978).

4. Interview with Sunnyland Slim (Albert Luandrew) by the author, Washington, D.C., Apr. 1977.

5. Muddy Waters, quoted in A. X. Nicholas, ed., *Woke Up This Mornin': The Poetry of the Blues* (New York: Bantam, 1973), p. 99.

6. Charles Peabody, "Notes on Negro Music," *Journal of American Folklore* 16 (1903):148–52.

7. Ibid., p. 149.

8. Ibid., p. 150.

9. Ibid., p. 151.

10. Ibid., p. 151.

11. Ibid., p. 152.

12. Howard W. Odum, "Folk Song and Folk Poetry as Found in the Secular Songs of the Southern Negroes," *Journal of American Folklore* 24 (1911):255–94.

13. Quoted in Lynne Fauley Emery, *Black Dance in the U.S. from 1619 to 1970* (Palo Alto, Calif.: National Press, 1972), p. 104.

14. Ibid.

15. Interview with Sam Chatmon by the author, Santa Cruz, Calif., Apr. 1973. The Chatmon brothers made a number of race records and played for dances in the Delta-Jackson region of Mississippi. The most prominent members of the group were Lonnie Chatmon, an excellent fiddle player, Bo Carter, a half-brother who played guitar and also made a number of solo recordings, and Sam Chatmon, who was the last surviving member of the Mississippi Sheiks. Also see Harry Oster, *Living Country Blues* (Detroit: Folklore Associates, 1969), p. 8; W. C. Handy, *Father of the Blues: An Autobiography* (New York: Macmillan, 1942), p. 5–6.

16. David Evans, "Afro-American One Stringed Instruments," *Western Folklore* 29 (1970):229–45. Also see William Ferris, *Blues from the Delta* (N.Y.: Doubleday, 1978), pp. 37–39, and Paul Oliver, *Savannah Syncopators: African Retentions in the Blues* (London: Studio Vista, 1970), pp. 84–88, for discussions on the influence of one-string instruments on the early rural blues.

17. Handy, *Father of the Blues*, p. 78.

18. Robert Palmer, *Deep Blues* (New York: Viking, 1981), p. 46.

19. Big Bill Broonzy, "Goin' Down the Road Feeling Bad," and "Mindin' My Own Business" on *The Big Bill Broonzy Story*, vol. 1, Verve Records U–300–5.

20. Big Bill Broonzy, "Joe Turner Blues," *Broonzy Story*, vol. 1.

21. Handy, *Father of the Blues*, pp. 151–53.

22. David Evans, "Charley Patton: Conscience of the Delta," in *The Voice of the Delta: Charley Patton*, ed. Robert Sacre (Liege, Belgium: Presses Universitaires, 1987), pp. 111–220.

23. Ibid., pp. 118, 125–31.

24. Ibid., pp. 132–33. Also see Palmer, *Deep Blues*, pp. 44–56.

25. Evans, "Charley Patton," pp. 140–41; David Evans, *Big Road Blues: Tradition and Creativity in the Folk Blues* (Berkeley: University of California Press, 1982), pp. 169–74; Jeff Titon, *Early Downhome Blues* (Urbana: University of Illinois Press, 1976), p. 7.

26. Hayes McMullen, quoted in Palmer, *Deep Blues*, p. 48.

27. Charley Patton, "Elder Green Blues," on *Charley Patton: King of the Delta Blues*, Yazoo L–1020. Most of Patton's recordings, made between 1929 and 1934, have been reissued on *Charley Patton*, Origin Jazz Library OJL6, OJL7, and *Charley Patton: King of the Delta Blues*.

28. Palmer, *Deep Blues*, p. 64.

29. The four "voices" can be heard on Charley Patton, "Spoonful Blues," on *Charley Patton: King*.

30. Cited by Evans in "Charley Patton," p. 139.

31. For a complete discography of Charley Patton's recordings, see John Fahey, *Charley Patton* (London: Studio Vista, 1970).

32. Evans, "Charley Patton," p. 175.

33. Charley Patton, "Pony Blues," on *Charley Patton: King*.

34. Charley Patton, "High Sheriff Blues," ibid.

35. Charley Patton, "Down the Dirt Road Blues," ibid.

36. Charley Patton, "34 Blues," ibid.

37. Charley Patton, "Revenue Man Blues," ibid.

38. Evans, "Charley Patton," pp. 184–87.

39. Charley Patton, "Tom Rushing Blues," on *Charley Patton: King*.

40. Charley Patton, "Mean Black Moan," on *Charley Patton*, OJL7.

41. Evans, "Charley Patton," p. 192.

42. Charley Patton, "High Water Everywhere," on *Charley Patton: King*.

43. Evans, "Charley Patton," pp. 170–72. Also see Samuel Charters, *The Bluesmen* (New York: Oak, 1967), pp. 34–56, and Palmer, *Deep Blues*, pp. 48–89, for additional discussions of Charley Patton's life and music.

44. See Palmer, *Deep Blues*, pp. 112–14.

45. Evans, *Big Road Blues*, pp. 176, 194; also Palmer, *Deep Blues*, pp. 79, 82–84.

46. Interview with Houston Stackhouse by Jim O'Neal, *Living Blues* 17 (Summer 1974):20–21.

47. Chatmon interview, Apr. 1973. Also see Charters, *The Bluesmen*, pp. 129–39.

48. Tommy Johnson, "Maggie Campbell," on *The Famous 1928 Tommy Johnson/ Ishman Bracey Sessions*, Roots RL–330.

49. Tommy Johnson, "Big Road Blues," ibid.

50. Tommy Johnson, "Canned Heat Blues," ibid.

51. Son House, "Preachin' the Blues," on *The Legendary Son House: Father of Folk Blues*, Columbia CL 2417.

52. Son House, "Dry Spell Blues," ibid.

53. See Charters, *The Bluesmen*, pp. 57–70. Also interview with Son House by Julius Lester, *Sing Out: The Folksong Magazine* 15, no. 3 (1965):38–45, and by Jeff Titon, *Living Blues* 13 (Apr.–May 1977):14–22.

54. Interview with Johnny Shines by Pete Welding, *Living Blues* 22 (July–Aug. 1975):28–32.

55. See Palmer, *Deep Blues*, pp. 111–31; Samuel Charters, *Robert Johnson* (New York: Oak, 1973); and Alan Greenberg, *Love in Vain: The Life and Legend of Robert Johnson* (Garden City, N.Y.: Doubleday, 1983).

56. Welding, Shines interview, p. 29.

57. Interview with Robert Jr. Lockwood by the author, Washington, D.C., Apr. 1977.

58. Charters, *Robert Johnson*, pp. 14–15.

59. Ibid., pp. 21–22.

60. Palmer, *Deep Blues*, p. 117.

61. Charters, *Robert Johnson*, pp. 11–25.

62. Robert Johnson, "Hellhound on My Trail," on *Robert Johnson: King of the Delta Blues Singers*, Columbia CL 1654.

63. Robert Johnson, "Love in Vain," on *Robert Johnson: King of the Delta Blues Singers*, Columbia CL 30034.

64. Robert Johnson, "Terraplane Blues," ibid.

65. Robert Johnson, "Preaching Blues," ibid.

66. Robert Johnson, "Crossroad Blues," ibid.

67. Robert Johnson, "Me and the Devil Blues," ibid.

68. See Janheinz Jahn, *Muntu: The New African Culture* (New York: Grove, 1961), p. 42. Also see Evans, *Big Road Blues*, p. 115.

69. Late in 1923, a black veteran named Joe Pullen had a dispute with his landlord, W. T. Saunders, over payment for his work as a sharecropper. Pullen felt he was being cheated. The confrontation led to a gun fight. Saunders was killed, and Pullen fled to a nearby swamp with his rifle and ammunition. A white posse estimated to have numbered close to a thousand men at its zenith descended on the area with an arsenal of rifles and machine guns. Gasoline was dumped into the swamp and set afire. Joe Pullen was eventually wounded by the posse, then captured, dragged through the streets of Drew by a mob, and lynched. According to the official body count, Pullen managed to kill four members of the posse and wound eight others; black sources in the area maintained that his marksmanship accounted for nineteen dead and forty wounded. The city of Drew responded to the incident by instituting a dusk-to-dawn curfew. See Evans, *Big Road Blues*, pp. 190–93.

A decade later, in nearby Cleveland, Mississippi, a deranged black man who murdered a white family was captured and put on trial. In order to prevent another public lynching, the governor called in the National Guard. The prisoner was convicted of murder and hanged legally. See Palmer, *Deep Blues*, pp. 89–92.

70. See John Cowley, "Shack Bullies and Levee Contractors: Black Protest Songs and Oral History," *Juke Blues* 3 (Dec. 1985):9–15.

71. Roy Wilkins, "Mississippi Slavery in 1933," *Crisis* 40, no. 4 (Apr. 1933): 81–82.

72. Interview with Peter Chatman by the author, Memphis, Sept. 1982.

73. Interview with Big Joe Williams by the author, Memphis, Nov. 1982.

74. Big Joe Williams, "Levee Camp Blues," on *Big Joe Sings the Blues*, Bluesville BVLP 1083.

75. Interview with Albert Luandrew by the author, Chicago, Aug. 1979.

76. John Van Deusen, *The Black Man in White America* (Washington, D.C.: Associated Publishers, 1944), p. 158.

77. Hortense Powderhouse, *After Freedom* (New York: Russell & Russell, 1968), pp. 86–87.

Chapter 3: "Po' Boy, Long Ways from Home": East Texas Blues

1. For details on this historic migration, see John Hope Franklin, *From Slavery to Freedom: A History of Negro Americans* (New York: Alfred A. Knopf, 1947), p. 183; Leon E. Litwack, *Been in the Storm So Long* (New York: Alfred A. Knopf, 1979), pp. 32–33; Samuel Charters, *The Bluesmen* (New York: Oak, 1967), pp. 167–71.

2. Mack McCormick, "Biography of Henry Thomas: Our Deepest Look at Roots," notes to *Henry Thomas: Ragtime Texas*, Herwin 209, pp. 4–5. Josh White was the first bluesman to make a commercial recording of "Red River Blues"; he did it for the American Recording Company in New York in 1932.

3. Willard "Rambling" Thomas, "Poor Boy Blues," on *Ramblin' Thomas: Chicago Blues, 1928*, Biograph BLP 12004.

4. Bengt Olsson, "Biography of Gus Cannon's Jug Stompers," notes to *Gus Cannon's Jug Stompers*, Herwin 208, p. 1.

5. The Texas penal system was finally reformed in the 1940s. See Bruce Jackson, *Wake Up Dead Man: Afro-American Work Songs from the Texas Prisons* (Cambridge, Mass.: Harvard University Press, 1972), pp. 38–44. Also see John Van Deusen, *The Black Man in White America* (Washington, D.C.: Associated Publishers, 1944), pp. 136–57.

6. Van Deusen, *Black Man in White America*, p. 156.

7. Jackson, *Wake Up Dead Man*, p. 8.

8. Ibid., p. 115.

9. Ibid., p. 93.

10. See John A. Lomax and Alan Lomax, *Folk Song U.S.A.* (New York: New American Library, 1947), p. 371.

11. Jackson, *Wake Up Dead Man*, p. 59.

12. Ibid., p. 315.

13. Henry Thomas, "Don't Ease Me In," on *Henry Thomas*.

14. McCormick, "Biography of Henry Thomas," p. 7.

15. Henry Thomas, "Railroadin' Some," on *Henry Thomas*.

16. Henry Thomas, "Shanty Blues" on *Henry Thomas*.

17. McCormick, "Biography of Henry Thomas," p. 7.

18. Gates Thomas, "South Texas Negro Work Songs: Collected and Uncollected," in *Rainbow in the Morning*, ed. J. Frank Dobie (Hatboro, Pa.: Folklore Associates, 1965), p. 160.

19. Ibid., pp. 172, 177–79; Will H. Thomas, "Some Current Folk Songs of the Negro," in *Folklore Society of Texas*, 1912, p. 12. E. C. Perrow, "Songs and Rhymes," *Journal of American Folklore* 28 (1915):190; Prescott Webb, "Notes to Folklore of Texas," *Journal of American Folklore* 28 (1915):290–99.

20. Charters, *The Bluesmen*, pp. 175–89; Pete Welding, notes to *Blind Lemon Jefferson*, Milestone M–47022; Stephen Calt, notes to *Blind Lemon Jefferson: King of the Country Blues*, Yazoo L–1069. Calt's most recent research has placed Blind Lemon Jefferson's birth in 1880. Also see Victoria Spivey, "Blind Lemon Jefferson and I Had a Ball," *Record Research* 78 (May 1966):9, and Roger S. Brown, "Recording Pioneer Polk Brockman," *Living Blues* 23 (Sept.–Oct. 1975):31.

21. Samuel Charters, *The Country Blues* (New York: Rinehart, 1959), p. 60.

22. Sam "Lightnin' " Hopkins, *My Life in the Blues*, Prestige PR 7370; Charters, *The Bluesmen*, p. 178.

23. Interview with Arron "T-Bone" Walker by Jim O'Neal, *Living Blues* 11 (Winter 1972–73):20.

24. Interview with Houston Stackhouse by Jim O'Neal, *Living Blues* 17 (Summer 1974):20–21.

25. Ibid., p. 21; interview with John Jackson by the author, Washington, D.C., Apr. 1980; Jeff Titon, *Early Downhome Blues* (Urbana: University of Illinois Press, 1976), p. 212; Charters, *The Bluesmen*, p. 188; Calt, notes to *Blind Lemon Jefferson: King of the Country Blues.*

26. Blind Lemon Jefferson, "Mosquito Moan," on *Blind Lemon Jefferson.*

27. Blind Lemon Jefferson, "Bad Luck Blues," ibid.

28. Blind Lemon Jefferson, "Matchbox Blues," ibid.

29. Blind Lemon Jefferson, "That Black Snake Moan," ibid.

30. Blind Lemon Jefferson, "That Crawling Baby Blues," ibid.

31. See Mary Berry and John Blassingame, "African Slavery and the Roots of Contemporary Black Culture," in *Chant of Saints: A Gathering of Afro-American Literature, Art, and Scholarship,* ed. Michael Harper and Stephen Stepto (Urbana: University of Illinois Press, 1979), p. 252.

32. Blind Lemon Jefferson, "Tin Cup Blues," on *Blind Lemon Jefferson.*

33. Blind Lemon Jefferson, "Rising High Water Blues," ibid. This song seems to be a cross between Charley Patton's "High Water Everywhere" and Bessie Smith's "Backwater Blues."

34. Blind Lemon Jefferson, "Prison Cell Blues," on *Blind Lemon Jefferson.*

35. Blind Lemon Jefferson, " 'Lectric Chair Blues," ibid.

36. Blind Lemon Jefferson, "Blind Lemon's Penitentiary Blues," ibid.

37. Blind Lemon Jefferson, "Lock Step Blues," ibid.

38. Ross Russell, "Illuminating the Leadbelly Legend," *Downbeat,* Aug. 6, 1970, pp. 17–19. *Leadbelly: The Library of Congress Recordings,* notes comp. and ann. by Lawrence Cohen, p. 7.

39. Moses Asch and Alan Lomax, eds., *The Leadbelly Song Book* (New York: Macmillan, 1944), p. 32.

40. Huddie Ledbetter, "Governor Pat Neff," on *Huddie Ledbetter,* Electra EKL-301.

41. David Goren, "Remembering Mother Scott: An Interview," *Sing Out: The Folksong Magazine* 27, no. 36 (1979):14.

42. See Serge Denisoff, *Great Day Coming: Folk Music and the American Left* (Urbana: University of Illinois Press, 1970), chs. 1–4, for an analysis of the proletarian folk revival and Leadbelly's role in it.

43. See Charters, *The Bluesmen,* pp. 197–203; Guido Van Rijn and Hans Verger, notes to *Alger "Texas" Alexander: Texas Troublesome Blues,* Agram Blues AB 2009, for details on Alexander's life.

44. Texas Alexander, "Section Gang Blues," on *Alger "Texas" Alexander.*

45. Texas Alexander, "Levee Camp Moan," ibid.

46. In an interview with Samuel Charters, Sam "Lightnin' " Hopkins recalled that

Texas Alexander was imprisoned for singing "bad songs" (Hopkins, *My Life in the Blues*). Another report stated that he was in prison from 1940 to 1945 for murdering his wife, but there is no record of this (Titon, *Early Downhome Blues*, p. 137).

47. Hopkins, *My Life in the Blues*.

## Chapter 4: "Pickin' Low Cotton": Piedmont Blues

1. See C. Van Woodward, *The Strange Career of Jim Crow* (New York: Oxford University Press, 1957), pp. 60–65, for a summary of Tom Watson's Populist views during this period. See. W. J. Cash, *The Mind of the South* (New York: Alfred A. Knopf, 1941), pp. 179–84, for an account of the importance of the Cotton Mill Campaign to the rise of the New South.

2. Jeff Titon, *Early Downhome Blues* (Urbana: University of Illinois Press, 1976), p. 29. Titon makes this assumption in his discussion of the regional origins of the rural blues. Also see Samuel Charters, *Sweet as the Showers of Rain* (New York: Oak, 1977), p. 137.

3. Howard W. Odum, "Folk Song and Folk Poetry as Found in the Secular Songs of the Southern Negroes," *Journal of American Folklore* 24 (1911):260–61, 272. Also see Titon, *Early Downhome Blues*, pp. 24–29.

4. Rudi Blesh and Harriet Janis, *They All Played Ragtime* (New York: Oak, 1966), p. 12.

5. Jim Jackson, "Travelin' Man," on *Country Blues Legends*, Yazoo 1002.

6. See Bruce Bastin, *Crying for the Carolinas* (London: Studio Vista, 1971), pp. 79–81, for Pink Anderson's version of "Travelin' Man."

7. Bruce Bastin, *Red River Blues: The Blues Tradition in the Southeast* (Urbana: University of Illinois Press, 1986), pp. 97–101.

8. Blind Blake, "Southern Rag," on *Blind Blake: Ragtime Guitar's Foremost Fingerpicker*, Yazoo 1068.

9. Blind Blake disappeared after touring with George Williams's Happy-Go-Lucky Road Show in the winter of 1932–33. An informant told me that Blake lived in Birmingham, Alabama, until his death in the 1950s.

10. Gus Cannon, quoted in Charters, *Showers of Rain*, p. 144.

11. Little Brother Montgomery interviewed by the author, Chicago, June 1982. Also see Bruce Bastin, *Red River Blues: The Blues Tradition in the Southeast* (Urbana: University of Illinois Press, 1986), pp. 40–43, and Paul Oliver, *Blues off the Record* (London: Baton, 1984), pp. 26–27, 80.

12. Blind Blake, "Diddie Wa Diddie," on *Blind Blake: Ragtime Guitar's Foremost Fingerpicker*.

13. Blind Blake, "Fightin' the Jug," on *Blind Blake*, vol. 1, Biograph BLP 12003.

14. Blind Blake, "Steel Mill Blues," on *Blind Blake*, vol. 2, Biograph BLP 12023.

15. Charters, *Showers of Rain*, pp. 103–11; interview with Joshua "Pegleg" Howell

by George Mitchell, *Nothing but the Blues*, ed. Mike Leadbetter (London: Hanover, 1971), pp. 258–59; Bastin, *Red River Blues*, pp. 102–5.

16. Joshua "Pegleg" Howell, "Fo' Day Blues," Columbia 14177.

17. Joshua "Pegleg" Howell, "Coal Man Blues," Columbia 14194.

18. Joshua "Pegleg" Howell, "Beaver Slide Rag," Columbia 14210.

19. Joshua "Pegleg" Howell, "Skin Game Blues," Columbia 14258.

20. Biographical information on Blind Willie McTell can be found in the interview tape recorded by John Lomax for the Library of Congress, 1940, which can be found in the Library of Congress folk archives. Also see Charters, *Showers of Rain*, pp. 121–31, and Bastin, *Red River Blues*, pp. 128–40.

21. Blind Willie McTell, "Mama 'Tain't Long 'fo' Day," on *Blind Willie McTell: The Early Years, 1927–33*, Yazoo L-1005.

22. Blind Willie McTell, "Statesboro Blues," ibid.

23. Lomax, McTell interview. Also see Bastin, *Red River Blues*, pp. 129–30.

24. Interview with John Jackson by the author, Washington, D.C., Feb. 1979.

25. Biographical information on Willie Walker is from Charters, *Showers of Rain*, pp. 140–41, and Bastin, *Red River Blues*, pp. 173–76.

26. Interview with the Reverend Blind Gary Davis by Samuel Charters, *Showers of Rain*, p. 158.

27. Biographical information on Blind Gary Davis is from Charters, *Showers of Rain*, pp. 157–69, and Bastin, *Red River Blues*, pp. 170–73, 241–51.

28. Bastin, *Crying for the Carolinas*, pp. 79–85. Ira Tucker, lead singer with the Dixie Hummingbirds, who grew up in Greenville, also remembers Dooley as the best bluesman in the area (interview by the author, Washington, D.C., Sept. 1979).

29. See Robert Shelton, *The Josh White Song Book* (Chicago: Quadrangle, 1963), pp. 1–12; Max Jones, "Josh White," *Blues Unlimited* 55–56 (June–Aug. 1968):8–11, Bastin, *Red River Blues*, pp. 166–78.

30. Josh White, "Blood Red River," ARC 13792–1.

31. Josh White, "Pickin' Low Cotton," ARC 13791–1.

32. Josh White, "Southern Exposure," on *Chain Gang Songs, Spirituals and Blues*, Electra 193.

33. See Erik Barnouw, *A Tower in Babel: A History of Broadcasting in the United States*, vol. 1 (New York: Oxford University Press, 1966), pp. 237–41, for a discussion of the rise of cigarette advertising in broadcasting before World War II.

34. See Bastin, *Red River Blues*, pp. 203–12.

35. As quoted, ibid., p. 209.

36. Zora Neale Hurston, *Dust Tracks on a Road* (Philadelphia: Lippincott, 1942), pp. 190–92.

37. See Bastin, *Red River Blues*, pp. 241–51.

38. For biographical information on Blind Boy Fuller see Charters, *Showers of Rain*, pp. 155–69, and Bastin, *Red River Blues*, pp. 214–38.

39. Interview with Sonny Terry by the author, Washington, D.C., Mar. 1982. For biographical information on Sonny Terry, see Charters, *Showers of Rain*, pp. 165–69, and Bastin, *Red River Blues*, pp. 262–69. Also see Barry Elmes, "Interview with Sonny Terry and Brownie McGhee," *Living Blues* 13 (Summer 1973):14–17.

40. Interview with J. C. Burris by Steve Hill, Santa Cruz, Calif., Oct. 1979.

41. Blind Boy Fuller, "Big House Blues," on *Blind Boy Fuller with Sonny Terry and Bull City Red*, Blues Classics II.

42. For biographical information on Brownie McGhee, see Bruce Bastin, *Red River Blues*, pp. 254–62. Also see Elmes, "Interview with Sonny Terry and Brownie McGhee," pp. 18–23.

43. Kip Lornell, "Virginia Traditions: Western Piedmont Blues," notes to *Virginia Traditions: Western Piedmont Blues*, Blue Ridge Institute LP 003, p. 2.

44. Ibid., pp. 8–13.

45. "Forty-second National Folk Festival," notes to the 1980 program, July 1980, Wolftrap, Va., p. 35.

46. Lornell, "Virginia Traditions," pp. 6, 10.

47. Quoted in Bastin, *Red River Blues*, p. 73.

48. Ibid., pp. 72–85.


# Introduction to Part II: Urban Blues


1. Robert C. Toll, *Blacking Up: The Minstrel Show in 19th Century America* (New York: Oxford University Press, 1974), p. 274.

2. See Robert Dixon and John Godrich, *Recording the Blues* (New York: Stein and Day, 1970), and Ronald Foreman Jr., "Jazz and Race Records, 1920–1932: Their Origins and Their Significance for the Record Industry and Society," Ph.D. diss., University of Illinois, 1972, for accounts of this period in the race record industry.

3. See Lewis A. Erenberg, *Steppin' Out: New York Nightlife and the Transformation of American Culture* (Chicago: University of Chicago Press, 1981); and Kathy Peiss, *Cheap Amusements: Working Women and Leisure in Turn-of-the-Century New York* (Philadelphia: Temple University Press, 1986), for discussions of the role of women in the commercialization of night-time leisure.

4. Richard Gambino, *Blood of My Blood* (Garden City, N.Y.: Doubleday, 1963), p. 113.

5. See Florette Henri, *Black Migration: Movement North, 1900–1920* (New York: Anchor/Doubleday, 1976), pp. 1–49, and John Hope Franklin, *From Slavery to Freedom: A History of Negro Americans* (New York: Alfred A. Knopf, 1947), pp. 435–51, for detailed discussions of this period of African-American history.

6. See Ronald L. Morris, *Wait Until Dark: Jazz and the Underworld, 1880–1940* (Bowling Green, Ohio: Bowling Green University Popular Press, 1980); and Leroy Ostransky, *Jazz City: The Impact of Our Cities on the Development of Jazz* (Englewood Cliffs, N.J.: Prentice-Hall, 1978), for historical studies of the role of black musicians in the urban underworld.

7. Richard Wright, *Twelve Million Black Voices* (New York: Arno, 1969), p. 128, and Ortiz Walton, *Music: Black, White and Blue* (New York: William Morrow, 1972), p. 29.

Chapter 5: "Laughin' to Keep from Cryin'": Vaudeville Blues

1. Langston Hughes and Milton Meltzer, *Black Magic: A Pictorial History of Black Entertainers in America* (Englewood Cliffs, N.J.: Prentice-Hall, 1967), pp. 67–72.

2. Edward A. Berlin, *Ragtime: A Musical and Cultural History* (Berkeley: University of California Press, 1980) p. 24; Chris Albertson, *Bessie* (New York: Stein and Day, 1974), p. 66.

3. Paul Oliver, *The Story of the Blues* (New York: Chilton Books, 1969), pp. 71–72; Hughes and Meltzer, *Black Magic*, pp. 67–69.

4. For more information on the TOBA, see Hughes and Meltzer, *Black Magic*, pp. 66–70; Giles Oakley, *The Devil's Music: A History of the Blues* (New York: Harcourt Brace Jovanovich, 1976), pp. 104–6; Oliver, *Story of the Blues*, pp. 69–72; Albertson, *Bessie*, pp. 26–32; Daphne Duval Harrison, *Black Pearls: Blues Queens of the 1920s* (New Brunswick, N.J.: Rutgers University Press, 1988), pp. 17–41.

5. John Ryan, *The Production of Culture in the Music Industry: The ASCAP-BMI Controversy* (New York: University Press of America, 1985), pp. 11–30, 53–75.

6. Ibid., p. 71.

7. John J. Niles, "Shout Coon Shout," *Musical Quarterly* 16 (Oct. 1930): 519–21.

8. David Ewen, *All the Years of American Popular Music* (Englewood Cliffs, N.J.: Prentice-Hall, 1977), pp. 219–28.

9. W. C. Handy, *Father of the Blues: An Autobiography* (New York: Macmillan, 1942), pp. 127–210; Ewen, *All the Years*, p. 221.

10. Roland C. Gelatt, *The Fabulous Phonograph* (New York: Appleton-Century, 1965), pp. 54–55; Perry Bradford, *Born with the Blues* (New York: Oak, 1965), p. 116; Robert Dixon and John Godrich, *Recording the Blues* (New York: Stein and Day, 1970), pp. 7–8.

11. Ewen, *All the Years*, pp. 186–87.

12. See Derrick Stewart-Baxter, *Ma Rainey and the Classic Blues Singers* (New York: Oak, 1968), pp. 10–31; Bill Malone, *Southern Music, American Music* (Lexington: University of Kentucky Press, 1979), p. 45; Jeff Titon, *Early Downhome Blues* (Urbana: University of Illinois Press, 1976), pp. 25–29, for discussions of vaudeville blues.

13. E. Simm Campbell, "Blues," in *Jazzmen*, ed. Frederic Ramsey and Charles Smith (New York: Harcourt Brace, 1939), pp. 110–11.

14. Handy, *Father of the Blues*, pp. 77–79, 103, 151–53.

15. Ibid., pp. 207–9; Albertson, *Bessie*, p. 44; Bradford, *Born with the Blues*, p. 98.

16. See Alan Lomax, *Mister Jelly Roll* (Berkeley: University of California Press, 1950), p. 21.

17. Bradford, *Born with the Blues*, p. 121.

18. Albertson, *Bessie*, p. 44; Bradford, *Born with the Blues*, p. 155.

19. Dixon and Godrich, *Recording the Blues*, pp. 10–13, 44; Titon, *Early Downhome Blues*, p. 204.

20. Dixon and Godrich, *Recording the Blues*, pp. 13–16; Ronald C. Foreman,

"Jazz and Race Records 1920–1932: Their Origins and Their Significance for the Record Industry" (Ph.D. diss., University of Illinois, 1972), pp. 60–62.

21. Jim O'Neal, "Guitar Blues: Sylvester Weaver," *Living Blues* 52 (Spring 1982):19–20.

22. Albertson, *Bessie*, pp. 39, 44–46; David Evans, *Big Road Blues: Tradition and Creativity in the Folk Blues* (Berkeley: University of California Press), pp. 74, 239, 271.

23. Albertson, *Bessie*, pp. 46; Lawrence Levine, *Black Culture and Black Consciousness: Afro-American Folk Thought from Slavery to Freedom* (New York: Oxford University Press, 1977), p. 478.

24. Albertson, *Bessie*, p. 46, 182. Columbia Records has reissued Bessie Smith's entire record output without compensating her estate.

25. Howard Odum and Guy Jonnson, *Negro Workaday Songs* (Chapel Hill: University of North Carolina Press, 1925), p. 34.

26. Jeff Titon, *Early Downhome Blues*, p. 205; Paula Dranov, *Inside the Music Publishing Industry* (White Plains, N.Y.: Knowledge Industry Publications, 1980), p. 101.

27. Dixon and Godrich, *Recording the Blues*, pp. 19, 22.

28. Sandra Lieb, *Mother of the Blues: A Study of Ma Rainey* (Amherst: University of Massachusetts Press, 1981), pp. 21–22, 50–52.

29. Interview with Thomas A. Dorsey by Jim O'Neal and Amy O'Neal, *Living Blues* 20 (Mar.–Apr. 1975), p. 23.

30. Titon, *Early Downhome Blues*, pp. 76–79. Also see Samuel Charters, *Sweet as the Showers of Rain* (New York: Oak, 1977), pp. 143–49.

31. Yannick Bruynoghe, *Big Bill Blues* (New York: Oak, 1969), p. 47. Several blues musicians have mentioned getting free liquor at recording sessions: see Titon, *Early Downhome Blues*, pp. 212–22; Evans, *Big Road Blues*, pp. 75–77.

32. Charles Wolfe, "The Birth of an Industry," in *The Illustrated History of Country Music*, ed. Patrick Carr (New York: Dolphin Books, 1980), pp. 30–2.

33. See Bill Malone, *Southern Music, American Music* (Lexington: University Press of Kentucky, 1979), pp. 65–66; Evans, *Big Road Blues*, pp. 72–74; Titon, *Early Downhome Blues*, pp. 210–11, 214, 218–21; Albertson, *Bessie*, p. 65. Also see chart, "Blues Centers and Locations," in Oliver, *Story of the Blues*, inside cover; Dixon and Godrich, *Recording the Blues*, pp. 106–7.

34. Dranov, *Music Publishing*, p. 101; Dixon and Godrich, *Recording the Blues*, pp. 64, 73, 94.

35. See Dranov, *Music Publishing*, p. 101; Dixon and Godrich, *Recording the Blues*, pp. 78–97; C. A. Schicke, *Revolution in Sound* (Boston: Little, Brown, 1974), p. 102.

36. Mike Rowe, *Chicago Breakdown* (London: Eddison Press, 1973), pp. 17–25.

37. Schicke, *Revolution in Sound*, p. 98; Dixon and Godrich, *Recording the Blues*, pp. 84, 87.

38. Schicke, *Revolution in Sound*, pp. 104–5; John Hammond, *John Hammond on Record* (New York: Summit Books, 1977), pp. 404–9.

39. Eugene Genovese, *Roll Jordan Roll: The World the Slaves Made* (New York: Random House, 1972), p. 249; Vincent Harding, *There Is a River: The Black Struggle*

*for Freedom in America* (New York: Harcourt Brace Jovanovich, 1981), pp. 153, 165, 199, 211, 233, 252.

40. See Robert Tallant, *Voodoo in New Orleans* (New York: Macmillan, 1946), pp. 20–21. The English translation of this Creole song was first printed in *New Orleans Times Picayune*, March 16, 1924. Also see Susan Cavin, "Missing Women on the Voodoo Trail to Jazz," *Journal of Jazz Studies* 3, no. 1 (Fall 1975):4–27.

41. See Linda Dahl, *Stormy Weather: The Music and Lives of a Century of Jazz Women* (New York: Pantheon, 1984), pp. 3–12.

42. For discussions of classic jazz and blues from a postwar perspective, see Rudi Blesh, *Shining Trumpets: A History of Jazz* (New York: Alfred A. Knopf, 1946), pp. 173–97; Andre Hodier, *Jazz: Its Evolution and Essence* (New York: Grove, 1956), pp. 21–38; Hugh Panisse, *The Real Jazz* (New York: Charles Scribner & Sons, 1958); Rex Harris, *Jazz* (London: Penguin Books, 1952), pp. 30–60.

43. LeRoi Jones, *Blues People: Negro Music in White America* (New York: William Morrow, 1963), pp. 81–82.

44. For biographical information on the classic blues women, see Stewart-Baxter, *Ma Rainey*; Dahl, *Stormy Weather*; Sally Placksin, *American Women in Jazz: 1900 to the Present* (New York: World View Books, 1982); Frank Taylor and Gerald Cook, *Alberta Hunter: A Celebration in Blues* (New York: McGraw-Hill, 1987).

45. James Lincoln Collier, *The Making of Jazz: A Comprehensive History* (New York: Dell, 1978), pp. 108–11.

46. Ibid., p. 111.

47. Mamie Smith, "That Thing Called Love," Okeh 4133-A.

48. Lil Johnson, "Hottest Gal in Town," Okeh 8162.

49. See William Francis Allen, Charles Pickard Ware, and Lucy McKim Garrison, *Slave Songs of the United States* (New York: Simpson, 1867), pp. 30–31.

50. Bertha "Chippie" Hill, "Trouble in Mind," Okeh 8312.

51. Sippie Wallace, "Section Hand Blues," Okeh 8232.

52. Victoria Spivey, "Dirty T.B. Blues," Victor V38570.

53. Alice Moore, "Prison Blues," Paramount 87911.

54. Sara Martin, "The Prisoner's Blues," Okeh 8326.

55. Victoria Spivey, "Bloodhound Blues," Okeh 8339.

56. Lottie Kimbrough, "Rolling Log Blues," Okeh 8138.

57. Maggie Jones, "Northbound Blues," Columbia 14902.

58. Alberta Hunter, "Michigan Water Blues," Paramount 12687.

59. Ida Cox, "Down South Blues," Paramount 12227.

60. Iva Smith, "Third Alley Blues," Columbia 12733.

61. Sippie Wallace, "Trouble Everywhere I Roam," Okeh 8244.

62. Bessie Jackson (Lucille Bogan), "Tricks Ain't Walkin' No More," Okeh 8456.

63. Lil Johnson, "Scuffling Woman Blues," Okeh 8134.

64. Merline Johnson, "Reckless Life Blues," Paramount 12456.

65. Lillian Green, "Packing House," in Paul Oliver, *Blues off the Record* (London: Baton, 1984), pp. 221.

66. Julia Moody, "Mad Mama's Blues," Columbia 14766.

67. Trixie Smith, "Trixie's Blues," Paramount 12261.

68. Jenny Pope, "Doggin' Me Around Blues," Paramount 12366.

69. Lil Johnson, "Press My Button," Okeh 8255.

70. Clara Smith, "Whip It to a Jelly," Columbia 14150.

71. Sara Martin, "Mean Tight Mama," Okeh 8324.

72. Ida Cox, "Wild Women Don't Get the Blues," Paramount 12228.

73. Alberta Hunter quoted in *Hear Me Talkin' to Ya: The Story of Jazz by the Men Who Made It*, ed. Nat Shapiro and Nat Hentoff (New York: Grove, 1957), pp. 223–24.

74. Victoria Spivey quoted in Dahl, *Stormy Weather*, pp. 119–20.

75. Ibid. Also see Placksin, *Women in Jazz*, pp. 28–38.

76. Interview with Victoria Spivey by the author, New York, July 1974.

77. See Taylor and Cook, *Alberta Hunter*, pp. 1–22. Also see Harrison, *Black Pearls*, pp. 147–63.

78. Ibid., p. 65.

79. Ibid., p. 149.

80. Lieb, *Mother of the Blues*, pp. 1–48; Stewart-Baxter, *Ma Rainey*, pp. 35–42; Dan Morganstern, notes to *Ma Rainey*, Milestone M-47021; Hans R. Rookmaker, notes to *Ma Rainey: Mother of the Blues*, Riverside RM8807.

81. John Work Jr., *American Negro Songs and Spirituals: A Comprehensive Collection of 230 Folksongs, Religious and Secular*. (New York: Negro University Press, 1915), pp. 32–33.

82. For material on the origin of the blues, see Chapter 1, n. 1, above.

83. Many people who saw Ma Rainey perform have published their recollections of her. Two who found her uniquely attractive are Thomas Dorsey and Victoria Spivey. See interview with Georgia Tom Dorsey by Jim O'Neal and Amy O'Neal, *Living Blues* 20 (Mar.–Apr. 1975):17–34; Oakley, *Devil's Music*, pp. 99–104; Dan Morganstern's notes to *Ma Rainey*. Two who found her unattractive, even ugly, are Little Brother Montgomery (interviewed by the author, Chicago, June 1977), and Champion Jack Dupree (quoted in Rookmaker, notes to *Ma Rainey*).

84. Langston Hughes, "Gospel Singing," quoted in Lawrence Levine, *Black Culture and Black Consciousness: Afro-American Thought from Slavery to Freedom* (New York: Oxford University Press, 1977), p. 180; interview with Sterling A Brown by the author, Washington, D.C., May 1980.

85. Sterling A. Brown, *Southern Roads* (New York: Harcourt Brace, 1932), pp. 52–64.

86. Ma Rainey, "Last Minute Blues," on *Ma Rainey: Queen of the Blues*, Biograph BLP 12032.

87. Ma Rainey, "Lost Wandering Blues" on *Ma Rainey*.

88. Ma Rainey, "Hear Me Talkin' to Ya," ibid.

89. Ma Rainey, "Black Eye Blues," ibid.

90. Ma Rainey, "Leavin' This Morning," ibid.

91. Ma Rainey, "Barrelhouse Blues," on *Ma Rainey: Queen of the Blues*.

92. Ma Rainey, "Prove It on Me," on *Ma Rainey*.

93. Albertson, *Bessie*, p. 104.

94. Interview with Sterling A. Brown by the author, Washington, D.C., May 1980.

95. Clyde Bernhardt quoted in Lieb, *Mother of the Blues*, p. 13.

96. Ma Rainey, "Lawd Send Me a Man Blues," on *Ma Rainey: Mother of the Blues*.

97. Ma Rainey, "Blame It On The Blues," on *Ma Rainey.*

98. Ma Rainey, "Boll Weevil Blues," ibid.

99. Ma Rainey, "Dead Drunk Blues," ibid.

100. Ma Rainey, "Countin' the Blues," ibid.

101. See Jarvis Anderson, "Bert Williams: The Jonah Man," *Notes on the Arts: Smithsonian Performing Arts*, Jan.–Feb. 1982:4–7.

102. Ma Rainey, "Those Dogs of Mine," on *Ma Rainey: Queen of the Blues.*

103. Cited in Lieb, *Ma Rainey*, p. 146.

104. Ma Rainey, "Lost Wandering Blues," on *Ma Rainey.*

105. Ma Rainey, "Southern Blues," on *Ma Rainey: Queen of the Blues.*

106. Stewart-Baxter, *Ma Rainey*, p. 44.

107. Source material on Bessie Smith includes Albertson, *Bessie*; Oliver, *Bessie Smith*; Hettie Jones, *Big Star Falling Mama: Five Women in Black Music* (New York: Dell, 1974), pp. 45–50; Richard Hadlock, *Jazz Masters of the Twenties* (New York: Macmillan, 1965), pp. 219–38.

108. See Oliver, *Bessie Smith*, pp. 3–7, for the theory that Ma Rainey was the dominant influence on Bessie Smith's style and repertoire; Albertson, *Bessie*, pp. 26–28, for the opposite view.

109. Albertson, *Bessie*, pp. 28–32.

110. Ibid., pp. 39, 42. Also see Bradford, *Born with the Blues*, pp. 35–37; Handy, *Father of the Blues*, p. 231.

111. Bessie Smith, "Tain't Nobody's Business If I Do," Columbia A3898.

112. Bessie Smith, "Mama Got the Blues," Columbia A3900.

113. Howard W. Odum, "Folk Song and Folk Poetry as Found in the Secular Songs of Southern Negroes," *Journal of American Folklore* 24 (1911):272.

114. Bessie Smith, "Jailhouse Blues," Columbia A3958.

115. Bessie Smith, "Gulf Coast Blues," Columbia A3844.

116. Albertson, *Bessie*, p. 46.

117. Ibid., pp. 48, 52.

118. Quoted in Perry Bradford, *Born with the Blues* (New York: Oak, 1965), p. 44. Also see Hadlock, *Jazz Masters*, pp. 219–38.

119. Ibid., pp. 227–30.

120. Bessie Smith, "Workhouse Blues," Columbia 14032-D.

121. Bessie Smith, "Poor Man's Blues," Columbia 14399-D.

122. Albertson, *Bessie*, pp. 148–49.

123. Bessie Smith, "Salt Water Blues," Columbia 14037-D.

124. Bessie Smith, "Sinful Blues," Columbia 14052-D.

125. Bessie Smith, "Young Woman's Blues," Columbia 14179-D.

126. Bessie Smith, "Reckless Blues," Columbia 14056-D.

127. Albertson, *Bessie*, pp. 117–20.

128. Ruby Smith quoted in ibid., p. 116.

129. Ibid., p. 122.

130. Sidney Bechet, *Treat It Gentle* (New York: Hill and Wang, 1960), p. 48.

131. Bessie Smith, "Nobody Knows You When You're Down and Out," Columbia 14853-D.

132. Handy, *Father of the Blues*, p. 267.

## Chapter 6: "Chocolate to the Bone": Urban Blues in the South

1. The city's madams, with the help of a local judge, won a verdict forestalling the licensing and taxing of prostitutes. The legal victory set off a celebration that turned into an erotic bacchanal in the French Quarter. See Jack Buerkle and Danny Barker, *Bourbon Street Black: The New Orleans Black Jazzman* (New York: Oxford University Press, 1973), p. 18. Also see Herbert Ashbury, *The French Quarter* (New York: Alfred A. Knopf, 1935).

2. Ronald L. Morris, *Wait Unitl Dark: Jazz and the Underworld, 1880–1940* (Bowling Green, Ohio: Bowling Green University Popular Press, 1980), p. 86.

3. See Ira Berlin, *Slaves Without Masters* (New York: Random House, 1974), pp. 108–32, for a discussion of the free "Creoles of color" in the antebellum period.

4. New Orleans mulattos remained a self-conscious social elite within the black community. P. B. S. Pinchbeck and O. J. Dunn were in the forefront of the struggle to enfranchise black men in Louisiana, a political battle that was won briefly in 1869. They also spearheaded local antisegregation agitation. The mulatto politicians allied themselves with the Republican party and urged the freedmen to do likewise. See John Blassingame, *Black New Orleans: 1860–1880* (Chicago: University of Chicago Press, 1973).

5. Morris, *Wait Until Dark*, p. 85; Pops Foster and Tom Stoddard, *The Autobiography of Pops Foster as Told to Tom Stoddard* (Berkeley: University of California Press, 1971), pp. 12–13; Buerkle and Barker, *Bourbon Street Black*, p. 163.

6. Buerkle and Barker, *Bourbon Street Black*, p. 147.

7. William Schafer, *Brass Bands and New Orleans Jazz* (Baton Rouge: Louisiana State University Press, 1977), pp. 28–29; Buerkle and Barker, *Bourbon Street Black*, p. 140.

8. Editorial in New Orleans newspaper quoted in George E. Cunningham, "The Italian: A Hindrance to White Solidarity in Louisiana: 1890–1895," *Journal of Negro History* 90 (1965):26.

9. In 1892 a general strike shut New Orleans down, as twenty-five thousand workers representing forty-nine unions walked off their jobs. Both black and white workers were involved in the strike, and they held together to win an arbitrated settlement despite the employers' attempts to divide them along racial lines. The same scenario was enacted in 1907, when ten thousand dock workers went on strike for three weeks before the owners agreed to a settlement. See Philip Foner, *Organized Labor and the Black Worker, 1819–1973* (New York: International Publishers, 1974), pp. 66–68, 90–91.

10. In 1890, members of the Provenzanos gang were put on trial for ambushing the

Matrangas gang. Each gang accused the other of belonging to the mafia. The Provenzanos were convicted but were granted a new trial. The Matrangas believed that a New
Orleans police inspector named Michael Hennessy had favored the rival gang and had
discovered evidence of perjury in the first trial. Detective Hennessy was subsequently
gunned down in the streets, gangland style. The Provenzanos were acquitted, and then
nineteen members of the Matrangas gang were charged with Hennessy's murder. When
a jury found six of the Matrangas not guilty and could reach no verdict on three others,
the white community was outraged. A large mob formed at the parish jail and lynched
eleven Matrangas gang members who were being held there. The mayor of New Orleans called the killings "necessary and justifiable," although "deplorable." No investigation of the lynchings was ever conducted, and no one was charged with the
Matrangas deaths. The incident strained relations between Italy and the United States.
See Thomas Pitkin and Francesco Cordosco, *Black Hand: A Chapter in Ethnic Crime*
(Totowa, N.J.: Adams, 1977), pp. 23–25.

11. Buerkle and Barker, *Bourbon Street Black*, pp. 18–19, 26; Foster and Stod-
dard, *Pops Foster*, pp. 19, 24; Morris, *Wait Until Dark*, pp. 91–93, 100–103; Leroy
Ostransky, *Jazz City: The Impact of Our Cities on the Development of Jazz* (Englewood
Cliffs, N.J.: Prentice-Hall, 1978), pp. 1–40.

12. Aaron Harris's brief career as the most ruthless black outlaw in Storyville is
illustrative of the violence endemic to the red-light district. He is remembered in a local
ballad for having killed his sister and brother-in-law in an argument over a cup of
coffee. He beat the rap, so the legend goes, with the help of Madame Papaloos. Harris
terrorized the residents of Storyville through his willingness to use his knife and his
gun to settle disputes. His prowess with weapons apparently intimidated the local police
as well. One source credits Harris with eleven murders before he was ambushed and
shot dead by two of his hoodlum associates. See Donald Marquis, *In Search of Buddy
Bolden: First Man of Jazz* (Baton Rouge: Louisiana State University Press, 1978), pp.
50–51; Alan Lomax, *Mister Jelly Roll* (Berkeley: University of California Press, 1950),
pp. 54–55, 105–7; Foster and Stoddard, *Pops Foster*, pp. 29–32.

13. See William Hair, *Carnival of Fury: Robert Charles and the New Orleans
Race Riot of 1900* (Baton Rouge: Louisiana State University Press, 1976), for an in-
depth study of the incident.

14. Foster and Stoddard, *Pops Foster*, pp. 36–37; Ostransky, *Jazz City*, p. 59;
Morris, *Wait Until Dark*, p. 100.

15. Roy Carew, "Remembering Tony Jackson," *Record Changer* 4 (Feb.
1943):34.

16. Lomax, *Mister Jelly Roll*, p. 269–91; also see Rudi Blesh and Harriet Janis,
*They All Played Ragtime* (New York: Oak, 1966), p. 169.

17. Reprinted in Lomax, *Mister Jelly Roll*, p. 51.

18. Ibid., pp. 269–71. Also see Blesh and Janis, *Ragtime*, p. 179.

19. Foster and Stoddard, *Pops Foster*, pp. 15–16, 92.

20. Marquis, *Buddy Bolden*, p. 100.

21. Ibid., p. 43–44.

22. Ibid., p. 105.

23. Danny Barker, "Memories of Buddy Bolden," *Evergreen Review* (Mar.
1965):67–74.

24. Marquis, *In Search of Buddy Bolden*, pp. 108–9. Also see *Jazzmen*, ed. Frederic Ramsey and Charles Smith (New York: Harcourt, Brace, 1939), p. 13.

25. Lomax, *Mister Jelly Roll*, pp. 17, 276.

26. Marquis, *Buddy Bolden*, p. 110.

27. Martin Williams, *Jazz Masters of New Orleans* (New York: Macmillan, 1967), pp. 1–26; Marquis, *Buddy Bolden*, pp. 99–112; Ramsey and Smith, *Jazzmen*, pp. 1–38.

28. Williams, *Jazz Masters*, p. 162.

29. John Dittner, *Black Georgia in the Progressive Era* (Chicago: University of Illinois Press, 1977), p. 13.

30. Ibid., pp. 83–87.

31. W. E. B. Du Bois referred to the "submerged tenth" as "the lowest class of criminals, prostitutes and loafers." See W. E. B. Du Bois, *The Philadelphia Negro* (Philadelphia: University of Pennsylvania Press, 1899), p. 311.

32. In September 1906, the local press began printing sensationalistic headlines about alleged black male assaults on white women. Thomas Dixon's race-baiting play *The Clansmen* had recently been staged in Atlanta before enthusiastic audiences. An outbreak of vigilantism suddenly engulfed Atlanta in terror for four days. Mobs descended on Decatur Street; they beat and in some instances killed black citizens indiscriminately. The next night, while the state militia patrolled Decatur Street, white vigilantes invaded a middle-class black neighborhood called Brownville and brutalized its residents. When the community tried to defend itself, the police were called in to disarm them. After one of their numbers was killed in a shootout, the Atlanta police resorted to terrorism; they arrested sixty black men in connection with the death of one white police officer and killed four more in the process. Overall, twelve black people were killed during the mayhem and another seventy were hospitalized with injuries. See Ray Stannard Baker, "Following the Color Line: A Race Riot and After," *American Magazine*, Apr. 1907. Reprinted in *Racism at the Turn of the Century: Documentary Perspectives, 1870–1910*, ed. Donald DeNevi and Doris Holmes (San Rafael, Calif.: Leswing Press, 1973), pp. 198–215. Also see Joseph Boskin, *Urban Racial Violence in the 20th Century* (Beverly Hills, Calif.: Glencoe Press, 1969), p. 68.

33. Dittner, *Black Georgia*, p. 13.

34. Perry Bradford, *Born with the Blues*, (New York: Oak, 1965), p. 18.

35. Lillian Glinn, "Atlanta Blues," Columbia 14421.

36. Interview with Thomas A. Dorsey by Jim O'Neal and Amy O'Neal, *Living Blues* 20 (Mar.–Apr. 1975):18–28.

37. Bob Koester, "The Saga of Speckled Red," *Jazz Report* 2 (Summer 1962):14–15. Also see David Mangurian, "Speckled Red," *Jazz Journal* 13 (June 1960):3.

38. Bradford, *Born with the Blues*, p. 19.

39. Quoted in Samuel Charters, notes to *The Atlanta Blues*, RBF Records, RBF 15, p. 1.

40. See Bruce Bastin, *Red River Blues: The Blues Tradition in the Southeast* (Urbana: University of Illinois Press, 1986), pp. 89–91.

41. See Mike Rowe, notes to *Chicago Breakdown: Big Maceo*, RCA Bluebird 0798.

42. Interview with William "Piano Red" Perryman by the author at Wolf Trap, Va., Aug. 1981.

43. Ibid.

44. Roger Brown, "Recording Pioneer Polk Brockman," *Living Blues* 23 (Sept.–Oct.):31.

45. See Bastin, *Red River Blues*, p. 106, for a discussion of this style and its origins.

46. Ibid., pp. 105–12; Samuel Charters, *Sweet as the Showers of Rain* (New York: Oak, 1977), pp. 112–20; Steve Calt, notes to *Barbecue Bob—Chocolate to the Bone*, on *Barbecue Bob—Chocolate to the Bone*, Mamlish s3808.

47. Robert Hicks, "Motherless Chile Blues," ibid.

48. Robert Hicks, "Chocolate to the Bone," ibid.

49. Bastin, *Red River Blues*, p. 110.

50. Ibid., pp. 112–21. Also see Charters, *Showers of Rain*, pp. 125–29, 133–34.

51. First and last verse of "Hard Road Blues" by Buddy Moss, reprinted in Charters, *Showers of Rain*, pp. 151–52. Also see Bastin, *Red River Blues*, pp. 125–28.

52. Interview with Roy Dunn by the author in Atlanta, Apr. 1984.

53. See Bastin, *Red River Blues*, pp. 140–42.

54. Interview with William "Piano Red" Perryman by the author at Wolf Trap, Va., Aug. 1981.

55. Foner, *Organized Labor*, p. 87.

56. Bradford, *Born with the Blues*, pp. 31, 93. Bradford also claims that Jelly Roll Morton acknowledged Lost John's contribution to the boogie-woogie style, but failed to mention him in his autobiography. Bob Eagle, "Lucille Bogan—Bessie Jackson," *Living Blues* 44 (Autumn 1979):25–28.

57. Bessie Jackson (Lucille Bogan), "B.D. Woman Blues," on *Blues Classics* Arhoolie #6.

58. Jaybird Coleman, "Mean Old Trouble Blues," on *Backwoods Blues*, Origin Jazz Library OJL8. Also see Charters, *The Bluesmen*, pp. 115–57.

59. Paul Oliver, *The Story of the Blues* (New York: Chilton Books, 1969), pp. 49, 52–53; Doug Seroff, "Black American Quartet Traditions," in *Program in Black American Culture* (Washington, D.C.: Smithsonian Institution, 1981), pp. 5–9, 14–16.

60. Ironically, Furry Lewis, a native of Memphis, was the first blues musician to use a slide guitar on a commercial recording, and "Roll and Tumble" was first recorded by "Hambone" Willie Newbern, a native of western Tennessee; see *The Roots of Rock*, Yazoo 1063. "Joe Turner" had several versions in circulation: W. C. Handy recalled a Memphis version; see W. C. Handy, *Father of the Blues: An Autobiography* (New York: Macmillan, 1942), pp. 151–53. Big Bill Broonzy had vivid memories of a Mississippi Delta version: Yannick Bruynoghe, *Big Bill Blues* (New York: Oak, 1969), pp. 52–59. Gus Cannon learned "Po' Boy, Long Ways from Home" in Clarksdale, Mississippi, before 1907, from a musician named Alex Lee; Bengt Olsson, "Biography," notes to *Cannon's Jug Stompers*, Herwin 208.

61. Shields McIlwaine, *Memphis down in Dixie* (New York: E. P. Dutton, 1948), pp. 18, 28, 45–54.

62. Crump was an anachronism in American politics. He was a late-blooming urban boss who came to power in the guise of a Progressive reformer, in keeping with the current political fashion. Yet he also continued the tradition of such southern Populists as Tom Watson and Ben Tillman. Crump was from the ranks of the uprooted poor

white farmers in the South and knew how to gain their political allegiance, especially in a new urban setting. He was equally adept at bringing others into the fold and relished his role as a political patriarch. Crump never gave a political speech in his entire life, but he managed to keep his name in the political limelight in Memphis by public relations ploys that ranged from personally sponsoring an annual Fourth of July picnic and fireworks show to naming a public park on Beale Street after W. C. Handy. During his later years, Crump was the benevolent despot of Shelby County politics. He was described by one observer as "a semi-literate old fellow with a steamed-apricot face and amazing, hairy eyebrows." Despite his background, he was one of the most powerful politicians in the South, much admired by men like Louisiana Governor Huey P. Long, who visited Crump in Memphis to get a first-hand look at his political machine. In addition to his political clout, Crump amassed a fortune through investments in real estate and insurance. He helped improve the quality of life in Memphis, but it was too often at the expense of the democratic process. See William D. Miller, *Mr. Crump of Memphis* (Baton Rouge: Louisiana State University Press, 1964), pp. 21–28; William D. Miller, *Memphis During the Progressive Era* (Memphis: Memphis State University Press, 1957), pp. 6–34; Robert Lanier, *Memphis in the Twenties* (Memphis: Zenda Press, 1979), pp. 2, 18, 21–26, 33–34.

63. Memphis police made regular Saturday night sweeps of black gathering places in the red-light district during which they arrested scores of African Americans for gambling, prostitution, disorderly conduct, and that favorite catchall charge—vagrancy. Those caught in the sweeps were routinely fined a standard amount of money. If they could not pay the fines, they were either sent to the county farm to do hard labor on the road gangs or rented out to local white cotton farmers. In Memphis, this was called the "fee system"; more generally, it was known as the convict-lease system. The planters would pay the fines of the black transgressors and then legally coerce them to work off the debt by laboring in the fields. See Lanier, *Memphis in the Twenties*, pp. 103–4, 111–12.

64. Margaret McKee and Fred Chisenhall, *Beale Street Black and Blue* (Baton Rouge: Louisiana State University Press, 1981), p. 17.

65. Ibid., pp. 136–37.

66. Alan Lomax, *Mister Jelly Roll* (Berkeley: University of California Press, 1950), pp. 137–39.

67. Ida B. Wells was forced to flee the city after speaking out against a lynching in an editorial in a weekly Baptist newspaper. Mary Church Terrell, the daughter of Robert Church, was jolted into a career of social activism when a close high-school friend of hers was lynched in Memphis. In 1917, white vigilantes burned a young black man at the stake and spread his remains along Beale Street. The man, Ell Parson, was accused of the rape and murder of a young white woman. Black residents of Memphis were outraged by the mob violence; many responded to a call to form a local NAACP chapter by attending a mass meeting. Memphis was an armed camp for a while; black and white citizens carried guns in the streets until a truce was worked out. See Miller, *Memphis During the Progressive Era*, p. 118–34; McKee and Chisenhall, *Beale Street Black and Blue*, p. 32.

68. McKee and Chisenhall, *Beale Street Black and Blue*, p. 38.

69. In 1922, there had been seventy-nine murders in the city; sixty-three of the

victims were black, and forty-nine were black men. Fifty-one of the deaths were caused by guns, and eighteen were caused by knife wounds. Those figures remained steady for the next two years, and then began to decline slightly. See Lanier, *Memphis in the Twenties*, p. 72–74.

70. Gus Cannon quoted in Bengt Olsson, "Biography," notes to *Cannon and His Jug Stompers*, Herwin 208, p. 1.

71. Reprinted in McKee and Chisenhall, *Beale Street Black and Blue*, p. 24.

72. Ibid.

73. In 1927, federal authorities arrested a gang of four Italian bootleggers led by John Bellomini at their warehouse. Along with a substantial haul of bootleg liquor, the agents also confiscated a payoff book listing over sixty Memphis law enforcement officers who had received eighty-four thousand dollars. The disclosure of its contents led to the indictment of thirty-eight policemen; they were all found "not guilty" by a jury of their peers, and the Memphis bootlegging operations returned to business as usual. See Lanier, *Memphis in the Twenties*, pp. 82–87.

74. Annette Church and Roberta Church, *The Robert R. Churches of Memphis: A Father and Son Who Achieved in Spite of Race* (Memphis: published privately, 1974), pp. 16–18.

75. Handy, *Father of the Blues*, pp. 97, 107.

76. Lomax, *Mister Jelly Roll*, pp. 92–97.

77. Interview with Peter Chatman by the author, Memphis, Sept. 1982. Edward Hatchett was another Memphis pianist, who played at the Midway Café before migrating to Chicago in the early 1930s. See Bengt Olsson, *Memphis Blues and Jug Bands* (London: Studio Vista, 1970), p. 32.

78. Samuel Charters, *Sweet as the Showers of Rain* (New York: Oak, 1977), pp. 15–16; Bengt Olsson, notes to *Memphis Jug Band*, Yazoo Records 1067.

79. Olsson, notes to *Memphis Jug Band*.

80. Memphis Jug Band, "Stealin'," on *Memphis Jug Band*.

81. Memphis Jug Band, "Cocaine Habit Blues," ibid.

82. Memphis Jug Band, "Overseas Stomp," on *The Jug Bands*, Folkways RF6.

83. Memphis Jug Band, "Whitewash Station," on *Memphis Jug Band*.

84. Charters, *Showers of Rain*, pp. 21–26; Olsson, notes to *Memphis Jug Band*.

85. Charters, *Showers of Rain*, pp. 27–41; Olsson, "Biography."

86. Gus Cannon quoted in Olsson, "Biography."

87. Charters, *Showers of Rain*, pp. 30–31.

88. Gus Cannon, "Can You Blame the Colored Man?" on *Gus Cannon's Jug Stompers*.

89. Gus Cannon's Jug Stompers, "Prison Wall Blues," ibid.

90. Gus Cannon's Jug Stompers, "Viola Lee Blues," ibid.

91. Richard Spottsword, notes to *The Great Jug Bands, 1926–1934*, Historical HLP-36; Charters, *Showers of Rain*, pp. 47–48, 64.

92. Jim Jackson, "Bootlegging Blues," on *Low Down Memphis Barrelhouse Blues (1928–1935)*, Mamlish s3803.

93. Frank Stokes, "Mister Crump Don't Like It," on *Frank Stokes: Creator of the Memphis Blues*, Yazoo Records 1056.

94. Frank Stokes, "You Shall," ibid.

95. Frank Stokes, "T'ain't Nobody's Business," ibid.

96. Frank Stokes, "Downtown Blues," ibid.

97. Furry Lewis quoted in Charters, *Showers of Rain*, p. 50.

98. Ibid., p. 51.

99. Furry Lewis, "I Will Turn Your Money Green," on *Furry Lewis in His Prime: 1927–1928*, Yazoo Records 1050.

100. Sleepy John Estes, "Diving Duck Blues," on *Sleepy John Estes: 1929–1940*, Asch Records RBF 8. Also see Charters, *Showers of Rain*, pp. 69–82.

101. Sleepy John Estes, "The Girl I Love, She Got Long Curly Hair," on *Sleepy John Estes: 1929–1940*.

102. Sleepy John Estes, "Sloppy Drunk Blues," ibid.

103. Sleepy John Estes, "Floating Bridge," ibid.

104. Sleepy John Estes, "Lawyer Clark Blues," ibid.

105. Sleepy John Estes, "Working Man Blues," ibid.

106. Interview with Robert Wilkins by Pete Welding in *Blues Unlimited* 53 (May 1968), and *Blues Unlimited* 54 (June 1968).

107. See Charters, *Showers of Rain*, pp. 83–95.

108. Interview with Big Joe Williams by the author, Memphis, Nov. 1982.

## Chapter 7: "Stormy Monday": Urban Blues in the Southwest

1. J. H. Owens, "Deep Ellum," *Dallas Gazette*, July 3, 1937. Also see Paul Oliver, *Blues off the Record* (London: Baton, 1984), pp. 162–63.

2. Tim Schuller, "Alex Moore, Whistling the Blues," *Living Blues* 35 (Nov.–Dec. 1977):8–10. Also see Paul Oliver, *The Story of the Blues* (New York: Chilton Books, 1969), pp. 137–38; Oliver, *Blues off the Record*, pp. 217–19; Alan Govenar, *Living Texas Blues* (Dallas: Dallas Museum of Art, 1985), p. 40.

3. Alex Moore, "Blue Bloomer Blues," on *Alex Moore in Europe*, Arhoolie 1048.

4. Bill Neely quoted in Govenar, *Living Texas Blues*, p. 24.

5. Ibid., p. 80.

6. Interview with T-Bone Walker by Jim O'Neal and Amy O'Neal, *Living Blues* 11 (Winter 1972–73):20–26; Part II, *Living Blues* 12 (Spring 1973):24–27.

7. See Helen Oakley Dance, *Stormy Monday: The T-Bone Walker Story* (Baton Rouge: Louisiana State University Press, 1987), for a detailed discussion of Walker's music and life.

8. Buster Smith quoted in Ross Russell, *Jazz Style in Kansas City and the Southwest* (Berkeley: University of California Press, 1971), pp. 75–76.

9. See Jesse O. Thomas, *A Study of the Social Welfare State of the Negro in Houston, Texas* (New York: NAACP, 1928); Edgar A. Schuler, "The Houston Race Riot, 1917," *Journal of Negro History* 29 (1944):300–36; Chandler Davidson, *Biracial Politics* (Baton Rouge: Louisiana State University Press, 1972), pp. 1–35.

10. Thomas, *Social Welfare State*, pp. 28–30.

11. Oliver, *Blues off the Record*, pp. 140–43, 198–201, 270–75.

12. Interview with Sippie Wallace by the author, Wolf Trap, Va., Aug. 1981. Also see Oliver, *Blues off the Record*, pp. 140–42.

13. Oliver, *Blues off the Record*, pp. 198–99.

14. Govenar, *Living Texas Blues*, pp. 41–42.

15. Buster Pickens quoted, ibid., p. 271.

16. Interview with Milt Larkin by the author, Houston, June 1983.

17. Oliver, *Blues off the Record*, p. 199.

18. Sam "Lightnin' " Hopkins, interviewed by Mack McCormick on *Lightnin' Hopkins: My Life in the Blues*, Prestige PR 7370. Also see Mack McCormick, "Lightnin' Hopkins Blues," *Jazz Review*, Jan. 1960; Kurt Loder, "Lightnin' Hopkins: 1912–1982," *Rolling Stone*, Mar. 18, 1982:17–18.

19. Sam Lightnin' Hopkins, "Tim Moore's Farm," on *Fast Life Woman: Lightnin' Hopkins*, Verve V-8453.

20. Sam Lightnin' Hopkins, "Stranger Here," on *Goin' Away: Lightnin' Hopkins*, Bluesville BV 1073.

21. William Reddig, *Tom's Town* (New York: J. P. Lippincott, 1947), p. 24.

22. Johnny Lazia was Kansas City's most flamboyant native gangster. Born of immigrant parents, he grew up in Kansas City's North End ghetto. At the age of eighteen, he was convicted of armed robbery and sentenced to fifteen years in the state prison. He was paroled in less that a year because of his friendship with the Pendergast brothers. He worked as a ward lieutenant in "Little Italy" for Mike Ross, an Irish business associate of the Pendergast machine. By 1928, Lazia had replaced Ross as the political kingpin of the North End and had negotiated a new arrangement with Tom Pendergast: Pendergast remained the machine's political boss, while Lazia was appointed the city's underworld czar, with control over the police of his district. This new authority enabled him to grant "safe passage" in Kansas City to notorious outlaws like Pretty Boy Floyd and Frank Nash. These sanctions precipitated the 1933 "Union Station Massacre," which left Nash and four FBI agents dead. See Lyle Dorsett, *The Pendergast Machine* (New York: Oxford University Press, 1968), and Maurice Milligan, *The Inside Story of the Pendergast Machine* (Lawrence: Kansas University Press, 1968), for detailed accounts of the rise and the fall of machine politics, vice, and corruption during the Pendergast era.

23. Edward R. Morrow quoted in Russell, *Jazz Style*, p. 8. Also see Dorsett, *Pendergast Machine*, pp. 66–68, 126–29, 135. Leroy Ostransky, *Jazz City: The Impact of our Cities on the Development of Jazz* (Englewood Cliffs, N.J.: Prentice-Hall, 1978), pp. 143–46.

24. Interview with Sterling A. Brown by the author, in Washington, D.C., Apr. 1979.

25. See Ross Russell, *Jazz Style*, pp. 10–24.

26. Rudi Blesh and Harriet Janis, *They All Played Ragtime* (New York: Oak, 1966), pp. 19, 112–20, 147.

27. See Russell, *Jazz Style*, pp. 74–81. Also see Gene Fernett, *Swing Out: Great Negro Dance Bands* (Midland, Mich.: Pendell, 1970), p. 49; Albert McCarthy, *Big Band Jazz* (New York: Putnam's Sons, 1974), pp. 134–39.

28. Count Basie quoted in Raymond Harricks, *Count Basie and His Orchestra* (New York: Citadel Press, 1958), p. 87. Also see "Ode to Jimmy," *Time*, Jan. 11, 1943, "Pack My Bags and Make My Getaway," *Downbeat*, Apr. 8, 1965.

29. Mary Lou Williams quoted in "Take Me to Froggy Bottom," *Negro Digest*, Dec. 1946:36.

30. Interview with Joe Turner by the author, in New York, June 1982.

31. Joe Turner quoted in Valerie Wilmer, *Jazz People* (New York: Bobbs-Merrill, 1971), pp. 148–49. Also see "Kansas City Moods," *Metronome*, Mar. 1945; "Boss of the Blues," *Downbeat*, Dec. 11, 1958; Peter Guralnick, "Big Joe Williams," *Lost Highway: Journeys and Arrivals of American Musicians* (Boston: David Godine, 1979), pp. 295–303.

32. Russell, *Jazz Style*, p. 50.

33. Joe Turner and Pete Johnson, "Cherry Red," on *The Boss of the Blues: Joe Turner Sings Kansas City Jazz*, Atlantic 1234.

34. Joe Turner and Pete Johnson, "Piney Brown Blues," ibid.

35. Gunther Schuller, *Early Jazz: Its Roots and Early Development* (New York: Oxford University Press, 1968), p. 284.

## Chapter 8: "Goin' Down Slow": Urban Blues in the Midwest

1. Oliver Johns, *Times of Our Lives* (New York: Macmillan, 1948), p. 98.

2. W. C. Handy, *Father of the Blues: An Autobiography* (New York: Macmillan, 1942), pp. 30–31.

3. Johns, *Times of Our Lives*, p. 98. Rudi Blesh and Harriet Janis, *They All Played Ragtime* (New York: Oak, 1966), p. 40.

4. Blesh and Janis, *They All Played Ragtime*, pp. 40–41, 55, 100–102.

5. Ibid., pp. 35–45, 52, 62; Edward Berlin, *Ragtime: A Musical and Cultural History* (Berkeley: University of California Press, 1980), pp. 136–39, 141–45, 154.

6. Florette Henri, *Black Migration: Movement North, 1900–1920* (New York: Anchor/Doubleday, 1976), p. 264; Joseph Boskin, *Urban Racial Violence in the 20th Century* (Beverly Hills, Calif.: Glencoe Press, 1969), p. 22.

7. Henri, *Black Migration*, pp. 264–68; Boskin, *Urban Racial Violence*, pp. 24–25. Also see Elliott Rudwick, *Race Riot at East St. Louis, July 2, 1917* (New York: Atheneum, 1972).

8. Stephen Papich, *Remembering Josephine Baker* (New York: Bobbs-Merrill, 1970), pp. 12–19.

9. Henri, *Black Migration*, pp. 267–68.

10. Ibid., p. 86; Paul Oliver, *The Story of the Blues* (New York: Chilton Books, 1969), pp. 89–90; Don Kent, notes to *Good Time Blues: St. Louis 1926–1932*, Mamlish s3805 LP; Leroy Pierson, notes to *Henry Mule Townsend*, Nighthawk 201 LP.

11. Oliver, *Story of the Blues*, p. 87; Michael Stewart and Don Kent, notes to *Hard Times Blues: St. Louis 1933–1940*, Mamlish s3806; James Lincoln Collier, *The Making of Jazz: A Comprehensive History* (New York: Dell, 1978), pp. 207–8.

12. Oliver, *Story of the Blues*, pp. 86–87; Paul Oliver, *Blues off the Record* (London: Baton, 1984), pp. 222–23; Kent, notes to *Good Time Blues*.

13. Interview with Little Brother Montgomery by the author, Chicago, May 1977; Samuel Charters, notes to *Roosevelt Sykes*, Folkways Records FS 3867; John Bently, "The Honey Dripper: Roosevelt Sykes," *Living Blues* 9 (Summer 1972):21–23.

14. Kent, notes to *Good Time Blues*.

15. James Odem and Sunnyland Slim, "Patience Like Job," RCA Bluebird 34–0727.

16. James Odem, "Goin' Down Slow," Bullet 27 UB2768B.

17. Paul Garon, "Remembering Lonnie Johnson," *Living Blues* 12 (Summer 1970); Bob Groom, "It's Too Late to Cry: A Tribute to Lonnie Johnson," *Blues World* 35 (Oct. 1970); Steve Calt, notes to *Mr. Johnson's Blues*, Mamlish s3807.

18. Lonnie Johnson, "There Is No Justice," on *Mr. Johnson's Blues*.

19. Lonnie Johnson, "Racketeers' Blues," ibid.

20. Lonnie Johnson, "Helena Blues," ibid.

21. Lonnie Johnson, "Why Women Go Wrong," RCA Bluebird B8322.

22. Lonnie Johnson, "When I Was Lovin' Changed My Mind," on *Mr. Johnson's Blues*.

23. Interview with Lonnie Johnson by Valerie Wilmer, *Jazz Monthly* Dec. 1963:28.

24. See Chris Albertson, *Bessie* (New York: Stein and Day, 1974), pp. 94–95, for an account of Lonnie Johnson's affair with Bessie Smith.

25. Peetie Wheatstraw, "The Peetie Wheatstraw Stomp," #1 and #2, on *Peetie Wheatstraw and Kokomo Arnold*, Classic Blues BC-4. Also see Paul Garon, *The Devil's Son-In-Law* (London: Studio Vista, 1971); Paul Garon, "Peetie's Brother," *Living Blues* 7 (Winter 1971–72):50.

26. Peetie Wheatstraw, "Mister Livingood," Decca 7473.

27. Peetie Wheatstraw, "Confidence Man," Decca 7647.

28. Peetie Wheatstraw, "Block and Tackle," Decca 7487.

29. Peetie Wheatstraw, "The First Shall Be Last and the Last Shall Be First," ibid.

30. Peetie Wheatstraw, "Road Tramp Blues," Decca 7389.

31. Ralph Ellison, *The Invisible Man* (New York: Signet Books, 1952), pp. 131–34.

32. Joe Stone (J. D. Short), "It's Hard Time," on *St. Louis Town, 1929–1933*, Yazoo L1003.

33. Interview with Big Joe Williams by the author in Memphis, Nov. 1982.

34. Blind Teddy Darby, "Pitty Pat Blues," on *Hard Times Blues*. Also see Leroy Pierson, "St. Louis Blues," *Living Blues* 3 (Autumn 1970):20–21.

35. Interview with Henry Townsend by the author, Washington, D.C., July 1982. Also see Leroy Pierson, notes to *Henry Mule Townsend*, Nighthawk Records 208.

36. J. D. Short, "She Got Jordan River in Her Hips," on *Good Time Blues*.

37. See Oliver, *Blues off the Record*, pp. 84–86; Steve Calt, Don Kent, and Pat Cont, notes to *Big Joe Williams: 1935–1941*, Mamlish s3810; Bob Koester, notes to "Piney Woods Blues: Big Joe Williams," on *Piney Woods Blues: Big Joe Williams*, Delmark 602.

38. Big Joe Williams, "Providence Help the Poor People," on *Big Joe Williams*.

39. See Leroy Pierson, notes to *Windy City Blues: 1935–1953*, Nighthawk Records 101; Leroy Pierson, notes to *Lake Michigan Blues, 1934–1941* Nighthawk Records 104.

40. Interview with Henry Townsend by the author, Washington, D.C., July 1982.

41. See Omer Carmichael, *The Louisville Story* (New York: Simon and Schuster, 1957), and Ann Braden, *The Wall Between* (New York: Monthly Review Press, 1958), for discussions of Louisville's culture, night life, and race relations during this period.

42. Rudi Blesh and Harriet Janis, *They All Played Ragtime* (New York: Oak, 1966), pp. 41, 94–95, 172–77, 248.

43. Carmichael, *Louisville Story*, pp. 69–81. Also see Joseph S. Cotter, *25th Anniversary of the Founding of Colored Parkland or Little Africa, Louisville Kentucky, 1891–1914* (Louisville: I. Willis Cole, 1934).

44. Henry Miles quoted in Jim O'Neal, "Kentucky Blues," *Living Blues* 51 (Summer 1981):36.

45. Ibid., pp. 25–30.

46. See notes to *Clifford Hayes and the Dixieland Jug Blowers*, Yazoo 1054; Samuel Charters, notes to *The Jugbands*, RBF RF 6; Jim O'Neal, "Kentucky Blues," pp. 25–36.

47. Henry Miles quoted in Jim O'Neal, "Kentucky Blues," p. 34.

48. Lafcadio Hearn, "Levee Life," *Cincinnati Commercial*, March 17, 1876. Reprinted in *The Selected Writings of Lafcadio Hearn*, ed. Henry Goodman (New York: Citadel Press, 1949).

49. See Chris Albertson, *Bessie* (Stein and Day, 1974), pp. 67–68; Joel Vance, *Fats Waller: Ain't Misbehaving* (New York: Dell, 1948), p. 106; Steve Tracy, "Going to Cincinnati," *Living Blues* 38 (Summer 1978):20–25.

50. Stargel Bull was a police officer who patrolled in the West End in the 1920s. Hog Head Joe's was the name of a restaurant that reputedly moved from place to place to avoid paying rent. There is no record of a Judge Landshaw, but Lockland Hollow was a local haven for moonshine operations. Walter Coleman, "I'm Going to Cincinnati," on *Blue Box #1*, MCA Coral 6–30106.

51. James Miles quoted in Tracy, "Going to Cincinnati," p. 21.

52. James "Pigmeat" Jarrett quoted ibid., p. 24.

53. See ibid., p. 25; "Cincinnati Boogie Woogie: Joe Duskin," *Living Blues* 17 (Summer 1974):18.

54. See Florette Henri, *Black Migration: Movement North, 1900–1920* (New York: Anchor/Doubleday, 1976), pp. 102–3, 112, 180–81; Paul Oliver, *The Story of the Blues* (New York: Chilton Books, 1969), p. 92. Also see Ida Webb Bryant, *Glimpses of the Negro in Indianapolis, 1863–1963* (Washington, D.C.: Howard University Press, 1964).

55. See Art Hodes and Chadwick Hensen, eds., *Selections from the Gutter: Portraits from the Jazz Record* (Berkeley: University of California Press, 1977), pp. 47–49.

56. See Kip Lornell, notes to *Leroy Carr*, Biograph 1005; Frank Driggs, notes to *Blues Before Sunrise*, CBS BPG 62266; Arthur Rosenblum, notes to *Scrapper Blackwell: Mr. Scrapper's Blues*, Bluesville 147.

57. Leroy Carr, "How Long, How Long Blues," on *Leroy Carr and Scrapper Blackwell, 1928–1934*, Yazoo L-1036.

58. Leroy Carr, "Blues Before Sunrise," on *Blues Before Sunrise*.

59. See Mike Stewart and Steve Calt, notes to *Leroy Carr and Scrapper Blackwell*; Mike Stewart and Steve Calt, notes to *Scrapper Blackwell*, Yazoo L-1019.

60. Champion Jack Dupree quoted in *Living Blues* 32 (May–June 1977):14. Also see Dave Holland, "A Naptown Blues Party," *Living Blues* 13 (Summer 1973):6, 28.

61. Henri, *Black Migration*, pp. 69, 169.

62. Quoted in Kenneth G. Weinberg, *A Man's Home Is His Castle* (New York: Saturday Review Press, 1971), pp. 22–24.

63. Albertson, *Bessie*, pp. 122–23.

64. Quoted in Eric Sackheim, *The Blues Line: A Collection of Blues Lyrics from Leadbelly to Muddy Waters* (New York: Schirmer Books, 1969), p. 492. For a historical account of the "Dozens," see Robert S. Gold, *Jazz Talk* (Indianapolis: Bobbs-Merrill, 1975), p. 76; Middleton Harris, ed., *The Black Book* (New York: Random House, 1974), p. 180.

65. Speckled Red, "The Dirty Dozens," on *Speckled Red: The Dirty Dozens*, Delmark DL 601.

66. See Thurgood Marshall, "The Gestapo in Detroit," *Crisis*, Aug. 1943:232–33, 246.

67. Interview with John Lee Hooker by the author in Washington, D.C., Aug. 1979. Also see interview with John Lee Hooker by Jim O'Neal and Amy O'Neal, *Living Blues* 44 (Autumn 1979):14–22.

68. Bobo Jenkins, "Bad Luck and Trouble," Chess 1565.

69. Bobo Jenkins, "24 Years on the Wrong Road," Big Star 1001.

70. Bobo Jenkins quoted in Rob Backus, *Fire Music: A Political History of Jazz* (Chicago: Vanguard, 1976), p. 53. Also see interview with Bobo Jenkins by Jim O'Neal and Amy O'Neal in *Living Blues* 3 (Autumn 1970):6–12; and Bruce Iaglauer, "Detroit Blues," *Living Blues* 3 (Autumn 1970):4–9.

## Chapter 9: "Looking Up at Down": Chicago Blues

1. Florette Henri, *Black Migration: Movement North, 1900–1920* (New York: Anchor/Doubleday, 1976), p. 83; Allan Spear, *Black Chicago: The Making of a Negro Ghetto, 1890–1920* (Chicago: University of Chicago Press, 1967); St. Clair Drako and Horace Clayton, *Black Metropolis: A Study of Negro Life in a Northern City*, vol. I (New York: Harper and Row, 1945), pp. 8, 21, 31–33.

2. Henri, *Black Migration*, pp. 151–52; Spear, *Black Chicago*, pp. 36–40.

3. Henri, *Black Migration*, pp. 62–66; Spear, *Black Chicago*, pp. 81–82, 114–15. For a detailed biography of Robert Abbott, see Roi Ottley, *The Lonely Warrior: The Life and Times of Robert S. Abbott* (Chicago: Chicago Defender, 1955).

4. Spear, *Black Chicago*, pp. 79, 187–89. Also see Lloyd Wendt and Herman Kogar, *Big Bill Thompson* (Indianapolis: Bobbs-Merrill, 1953); Harold Gosnell, *Negro Politicians: The Rise of Negro Politicians in Chicago* (Chicago: University of Chicago Press, 1935).

5. Henri, *Black Migration*, pp. 83–87, 320–21; Spears, *Black Chicago*, pp. 218–19, 206, 212–16; Drake and Clayton, *Black Metropolis*, 1:65–66, 110; Joseph Boskin, *Urban Racial Violence in the 20th Century* (Beverly Hills, Calif.: Glencoe Press, 1969), pp. 30–37; Chicago Commission on Race Relations, *The Negro in Chicago* (Chicago, 1922).

6. John Landesco, *Organized Crime in Chicago* (Chicago: University of Chicago Press, 1928), pp. 31–38.

7. Ronald Morris, *Wait Until Dark: Jazz and the Underworld, 1880–1940* (Bowling Green, Ohio: Bowling Green University Popular Press, 1980), pp. 6, 25, 59, 61, 108, 117, 121, 141, 183.

8. Interview with Hammie Nixon by the author, Memphis, Sept. 1, 1982.

9. Perry Bradford, *Born with the Blues* (New York: Oak, 1965), p. 34.

10. Henri, *Black Migration*, p. 143; Spear, *Black Chicago*, p. 26.

11. Earl Hines, "How Gangsters Ran the Band Business," *Ebony*, Sept. 1949:112.

12. Spear, *Black Chicago*, pp. 76–77; Morris, *Wait Until Dark*, p. 112.

13. Chris Albertson, *Bessie* (Stein and Day, 1974), p. 75.

14. Langston Hughes, *The Big Sea* (New York: Random House, 1948), p. 45.

15. Robert Dixon and John Godrich, *Recording the Blues* (New York: Stein and Day, 1970), p. 27.

16. Ibid., pp. 44, 60–61, 71.

17. Clarence Lofton, "Strut That Thing," Vocalion 24678. Also see Oliver, *Story of the Blues*, pp. 82–83.

18. William Russell, "Boogie Woogie," in *Jazzmen*, ed. Frederic Ramsey and Charles Smith (New York: Harcourt Brace, 1939), pp. 196–97.

19. Interview with Thomas Dorsey by Jim O'Neal and Amy O'Neal, *Living Blues* 20 (Mar.–Apr. 1975):17–34.

20. Russell, "Boogie Woogie," pp. 185–86. Also see Oliver, *Story of the Blues*, p. 83.

21. Charles "Cow Cow" Davenport, "I'm Goin' Up North" Brunswick 10–356.

22. See Art Hodes and Chadwick Hansen, eds., *Selections from the Gutter: Portraits from the Jazz Records* (Berkeley: University of California Press, 1977), pp. 39–47.

23. Russell, "Boogie Woogie," p. 198.

24. Samuel Charters, note to *Piano Blues*, RBF Records, RF312; Russell, "Boogie Woogie," pp. 187–88; Oliver, *Story of the Blues*, p. 84.

25. Russell, "Boogie Woogie," pp. 192–93; Oliver, *Story of the Blues*, p. 84; John Hammond, *John Hammond on Record* (New York: Summit Books, 1977), pp. 164–65.

26. Yannick Bruynoghe, *Big Bill Blues* (New York: Oak, 1969), pp. 29–49.

27. Ibid., pp. 68, 69.

28. Ibid., p. 71.

29. Big Bill Broonzy, "When Will I Get to Be Called a Man?" on *Big Bill Broonzy Sings the Country Blues*, Folkways Records FA 2326.

30. Big Bill Broonzy, "Black, Brown and White," on *Big Bill Broonzy*, Folkways Records FG 3586.

31. Big Bill Broonzy, "Stump Blues," on *The Big Bill Broonzy Story*, vol. 2, Verve Records V–300–5.

32. "Plowhand Blues," Big Bill Broonzy, ibid.

33. Big Bill Broonzy, "Key to the Highway," on *The Big Bill Broonzy Story*, vol. 1.

34. Big Bill Broonzy, "Looking Up at Down," Okeh 05698.

35. Jim O'Neal, notes to *Tampa Red: The Guitar Wizard*, Arhoolie BC 25; Steve

Calt, liner notes to *Tampa Red: Bottleneck Guitar Wizard*, Yazoo L 1039. Also see interview with Thomas Dorsey by Jim O'Neal and Amy O'Neal, *Living Blues* 20 (March–Apr. 1975):25.

36. Blind John Davis quoted in notes to *Tampa Red: The Guitar Wizard*, RCA Bluebird AXM2-5501.

37. Drake and Clayton, *Black Metropolis*, 2:481; "Negro Population of Chicago," *History Statistics of the U.S.*, table 8 (C25–73).

38. Bruynoghe, *Big Bill Blues*, p. 138.

39. Ibid., pp. 141–42.

40. Ibid., p. 142.

41. Interview with Arthur Crudup by Mike Leadbetter, *Blues Unlimited* (UK), Sept. 1970:25–27. Also see Arnold Shaw, *Honkers and Shouters: The Golden Years of Rhythm and Blues* (New York: Macmillan, 1978), pp. 31–35; Steve Calt, notes to *Arthur Crudup: Father of Rock & Roll*, RCA Vintage Series LPV-573.

42. See David Evans, "Folk and Popular Blues Styles from the Beginning to the Early 1940s," notes to *Let's Get Loose*, New World Music NW 290, 1978, p. 5.

43. See Paul Oliver, "Kokomo Arnold," *Jazz Monthly*, May 1962:10; Chris Strachwitz, notes to *Kokomo Arnold/Peetie Wheatstraw*, Blues Classics 4.

44. Blind Lemon Jefferson, "Tin Cup Blues," on *Blind Lemon Jefferson*, Milestone M47022.

45. Big Bill Broonzy, "Starvation Blues," on *The Young Bill Broonzy 1928–1936*, Yazoo 11011.

46. Tampa Red, "Depression Blues," Vocalion 1656.

47. Sleepy John Estes, "Hobo Jungle Blues," Decca 7354.

48. Carl Martin, "Let's Have a New Deal," on *Country Blues Classic*, vol. 4, Blues Classics 14.

49. Sonny Boy Williamson, "Welfare Store," on *Sonny Boy Williamson* vol. 1, Blues Classics 3.

50. Floyd Council, "Don't Want No Hungry Woman," reprinted in Eric Sackheim, *The Blues Line: A Collection of Blues Lyrics from Leadbelly to Muddy Waters* (New York: Schirmer Books, 1969), p. 421.

51. Jazz Gillum, "Down South Blues," Bluebird B9004.

52. Little Bill Gaither, "Creole Queen," Okeh OG561.

53. Washboard Sam, "I'm on My Way," on *Washboard Sam*, Blues Classics 10.

54. Washboard Sam, "I Been Treated Wrong," on *The Country Blues*, RBF–1. Also see Paul Oliver's notes to *Washboard Sam*, and Don Kent's notes to *Washboard Sam*, RCA Victor Vintage Series LP0577.

55. Interview with Memphis Slim by the author, Memphis, July 1982.

56. Samuel Charters, notes to *Blues Roots: Chicago in the 1930's*, RBF–16; Mike Rowe, notes to *Chicago Breakdown: Big Maceo Merriweather*, RCA Victor Vintage Series AxM2-5506; Tom Pomposello, notes to *Memphis Slim: I'll Just Keep on Singing the Blues*, Muse 5219. Also see Bruynoghe, *Big Bill Blues*, pp. 112–16, 126–37; Shaw, *Honkers and Shouters*, pp. 42–45.

57. Langston Hughes, "Here to Yonder: Music at Year's End," *Chicago Defender*, January 9, 1943. Reprinted in *Living Blues* 19 (Jan.–Feb. 1975):7.

58. Quoted in Mike Rowe, *Chicago Breakdown* (London: Eddison Press, 1973), p. 43.

59. See Paul Oliver notes to *Sonny Boy Williamson*, vol. 1–3, Blues Classics 3, 20, 24; Mike Rowe, *Chicago Breakdown*, pp. 20–25, 40–45, 67–70; Bruynoghe, *Big Bill Blues*, pp. 120–23.

60. Sonny Boy Williamson, "Insurance Man Blues," on *Bluebird Blues: Sonny Boy Williamson*, RCA International 1088.

61. Sonny Boy Williamson, "Collector Man," on *Sonny Boy Williamson*, vol. 1.

62. Sonny Boy Williamson, "Moonshine," on *Bluebird Blues*.

63. Sonny Boy Williamson, "Alcohol Blues," on *Sonny Boy Williamson*, vol. 3.

64. Sonny Boy Williamson, "Bad Luck Blues," ibid.

65. Sonny Boy Williamson, "I Have Got to Go," ibid.

66. Sonny Boy Williamson, "Christmas Morning Blues," on *Bluebird Blues*.

67. Sonny Boy Williamson, "Elevator Woman," ibid.

68. Sonny Boy Williamson, "Stop Breaking Down," on *Sonny Boy Williamson*, vol. 2.

69. Sonny Boy Williamson, "Hoodoo Hoodoo," ibid.

70. Interview with Sunnyland Slim by the author, Chicago, May 1978.


## Conclusion


1. Interview with Henry Townsend by the author, Wolf Trap, Va., Aug. 1983.

2. Molefi Kete Asante, *The Afrocentric Idea* (Philadelphia: Temple University Press, 1987), p. 84.

3. Ibid., pp. 54–55.

4. Ibid., pp. 193–94.

5. See Mike Rowe, *Chicago Breakdown* (London: Eddison Press, 1973), pp. 40–62, 174–205.

6. See Norman Spaulding, "History of Black Oriented Radio in Chicago, 1929–1963" (Ph.D. diss., University of Illinois, 1981), pp. 71–78.

7. Ibid., pp. 78–86. Benson did shows on WGES, WAAF, and WJJD.

8. See Rowe, *Chicago Breakdown*, pp. 40–78, 98–125. Other important independent record labels operating out of Chicago during this period included Art Sheridan's Chance and Sable labels, which recorded John Lee Hooker, Little Walter Jacobs, and Eddie Boyd, among others; the National/State labels, which featured releases by Robert Nighthawk, Big Walter Horton, and Junior Wells; and the Vee Jay label, whose major blues artist was Jimmy Reed.

9. Ibid., pp. 79–92. Also see Jim Rooney, *Bossmen: Bill Monroe and Muddy Waters* (New York: Dial Press, 1971); Peter Guralnick, "Muddy Waters: Gone to Main Street," in his *Feel Like Going Home* (New York: Outerbridge & Dienstfrey, 1971), pp. 42–66; Robert Palmer, "Muddy Waters: The Delta Son Never Sets" in *Rolling Stone*,

Oct. 5, 1978:53–56; Jim O'Neal and Amy O'Neal, "Muddy Waters Interview" in *Living Blues* 64 (Mar.–Apr. 1985):15–40.

10. See Robert Palmer, *Deep Blues* (New York: Viking, 1981), pp. 173–98; Rowe, *Chicago Breakdown*, pp. 140–44.

11. See Palmer, *Deep Blues*, pp. 231–38; Rowe, *Chicago Breakdown*, pp. 134–39; Guralnick, "Howling Wolf: Don't Laugh at Me," in *Feel Like Going Home*, pp. 120–37.

12. See Guralnick, "Boppin' the Blues: Sam Phillips and the Sun Sound," in *Feel Like Going Home*, pp. 138–45; Colin Escott and Martin Hawkins, *Sun Records: The Brief History of the Legendary Record Label* (London: Quick Fox, 1975); Charles Sawyer, *The Arrival of B. B. King* (New York: Doubleday, 1980).

13. See Arnold Shaw, *Honkers and Shouters: The Golden Age of Rhythm and Blues* (New York: Macmillan, 1978), pp. 479–88.

14. Ibid., pp. 179–210, 247–60.

15. Ibid., pp. 144–68. Also see Jim Huskins, *Queen of the Blues: A Biography of Dinah Washington* (New York: William Morrow, 1987).

16. Shaw, *Honkers and Shouters*, pp. 58–85.

17. Ray Charles and David Ritz, *Brother Ray: Ray Charles' Own Story* (New York: Dial Press, 1978). Also see Shaw, *Honkers and Shouters*, pp. 129–40, 194–211; Charlie Gillett, *Making Tracks: The History of Atlantic Records* (London: Panther Books, 1975); Richard Harrington, "Atlantic's Bow to the Blues Heritage," *Washington Post*, May 12, 1988.

18. See Charlie Gillett, *The Sound of the City: The Rise of Rock and Roll* (New York: Outerbridge & Dienstrey, 1970).

19. See Gerri Hershey, *Nowhere to Run: The Story of Soul Music* (New York: Penguin Books, 1985), pp. 117–227; Peter Benjaminson, *The Story of Motown* (New York: Grove Press, 1979); Simon Frith, "You Can Make It If You Try: The Motown Story," in Ian Hoare, ed., *The Soul Book* (New York: Dell, 1976), pp. 39–73.

20. See Peter Guralnick, *Sweet Soul Music: Rhythm and Blues and the Southern Dream of Freedom* (New York: Harper & Row, 1986), pp. 97–219, 332–52.

21. See Paul Oliver, *The Story of the Blues* (New York: Chilton Books, 1969); Giles Oakley, *The Devil's Music: A History of the Blues* (London: Ariel Books, 1978); John Godrich and Robert Dixon, *Blues and Gospel Records 1902–1942*; Mike Leadbetter and Neil Slaven, *Blues Records 1943–1966* (London: Hanover Books, 1968).

22. See Bruce Bastin, *Red River Blues: The Blues Tradition in the Southeast* (Urbana: University of Illinois Press, 1986); David Evans, *Big Road Blues: Tradition and Creativity in the Folk Blues* (Berkeley: University of California Press, 1982); Bill Ferris, *Blues from the Delta* (Garden City, N.Y.: Anchor Books, 1978); Charles Keil, *Urban Blues* (Chicago: University of Chicago Press, 1966); Barry Lee Pearson, *Sounds So Good to Me* (Philadelphia: University of Pennsylvania Press, 1985); Jeff Titon, *Early Downhome Blues* (Urbana: University of Illinois Press, 1976).

23. Houston Baker Jr., *Blues, Ideology and Afro-American Literature* (Chicago: University of Chicago Press, 1986), p. 5. Also see Sterling A. Brown, "The Blues as Folk Poetry," *Folk-Say: A Regional Miscellany, 1930*, ed. B. A. Botkin (Norman: University of Oklahoma Press, 1930), pp. 324–39; Albert Murray, *The Hero and the Blues*

(Columbia: University of Missouri Press, 1973); Albert Murray, *Stomping the Blues* (New York: McGraw-Hill, 1976); W. Lawrence Hogue, *Discourse and the Other: The Production of the Afro-American Text* (Durham: Duke University Press, 1986), pp. 107–31.

24. See Palmer, *Deep Blues*; Guralnick, *Feel Like Going Home*; Samuel Charters, *The Country Blues* (New York: Rinehart, 1959); Samuel Charters, *Robert Johnson* (New York: Oak, 1973); and Samuel Charters, *Sweet as Showers of Rain* (New York: Oak, 1977); Lawrence Levine, *Black Culture and Black Consciousness: Afro-American Folk Thought from Slavery to Freedom* (New York: Oxford University Press, 1977).

# General Index

African music, traditional, 3, 5, 15
Agriculture, in Piedmont region, 79–80
Ajax record company, 128
Akers, Garfield, 54
Alcoholism, 43
Alexander, Alger "Texas," 60, 75–78, 230, 238
Allen, Fulton. *See* Fuller, Blind Boy
Allen, Jap, 245
Allen, O. K., 74
Alligator Records, 341–42
Altheimer, Josh, 134, 306
American Record Company, 103
American Society of Composers, Authors, and Publishers (ASCAP), 122
Ammons, Albert, 135, 298–99
Ananse, 22
Anderson, Pink, 83, 97, 98
Andrews, Dope, 127
Andy Boy, 236–237
Anthony, Eddie, 90–91, 92, 198
Antiphony, 24
Antoine, Ike, 28
Apollo record company, 335–36
Arhoolies, 17–18, 23–24
Aristocrat Records, 329–30
Armstrong, Louis, 164, 171–72, 260
Arnold, James "Kokomo," 45, 47, 135, 309–10
Arnold, John Henry "Big Boy," 97, 98
Arto record company, 128
ASCAP. *See* American Society of Composers, Authors, and Publishers
Atlanta, 191–92; blues legends of, 195–98; piano players of, 193–95
Austin, Lovie, 154, 163–64, 294

Bailey, Buster, 164, 171
Bailey, Deford, 103
Bailey, Kid, 35, 54
Ballads, 7; African-American, 18–20, 23–24; Anglo-American,

transformation by African Americans, 19; "bad nigger," 21–22; boll weevil, 22–23; folk heros in, 19–20; John Henry, 20–21
Banjo, 30
Bankston, Dick, 35
Barrasso, Anselmo, 120
Barrasso, F. A., 120
Barrelhouse blues, 73, 194
Basie, Count, 135, 245, 247, 248
Bates, Deacon L. J., 66. *See also* Jefferson, Blind Lemon
Bates, Will, 210, 217
Beale Street, 205, 228–29
Beale Street Blues Boys, 332
Beamon, Lottie. *See* Kimbrough, Lottie
Bechet, Sidney, 156
Bell, John, 199
Bell, "Red Eye" Jesse, 257
Benson, Al, 328–29
Bertrand, Jimmy, 86
Bigeou, Esther, 139
Birmingham, blues of, 198–202
Birmingham Jug Band, 201
Black Bob, 134
Black communities, southern, in blues recordings, 147
Blackface minstrels, 113–14, 120
Black freedmen, political ascendency of, 25
Black magic theme, 162
Blackman, Tee Wee, 210, 211, 212
Black oral tradition, 15; in Africa, 13; black ballads and, 19; griots and, 7–8
Black Patti record company, 129
Black preachers, 5
Black record market, 128–29
Blacks, status of, 50–51
Black Storyville, 184–85
Black Swan record company, 128, 154, 166
Blackwell, Scrapper, 45, 263, 280–82

383

# Song Index

# Permissions